THE RISE OF COTTON MILLS
IN THE SOUTH

SOUTHERN CLASSICS SERIES

John G. Sproat, General Editor

THE RISE OF COTTON MILLS IN THE SOUTH

BROADUS MITCHELL

with a new introduction by David L. Carlton

UNIVERSITY OF SOUTH CAROLINA PRESS

Published in cooperation with the Institute for
Southern Studies and the South Caroliniana Society
of the University of South Carolina.

UNIVERSITY OF SOUTH CAROLINA *BICENTENNIAL*

© 2001 University of South Carolina

Published in Columbia, South Carolina, by the
University of South Carolina Press

Manufactured in the United States of America

05   04   03   02   01   5   4   3   2   1

Library of Congress Cataloging-in-Publication Data

Mitchell, Broadus, 1892–
    The rise of cotton mills in the South / Broadus Mitchell ; with a
new introduction by David L. Carlton
        p.   cm. — (Southern classics)
    Originally published: Baltimore : Johns Hopkins Press. 1921.
    Includes bibliographical references.
    ISBN 1-57003-421-4 (pbk. : alk. paper)
    1. Cotton textile industry—Southern States. 2. Cotton
manufacture—Southern States. 3. Textile workers—Southern
States. 4. Working class—Southern States. I. Title. II. Series.
    HD9877.S85 M58   2001
    338.4'767721'0975—dc21   00-069093

CONTENTS

GENERAL EDITOR'S PREFACE

Aside from the sectional conflict, few topics stir more controversy among historians of the American South than the record of the region's industrialization. Going well beyond conventional economic history, moreover, the topic interacts directly with the social, political, cultural, and racial development of the region, especially in the twentieth century. In 1921, Broadus Mitchell established a bold pattern for dealing with the subject with his classic study of southern cotton mills—a book that, as David Carlton attests in his splendid introduction to this new edition, remains the starting point for all subsequent explorations of the subject.

Carlton's introduction further reveals Mitchell as a fascinating scholar-citizen, whose personal intellectual and political development over the years offers insights into the metamorphosis of the South from "old" to "new" and "newer."

Southern Classics returns to general circulation books of importance dealing with the history and culture of the American South. Sponsored by the Institute for Southern Studies and the South Caroliniana Society of the University of South Carolina, the series is advised by a board of distinguished scholars who suggest titles and editors of individual volumes to the general editor and help establish priorities in publication.

Chronological age alone does not determine a title's designation as a Southern Classic. The criteria also include significance in contributing to a broad understanding of the region, timeliness in relation to events and moments of peculiar interest to the American South, usefulness in the classroom, and suitability for inclusion in personal and institutional collections on the region.

JOHN G. SPROAT
General Editor

INTRODUCTION

Nearly half a century after the publication of *The Rise of Cotton Mills in the South,* Broadus Mitchell was asked to write an introduction to a reprint edition, a task he approached with some bemusement. The book, he freely admitted, was a piece of "student work," the product of a raw doctoral candidate whose first outing gave only the most tentative promise of the long, full, and productive life he would ultimately lead (Mitchell died at age 95, in 1988). The later author of a magisterial two-volume study of Alexander Hamilton may have inwardly winced at the sometimes awkward scholarship; the bold activist who subsequently risked his career repeatedly in behalf of "progressive" causes and civil liberties may have harbored some unspoken doubts about his youthful enthusiasm for the beneficent character of southern industrialists. The most he actually volunteered at the time, though, was that there are "shortcomings in the text of which I am well aware."[1]

Ironically, despite its youthfulness, and notwithstanding a tradition of criticism almost as old as the book itself, *The Rise of Cotton Mills in the South* remains not only the most influential book Mitchell ever wrote, but also one of the most influential works in the historical literature of the twentieth-century South. As the first full-dress scholarly effort to come to terms with the industrialization of the South, especially the rise of its bellwether cotton-textile industry, it has been the starting point for all subsequent explorations of the subject. More important, to the generation of southern intellectuals who in the 1920s and 1930s laid the groundwork for modern southern studies, Mitchell offered satisfying ways of understanding the South's poverty and its industrial lag behind the nation, the differences between the so-called "Old" and "New" Souths, and, most espe-

---

[1]Broadus Mitchell, "Introduction," in *The Rise of Cotton Mills in the South* (reprint ed; New York: Da Capo Press, 1968), v.

cially, the deeper continuities that gave the region's industrial society a distinct "southern accent."

Finally, Mitchell offered an interpretation of southern industrialization that was mythic in its sweep; indeed, the book reads as much like a fervent sermon as a sober analysis. Rooted in the militant modernizing ethos of the Progressive-era reform milieu in which he grew up, Mitchell offered a vision of a South transcending its past to remake itself as a "modern" society, but at the same time drawing upon its heritage of paternalism and *noblesse oblige* to define a "separate path" to a more humane and just industrial order. If the actual order arising from industrialization proved neither particularly humane nor particularly just, the problem was not with modernity itself, nor with the basic character of southern society, but with the abandonment by industrial leaders of the values of their ancestors. Such ills as child labor and the "stretchout" could thus be remedied without recourse to social upheaval, by invoking the community solidarity and humanitarian concern of the storied southern past.

In time this vision would come under sharp criticism, as later South-watchers would come to repudiate the elitism at its core, and much of it would be abandoned even by Mitchell himself; yet it has retained much of its power even to the present day. Moreover, as we shall see, Mitchell's distaste for explanations that reduced the driving force of industrialization to simple lust for gain led him to some striking insights into the social character of industrialization, insights that, reexamined in recent years, continue to enlarge our understanding. Finally, viewed as a historical document as well as a historical account, *The Rise of Cotton Mills in the South* can open a window for us onto the religiously infused optimism of the Progressive-era milieu from which the book, and its author, arose.

John Broadus Mitchell (he dropped his first name early on) was born into one of the more remarkable family connections in the post-Civil War South.[2] His father, Samuel Chiles Mitchell,

---

[2]Biographical materials on Broadus Mitchell are abundant. They include three extensive interviews, two conducted by Daniel Singal on 11 November and 29 December 1971 for the Southern Intellectuals Project of the Columbia University Oral History Program (hereafter Singal interviews), and one con-

was the son of Morris Randolph Mitchell, a Memphis cotton factor, and was born in 1864 in Coffeeville, Mississippi, whence his mother had fled following the federal occupation of Memphis. Samuel's father, who had ridden with Nathan Bedford Forrest, came out of the Civil War with both health and finances ruined, and the family ultimately had to move to Texas. At an early age Samuel went to work for a Galveston merchant, William Terry. Impressed by the young man, Terry offered to finance his college education and in 1882 sent him to Georgetown College, a Baptist school near Louisville, Kentucky. After graduation in 1888 he taught Latin and Greek at Georgetown and at Mississippi College. In 1891 he married Alice Virginia Broadus, whose father, John A. Broadus of Louisville, was the most celebrated Southern Baptist seminarian of the time; nationally known and well connected, Broadus afforded his energetic son-in-law his first entrée into national academic and philanthropic circles. It was while Samuel and Alice were at Georgetown that their first child was born, on 27 December 1892, and given the name of his maternal grandfather.[3]

In 1895, when Broadus was two years old, Samuel joined the faculty of Richmond College (now the University of Richmond) and moved his family to the Virginia capital, where the future historian spent most of his youth. His upbringing was in many ways typical of a faculty brat at a church-related school in the late-nineteenth-century South. The family lived on campus; the

ducted by Mary Frederickson on 14 August 1977 for the Southern Oral History Program of the University of North Carolina at Chapel Hill (hereafter Frederickson interview). Transcripts of all three are available in the Southern Oral History Program Collection, B-23 and B-24, Southern Historical Collection, University of North Carolina Library, Chapel Hill (hereafter SHC). Mitchell himself wrote an extensive, but unpublished, autobiography, which can be found in the Broadus Mitchell Collection, Box 6, Series 2.4, Folders 58 and 59, SHC (hereafter Mitchell autobiography). Among the most important biographical treatments of Mitchell are Daniel J. Singal, "Broadus Mitchell and the Persistence of New South Thought" *Journal of Southern History* 45 (August 1979): 353–80; Singal, *The War Within: From Victorian to Modernist Thought in the South, 1919–1945* (Chapel Hill: University of North Carolina Press, 1982), chap. 3; and Jacquelyn Dowd Hall, "Broadus Mitchell," *Radical History Review* 45 (August 1989): 31–38.

[3]Singal interviews, 1–8; Mitchell autobiography, 4; "Samuel Chiles Mitchell," *National Cyclopedia of American Biography*, vol. 14, pp. 88–89; John Carroll Presley, "Samuel Chiles Mitchell: A Biography of a Southern Educator" (Ph.D. dissertation, University of Virginia, 1992), chap. 1.

children (ultimately five in all) were barred from leaving the College compound, and their choice of playmates was limited to other faculty children. Schooling was likewise on campus, first at a primary school kept by a professor's daughter, then at a Preparatory (or "Fitting") School maintained by the College (and indeed most southern colleges of that time) to remedy the common failure of southern public schools to prepare students for college-level work. Faculty families were hardly well-to-do, and Broadus recollected a life of "plain living and high thinking," although the family could nonetheless afford black servants.[4]

In one sense, then, Broadus's upbringing was sheltered and constricted; for all his later sympathies with the poor, the working class, and blacks, he made acquaintance with few of them apart from the servants. In another sense, though, his childhood was open to all the intellectual breezes beginning to blow through the world of the "New South" elite. By the late 1890s Samuel became convinced that the traditional classical curriculum of the College needed to be broadened, and in 1898–1899 took his Ph.D. in history at the newly established University of Chicago. Samuel was little interested in scholarship, though; his great passion was for the improvement and uplift of the community, and more largely the South. He was president of the Virginia Anti-Saloon League, and became increasingly concerned with the state of southern public education, a preoccupation that brought him into contact with other prominent southern educators and such prominent members of the northern philanthropic establishment as Robert Ogden and George Foster Peabody. The Mitchell home in Richmond was a frequent stop for these luminaries, along with such literary celebrities as the muckraking journalist Ray Stannard Baker. The year before Broadus entered college, Samuel spent a year as Visiting Professor at Brown, introducing Broadus to another part of the country and to still other eminent people, such as the publisher George Plimpton and Helen Keller.[5]

---

[4]Mitchell autobiography, 7–25; Singal interviews, 22, 29–35.
[5]Presley, "Samuel Chiles Mitchell," chaps. 2–4; Mitchell autobiography, 33–41; Singal interviews, 10–17, 35–40; S. C. Mitchell, ed., *The South in the Building of the Nation*, vol. 10: *History of the Social Life* (Richmond, Va.: Southern

By the standards of his time and place, then, Broadus was from childhood drenched in cosmopolitan influences. These influences, though, were filtered through the ethos of the progressive southern middle class, a deeply earnest mind-set shaped by evangelical Protestantism. Samuel was an ordained Baptist minister, and, while his faith may have become attenuated in later years, his fervent sense of vocation never faltered. His devotion to uplifting the South was manifested not only in his activism but also in his writing, which in its tone was more hortatory than scholarly. He edited the *Social Life* volume of the multi-volume *The South in the Building of the Nation,* a massive survey of the state of southern life as of the early twentieth century. He wrote numerous articles for newspapers and magazines such as *The Outlook, The Sewanee Review,* and *The South Atlantic Quarterly.*

At the core of Samuel's analysis of the South was his repudiation of the slave regime. In his eyes, secession was a disaster visited upon the region by a backward political leadership presuming to stand athwart the three great progressive currents of the age: liberty, nationalism, and industrialism. The failure of the Confederate project thus displayed the bankruptcy of a regional leadership that stood for slavery, for localism, and for agrarianism. Accordingly, the great need of the South was to disavow those leaders and their obsession with using political devices to block progress, and turn to a new class of leaders skilled in the useful arts of industry, technology, and, especially, education. Teachers and "publicists" held center stage in Samuel's vision; "and by this [latter] term I mean, not office-seekers—they, alas! Are legion—but men who can bring scientific intelligence to bear upon the economic, social, and political conditions confronting us." Southern politicians he considered mere "demagogues"; shut out from responsible power by the outcome of the War, lacking the discipline of a two-party system, their "powers have become contracted to the limits of the prejudices which [they have] tried to congeal." In the process, southern democracy had "ceased to become educative—losing

---

Historical Publication Society, 1909). Cf. William A. Link, *The Paradox of Southern Progressivism, 1880–1930* (Chapel Hill: University of North Carolina Press, 1992).

thereby its essential virtue." To Samuel's mind, the future of the South was properly in the hands, not of democratic reformers, but of its nonpolitical elites: the "statesmen" of the press, of education, and of commerce and industry.[6]

This analysis had a profound influence on the young Broadus, who later in life recalled Richmond's Monument Avenue, adjoining the College, and its statuary pantheon of Lost Cause heroes, with unveiled contempt: "It's a pity that Virginia, that Richmond has chosen these Confederate heroes for the embellishment of its principal residential avenue, that while they were all men of personal integrity, they led us into trouble, and that really we would do better to melt these monuments down, that the bronze makes splendid gutters and downspouts—it isn't corroded at all—and if we remove from the admiration of the southern people these servants of a wholly wrong contention, that it would be desirable." From fairly early in his life, then, Broadus was imbued with his father's faith in material and moral progress, his father's passion for uplift—and his father's suspicion of democratic politics and politicians.[7]

The Mitchells' preoccupation with the need for fresh southern leadership, and their preference for "useful men" over politicians, were enhanced by their experiences in the years 1909–1913, when Samuel served as president of the University of South Carolina in Columbia. The elder Mitchell threw himself into the task of dragging the university, and South Carolina education generally, into the twentieth century, bringing in new faculty and guest lecturers, breaking down barriers between the campus and the community, and constantly touring the state in

---

[6]Samuel Chiles Mitchell, "The Educational Needs of the South," *The Outlook* 76 (13 February 1904): 415–19; the quotes appear on p. 418. This article, published earlier in the *Religious Herald,* 16 April 1903, under the title "Appomattox and the Age," (Presley, "Samuel Chiles Mitchell," 66) was adapted from an address Samuel delivered at a Southern Education Board dinner in New York. Broadus cited it in *The Rise of Cotton Mills in the South* (p. lvii below) as an illustration of his father's influence on his own thinking; as late as the 1970s he described this short piece as "one of the most apt interpretations of Southern history that I know." Singal interviews, 12. The word "publicist," a favorite of Samuel's, had not yet acquired its modern public-relations sense. Its original meaning was "an expert commentator on public affairs"; Samuel seems to have used it more broadly as a well-equipped person engaged in public affairs, either as an actor or as a commentator.

[7]Singal interviews, 14.

behalf of school reform. In the process, he cultivated a network of local elite Progressives, including the "welfare capitalist" Thomas F. Parker, the Charlotte engineer and "New South" promoter Daniel Augustus Tompkins, the welfare worker L. P. Hollis, and the journalist/industrial apologist August Kohn. Representatives of the progressive middle class of South Carolina, they were both eager to modernize the state and convinced that people of their attainments were its proper guides. These were just the sort of "publicists" in whom Samuel—and increasingly his son—were inclined to place their hopes for the southern future.[8]

In the meantime, Broadus entered the University of South Carolina, graduating in 1913. He was by his own description an indifferent student, far more interested in extracurricular activities than in his studies. He was active in the Euphradian Society, one of the university's two debating societies, and was in 1912 an active Wilson Democrat. More important was his budding involvement in journalism. As a child growing up in Richmond he had become a regular correspondent for the Children's Page of a Richmond newspaper; at South Carolina he wrote for the student newspaper, helped organize the Southern Collegiate Press Association, and, after his freshman year, became campus correspondent for the *Columbia Record,* later doing police reporting and book reviewing for the *Record* and the major Columbia daily, *The State.* In journalism, it appeared, he'd found his vocation; for some years after his life took its turn into academe, he would vacillate between the classroom and the newsroom. When, ensconced later at Johns Hopkins, he received news that McDavid Horton, his journalistic mentor in Columbia, had been killed fighting in France, he eulogized his friend in a way that revealed his ambivalence about the choices he made in his life:

> When I compare him with the people I know here in the
> University, and moreover when I think of all the newspa-

---

[8]Presley, "Samuel Chiles Mitchell," chap. 5; Daniel W. Hollis, "Samuel Chiles Mitchell, Social Reformer in Blease's South Carolina," *South Carolina Historical Magazine* 70 (January 1969): 20–37; Singal interviews, 22–28, 53, 56–59; Mitchell autobiography, 44–47.

per people I have known as compared with all the academic friends I have, I think that maybe the former have
accomplished more than the latter. . . . [Horton] learned
more about things and men then [*sic*] some of these University students and professors will ever know. . . . He was
not tempted to analyze, but to create. He did not know
why he reached conclusions, but he had good judgment.
His alchemy was worth all the 'legitimate' method of the
school masters. He held the trick against them all, because
he knew how to love.[9]

While by this time committed to academe, his writing would
throughout his life be leavened by a newsman's flair for vivid
language and human interest.

In 1913, the year of Broadus's graduation, Samuel underwent
the most traumatic crisis of his mature life. Having recommended to the administrators of the Peabody fund that they
concentrate their funds on improving South Carolina State College, the impoverished state college for blacks, he ran afoul of
David B. Johnson, president of Winthrop College, the state
school for white women. Johnson complained to Governor Cole
L. Blease, a classic "southern demagogue" eager to seize any
opportunity to discredit his "respectable" opponents. Denounc-
ing Samuel for diverting education funding from white women
to blacks, he demanded a legislative hearing, which he person-
ally attended and lobbied. While the state General Assembly,
and later the University Board of Trustees, ultimately vindicated Samuel, the elder Mitchell felt that his effectiveness as a
"publicist" had been compromised. Fortuitously, he received an
invitation to head the Medical College of Virginia in Richmond,
and closed out his brief encounter with the Deep South.[10]

The episode left a strong, bitter aftertaste in the mouth of his
son, however. It gravely exacerbated Broadus's contempt for
politics and politicians, and undoubtedly reinforced his preference for the mugwumpish "respectables" who had supported his

---

[9]Mitchell autobiography, 22, 47–50; The quote comes from Broadus Mitchell
to Mother, 1919? Samuel Chiles Mitchell Papers, SHC.

[10]Presley, "Samuel Chiles Mitchell," chap. 6; Hollis, "Samuel Chiles Mitchell,"
30–37; Singal interviews, 59–67.

father against Blease. It left him, too, with a lasting disdain for Blease's supporters—a telling disdain, since Blease was notable for his appeal to cotton-mill workers. Millhands lived in isolation from middle-class folk, especially the circles in which the Mitchells moved; Broadus knew only two, fellow students at the university, and recalled them as curiosities. Most of what he knew about the white southern working class, therefore, he learned from family friends such as Parker and Kohn, from whom he acquired, for all his later sympathies with their plight, a patronizing sense that they were people who could not be trusted with self-government, who required guidance and protection from their "betters."[11]

Following his graduation from the University of South Carolina, Mitchell (as Broadus will henceforth be referred to here) returned to Richmond and took employment as a reporter for the Richmond *Evening Journal.* He planned after a year to further his journalistic career with graduate work at the Columbia University School of Journalism, and was in fact accepted there. In the course of his stint with the *Evening Journal,* however, he had been moved to the business beat, and, feeling his lack of specialized knowledge, decided instead to pursue graduate work in "political economy" at The Johns Hopkins University in Baltimore. In our own heavily credential-conscious and career-tracked age, the decision seems astonishingly casual. He was entering a Ph.D. program in a specialized discipline in which he had never taken a course; while Hopkins-style "political economy" was far from the highly mathematical and theoretical discipline we now know as economics, it was an odd move for one who had been an undergraduate English major and had by his own admission never been good at math. Further, he planned no long-term commitment to an academic career. Nonetheless, it proved to be the pivotal decision of his life.[12]

Situated in the border-state city of Baltimore, Johns Hopkins was, in a manner of speaking, a southern university. It was cer-

---

[11]Singal interviews, 60–62, 94; Frederickson interview, 33–34. On the social separation of "mill people" and "town people," see also David L. Carlton, *Mill and Town in South Carolina, 1880–1930* (Baton Rouge: Louisiana State University Press, 1982), esp. chaps. 4–6.

[12]Mitchell autobiography, 58–66; Singal interviews, 75–78.

tainly a logical choice for a young southerner wishing to do graduate work; a Hopkins graduate had been Samuel's mentor at Georgetown, and the elder Mitchell had sent the school a number of students, notably the future editor-historian Douglas Southall Freeman.[13] At the same time, in an era when "southern" meant "third-rate" in higher education, Johns Hopkins was truly eminent. Founded in 1877 with railroad stock from the estate of a wealthy Baltimore merchant, its founding president, Daniel Coit Gilman, introduced the model of the German research university to the United States. The modern academic study of history in America was profoundly shaped by the "seminary" created by Herbert Baxter Adams. Likewise the study of "political economy" was molded by the reform-minded Richard Ely, who used historical method to criticize laissez-faire and classical theory, as well as by his opponent, the mathematician and pioneering neoclassicist Simon Newcombe.[14]

By the time Mitchell arrived, political economy at Johns Hopkins was no longer on the intellectual cutting edge of the discipline. Nonetheless, the historicist tradition was carried on by Jacob H. Hollander, a student of Adams and Ely, who in 1901 established the first independent "seminary" in political economy with his colleague George E. Barnett. Hollander, the dapper, cosmopolitan scion of a wealthy German-Jewish Baltimore manufacturing family, divided his time between the academy and public service, playing a major role in revamping the public finances of Puerto Rico, Indian Territory, and the Dominican Republic. His scholarship was varied, but his central passion was for the history of economic ideas, a devotion that combined his research interests with his zeal for book collecting; he amassed one of the first great American collections of economic treatises. Barnett was the son of a Methodist minister on the Eastern Shore, who like Hollander moved from Hopkins student to Hopkins teacher. A Democratic foil to the Progressive Republican Hollander, the two were famous for their "sham

---

[13]Presley, "Samuel Chiles Mitchell," 23–25; Singal interviews, 75–76.

[14]Hugh Hawkins, *Pioneer: A History of the Johns Hopkins University, 1874–1889* (Ithaca, N.Y.: Cornell University Press, 1960), chap. 10; William J. Barber, "Political Economy in the Flagship of Postgraduate Studies: The Johns Hopkins University," in *Breaking the Academic Mould : Economists and American Higher Learning* (Middletown, Ct.: Wesleyan University Press, 1988), 203–24.

battles" in seminar, but they were warm friends and close col-
laborators. They believed that the best way to train graduate
students was to focus the attention of the group on a single topic,
allowing for fruitful exchange of information and ideas among
students and mentors. The topic they specifically chose was
labor economics—the field of Barnett's own primary focus.
Importantly, they steered students away from theoretical mod-
eling (thus going against the discipline's increasing neoclassi-
cism) toward empirical investigation of practical problems,
based on documentary evidence and interviews with actual
union leaders. Barnett (and, less reliably, Hollander) was sympathetic to the labor movement, seeing unions as important to
the proper distribution of wealth in a market economy; he
played an active part in Baltimore's social-reform community,
to which he would soon introduce his new student from the
South.[15]

In its historical, empirical approach, the Johns Hopkins Seminary in Political Economy was a congenial fit for Mitchell. Both
traditional classical economics and the newly ascendent mar-
ginalist, or neoclassical, school, put him at sea; assigned F. W.
Taussig's popular *Principles of Economics* as, in effect, a reme-
dial text, "I found it very hard going, hard going." For that reason alone he would be disinclined to seek a future in theoretical
economics; as he told his mother, "political economy is as hard
as mathematics, as colorful as this rainy day, and a great deal
more dry. . . . What a pity that the science which treats of getting a living, should be so hopelessly depressing!"[16]

But his lack of mathematical aptitude was only the beginning

---

[15]Broadus Mitchell, "Jacob Harry Hollander," *Dictionary of American Biography*, supp. 2, 310–12; G. Eberton Evans Jr., "George Ernest Barnett," *DAB*,
supp. 2, 23–24; Joseph Dorfman, *The Economic Mind in American Civilization*,
vol 5: *1918–1933* (New York: Viking Press, 1959), 516–18, 586–87; Arthur H.
Cole, "Economic History in the United States: Formative Years of a Discipline,"
Journal of Economic History 28 (December 1968): 556–89, esp. p. 564; Singal
interviews, 81–84, 86–87. On Hollander's consulting work, see Emily S. Rosenberg and Norman L. Rosenberg, "From Colonialism to Professionalism: The
Public-Private Dynamic in United States Foreign Financial Advising,
1898–1929," *Journal of American History* 74 (June 1987): 59–82. On Hollander's
approach to graduate instruction, see Jacob H. Hollander, "Graduate Instruction in Political Economy" (in Seminar Methods of Economic Instruction: A
Symposium) *Journal of Political Economy* 20 (February 1912): 175–79.

[16]Singal interviews, 78–79; the quote is from Broadus Mitchell to Mother,
November 1916. Samuel Chiles Mitchell Papers, SHC.

of his problem with the neoclassical approach; its materialistic, hedonistic assumptions about human nature, and the smug assurance of many of its practitioners that the apparent chaotic amorality of capitalism masked a deeper, beneficial order that it was foolish to tamper with, offended both his idealism and his faith in the primacy of moral purpose in shaping social life. "The most thoughtful expounders of economic theory and life have shown crimps in their minds, and the world has abundantly suffered from their false dogmas, false and sincere. Look what laissez-faire did for England, in preventing, over a period of fifty years, that interference with factory conditions on the part of Parliament which, though an invasion of the dogma of freedom of contract, was yet the only means of shortening working hours and helping housing conditions that sorely needed change."[17] An early encounter with the British socialist John Spargo introduced him to socialism and led him to read volume 1 of *Capital*, but his own critique of possessive individualism and the free market drew more heavily on native sources. Henry George, the advocate of using a "single tax" on land to break up concentrations of private power and underwrite a "cooperative commonwealth," held a special attraction; in a talk given to a Baltimore YMCA in 1919, he extolled the "principle, so clearly expressed in 'Progress and Poverty,' that the world is built not on selfishness and exclusiveness, but on generosity and cooperation."[18]

Prompted by Hollander's interest in the history of economic ideas, Mitchell was soon discovering Friedrich List, the German nationalist economist: "His work is the clearest I have nearly ever read, and full to the brim with patriotism. . . . His are the calmest and finest criticisms of Adam Smith from an opponent of his essential doctrines that I know." Mitchell then proceeded to study the antebellum American nationalist economists, whose approach had inspired List. The nationalists were favorites of Hollander, who saw in them precursors to his own protectionist Republican principles, and who encouraged his students to explore their ideas. Mitchell found himself drawn to the nationalists' critique of liberal capitalism, which argued that, without

---

[17]Broadus Mitchell to Mother, 14 November 1919.
[18]Mitchell autobiography, 74–75; on Mitchell and Henry George, Broadus Mitchell to Father, prob. 1919. Samuel Chiles Mitchell Papers, SHC.

direction, the workings of the free market would produce neither a properly balanced economic development nor an equi-
table distribution of economic opportunity. In its insistence that
the market economy must ultimately serve the welfare of the
community, their thought appealed to his increasingly ardent
sympathies for the poor and the working class; it also beckoned,
though, because of its appeal to social order and its emphasis on
the role of the "economic statesman" in leading the way to the
Good Society. For Mitchell, passion for social justice and faith in
the efficacy of moral action to counter the free-market jugger-
naut, traits that would make him a socialist, paradoxically also
generated in him an admiration for enterprising elites, be they
southern industrialists or, later in his career, Alexander Hamilton.[19]

As a research-oriented program, the Johns Hopkins "seminary" expected its students to develop a dissertation topic in the
first year, and Mitchell was already discussing possible topics
with Hollander during his first semester. Hollander rejected one
of his initial suggestions, a study of rural credit, as a subject
already overworked. Mitchell's second proposal struck him as
more promising. During his father's year at Brown, Mitchell
had encountered the New England textile industry, one of the
seedbeds of the American Industrial Revolution; as a student at
South Carolina, he had been struck by the mill district of
Columbia, socially isolated but highly visible on the plain south
of the bluff on which the University stood. Recognizing that a
momentous extension of industrial society to the heart of the
agrarian South was underway (and thoroughly imbued with his
father's quasi-religious faith in industrial modernization), he
proposed a comparative study of cotton mills in New England

---

[19]On Hollander and the nationalists, see Dorfman, *Economic Mind in American Civilization* 5: 586–88; Mitchell autobiography, 75; the quote on List is from
Broadus Mitchell to Mother, 19 January 1916. Samuel Chiles Mitchell Papers,
SHC. On Mitchell's attraction to the nationalists, see Broadus Mitchell, "American Radicals Nobody Knows," *South Atlantic Quarterly* 34 (October 1935):
394–401; and his remarks at two Round Table Conferences at the 1930 and 1932
Meetings of the American Economic Association, printed under the titles "Economic History: The Decline of Laissez-Faire," *American Economic Review* 21
(March 1931): 3–10 (Mitchell's remarks appear on pp. 6–7); and "American Economic Thought," *American Economic Review* 23 (March 1933): 85–90 (Mitchell's
remarks appear on pp. 87–88).

and the South. Hollander, having sized up his reporter-protégée, feared that a comparative approach would quickly degenerate into a "mere series of pen pictures and snapshots," and suggested instead that Mitchell concentrate on the southern industry, "considered as an exploitation of natural resources and of labor," and that he organize his inquiry around the role of the entrepreneur. Mitchell, still the journalist, rankled at Hollander's exaltation of academic rigor over "popular treatment," but agreed to explore the matter further.[20]

By March 1915 he was beginning to define his principal thesis, characteristically in disagreement with his mentors. Regarding Barnett's hypothesis that the construction of railroads in the post-Civil War South opened up a pool of mountain labor to exploitation by Piedmont mills, Mitchell remarked that "I am giving him attention," but he clearly found such economistic explanations insufficient. One needed to factor in "a new spirit in the South which, by 1880 when the country had begun to recover from the war, showed itself in the establishment of cotton mills, or, in other words, abandonment of an exclusive policy of agriculture; in the employment of poor whites in place of incompetent emancipated blacks; in a general desire to reorganize the section in the light afforded by sad experience."[21] Here was the germ of Mitchell's subsequent argument about southern textile industrialization; that he expressed it at the outset of his project, well before he began serious research, shows that his interpretation of the rise of the mills owed less to his empirical observation than to his intellectual predispositions: his resistance to economic determinism, his intellectual debt to his father, and his endowment of modernization with sacred significance.

In the summer of 1915 the heavy work began. Mitchell located a rooming house in Washington, D.C., and, in the middle of a hot summer, began reading southern newspapers housed in the Library of Congress. Discovering quickly enough how massive a task it would be to read through a representative sample of daily newspapers over a considerable period, and having

---

[20]Mitchell autobiography, 73; Singal interviews, 93–95; Frederickson interview, 33–34; Broadus Mitchell to Mother, 1914 (probably prior to 18 December). Samuel Chiles Mitchell Papers, SHC.

[21]Broadus Mitchell to Mother, March 1915. Samuel Chiles Mitchell Papers, SHC. Note, too, the racial stereotyping, see below, xlvii–l.

already hypothesized that 1880 was the great turning point in southern industrial history, he limited his attention to the years around 1880—thus assuming, rather than testing, his hypothesis. At first his quest was frustrating, for while he was finding in those yellowed columns lively interest in material progress, especially in railroad projects, references to new cotton mills were casual and failed to explore the motivations for building them. It was "all very fragmentary and unconscious. . . . It is pitiful to see the pride the people had, and yet the little germs of material progress are encouraging. If they could only have seen that salvation lay in education, in industries, in hard work!"[22]

As he moved from North Carolina to South Carolina papers, though, he felt himself hitting pay dirt, and in a letter to his father (Mitchell used his parents, perhaps more than his mentors, as sounding boards) began pouring out more of the ideas that would underlie the future book. He now saw 1880 as the culmination of what could only be described as a classic religious conversion experience. Two events—the Civil War, and the Garfield-Hancock election of 1880—bracketed the process. The War produced initial conviction of sin; Confederate defeat impressed upon the South that it had followed the wrong path. There followed, though, during Reconstruction, a phase when the region resisted the Call of the Spirit: "a period of delirium, filled with enmity against the North, sulky despondency at home, hopeless, dogged persistence in an order that had to pass." The near-victory of the Democrats in the Presidential election of 1876 encouraged the South to believe that it could restore its fortunes through a return to political ascendency—an illusion wiped out by General Winfield Scott Hancock's defeat by James Garfield in 1880. That event, Mitchell was now convinced, made clear to the South the truth that his father preached—that politics was a false god and that the true path lay in material progress and modernization.

They come to see all at once that a 'solid South' must come about, a South solid for material progress, bent upon hard work, trained in things economic, declaring for a host

---

[22]Mitchell autobiography, 76; the quote is from Broadus Mitchell to Mother, Summer 1915. Samuel Chiles Mitchell Papers, SHC.

of [unclear] changes at once: public education, temperance, fair elections, abolition of the duel, construction of
railways, support of county and state and world fairs. . . .
I can tell almost the day the idea came into North Carolina, and the South Carolina papers, unconsciously, show
a new gospel passing over the state as clearly as you sometimes see the shadow of a cloud float from one end of a
field to another. It got to be a 'cotton mill campaign' as the
News and Courier called it.

Thus the South, in Mitchell's actual words, was "born again."

Mitchell's notion that he could "tell almost the day" of the
beginning of the southern industrial revolution—and that the
moment was linked so decisively with the relatively inconse-
quential Garfield-Hancock race—has not fared well with later
historians, as we will see; but here he was reading the historical
record as a minister might, as support for an essentially spiritual
view of southern modernization. Accepting literally the elder
Arnold Toynbee's declaration of a British "industrial revolution," Mitchell expected to find for the southern industrial revolution a date as decisive as the storming of the Bastille was to
the French Revolution. Moreover, such a fundamentally new
economic departure, he believed, fraught with unknown risk
and self-doubt, needed a fundamental reorientation of spirit.
"Water powers, cheap labor, proximity to the raw cotton, low
taxes, favorable freight rates, fuel in abundance—these things
were helps to the building of mills, but they did not build them.
Their establishment is deeper seated. It came from the bottom
of their hearts. Advantageous circumstances were welcomed
and employed to the utmost, but they were helps rather than
stimuli. The development was internal, not external." By reading the "Industrial Revolution" in the South as a conversion
experience, as a flash of light on a Road to Damascus, he was
reintroducing Grace and moral meaning into the grubby chaos
of economic history. If materialistic factors were necessary to
economic change, it was the spirit that gave it life and a purpose
beyond the selfish pursuit of profit.

But could a whole people be regenerated in an instant? Conceivably, but Mitchell was well aware from his own family's vicissitudes that not all southerners were among the regenerate. In his experience, it was the circles in which his family moved— the educated professional elite, the leading business and commercial men, the "new women," and their well-heeled and well-connected northern sympathizers—who had caught the vision of modernity, and who were seeking to evangelize their southern sisters and brothers. In the 1880 conversion Mitchell now saw the origins of his own class, and of the charge given the elect to lead in modernizing the region: "Once the leaders got the conception of an industrial South, the thing amounted to little less than a religion with them. They were transformed from capitalists merely into philanthropists; directors of a bank, a railroad and cotton mill were not business men only. They were patriots."[23]

That high estimation of the "useful citizens" of the South was reinforced the following summer. The Johns Hopkins "seminary" stressed the gathering of information about the "real world" from active participants such as labor leaders and entrepreneurs, and Mitchell was expected to do much the same. Accordingly, in the late summer of 1916 he set forth on a lengthy interview trip through the Carolina Piedmont, using a rail pass purchased by his father. It was a grueling expedition; he found the accommodations bad, and trains scarcely ever on time, probably because the boom accompanying the war in Europe was straining southern rail capacity. He customarily interviewed from morning until well into the evening, frequently approaching without introduction total strangers running enterprises swamped with wartime business. Nonetheless, he generally reported being cordially received, partly because of his social background (his letters repeatedly reported some family acquaintance with his interviewees), partly, one suspects, because of his unabashed admiration for their role in modernizing the South. In Salisbury, North Carolina, he uncovered one of the most striking stories of the mill-building effort, the tale of

---

[23]All the above quotes are from Broadus Mitchell to Father, Summer 1915. Samuel Chiles Mitchell Papers, SHC. For the origin of the concept of an "industrial revolution," see Arnold Toynbee, *Lectures on the Industrial Revolution in England* (London: Rivington's, 1884).

a cotton mill born out of a religious revival; in Concord, he encountered Charles A. Cannon, founder of what later became Cannon Mills, who he subsequently depicted as the agent of a community effort.

Entering South Carolina, though, Mitchell was graphically reminded of the magnitude of the modernizers' task. The state was in the throes of a hot gubernatorial campaign, with his father's old nemesis Cole Blease threatening to return to the governor's office. He described the scene to one of his brothers: "On the car last night were many drunken cotton mill operatives wearing buttons with his pirate face on them. He spoke at Greenville yesterday, and the streets were filthy with his poor, deluded supporters. When I saw them, I thought how truly the Civil War has lasted us to the present." Strikingly for a young man whose political views were even then moving rapidly left-ward, his views of the southern textile working class continued to fit perfectly with those of his interviewees. He reported with approval the observations of a prominent Greenville mill attorney ("whose father is known to Mother") expressing the fear (common at the time among the South Carolina elite) that with the gathering of rural workers into mill villages they had developed a class consciousness that was dangerous to the continued progress, even safety, of the State. "Schools were established for them, Y.M.C.A. and playground facilities were given them and the welfare work generally was entered upon. It now begins to occur to some that these people need not to be given advantages in their villages only, but that they need to be assimilated back to the general population. . . . The trouble with the people is now that, with some education in their own mill schools, they have received no real education as members of society."

While on one level Mitchell was being critical of the mistakes of the modernizers (and his criticism would get sharper in subsequent years), his chief complaint against them was that they were failing in their duties toward their charges. As for the southern mill workers, the increasingly "radical" Mitchell continued to view them paternally, as unformed citizens in need of "uplift."[24]

---

[24]Mitchell autobiography, 77; Singal interviews, 95–103; Frederickson interview, 34–37; the quotes are from Broadus Mitchell (in Anderson, S.C.) to Terry

There remained much more to do: further work in newspaper files, notably those of the Baltimore *Manufacturers' Record;* a Christmas interview trip to Charleston and Augusta, Georgia; mastery of the then-scanty secondary literature. As a pioneer investigator of what at the time was a poorly understood historical development, and as a neophyte scholar to boot, Mitchell found himself ever more confused as he delved further into his subject. In a moment of discouragement he confessed to his mother, "Like the cow in Mother Goose, I have tried to jump over the moon. No student, with his limited resources in years and money, can hope to do justice to any subject not the most minute."[25] Even though his argument had existed in embryo from the beginning, Mitchell took his task seriously. While believing, for instance, that the South was unable to industrialize without being prompted by the Spirit, he was aware that such important precursors as the reformer Edgar Gardner Murphy and the historian Victor S. Clark had regarded postbellum industrialization as a continuation of earlier developments; wedded to the notion of a southern "industrial revolution," he needed nonetheless to refute the claim that, even while possessed by the incubus of slavery, southerners had developed their own tradition of industrial enterprise. This, in the end, he believed he could do, for he felt that Clark lacked his own "native appreciation of the spiritual elements involved": "Faultlessly analytical, accurate to the minutest detail, splendidly balanced in all his judgments, I feel he has, after all, missed the secret."[26]

In the meantime, Mitchell had career issues to concern him. Hollander was pressing him to complete his dissertation and

---

Mitchell (brother), 10 September 1916; see also Broadus Mitchell to Mother, 16 September 1916. Samuel Chiles Mitchell Papers, SHC. On Blease, mill workers, and middle-class anxieties about mill culture, see David L. Carlton, *Mill and Town*, esp. chap. 6.

[25]Broadus Mitchell to Mother, 28 December 1916; Broadus Mitchell to Father, 24 March 1917; the quote is from Broadus Mitchell to Mother, 16 September 1916. Samuel Chiles Mitchell Papers, SHC. For views of the antebellum industrial past contrary to Mitchell's, see Edgar Gardner Murphy, *Problems of the Present South* (New York: Longmans, Green and Co., 1909); and Victor S. Clark, *History of Manufactures in the United States, 1607–1914*, 2 vols. (Washington: Carnegie Institution, 1916), vol 1: 553–58.

[26]Broadus Mitchell to Father, 12 December 1916; the quotes are from Broadus Mitchell to Mother, 1920. Samuel Chiles Mitchell Papers, SHC.

enter academe; Johns Hopkins was expanding its offerings in political economy, notably by adding evening classes, and he was beginning to find in the classroom an outlet for his enthusiasm and his zest for "progressive" evangelizing. But he still had hopes of returning to journalism; indeed, in early 1917 he was offered a chance to become heir apparent to Richard Hathaway Edmonds, the longtime editor of the *Manufacturers' Record.* In view of Mitchell's already lively interest in socialism, the offer from the boosterish, impeccably right-wing *Record* is in retrospect astonishing; yet its managers were attracted to Mitchell by his "intense sympathy with the South," and apparently Mitchell himself saw as yet no serious difference between the *Record*'s modernizing agenda and his own.[27] American entry into World War I made Edmonds reluctant to hire, but Mitchell continued to juggle the academy and the press, dividing his time between Johns Hopkins (he defended his dissertation in February 1918) and work for Douglas Southall Freeman's Richmond *News Leader* until he was drafted in June 1918, taking a clerical assignment at Fort Dix, New Jersey. After demobilization in January 1919, he returned briefly to the *News Leader,* but his attitudes were shifting; he found his reporter colleagues "a sorry lot, and yet they can all do what I am doing as well as I can." When Hollander soon offered him a position as instructor in political economy, he accepted. Even though the pay was only half his *News Leader* salary, his father, on whom he relied closely for advice, believed its security preferable to "the hazards of newspaper life," and in any case, Mitchell believed, "there are other compensations." When, later in 1919, the *Manufacturers' Record* offered him an editorial post, he declined. Moving rapidly to the left in the wake of the War, he was reluctant to go there except for a good salary and a free hand: "I have perhaps the best thing here anyhow."[28]

Thus Mitchell committed himself to academic life, although

---

[27]Broadus Mitchell to Father, 12 December 1916, 24 March 1917, 27 May 1917; Broadus Mitchell to Mother, 14 March 1917, April 1917, 18 May 1917. Samuel Chiles Mitchell Papers, SHC. On the *Manufacturers' Record* offer, see Singal, *War Within,* 63.

[28]Mitchell autobiography, 79–95; Broadus Mitchell to Father, 22 June 1917, 29 June 1917, 20 February 1918, 5 April 1918, 25 May 1919; Broadus Mitchell to Mother, 14 January 1919, 22 January 1919. Samuel Chiles Mitchell Papers, SHC.

characteristically defining his role to suit himself. As a graduate student he had not only become interested in socialism, but had also been introduced by Barnett to a whole community of welfare workers, social-gospel ministers, and labor reformers, notably Elisabeth Gilman, the daughter of Johns Hopkins's founding president, who became the most prominent radical in interwar Baltimore.[29] Soon after he joined the Hopkins faculty Mitchell began a night school for workers in collaboration with an official of the Amalgamated Clothing Workers of America. His increasingly visible radicalism destroyed his relationship with the *Manufacturers' Record,* now in his mind "a most excellent example of economic narrow-mindedness and selfishness," and whose managing editor surreptitiously attempted to undermine his career. To his father's alarm that Mitchell might be sacrificing his "larger purpose" for the sake of his interest in workers' education, the bumptious son reassured him that his position at the University was in no danger, that maintaining the good will of the *Record* was not worth the trouble, and, most important, that "political economy to me means help for the majority of the people, and that, so long as my teaching the subject lasts, will remain my purpose."[30]

Mitchell's increasingly open radicalism coincided with his work on revision of his dissertation for publication, undertaken mainly in the summer of 1920 in North Carolina. Unless other arrangements were made, all Hopkins social science dissertations were published in a periodical series, The Johns Hopkins University Studies in Historical and Political Science, which had been established in 1882 by Herbert Baxter Adams. The MacMillan Company had shown some interest in the manuscript, but wished a more broadly-gauged treatment of southern economic history, and it was in the Hopkins series that the book would come out in 1921.[31]

---

[29]On Gilman, see Broadus Mitchell, "Gilman, Elisabeth," in Edwin T. James et al., eds., *Notable American Women*, 3 vols. (Cambridge, MA: Belknap Press of Harvard University Press, 1971), vol. 2: 42–43; Singal interviews, 87–89.

[30]On Mitchell's worker education interests, see Mitchell autobiography, 98–99; Broadus Mitchell to Mother, 18 February 1920, 9 August 120; Broadus Mitchell to Father, 24 April 1920, the quotes are from Broadus Mitchell to Father, 1920. Samuel Chiles Mitchell Papers, SHC.

[31]On the origins of the Johns Hopkins Studies, see Hawkins, *Pioneer*, 108–9; on MacMillan's interest, see Broadus Mitchell to Mother, 9 August 1920. Samuel Chiles Mitchell Papers, SHC.

As he moved leftward, Mitchell's attitudes toward the contemporary southern textile industry were souring much as they
had toward the *Manufacturers' Record;* in 1919 he had published in the progressive magazine *Survey* a blistering attack on
southern mill owners' opposition to child labor reform. Yet his
increasing distaste for industrialists' conservatism, and his rising sympathy with the wave of textile-worker militance that
succeeded World War I, did not force any wholesale change in
the argument of *Rise of Cotton Mills.* Why? In Mitchell's mind,
both his admiration for the "industrial statesmen" of the "Cotton-Mill Campaign" of 1880 and his passion for the unionists'
campaign of 1919 stemmed from their common contribution to
the material advance of the South. To explain how the two
antagonistic tendencies were related, he developed a theory of
stages. In their time and place, the cotton-mill campaigners
were lifting the South out of the wretched poverty and lassitude
to which slavery had consigned it; lacking the resources to lift
child workers to a higher level of welfare, he argued, child labor
was actually philanthropy. As the southern industrial revolution
energized and enriched the region, though, child labor and the
other forms of cheap labor underwriting the South's industrialization became drags on the advancement of regional welfare,
while the vision animating the pioneering generation of southern mill men failed in their successors. In this respect, Mitchell
believed, the South was recapitulating the experience of older,
industrialized parts of the world. Now that it was launched on
its industrializing course, it was the duty of a new corps of
visionaries, including presumably Mitchell himself, to nudge it
along to the next stage. Both by praising the earlier generation
of industrial heroes and criticizing their heirs, Mitchell was following his father's vocation of "publicist" for a new and better
South.[32]

With the publication of *Rise of Cotton Mills in the South,*
Mitchell's interpretation of southern textile industrialization
was present in outline. During the following decade he fleshed

---

[32]Broadus Mitchell, "The End of Child Labor" *Survey* 42 (23 August 1919),
747–50, reprinted in Broadus Mitchell and George Sinclair Mitchell, *The Industrial Revolution in the South* (Baltimore: Johns Hopkins University Press,
1930), 217–32. Mitchell's "stage" model of southern industrial progress is discussed in Hall, "Broadus Mitchell," 36–37.

it out along two lines. The first involved exploring in greater detail the backwardness of the slave South. As an extension of his earlier studies of pioneer industrialists he decided to write a biography of William Gregg, the South Carolina cotton manufacturer who became the antebellum South's best-known industrialist and industrial propagandist, and whose whiggish *Essays in Domestic Industry* had long before piqued Mitchell's interest. Gregg he depicted as an industrial prophet—a man who saw well before the catastrophes of the 1860s that the South was being left behind by the modern world, and proposed a sound program of industrial development to help it regain lost ground. Mitchell was especially struck by Gregg's concern for the uplift of the "poor whites," and compared the regime at his mill village, Graniteville, to that of the pioneer Scottish socialist-mill owner Robert Owen at New Lanark. Alas, Gregg was a prophet without honor in his own country—in pre-secession South Carolina, the arguments of practical "publicists" counted for too little, the fantasies of politicians for too much.[33]

Before completing *Gregg,* though, Mitchell wrote a biography of another of his antebellum alter egos. In *Frederick Law Olmsted: A Critic of the Old South (1924)* he lauded the great antislavery journalist as a hard-headed observer of the "peculiar institution" in its actual workings: "his portrayal was vivid and dispassionate because he reported particulars, gave an inventory of what he saw and what was said in his presence. He offered a photograph, not a sermon." Olmsted was chiefly interested in the institution's deleterious effects on southern regional progress, and Mitchell saw in him a fellow modernizer, condemning the backwardness whose twentieth-century aftereffects Mitchell himself lamented. But he also liked Olmsted's distrust of moralizing abolitionists. Mitchell, already drifting far from his evangelical roots, was, like many of his fellow 1920s liberals, increasingly upset with evangelicals, whom he now ranked with politicians as "retrograde" forces in southern life. A similar revulsion at the preachers and politicians who had brought on the Great War would by the 1930s produce the so-

---

[33]Broadus Mitchell, *William Gregg, Factory Master of the Old South* (Chapel Hill: University of North Carolina Press, 1928). On the origins of *Gregg* see Singal interviews, 140–41; Mitchell autobiography, 73, 113–14.

called "revisionist" school of Civil War history, which declared
that war to be a "needless tragedy" stirred up by venal office-
seekers and fanatics. The message Mitchell gained from Olmsted anticipated the "revisionist" case: that slavery could have
been eased from the scene had reasonable southerners recognized its inviability, but that their thinking had been hopelessly
confused by the fanatics of the North and the demagogues of the
South. Given that slavery was eventually bound to give way to
the march of Progress, the Civil War was but a bloody hasten-
ing of the inevitable. A shift was beginning to occur in Mitchell's
thinking; the antideterminist young scholar of *Rise of Cotton
Mills* was putting increasing faith in economic determinism.[34]

That shift became increasingly apparent in his commentary
on the contemporary industrial South. Throughout the 1920s he
published numerous articles in various venues, including not
only specialty journals but also middlebrow magazines such as
The Outlook, religious journals such as *Commonweal,* and quar-
terlies, such as *Virginia Quarterly Review* and *South Atlantic
Quarterly,* with considerable readership among the southern
intelligentsia. In these pieces he both popularized his "sacred
history" of the southern industrial revolution and broadened his
criticism of the contemporary industry. The South, he argued,
was still suffering from cultural lag; while its productive capacities had been revolutionized, its social relations remained retrograde, as evidenced not only in child labor but in low wages,
poor working conditions, and resistance to unionization. While
in this regard it was following in the footsteps of older industrial
regions such as Old and New England, it now had to proceed to
the next stage of spreading the benefits of industrial society to

---

[34]Broadus Mitchell, *Frederick Law Olmsted: A Critic of the Old South* (Baltimore: Johns Hopkins University Press, 1924). The quote is from Mitchell autobiography, 104. On the "revisionist" school of Civil War historians, see Thomas
J. Pressley, *Americans Interpret Their Civil War,* (New York: Collier Books,
1962), 291–328. Mitchell's views probably drew more directly on U. B. Phillips's
argument (in *American Negro Slavery* [New York: D. Appleton and Co., 1918],
esp. chap. 19) that the plantation slave-labor system lacked long-term economic
viability, and on a new school of "southern vindicators" who concluded from the
arguments of Phillips and of Charles A. and Mary R. Beard (in *The Rise of
American Civilization,* 2 vols. [New York: The MacMillan Co., 1927], vol. 2:
chaps. 17 and 18) that the slavery issue was either an irrational invention of abo-
litionist "fanatics" or a smokescreen for aggression by northern industrial interests. On these latter, see Pressley, *Americans Interpret Their Civil War,* 273–87.
Unlike these defenders of the South, Mitchell found madmen on both sides.

the workers whose sacrifices had built up the industry, and its leadership had to extend the modernizing vision of the pioneer industrialists to accommodate social, as well as economic, progress. In this argument he was joined, toward the end of the 1920s, by his younger brother George, who had followed Broadus to the Johns Hopkins political economy program and had written a dissertation under Barnett on southern textile unions. As a Rhodes scholar from 1926 to 1929, he had written some pieces for the British press on southern labor, particularly explaining the strike wave of 1929. At the end of the 1920s the two brothers collected their articles into a book, published as *The Industrial Revolution in the South* (1930).[35]

Through the 1920s, then, Mitchell continued to be actively engaged with his native region. In the 1930s, though, he began to move away from the concerns of his youth, and indeed began to disengage from the South itself. One reason for the shift was his increasing immersion in Baltimore and Maryland social activism. A protest against a brutal lynching on the Eastern Shore led him in 1934 to run for Governor of Maryland on the Socialist ticket (he campaigned with Elisabeth Gilman, running as Socialist candidate for the U.S. Senate). Explaining this temporary abandonment of his antipolitical prejudices as "educational" in purpose, he took pride less in his paltry showing than in his role in defeating the Democratic incumbent, a man he esteemed scarcely more highly than he had Cole Blease. Increasingly rancorous relations with the Johns Hopkins administration (aggravated both by his idealism and his lifelong impetuosity) led him to resign in 1938, and he left the South for good, ultimately settling in New York City and doing wartime work for the International Ladies' Garment Workers' Union before resuming his academic career at Rutgers and then at Hofstra.[36]

Some historians have seen a deeper significance to Mitchell's

---

[35]Mitchell and Mitchell, *Industrial Revolution in the South*. George Mitchell's dissertation was published the same year as *Textile Unionism and the South* (Chapel Hill: University of North Carolina Press, 1930). He went on to a varied career in academe and government service, ending his active career in the 1950s as director of the Southern Regional Council, the premier organization of southern white liberals during the Civil Rights Era. He died in 1962. Presley, "Samuel Chiles Mitchell," 295–98.

[36]Mitchell autobiography, esp. 118ff.

turn away from the South, attributing it to an increasing aware-
ness that his admiring picture of the early industrialists had led
him into an intellectual dead end—that his apotheosis of white
social solidarity obscured both the reality and the necessity of
class conflict in the industrial South. Certainly the era of deep
labor conflict beginning in 1929 could well have suggested to
him that his faith in the vision of the old industrial leadership of
the South had been misplaced from the beginning. Mitchell
never repudiated his rosy estimate of the first mill builders,
however; indeed, he never really accepted the socialist notion
that class conflict was central to economic progress.[37] More
likely, his detachment stemmed from simple frustration with the
failure of his native region to follow the path of modernization
blazed by historical precedent. First, the industrialists of the
1920s ignored his pleas to be statesmen as well as businessmen;
convinced that they *were* following their ancestors' footsteps,
they reviled Mitchell as another "outside" radical agitator. Nor
did southern workers fulfill his postwar hopes that they would
enlist behind a union vanguard. The nonsouthern workers he
encountered in his labor-education work in the 1920s and 1930s
were cosmopolitan, feisty, and ideologically committed—in
other words, much like Mitchell himself; by contrast, the textile
workers he taught in the Southern Summer School for Women
Workers seemed to him passive, and the atmosphere "primary-
grade."[38] While service as an observer at a major rayon-plant
strike at Elizabethton, Tennessee, in 1929 gave him a respect for
southern workers' "pertinacity" he had not previously shown, in
the end the labor conflicts of the 1930s only confirmed his disappointment. In 1937 he recalled attending a strike meeting
"where a committee of local workers, which had been sent to the
employer for moral effect, was supposed to make a report. One
got the impression that they were dazed, not knowing what it

---

[37]This argument was made specifically by Singal, *War Within*, chap. 3. When
responding to such critics as C. Vann Woodward, Mitchell graciously allowed
that "doubtless he is correct," but gave no substantive ground on the central contentions of *Rise of Cotton Mills*. Singal interviews, 97–101. Singal's argument is
countered by Hall, "Broadus Mitchell," 36–37.

[38]The quotes are from Frederickson interview, 53–58. On the Southern Summer School, see Mary E. Frederickson, "A Place to Speak Our Minds: the Southern School for Women Workers" (Ph.D. dissertation, University of North
Carolina at Chapel Hill, 1981).

was all about. They were tongue-tied. Not only did they have to be steered and prodded and upheld by the visiting union officials, but at the same time their weakness had to be treated with patience and tact. The generalship had to come from the outsiders."[39] Southern workers and their culture, paradoxically, seemed more alien to this son of the southern middle class than did the ethnic radicals of Baltimore.

In short, Mitchell could find no heroes in the current southern scene, no vanguard to lead the way to the Better Society. Thus he tended increasingly to appeal to precisely those inexorable economic forces that he found so inadequate in explaining the beginnings of industrialization. A common theme to many of the pieces collected in *Industrial Revolution in the South* was an insistence, not simply on the social desirability of industrial improvement, but on its inevitability. If the South, as he increasingly contended, was simply following in the footsteps of more "progressive" regions, then efforts to retard (or hasten) social change would only produce social disturbance. Had not his study of Olmsted and the Civil War shown him that attempts to impede social change by political means do more harm than good? Just as "slavery was dissipating itself at the very time it was most frantically defended[,] similarly, child labor in southern cotton mills . . . is well on the road to extinction," he declared. Hard-headed managers would eventually abandon child labor as uneconomical; industrial expansion and diversification would expand opportunities and place upward pressure on wages; workers would gain new aspirations and desires, and would organize to demand better treatment. Where, then, was there need for the old "philanthropy"? The pioneers Mitchell had so adulated in his youth he now relegated to a vanished heroic age; indeed, responding to the welfare-capitalist rhetoric of their successors, he increasingly saw their legacy as retrograde, as the lingering influence of the plantation mentality. Whereas *Rise of Cotton Mills* found diversity in the origins of the mill-builders, the articles in *Industrial Revolution in the South* asserted that their roots had been in the old slaveholding elite, and their values those of the "aristocratic" slave regime—

---

[39]Broadus Mitchell, *General Economics: An Introductory Text* (New York: Henry Holt and Co., 1937), 444.

values that aided the industrial process then, but were now impediments to further modernization. The New South no longer needed statesmen of that order, only people willing to abandon reactionary religion and politics and come to terms with social progress.[40]

Unsurprisingly, Mitchell's paeans to the unalloyed good of industrial modernization failed to sit well with the most important group of anti-modernists in the interwar South—the so-called Southern Agrarians, a group of intellectuals loosely connected with Vanderbilt University, who in 1930 launched a movement opposed to further industrialization of the South and championing the reestablishment of a society of independent freeholding farmers reverent toward Nature and Nature's God.[41] Mitchell, as one might expect, had little use for the Nashville back-to-the-land enthusiasts, and said so in a contribution to W. T. Couch's symposium *Culture in the South* (1934). The old rural regime for which they pined, he said, was worthless, and the "culture" it allegedly produced "was so elusive that the observer today can not find it. It did not take form in music, poetry, prose, building, works of engineering, jurisprudence, science, or theology, let alone the infinitely more difficult matter of decent human comfort and independence for the average man within the South."[42]

The Agrarians responded in kind. "I have tried for years to understand what is wrong with Mr. Mitchell," said the poet and Agrarian attack dog Allen Tate: "The farmers are in wretched condition; but this does not concern Mr. Mitchell; he can do nothing for them. Although labour troubles in the South have been grievous, they have not been grievous enough. We must catch up with the world; we must completely industrialize the South so that we shall have a problem that must be solved in socialist terms."[43] "Good God! That is actually his reasoning!"

---

[40]Mitchell and Mitchell, *Industrial Revolution in the South*, passim. The quote appears on p. 51.

[41]The best account of the Southern Agrarian movement is Paul K. Conkin, *The Southern Agrarians* (Knoxville: University of Tennessee Press, 1988).

[42]Broadus Mitchell, "A Survey of Industry," in W. T. Couch, ed., *Culture in the South* (Chapel Hill: University of North Carolina Press, 1934), 80–92; the quote appears on p. 81.

[43]Allen Tate, "A View of the Whole South," *American Review* 2 (February 1934), 411–32; the quote appears on p. 420.

shrieked Tate to his fellow Agrarian Donald Davidson.[44] But the Agrarian also put his finger on a more profound problem: Mitchell was far more intent on seeing the southern "poor whites" "uplifted" than he was on appreciating them for what they were and understanding what they themselves might want. For Mitchell—the faculty brat turned Hopkins professor and resident of H. L. Mencken's Baltimore—"culture" was "high culture," a product of formal education and an object of consumption; it was that "culture" that was "so elusive that the observer today can not find it." By comparison the culture of the white rural and mountain South was simply "backward" and "primitive," and sweeping it aside could only be a benefit.[45] Tate thought differently. Echoing early Appalachian commentators such as John C. Campbell and J. Wesley Hatcher, and anticipating a major modern theme in Appalachian social and cultural criticism, he saw in Mitchell's faith in modernization and denigration of the premodern South a prettied-up version of an older and more sinister agenda: "Industry has advertised the mountaineer as a debased creature whose life deserves no respect but to whom, for some mysteriously humanitarian reason, should be given the improvements of the bathroom and the kitchen sink."[46] In important respects Tate's criticism was

---

[44]Allen Tate to Donald Davidson, 9 January 1934; John Tyree Fain and Thomas D. Young, *The Literary Correspondence of Donald Davidson and Allen Tate* (Athens: University of Georgia Press, 1974), 287.

[45]Mitchell owed an obvious debt here to H. L. Mencken's famous essay "The Sahara of the Bozart," (in *Prejudices, Second Series* [New York: Alfred A. Knopf, 1920]), which argued much the same thing.

[46]Tate, "A View of the Whole South," 417. For early critiques of the "modernizer" assault on Appalachia, see John C. Campbell, *The Southern Highlander and His Homeland* (New York: Russell Sage Foundation, 1921), esp. 299–322; Campbell, "From Mountain Cabin to Cotton Mill," *Child Labor Bulletin* 2 (1913): 74–84; and J. Wesley Hatcher, "Appalachian America," in Couch, ed., *Culture in the South,* 374–403 (Tate regarded Hatcher's contribution to *Culture in the South* to be the best piece in the volume). Mitchell persistently perceived ordinary rural southern whites, especially Appalachian mountain folk, as "backward"; in 1979 he recalled a trip forty years before on the newly built Skyline Drive in Virginia: "We saw how a modern highway, well engineered through backward mountainous country can portend the drawing of people out of their fastnesses of terrain and manner of life." Modern Appalachian scholars have decried the construction of the Skyline Drive for its dispossession of small farmers and its disruption of communities. Mitchell autobiography, 186–87. An expanding literature has examined the use of the "backward mountaineer" stereotype to justify exploitation and heedless "modernization" in Appalachia; the best, most general treatments of Appalachian image-making are Henry

grossly unfair; Mitchell had the welfare of poor white southerners very much at heart. But his adulation of material progress as a cure-all was, in its own way, as blind to the larger needs of the southern people as the religious and economic dogmas he opposed.

However, if Mitchell was counseling his native region to give itself over to the workings of a linear "progress," he was hardly abandoning his old quest for a tradition of economic statesmanship critical of chaotic, brutalizing capitalism. Arguing in 1939 that the teacher of economics should be an advocate, not simply an expositor, he crucially qualified his determinism: "Economic determinism, which is the loose formula of the collectivist, means that prior conduct has a bearing upon subsequent development, but does not forget that what we do now helps to shape the compulsions under which we will some day rest. The wish need not be impotent in economic affairs. Exhortation may be quite as powerful as the savings of large-scale production. . . . Moral force may have its place beside magnitudes susceptible of more precise statement."[47] Mitchell might use economic-determinist arguments for polemical effect, but in his deepest thought the middle-aged economist, like the young graduate student, insisted on inserting moral purpose into the machinery.

If he could no longer find visionaries to admire in the contemporary South, he found them elsewhere, for instance in a growing enthusiasm for the Soviet experiment. In his own country, though, he found his heroes chiefly in the past, safely beyond disillusionment, and they were, at least at first blush, the very opposite of Bolsheviki. As noted earlier, in graduate school he had become fascinated with the nationalist school of antebellum American political economists, the school that had inspired the German economic thinker Friedrich List. As he began to take on graduate teaching at Hopkins in the 1920s, he developed a

---

Shapiro, *Appalachia on Our Minds: The Southern Mountains and Mountaineers in the American Consciousness, 1870–1920* (Chapel Hill: University of North Carolina Press, 1978); and Allen Batteau, *The Invention of Appalachia* (Tucson: University of Arizona Press, 1990).

[47]Broadus Mitchell, "Treatment of Controversial Questions in the Teaching of Political Economy," *American Economic Review* 30 (June 1940): 339–43; the quote appears on p. 342.

seminar around the nationalist school, and directed a number of dissertations exploring their thought.[48]

By the 1930s, encouraged by his mentor Hollander, he was touting nationalist economics as a basis for an authentic American "collectivism." The Great Depression, he believed, had shown neoclassical theory, and more particularly the new mathematical economics, to be incapable of anticipating economic change or of handling historical contingency.[49] At the same time he was appalled by the early New Deal and its policies of induced scarcity.[50] Against both he placed the nationalists. Unlike the theorists, he argued, they learned inductively, through experience, and in their hands economics was no "science," but an art akin to statecraft. Moreover, while the classical and neoclassical traditions were, in Mitchell's view, essentially pessimistic, focused on minimizing scarcity (or, in the case of the New Dealers, managing scarcity), the nationalists were optimists, concerned less with the present economic viability of their schemes for large-scale internal improvements and the nurturance of infant industries than with their potential to develop the long-term economic capacities of the nation. Neoclassical economics narrowed the vision of the statesman, warning him

---

[48]Singal interviews, 113–14, 158; Mitchell autobiography, 134–35. Although Mitchell's dissertation was the first ever produced at Johns Hopkins in economic history, by the 1930s Hopkins was an important center of instruction in the field; see Cole, "Economic History in the United States," 564.

[49]One hapless econometrician, who, following his models, had told subscribers to his investment service to "buy" on the eve of the 1929 Crash, became the target of an especially savage, sexually charged, Mitchell lampoon: with his debacle, "the slide rule, which has been the emblem of the old faith, became limp, its graduations blurred beyond recognition. The rod of Aaron was flung down, and wriggled like a snake." Mitchell, "Treatment of Controversial Questions," 341. This article was revised from a paper delivered at a "Round Table on Problems in the Teaching of Economics" held at the 1939 Meeting of the American Economic Association and reported in *American Economic Review* 30 (March 1940): 106–11; a summary of Mitchell's paper appears on pp. 106–7.

[50]Mitchell delivered a sharply worded indictment of these policies in a radio address, "Security and Capitalism," delivered 9 May 1935 over the NBC Blue Network and co-sponsored by the National Advisory Council on Radio in Education and the League for Industrial Democracy; a transcript of the talk is enclosed in Broadus Mitchell to Mother, 25 May 1935, Samuel Chiles Mitchell Papers, Folder 192, SHC. A later, more balanced estimate of the New Deal can be found in his *Depression Decade: From New Era Through New Deal, 1929–1941* (New York: Holt, Rinehart and Winston, 1947).

against intervening in the marketplace; the nationalists broadened his vision, and promoted the ability of the imaginative leader to foster the expansion of human welfare through economic organization.

Mitchell thus saw the nationalists as the first American "collectivists," and in that regard much like socialists. There were differences as well, of course. Nationalists had no interest in class struggle, preferring to emphasize a harmony of interest among classes. More importantly, they were less concerned with democratic control of the economy than with the mobilization of productive power—less concerned with distribution of goods, let alone the character of the goods to be distributed, than with developing the capacity to produce them. Tellingly, in both respects Mitchell preferred the nationalist position to that of his socialist contemporaries: "There is often reason to think, nowadays, that the yearning for democratic expression in economic life is unwisely allowed to overshadow the preliminary problem of accomplishing technical proficiency." His admiration for socialism and his persistent enthusiasm for the Soviet Union thus had relatively little to do with an ideal of "industrial democracy"; rather, he saw socialism as yet another stage in the unfolding of the modernizing vision he grew up with, in which progress was achieved through centralized organization overseen by broad-minded statesmen.

> The American economic nationalists had in mind, to be sure, the prosperity of the whole country, but their philosophy was predicated upon a harmony of interests, not upon class cleavage. Theirs was in the main a physical task, and it could not be pushed through successfully without intelligent and resourceful leadership. This meant reliance upon the only group which possessed economic capacity and unity of purpose, namely, upon men of means. These would not consult the masses, in whose ultimate interest, however, they would be working. Much the same is true, be it noted, of present proposals for the transition stage between capitalism and collectivism; most radicals will admit that there must be a benevolent dicta-

torship as the stepping-stone from individualism to the common ownership and control of the means of production.[51]

The persistently elitist character of his modernizing vision was ultimately expressed in his deepening admiration for the progenitor of American nationalistic economic thought, Alexander Hamilton. Mitchell discovered Hamilton in graduate school and made him the focus of his postwar scholarship. His two-volume biography of Hamilton became the crowning scholarly achievement of Mitchell's life. An oddly appropriate fascination, this—the socialist Mitchell, who in the 1950s was vocally protesting academic blacklisting, for the conservative Hamilton, who Mitchell regarded as, at heart, a "collectivist"—a man who felt that his adopted country would never attain the greatness and prosperity it needed if it relied on the automatic workings of the free market, and who insisted that the economic statesman needed deliberately to foster and plan its development. In Hamilton, Mitchell, the paternalistic apostle of social concern, the southern progressive modernizer, found his ultimate object of veneration.[52]

In a very real sense, Broadus Mitchell, his "radicalism" notwithstanding, can be said to have been a man who lived much of his life as an emissary from another time, a time when "modernity" in the South was more a battle cry than a fact of life. A reader might be excused for thinking much the same of his most famous book. More than three quarters of a century old, *The Rise of Cotton Mills in the South* sounds antique to a modern ear, more like a revival sermon than what we've come to regard as dispassionate scholarship. Its unabashed hero worship grates on sensibilities reflexively suspicious of figures held up insistently for admiration. Its racial attitudes and views of

---

[51]Mitchell, "American Economic Thought"; Mitchell, "Decline of Laissez-Faire"; Mitchell, "American Radicals Nobody Knows"; the quotes are on p. 397. Hollander, who (incestuously) served as a discussant on the American Economic Thought Round Table, declared Mitchell's paper "brilliant"; "American Economic Thought," 90.

[52]Singal interviews, 158–63; Broadus Mitchell, *Alexander Hamilton*, 2 vols. (New York: The Macmillan Company, 1957–62).

southern history, while liberal for its time, look hopelessly retrograde to us. Finally, it is a book whose central contentions have
come under withering assault, especially in the years since
World War II.

Yet our hypothetical reader dismisses the book at her peril.
For all its flaws and vicissitudes, *Rise of Cotton Mills* was
penned by an author close to the events and people he was writing about. Behind the hortatory rhetoric lies a good deal of
sound observation about the practical problems of introducing
industry to a preindustrial society; Mitchell, after all, was a budding economist and an experienced business reporter as well as
a Progressive exhorter. Even in his most widely criticized contention, that the generals of the "Cotton-Mill Campaign" were
community-minded economic statesmen, he was on to something important about the social character of these early southern industrial entrepreneurs, something that later debunkers,
pursuing agendas of their own, failed to appreciate.[53]

On publication in 1921, *The Rise of Cotton Mills in the South*
immediately became the standard work on southern textile
industrialization. No one prior to Mitchell had delved as extensively or written more comprehensively about the creation of
the southern textile industry. Certainly no one had imbedded the
story of southern industrialization in so comprehensive a view of
the region's history; for perhaps the first time, the legitimating
myths of the "New South" received rigorous scholarly under-
pinning, just at a time when the writers of the "Southern Renaissance" were beginning to break clear of the stifling pieties of the
"Lost Cause."

It also appeared at a moment when the southern textile industry became a national issue. In the 1920s the traditional centers
of American cotton textile production, which were also the cra-
dles of the American Industrial Revolution, suddenly found
themselves in catastrophic decline. Giant mills closed their
doors, and entire cities in New England went bankrupt. In the
meantime, the southern industry continued to grow, and by
1930 the South had supplanted New England as the major cot-

---

[53]Singal, *War Within*; George B. Tindall, "The Benighted South: Origins of a
Modern Image," in Tindall, *The Ethnic Southerners* (Baton Rouge: Louisiana
State University Press, 1976), 43–58.

ton-textile center of the nation. That a region long considered industrially backward could thus seize control of a historic core industry from "Smokestack America" sent disturbed northern manufacturers, politicians, and labor leaders scrambling to find out just how the South had done it. And for guidance the preeminent authority was Mitchell, with his contention that the South had industrialized essentially through adopting a sort of "industrial policy," a "deliberately planned" manufacturing development.[54]

Mitchell's argument that industrialization had proceeded out of a sense of social solidarity that transcended class divisions among whites proved to have other uses as well, specifically to explain the "docility" of southern workers. On the one hand, his work served (to his discomfort) to bolster the arguments of southern textile industry apologists that the mills were socially uplifting enterprises; that, in the words of one manufacturer, "we make American citizens and run cotton mills to pay the expenses."[55] On the other, especially as the 1930s wore on, prolabor liberals were increasingly distressed at the chronic failure of southern workers, the sometimes massive labor conflicts of the 1930s notwithstanding, to move to the "next stage" of organizing unions. To one such observer, the North Carolina journalist W. J. Cash, Mitchell's view of the origins of the mills suggested the answer. In a society schooled by Civil War and Reconstruction to militant solidarity, facing impoverishment and erosion of its bedrock principle of white supremacy, leaders arose to tout Progress as the means both to restore prosperity and to bolster the "proto-Dorian bond" among white men. As the "New South" progressives moved to build mills, and to limit mill employment to whites, the old yeomanry, sliding into tenancy or worse, responded with gratitude—and continued to do so to Cash's own day. In this way Mitchell's argument became an integral part of Cash's sweeping synthesis of southern history, *The Mind of the South* (1941)—probably the single most

---

[54]Mitchell and Mitchell, *Industrial Revolution in the South*, passim; Claudius T. Murchison, *King Cotton Is Sick* (Chapel Hill: University of North Carolina Press, 1930); Gavin Wright, "Cheap Labor and Southern Textiles, 1880–1930" *Quarterly Journal of Economics* 96 (November 1981): 605–29.

[55]Liston Pope, *Millhands and Preachers: A Study of Gastonia,* (New Haven: Yale University Press, 1941), 16.

commanding book ever written on the region, and one that spread Mitchell's influence far beyond his own readership and well past World War II.[56]

But even before the end of the 1920s, dissenting voices began to appear. Harriet Herring, a former mill welfare worker who became the resident textile expert at Howard W. Odum's Institute for Research in Social Science at the University of North Carolina at Chapel Hill, accepted Mitchell's historical account in her book *Welfare Work in Mill Villages* (1927), but by 1931 was beginning to express some doubts. Commenting on the efforts of the Mitchells in *The Industrial Revolution in the South* to use the example of the old-time industrial statesmen to shame their money-grubbing successors, Herring pointed out that in fact the ills they were criticizing—child labor, low wages and long hours, use of the mill village to control workers—had been worse in the Good Old Days, and that pioneer industrialists "were often pretty harsh masters."[57]

Herring's critique was mild and friendly. A more serious problem for the book's reputation arose in the 1930s, as many commentators began to question Mitchell's bedrock faith in the beneficence of industrialization itself. As the rural South sank into depression, and as leading southern industries such as cotton textiles became "sick," observers became impressed, not with the "revolutionary" character of southern industrialization, but with its failure to achieve its promise. Half a century after the "Cotton-Mill Campaign," the bulk of southern income continued to be generated by agriculture and extractive industry; the manufacturing sector remained stunted. Not only had modernization failed to deliver on its promises, but many—and not just Agrarians—began to suspect that the problem was not with

---

[56]W. J. Cash, *The Mind of the South* (New York: Alfred A. Knopf, 1941), 148–89, esp. the reference to "the celebrated monograph" on p. 180; see also C. Vann Woodward's critique of Cash, "The Elusive Mind of the South," in Woodward, *American Counterpoint: Slavery and Race in the North-South Dialogue,* (Boston: Little, Brown, and Co., 1971), 261–86, which is in passing a critique of Mitchell as well. See also Gavin Wright, "Economic Progress and the Mind of the South," in Paul D. Escott, ed., *W. J. Cash and the Minds of the South,* (Baton Rouge: Louisiana State University Press, 1992), 187–206, esp. 196–98.

[57]Harriet Laura Herring, *Welfare Work in Mill Villages* (Chapel Hill: University of North Carolina Press, 1929), esp. 13–20; Herring, "The South Goes to the Bindery," *Social Forces* 9 (March 1931): 427–31; esp. 428; the quote appears on p. 428. See also Pope, *Millhands and Preachers*, 16–20.

the dead weight of the past, as Mitchell claimed, but was rooted in a serious flaw with modernization itself. Southern manufacturing looked less like the first stage of a universally valid and progressive process than like a dead end, saddling the region with low wages, low skills, and "colonial" dependence on outsiders. To such observers Mitchell's standard prescription for southern ills—that the region would grow its way out of its troubles—seemed increasingly irrelevant.[58]

It actually appeared worse than irrelevant to the historian C. Vann Woodward, who in the 1930s began his massive rewriting of post-Civil War southern history, a project that would culminate with the 1951 publication of *Origins of the New South.* To be sure, both Mitchell and Woodward accepted the premise that there *was* a "New South," one dramatically different from the Old Regime. Their major difference lay in their sympathies. Woodward's were placed, not with the modernizing elite, but with those whom he saw as their victims, the white and black common people of the South; his heroes, the Populists, were as radically democratic as Mitchell's family network had been firmly elitist.[59]

Believing in the possibility of a better, more democratic, and more egalitarian South than the one that arose under the New South modernizers, Woodward proceeded to unmask the modernizers' pretensions to "statesmanship." First, he showed, there was no "Industrial Revolution" in the South. While few factories existed in the region before the Civil War, and while the pace of

---

[58]See, for instance, Clarence H. Danhof, "Four Decades of Thought on the South's Economic Problems," in Melvin L. Greenhut and W. Tate Whitman, eds., *Essays in Southern Economic Development* (Chapel Hill: University of North Carolina Press, 1964), 7–68; National Emergency Council, *Report on Economic Conditions of the South* (1938), reprinted, with an introduction, in David L. Carlton and Peter A. Coclanis, *Confronting Southern Poverty in the Great Depression* (Boston: Bedford Books of St. Martin's Press, 1996). The "colonial economy" argument was first set forth by Rupert B. Vance in *Human Geography of the South: A Study in Regional Resources and Human Adequacy* (Chapel Hill: University of North Carolina Press, 1932), 467–81.

[59]For an overview of the larger project in which Woodward was engaged, see C. Vann Woodward, *Thinking Back: The Perils of Writing History* (Baton Rouge: Louisiana State University Press, 1986); also, Michael O'Brien, "C. Vann Woodward and the Burden of Southern Liberalism" *American Historical Review* 78 (June 1973), 589–604. Woodward, mistakenly in my view, characterizes Mitchell as a "continuitarian," one who essentially saw the Old South merging seamlessly into the New; *Thinking Back*, 25, 63, 72.

industrialization quickened around 1880, the South nonetheless had a long heritage of manufacturing enterprise, and the "Cotton Mill Campaign" itself yielded paltry results even as late as the early twentieth century. Industrialization was a slow, evolutionary development, hardly the result of a consciously designed crusade, and was limited to cheap-labor, low-value-added "colonial" sectors—hardly the recipe for the modern industrial society promised by Mitchell's scheme of linear progress.

More important, Mitchell's "religious" view of mill building downplayed the fundamental reason for all business enterprise: profit. In Woodward's eyes, Mitchell was collaborating in a massive fraud, in which buccaneering "new men," arisen from the ashes of the Old Order, posed as the South's saviors when they were in fact its rapists. In opposition to Mitchell's exaltation of class harmony among whites, Woodward insisted that conflict was essential to protecting "the people" from "the interests." In contrast to Mitchell's disdain for "demagogic" politicians, Woodward placed a "demagogue," Georgia's Tom Watson, at the very center of his narrative, and offered Watson and his political crusade as emblematic of a South in which the values of democracy and equality, not "the achievement of productive abilities," would be assigned priority.[60]

The publication of *Origins of the New South* was a major turning point in the influence of Mitchell's interpretation of southern industrialization; in the years following, many of *Rise of Cotton Mills*'s central contentions have come under question. One point of attack has been his, and others', insistence on the industrial backwardness of the slave regime. Historians Richard W. Griffin and Ernest McPherson Lander have challenged his argument that slavery had stifled industrial enterprise by demonstrating the presence of a considerable antebellum southern cotton-textile industry. More broadly, Kenneth M. Stampp has applied a critical version of "consensus" analysis to declare the slave South thoroughly capitalistic; and in the 1960s and after, so-called cliometric historians such as Robert W. Fogel,

---

[60]C. Vann Woodward, *Origins of the New South, 1877–1913* (Baton Rouge: Louisiana State University Press, 1951), esp. chap. 5 ("The Industrial Evolution") and chap. 11 ("The Colonial Economy").

Stanley Engerman, and Claudia Goldin, along with noncliometricians Robert Starobin and Charles B. Dew, have found the slave economy to be both dynamic and thoroughly compatible with industrialization.[61]

Other economic historians, however, have been inclined to agree with Mitchell's treatment of southern plantation society as economically stagnant. In the 1960s the then-Marxist historian Eugene D. Genovese reasserted the "precapitalist" character of the slave South in a manner not unlike Mitchell, although, as one harshly critical of the "bourgeois" culture of the antebellum North, he was hardly friendly to Mitchell's condemnation of southern "backwardness." Even economic historians in the neoclassical tradition, though, such as Gavin Wright, Fred Bateman, and Thomas Weiss, have reaffirmed Mitchell's basic position, albeit with more sophisticated arguments drawn from modern economic and economic-development theory. To be sure, no longer can historians declare plantation slavery to have been inimical to the "industrial spirit," as Mitchell did; the newer arguments have stressed structural rigidities in plantation societies that inhibit industrial development, such as orientation toward outside markets, over-specialization in agriculture, lack of urbanization, and deficiencies in entrepreneurial and labor skills, commercial development, and market articulation. Nonetheless, for probably the majority of those concerned with making sense of southern economic history, Mitchell's belief that the South's plantation heritage was a disability that needed

---

[61]Richard W. Griffin's numerous articles are best represented by his "Ante-Bellum Industrial Foundations of the (Alleged) New South" *Textile History Review* 5 (1962): 33–43; see also Ernest McPherson Lander, *The Textile Industry in Antebellum South Carolina* (Baton Rouge: Louisiana State University Press, 1969). Kenneth M. Stampp Jr., *The Peculiar Institution: Slavery in the Ante-Bellum South* (New York: Alfred A. Knopf, 1956), insists on the liberal-capitalist underpinnings of slavery. The case for the dynamism and flexibility of the antebellum slave regime is made most comprehensively by Robert W. Fogel and Stanley Engerman, *Time on the Cross: The Economics of American Negro Slavery* (Boston: Little, Brown and Co., 1974); Robert W. Fogel, *Without Consent or Contract: The Rise and Fall of American Slavery* (New York: W. W. Norton, 1989); on industrial slavery more particularly, see Claudia Dale Goldin, *Urban Slavery in the American South: A Quantitative History* (Chicago: University of Chicago Press, 1976); Robert S. Starobin, *Industrial Slavery in the Old South* (New York: Oxford University Press, 1970); and Charles B. Dew, *Bond of Iron : Master and Slave at Buffalo Forge* (New York: W. W. Norton, 1994).

to be overcome, if not necessarily consciously repudiated, before the region could advance remains fundamentally sound.[62]

Other work of the 1950s and 1960s has undermined *Rise of Cotton Mills* in less direct ways, particularly with respect to the one quality of the book most likely to disturb modern readers: its treatment of race. Mitchell basically accepted the prevailing southern view of Reconstruction, for instance, as a time of "misrule" by carpetbaggers, scalawags, and blacks incapable of democratic citizenship. His understanding of the period essentially followed that of the pro-southern Columbia University historian William A. Dunning and his "school," whose guiding presumption—that the Reconstruction effort to establish full citizenship rights for African Americans was an offense to nature and good government—has since been roundly repudiated.[63]

More seriously, Mitchell's general attitude toward black southerners falls considerably short of what today would be mainstream, let alone liberal, views. African Americans are, with rare exceptions, ghostly presences in *Rise of Cotton Mills*. Mitchell's central indictment of the slave regime had far less to do with its impact on the slaves than with its retarding influence on the southern economy, and especially its failure to foster the improvement of the nonslaveholding white population, which he depicted (following Olmsted) as mired in a slavery-induced

---

[62]Eugene D. Genovese, *The Political Economy of Slavery: Studies in the Economy and Society of the Slave South* (New York: Vintage, 1965); Gavin Wright, *The Political Economy of the Cotton South: Households, Markets and Wealth in the Nineteenth Century* (New York: W. W. Norton, 1978); Fred Bateman and Thomas Weiss, *A Deplorable Scarcity: The Failure of Industrialization in a Slave Society* (Chapel Hill: University of North Carolina Press, 1981); Peter A. Coclanis, *The Shadow of a Dream: Economic Life and Death in the South Carolina Low Country, 1670–1920* (New York: Oxford University Press, 1989). These structural arguments were in fact anticipated by Mitchell, but were subordinate to his main thesis.

[63]For the "Dunning School" version of Reconstruction, see William A. Dunning, *Reconstruction, Political and Economic, 1865–1877* (New York: Harper and Brothers, 1907); for Mitchell's reliance on this work, see *Rise of Cotton Mills*, 79. The "revisionist" literature on Reconstruction is vast; representative general treatments include W. E. B. DuBois, *Black Reconstruction* (New York: Harcourt, Brace and Co., 1935); John Hope Franklin, *Reconstruction After the Civil War* (Chicago: University of Chicago Press, 1961); Kenneth M. Stampp, *The Era of Reconstruction, 1865–1877* (New York: Alfred A. Knopf, 1965); and Eric Foner, *Reconstruction: America's Unfinished Revolution, 1863–1877* (New York: Harper and Row, 1988).

slough of backwardness. By the same token, a central feature of his case for the "philanthropic" motives of the mill builders lay precisely in the fact that the postbellum textile industry reserved the new mill jobs for poor whites—in his view, the great neglected resource of the region, and a people whose uplift was essential to the region's economic and social progress. At times he actually seems to regard the provision of employment opportunity to black workers in the mills with hostility; he expressed "some surprise" at advocacy of black mill labor by his hero William Gregg, and could only attribute it to the deadening influence of living in a slave society on even such a visionary as him.[64]

In this regard he was, again, very much a creature of his family and class. Samuel Chiles Mitchell was more "liberal" than many white southerners of his day, speaking out against lynching and supporting (at some personal cost, as we have seen) greater provision for black education. But the education he advocated was of the "industrial" sort championed by Booker T. Washington: "It is of course understood that by education and religion for the negro [sic] I mean very practical things. His education must be both mental and manual, and his religion must be wholly moral." In keeping with Samuel's general hostility toward politics, he viewed Reconstruction as a "blunder-crime," and regarded efforts of blacks to seek improvements in their position through political agitation as worthless. He applauded disfranchisement for showing blacks that "suffrage is a privilege to be gained only by the worthy, reckoned according to property and intelligence," and hoped that, by taking racial issues out of politics, it would cool the passions stirred by demagogues: "to hold the wolf by the ear is no longer our sole duty."[65] The elder Mitchell's views were representative of a standard southern progressive approach to the problem of race, which one histo-

---

[64]Mitchell, *Rise of Cotton Mills*, p. 210.

[65]S. C. Mitchell, "Educational Needs of the South"; the "property and intelligence" quote appears on p. 414. Samuel C. Mitchell, "The Nationalization of Southern Sentiment" *South Atlantic Quarterly* 7 (April 1908): 107–13; the "blunder-crime" and "wolf" quotes appear on p. 109. Presley, "Samuel Chiles Mitchell," stresses Samuel's racial "liberalism," especially with respect to lynching, but fails to acknowledge his endorsement of disfranchisement and his generally paternalistic approach to black education.

rian has termed "accommodationist racism"; while racial radicals such as Cole Blease regarded blacks as beasts to be
restrained, if not exterminated, accommodationists regarded
them as children capable of (slow) development, but only if kept
in their "place."[66]

The limits posed on the young Broadus's racial vision by his
time, place, and social class, though, were alloyed in *Rise of Cotton Mills* by his efforts to be "scientific" and judicious. Thus, in
discussing the prospects for black workers in the textile industry, he balanced claims that blacks were racially unsuited for
mill work with extensive treatment of several early-twentieth-
century "experiments" with black labor, including one launched
by an African American entrepreneur in Concord, North Carolina. While these "experimental" enterprises failed, he found
that factors unrelated to the race of the work force were more
culpable, and concluded that the case against black labor was
not yet proven—an "advanced" position for his time.[67]

More importantly, the racial inadequacies of *Rise of Cotton
Mills* were transcended in time by the Mitchells themselves.
"Accommodationist racists" were, of all white southerners, those
most likely to liberalize their views over time, and the Mitchells,
in particular, moved very far, very fast. In the 1930s Broadus
became president of the Baltimore Urban League, and the issue
precipitating his rupture with Johns Hopkins involved his
efforts to gain admission to the political economy program for
the League's African American secretary. In the 1950s his
younger brother George served as executive director of the
Southern Regional Council, the preeminent organization of
southern white liberals during the Civil Rights era, at a time
when open advocacy of a racially integrated South required
enormous moral stamina. If the racial attitudes of *Rise of Cot-*

---

[66]On "accommodationist racism," see George M. Fredrickson, *The Black
Image in the White Mind: The Debate on Afro-American Character and Destiny,
1817–1914* (New York: Harper and Row, 1971), chap. 10.

[67]Mitchell, *Rise of Cotton Mills*, pp. 215–21. More recent treatments of black
cotton-mill labor and entrepreneurship include Allen Heath Stokes Jr., "Black
and White Labor and the Development of the Southern Textile Industry,
1800–1920" (Ph.D. dissertation, University of South Carolina, 1977); and Allen
Edward Burgess, "Tar Heel Blacks and the New South Dream: The Coleman
Manufacturing Company, 1896–1904" (Ph.D. dissertation, Duke University,
1977).

ton Mills give us unease, we can nonetheless see in the book's relative generosity (for its time) toward blacks, and its fervent commitment to "uplift" and "progress," the motives that would later impel its author to help lead the way to a more racially just South[68]

As we have seen, Mitchell suffered from another blind spot: class. Mitchell never really knew mill workers, and indeed never felt he needed to; like most modernizers, he believed that what was good for them was self-evident, and only needed realization by those in charge, or else advancement through the inexorable forces of Progress. Thus a reader would be ill-advised to pick up *Rise of Cotton Mills* expecting to learn much about the lives of workers. One learns, to be sure, about workers as "labor sources," and also about the benefits they gained by moving to the factories; but the worker experience itself gets short shrift. In the 1930s, when the southern textile industry erupted in recurrent labor conflict, sociologists and economists attempted to fill the gap, but extensive exploration of the mill workers' world came only after the 1960s, when historians began consciously to write "history from the bottom up." In the early 1970s Melton McLaurin punctured the myth of worker docility during the late-nineteenth-century "pioneer phase" of the industry; in the 1980s David L. Carlton and the group associated with the Southern Oral History Program at the University of North Carolina at Chapel Hill uncovered, in different ways, a "cotton mill culture" that was no mere adoption of "modern" values, but one that used tradition in creative (and not always lovely) ways to cope with a world the workers could help make, although not as they pleased. The outpouring of work on mill life in all its aspects has continued to the present, and shows no sign of abating.[69]

---

[68]Mitchell autobiography, pp. 176–84; Presley, "Samuel Chiles Mitchell," 295–98. Daniel Singal describes Mitchell's resignation from Johns Hopkins as "a gesture . . . no other southern-born intellectual of that day would conceivably have made." Singal, *War Within,* 81.

[69]Melton A. McLaurin, *Paternalism and Protest; Southern Cotton Mill Workers and Organized Labor, 1875–1905* (Westport, Ct.: Greenwood Publishing Corp., 1971); Carlton, *Mill and Town;* Jacquelyn Hall et al., *Like a Family: The Making of a Southern Cotton Mill World* (Chapel Hill: University of North Carolina Press, 1987). Another major recent works include Idus A. Newby, *Plain Folk of the New South* (Baton Rouge: Louisiana State University Press, 1989);

Curiously, *Rise of Cotton Mills* was attacked from an altogether different quarter in the 1970s, as a newer generation of historians began to challenge the hegemony of Woodward's view of the "New South." Contending that southern industrialization had been sponsored, not by "new men," but by a reactionary planter elite persisting from antebellum times, and that the cotton mills had carried the values of the slave plantation into the twentieth century, the sociologist Dwight B. Billings Jr. criticized *Rise of Cotton Mills* for its contention that the "New South" was truly new. Building on Griffin's North Carolina studies, Billings complained that Mitchell overplayed the difference between the "backward" Old South and the "progressive" New South. Further, Billings contended that *Rise of Cotton Mills* wrongly attributed the "Cotton-Mill Campaign" to the advent of a new middle class in the postbellum South. The articles in *The Industrial Revolution in the South,* he argued, were more nearly correct in their declaration that southern industrial pioneers were "generally gentlemen, not operatives or mechanics as in England."[70]

Certainly, the Mitchell of *Industrial Revolution in the South,* with his polemical emphasis on the "retrograde" elements in southern industrial life, fitted Billings's argument well. But the Mitchell of *Rise of Cotton Mills* was little interested in "class" issues. While in his polemical pieces he was willing to evoke the myth of Old South *noblesse oblige* to shame the allegedly more

---

Allen Tullos, *Habits of Industry: White Culture and the Transformation of the Carolina Piedmont* (Chapel Hill: University of North Carolina Press, 1989); Douglas Flamming, *Creating the Modern South: Millhands and Managers in Dalton, Georgia, 1884–1984* (Chapel Hill: University of North Carolina Press, 1992); and Bryant Simon, *A Fabric of Defeat: The Politics of South Carolina Millhands, 1910–1948* (Chapel Hill: University of North Carolina Press, 1998).

[70]Dwight B. Billings Jr., *Planters and the Making of a "New South": Class, Politics, and Development in North Carolina, 1865–1900* (Chapel Hill: University of North Carolina Press, 1979), esp. 53–57, 101–4. The Griffin articles on which Billings built are Richard W. Griffin and Diffee W. Standard, "The Cotton Textile Industry in Ante-bellum North Carolina: Part I: Origin and Growth to 1830" *North Carolina Historical Review* 34 (January 1957): 15–35; and Griffin and Standard, "The Cotton Textile Industry in Ante-bellum North Carolina: Part II: an Era of Boom and Consolidation, 1830–1860" *North Carolina Historical Review* 34 (April 1957): 131–64. Mitchell and Mitchell, *Industrial Revolution in the South,* 122; cited in Billings, *Planters and the Making of a "New South,"* 103.

crass modern generation of industrialists (or, conversely, to complain of it as an archaic carryover), he was generally quite careless about attributing "class" origins to his industrialists. Whether they began as planters or as country storekeepers mattered less to him than that they were community leaders. And, in the end, it was a revolution in community spirit, not "class interest," that explained industrialization for Mitchell.

In this respect the young Mitchell was on to something that eluded his detractors. Commentators from Woodward to Billings commonly brought to their critiques an understanding of "classic" industrialization that identified it with *laissez-faire* capitalism, "rugged individualist" entrepreneurs obsessed with profit, and a mobile proletariat selling its labor-power on an open "labor market." Informed by that model, Woodward attacked *Rise of Cotton Mills* for romanticizing bottom-line-driven entrepreneurs, and Billings faulted it for failing to understand that southern industrialization was fundamentally different from the "liberal" process followed in the North. But by the 1970s new work was beginning to raise questions about the historical usefulness of distinctions between "precapitalist" and "capitalist," between "paternalistic" and "profit-minded," and between "northern" and "southern" patterns of industrialization. Northern textile historians such as Barbara Tucker, Jonathan Prude, and Anthony F. C. Wallace recovered the half-forgotten tradition of paternalism in early northern textiles. More broadly, the business historian Philip Scranton, drawing in part on similar work done in England by Patrick Joyce, developed a theory of industrial paternalism that related it as much to business imperatives as to traditional social values and systems, and found similar patterns of industrial paternalism across American regions. "Paternalism," which Woodward viewed as inconsistent with hard-nosed capitalism, was increasingly seen as an *aid* to it—a means of mobilizing, screening, and disciplining labor that was common to a broad range of societies in the initial stages of industrialization. Still others have found "paternalism" to have been useful to workers as well, both as a means of cushioning the social disruption attendant on the move to the factory and as an ethos that could be appealed to for protection against arbitrary management.[71]

As the boundaries between "traditional" and "modern" values have gotten fuzzier, Mitchell's own infusion of "uplift" rhetoric into his account of southern industrialization has begun to make more sense. Thus the economic historian Cathy McHugh has argued that in Alamance County, North Carolina, paternalism served the labor mobilization needs of a newly developing industry. Mitchell's attribution of religious motives for the "Cotton-Mill Campaign," previously dismissed as hypocritical window-dressing for exploitation, has been reexamined and to some degree rehabilitated. Gary R. Freeze's work on the life of a leading nineteenth-century North Carolina industrialist, John Milton Odell, has found his business practices suffused with a paternalistic Methodism acquired, in part, from a New England immigrant. The famous case of the Salisbury Cotton Mill, born in a revival, has been revisited and found to have substance. For evangelicals of the late-nineteenth-century South, Christian faith called for salvation in this world as well as the next; the Rev. Robert Gamaliel Pearson, who saw cotton mills as teaching habits of self-control and inner direction to his Salisbury revival audience, was both credible and typical of his time and place.[72]

---

[71]Barbara M. Tucker, *Samuel Slater and the Origins of the American Textile Industry, 1790–1860* (Ithaca, N.Y.: Cornell University Press, 1984); Jonathan Prude, *The Coming of Industrial Order: Town and Factory Life in Massachusetts, 1810–1860* (New York: Cambridge University Press, 1983); Anthony F. C. Wallace, *Rockdale: the Growth of an American Village in the Early Industrial Revolution* (New York: Alfred A. Knopf, 1978); Philip Scranton, "Varieties of Paternalism: Industrial Structures and the Social Relations of Production in American Textiles" *American Quarterly* 36 (Summer 1984): 235–57; Gerald Zahavi, *Workers, Managers, and Welfare Capitalism : the Shoeworkers and Tanners of Endicott Johnson, 1890–1950* (Urbana: University of Illinois Press, 1988).

[72]Cathy M. McHugh, *Mill Family: The Labor System in the Southern Cotton Textile Industry, 1880–1915* (New York: Oxford University Press, 1988); Gary Richard Freeze, "Model Mill Men of the New South: Paternalism And Methodism in The Odell Cotton Mills of North Carolina, 1877–1908" (Ph.D. dissertation, University of North Carolina at Chapel Hill, 1988); Freeze, "God, Cotton Mills, and New South Myths: A New Perspective on Salisbury, North Carolina, 1887–1888," in Elizabeth Jacoway et al., eds., *The Adaptable South: Essays in Honor of George Brown Tindall* (Baton Rouge: Louisiana State University Press, 1991), 44–63. For more on "paternalism," see Flamming, *Creating the Modern South;* David L. Carlton, "Paternalism and Southern Textile Labor: A Historiographical Review," in Gary M. Fink and Merl E. Reed, eds., *Race,*

If paternalism and evangelical religion were intrinsic to industrialization and modernization, rather than being opposed to them, the public-spiritedness that Mitchell found in the cotton-mill crusade turns out not to have been particularly incompatible with pecuniary motivation. In *Mill and Town in South Carolina* (1982) and other writings, David L. Carlton has found that many, if not all mills, were indeed the creations of community efforts. To be sure, these "community projects" lacked the purely altruistic motives that Mitchell tended to ascribe to them. Their "philanthropic" aims, for instance, were directed less toward worker welfare than toward the improvement of the largely middle-class business communities of the proliferating small towns. If the prospect of large profits were not always paramount to industrial promotions, indirect pecuniary benefits, such as expanded population and trade or speculative gains in land values, commonly were. Mills were commonly "booster" enterprises, designed more to make the collective fortunes of communities than to make the individual fortunes of entrepreneurs; but making fortunes was ever their intent.[73]

While Mitchell may have misunderstood the social dimension of the "rise of the mills," he nonetheless was the first to spot it, and to document it with the testimony of active participants. Thus he saw something that many of his critics have missed— that industrialization, commonly viewed as a disruption visited on societies by "creatively destroying" (or simply destroying) entrepreneurs, in fact grows out of societies, and is dependent on social organization for its success. It was the task of his and his father's generations to reform southern institutions as a prerequisite to material and social progress, and in that project they had good reason to regard industrialists as allies, not opponents. If Mitchell emerged later as an industrial critic, he was motivated at least in part by a sense of betrayal, a belief that the textile men of his time had opted to shirk their earlier social roles

Class, and Community in Southern Labor History (Tuscaloosa: University of Alabama Press, 1994), 17–26.

[73]Carlton, *Mill and Town*; see also Carlton, "The Revolution From Above: The National Market and the Beginnings of Industrialization in North Carolina," *Journal of American History* 77 (September 1990): 445–75; Edward L. Ayers, *The Promise of the New South: Life after Reconstruction* (New York: Oxford University Press, 1992); Wright, "Economic Progress," 196–98.

as leaders of a great social transformation. But, unlike his critics, he never accepted the notion that industrialists were by
nature exploitive—partly because he was blinded by admiration, but also because he was genuinely appreciative of the role
they played in advancing the South toward modernity. To
Mitchell, the impulse to industrialize could never be rooted in
mere lust for profit—the risks of startup enterprises in an under-
developed region were simply too great, and safer investments
too plentiful, for that. If he overdid the claim that mill men were
"philanthropists," he did capture *something* important: that the
highly public nature of mill building, with its widely held share-
holdings, its mass meetings and newspaper campaigns, made
local mills into sorts of public utilities, which were expected to
serve goals broader than those signified on a flush balance sheet.
He rendered, from the inside, the experience of communities
accustomed to thinking of social change in terms of conversion
and revival, communities that made industrialization a sort of
religious crusade and the factory a symbol of their aspirations.
Anyone wishing to comprehend the industrialization of the
South needs to understand it as a product of communities, of a
society, as well as of individuals—and *The Rise of Cotton Mills
in the South* will remain their indispensable starting point.

PREFACE TO THE FIRST EDITION

In prefacing some observations on the history of the South a writer has said: "It will be something if these papers shall make it plain that my subject is a true body of human life—a thing, and not a mass of facts, a topic in political science, an object lesson in large moralities. To know the thing itself should be our study; and the right study of it is thought and passion, not research alone."[1] The same is true of the present story of the South's espousal of manufactures in place of whole devotion to agriculture. Rightly set forth, it is not only an industrial chronicle, but a romance, a drama as well. One who himself bore a part in the events here described, at the outset of my project hoped that I would grasp both the economic and the spiritual aspects of the period under review.[2] This I have tried to transmit to the reader, and I have found that the fuller the account of material circumstance, just so much the clearer becomes the spiritual significance.

In point of view I owe most to my Father, accepting his concise explanation that the South was overcome at Appomattox because it placed itself in opposition to the compelling forces of the age—by agency of the invention of the cotton gin held to slavery instead of liberty, insisted upon States' rights in place of nationality, and chose agriculture alone rather than embracing the rising industrialism. As a result, the task since 1865 has been to liberalize the South in thought, nationalize it in politics, and industrialize it in production. "Would we make cotton king? Let us aspire to spin every fibre of our exhaustless fields. By such alignments with this wondrous mother-age, we shall enable the South to take her rightful part in determining the national destiny."[3] My study is little more than illustration of this analysis of the past, this interpretation of the present and future.

[1] William Garrott Brown, The Lower South in American History.
[2] Mr. J. C. Hemphill.
[3] Samuel Chiles Mitchell, "Educational Needs of the South," in the Outlook, N.Y., vol. lxxvi, no. 7, p. 415ff.

Formerly, a landed aristocracy shut out the average man from economic participation; but with the rise of cotton mills, the poor whites were welcomed back into the service of the South. As a conclusion from my survey I cannot but express the anxiety that through lessons of the old mistake we shall avoid the new error, insuring that an aristocracy of capital shall not now preclude industrial democracy.

My purpose has been to describe the birth of the industry in the South rather than its development. In only a small number of instances has this plan been departed from; many topics rich in interest have not been broached.

I regret that two books did not come into my hands in time to be used in this study. Holland Thompson's "The New South," and George T. Winston's "A Builder of the New South" (the story of the life work of D. A. Tompkins), are contributions which will be found valuable.

I owe thanks for special assistance to Professor Jacob H. Hollander and Professor George E. Barnett, of The Johns Hopkins University, who guided the investigation; the proprietors of the Manufacturers' Record, who permitted me to use the early files of the paper; Mr. T. S. Raworth, of Augusta; Mr. William M. Bird, of Charleston; Professor Yates Snowden and Mr. August Kohn, of Columbia, all of whom made documentary material available to me. Others have given me hardly less generously of their time and thought; footnote references to interviews and correspondence with these must serve as acknowledgment in each case.

B. M.

THE RISE OF COTTON MILLS
IN THE SOUTH

THE RISE OF COTTON MILLS IN THE SOUTH

CHAPTER I

THE BACKGROUND

This opening chapter undertakes a brief survey of the historical and economic background out of which the cotton manufacturing industry of the South, as a distinct development, emerged. It may be said that thus to begin the story of the rise of the mills with discussion of a period which lies a century in advance, is not unlike the production of a play hopeful in conception, robust in theme and rapid in action, but in which the curtain first lifts to show a stage which, except for a few unrelated characters, remains empty throughout an entire act.

It is a purpose here to refer to the views of some observers who believe they have caught glimpses of men and facts in these prior years not only presaging but causally related to the main action later. The total of this chapter will show, however, that the development, as such, first substantially showed itself and had its complete genesis about the year 1880.

In the neglect of Southern economic history, information of the early period is not abundant, yet there is less dispute as to findings of fact than as to right interpretation of material evidences agreed upon. In bringing the several beliefs into parallel presentation it will be seen that concerning the rise of cotton mills in the South a little body of theory exists. Several of the statements that will be given are not well-informed, and others are almost too studied, so that they lose perspective. Interpretations will be cited in connection with the different stages under discussion, so that the relative weighting of these stages, as intended by writers, will appear.

9

It is first useful to notice the limits of divergence of views. One who wrote with empirical purpose and may be believed to have been not deeply interested in the historical setting of the mills, has said of one State, taken by him as typical: "The story of the development of the cotton manufacturing industry in South Carolina is not wanting in impressive elements. From the beginning in 1790 till 1900 it was a struggle of gradually increasing intensity and extension."[1] This conception of continuity is in marked contrast with a representative expression of another Southerner likewise for some time a resident of the North. After referring to promising industrial beginnings it is declared that: ". . . a manufacturing development throughout the Piedmont region of the South might have continued parallel with that which has taken place in Pennsylvania, except for the . . . combined influence of the invention of the cotton gin, the institution of slavery, and the checking of . . . immigration. As late as 1810 the manufactured products of Virginia, the Carolinas and Georgia exceeded in value those of the entire New England states. By Whitney's invention . . . cotton planting became so profitable, that for a period of forty years the price remained above twenty-five cents a pound. Factories were abandoned. . . . As cotton and slavery advanced, the population of free white work people were driven further and further into the mountain country, and thus many of the white industrial workers of 1800 became the poor mountain farmers of 1850 . . . the owners of factories who operated with free white labor in 1800 had become in 1850 the cotton planters operating with black slave labor. . . . When the abolition of slavery removed one great difficulty of industries and the white people who had formerly deserted manufactures for agriculture went back to the pursuits of their fathers, these mountaineers formed the labor supply."[2]

[1] P. H. Goldsmith, The Cotton Mill South, p. 4.
[2] D. A. Tompkins, in The South in the Building of the Nation, vol. ii, p. 58. For a more summary statement, cf. ibid., Cotton Mill, Commercial Features, pp. 108–109. Cf. also ibid., History of Meck-

Not so categorical as one opinion that "from 1810 to 1880 the South was industrially a desert of Sahara," this view still makes it clear that from a point early in the century until a date subsequent to the Civil War, absorption in cotton culture threw manufacturing of all sorts into the discard.

There is sufficient evidence that in what may be roughly called the Revolutionary Period, the South was well started toward a balanced economic development, with manufactures as well as agriculture.[3] In South Carolina early encouragement was given to the manufacture of cotton specifically; one Hugh Templeton, seeking inventor's privileges, in 1789 deposited with State authorities a plan for a carding machine and "a complete draft of a spinning machine, with eighty-four spindles, that will spin with one man's attendance ten pounds of good cotton yarn per day."[4] In 1795 the legislature authorized commissioners to project a lottery for the benefit of William McClure in his effort to establish a cotton manufactory to make "Manchester wares."[5] The

---

lenburg County, vol. i, pp. 133–137; The Tariff and Reciprocity; Road Building and Repairs, p. 24; W. L. Trenholm, The Southern States, quoted in C. D. Wright, Industrial Evolution of the United States, pp. 145–146; J. A. B. Scherer, Cotton as a World Power, p. 168 ff.; Walter H. Page, The Rebuilding of Old Commonwealths, p. 139.

[3] "Upon the whole, the last half of the Eighteenth century, before the influence of the cotton gin and Arkwright's inventions were fully felt in the South, was a period when agriculture yielded some ground in primary manufactures and household industries." (V. S. Clark, in South in Building of Nation, vol. v, p. 308). Cf. Tompkins, The South's Position in American Affairs, p. 1. Of North Carolina a careful student has said: "Though there were no towns of any size, the number and skill of the artisans was such that, in 1800, it seemed probable that the logical development would be into a frugal manufacturing community, rather than into an agricultural state" (Holland Thompson, From the Cotton Field to the Cotton Mill, p. 25). See, especially with reference to iron making in this period, Richard H. Edmonds, Facts About the South (ed. 1894), p. 3 ff. There is importance in the founding of the Manumission Society, with 1600 active members as late as 1826 (ibid., pp. 26–27).

[4] August Kohn, The Cotton Mills of South Carolina, pp. 10–11.

[5] Ibid., pp. 9–10. In an appropriation bill of 1809, the sum of $1000 was advanced to Ephraim McBride "to enable him to construct a spinning machine on the principles mentioned in a patent he holds from the United States" (ibid., pp. 10–11). In the same

South shared in the national impulse toward economic self sufficiency consequent upon the stoppage of colonial commerce with England and the Revolution. Proceedings of the Safety Committee in Chowan County, North Carolina, for March 4, 1775, show that "the committee met at the house of Captain James Sumner and the gentlemen appointed at a former meeting of directors to promote subscriptions for the encouragement of manufactures, informed the committee that the sum of eighty pounds sterling was subscribed by the inhabitants of this county for that laudable purpose." The chairman offered ten pounds to the first producer in a certain time of fulled woolen cloth. The provincial congress took steps the same year to stimulate, by bounties, the manufacture of gunpowder, rolling and slitting mill products, cotton cards, steel, paper, woolen cloth and pig iron.[6]

Although their objects were possibly political as well as industrial, mechanics' societies existed at Charleston and Augusta before and about the year 1810; in Augusta were made some of the earliest attempts in this country to improve the steam engine.[7] As early as 1770 there was formed in South Carolina a committee to establish and promote manufactures, with Henry Laurens as chairman.[8] The purchase by Southern States of the patent rights of Whitney's cotton gin is to be interpreted not as a design to leave off cotton manufacturing, but rather as evidence of a prevalent spirit for mechanical improvement.

Glimpses at individual establishments show the textile industry of the South in this Revolutionary Period to have

year the request of the president of the Homespun Company of South Carolina for a loan on account of a patent was unfavorably received by a legislative committee, but it was recommended that he be allowed until the next meeting of the legislature "to report on the utility of the machine called the Columbia Spinster, so as to entitle, in case the same be approved, the inventor of the same to the sum provided by law for his benefit" (ibid., p. 11). Cf. ibid., pp. 11-13.

[6] For these facts the writer is indebted to a MS. of M. R. Pleasants, "Manufacturing in North Carolina before 1860."

[7] Clark, in South in Building of Nation, vol. v, p. 310.

[8] Kohn, Cotton Mills of South Carolina, p. 7.

been generally of the domestic character. Manufacturing was conducted by individuals rather than corporations, and was usually directly connected with plantations. Daniel Heyward, a planter, in a letter in 1777, declared with reference to his "manufactory" that if cards were to be had "there is not the least doubt but that we could make six thousand yards of good cloth in the year from the time we began."[9] Domestic production is clearly seen in a statement the same year that a planter in three months trained thirty negroes to make one hundred and twenty yards of cotton and woolen cloth per week, employing a white woman to instruct in spinning and a white man in weaving, and it was said: "He expects to have it in his power not only to clothe his own negroes, but soon to supply his neighbors."[10]

A few plants may have approached a commercial character. In 1790 it was related that "a gentleman of great mechanical knowledge and instructed in most of the branches of cotton manufactures in Europe, has already fixed, completed and now at work on the high hills of the Santee, near Stateburg, and which go by water, ginning (?) carding and slubbing machines, with 84 spindles each, and several other useful implements for manufacturing every necessary article in cotton." This establishment was coincident with Slater's famous factory at Pawtucket, Rhode Island, founded in 1790, and may have antedated it, though comparative credit to the Stateburg enterprise is perhaps diminished by information that while some long staple cotton was imported from the West Indies, and a variety of goods were made, it was conducted as an adjunct to a plantation, parts of its equipment were later removed to and set up on another plantation, and much of its yarn was spun for persons in the vicinity. It is notable, however, that the machinery was made in North Carolina.[11]

---

[9] Ibid., p. 7.
[10] South Carolina and American General Gazette, Jan. 30, 1770, quoted in ibid., p. 7. Cf. ibid., pp. 6–7.
[11] American Museum, viii, Appendix iv, part 2, July 1, 1790, cited in ibid., p. 8. The question mark is Mr. Kohn's. If Mr. Kohn is correct in believing that "a regular cotton mill" was established by

The textile industry in the South in the latter part of the eighteenth and earlier part of the nineteenth centuries was stamped with the hallmark of domestic production.[12]   However, it is to be remembered that a century and a half ago this and other manufactures in every part of America and in England too bore very much of the domestic character,[13] and that probably Southern States showed instances of power-driven machinery before Slater set up the first Arkwright mill in Rhode Island. The South had planter-manufacturers it is true, but this link between agriculture and industry as contrasted with New England is easily explained in the more general fertility of the soil and the effect this of course had upon the occupation of the people. Furthermore, the very fact of this coupling indicates the inclination toward economic balance and the promise in these years of a rational development.[14]

Mrs. Ramage, a widow, on James Island, Charleston District, in 1778, the fact is highly interesting, because the date is nine years antecedent to that of America's "first factory," at Beverly, Massachusetts. The South Carolina mill was operated by mule power; no traces survive (ibid., p. 8. Reference is particularly to the City Gazette and Daily Advertiser, Charleston, Jan. 24, 1779).

[12] Referring especially to the establishments just noticed and to water-driven spindles near Fayetteville, Mr. Clark has said: "Small mills may have started in the Carolinas and Georgia, and after a brief infancy have vanished and left no name; but, if so, the fact is curious rather than significant, for it had no relation to the subsequent history of the industry" (History of Manufactures in the United States, 1607-1860, p. 537). As indicating further the lack of causation in these ventures, it is observed: "Maryland is hardly typical industrially of the Southern states. Its factories date from the Revolution . . ." (ibid., in South in Building of Nation, vol. v, pp. 328-329). ". . . prior to the war of 1812 the advance of Southern manufactures was principally in what were then household arts —those that produced for the subsistence of the family rather than for an outside market. These manufactures continued generalized and dispersed rather than specialized and integrated" (ibid., p. 312). Cf. ibid., p. 310, and W. W. Sellers, A History of Marion County, p. 26.

[13] Carroll D. Wright, "The Factory System of the United States," p. 6, in U. S. Census of Manfactures, 1880.

[14] The Bolton Factory was built in 1811 on Upton Creek, Wilkes County, Ga. In 1794 on this site had been erected one of Whitney's first cotton gins, propelled by the water power that later ran the cotton mill. It is said that Lyon here conceived important improvements in the Whitney invention, making a saw gin (Southern Cotton Spinners' Association, proceedings, seventh annual convention, p.

The nature of the mills up to 1810, then, is clear. Coming now to those established in decades just following, a subject is entered in which some controversy is involved. These plants I have chosen to call the "old mills." A distinction is to be observed between influence of these factories upon the later great development and the proper character to be ascribed to them as of themselves. A manufacture which is forerunner in time is not necessarily antecedent in effect. To substantiate a view that the Civil War interrupted a course which was clearly laid down in years previous, it ought to be demonstrable that the old mills had essentially the same features as those of the later development, with only those lacks which were inherent in an industry in formative stage.[15] The South had small cotton farmers of a prevalent sort before ever Knapp taught efficient production. If the old mills were of a notably different stripe from those of the period fifteen years after the War, the genesis of the industry, economically speaking, lies in

---

41 ff.). Here is a suggestion of the fact that the South was on the right road—a gin, so far from diverting attention entirely to the cultivation of the staple, was succeeded by a cotton mill on the same spot, operated by the same power. Perhaps Helper was in bounds when the declared: "Had the Southern States, in accordance with the principles enunciated in the Declaration of Independence, abolished slavery at the same time the Northern States abolished it, there would have been, long since, and most assuredly at this moment, a larger, wealthier, wiser, and more powerful population, south of Mason and Dixon's line, than there now is north of it" (H. R. Helper, The Impending Crisis of the South, ed. 1860, pp. 161–162).

[15] A North Carolinian of post-bellum experience, but who has been identified with one of the foremost industrial communities of the South, thought it had been "a clear case of arrested development; it would have all come sooner, but for the War. It might be said that had slavery continued, manufacturing would never have come in the South, but it is also true that slavery was doomed. There is no use in talking about what might not have happened had slavery continued" (W. F. Marshall, interview, Raleigh, N. C., Sept. 16, 1916). Loose, unsupported statements are frequent: "The first cotton mill . . . in North Carolina was built at Lincolnton in 1813 by Michael Schenck. . . . This mill was the forerunner of that remarkable industrial development which has taken place in North Carolina since that time" (Pleasants MS.).

the later date. The mere fact that the old mills were known to the later builders is hardly enough.[16]

Not a few plants in the South have been in continuous operation since an early date. But this does not mean that many of these, so far from inspiring the later development, were not themselves by its stimulus so greatly changed as to be radically different from their former character.[17] In the light of the spirit in which mills were built about 1880 and the demonstrated total newness of the hands to the processes and even the idea of textile manufacture, it seems unnecessary to controvert an opinion that not only did the ante-bellum factories furnish a starting point for the later development, but domestic weaving had accustomed the people to the industry.[18]

The history of the mills of the thirty years following 1810 is rather hazy.[19] Important facts, however, stand out.

---

[16] "In the older mills, before the War, the seed had been planted, and cultivation was renewed after the War. The ante-bellum mills were pretty well known throughout the country. The woolen mills at Salem, and the cotton mills in Alamance and a few in Gastonia were known. The fact that such goods as 'Alamance' had a name already was an advantage" (John Nichols, int., Raleigh, N. C., Sept. 16, 1916). He continued to speak of these mills in close conjunction with the names of the families and manufacturers who owned them —the personal factor stood out in his mind more strongly than any other.

[17] Mr. Kohn believes that the one with the longest record is that founded at Autun, near Pendleton, S. C., in 1838, by B. F. Sloan, Thomas Sloan, and Berry Benson (Cotton Mills of S. C., p. 15). Cf. Charlotte (N. C.) News, Textile Industrial Edition, Feb., 1917, with reference to the Rocky Mount Mill. One long-established enterprise fell under local dislike as late as the seventies, a generous-minded father being suceeded in the management by reckless sons; the strength of the personal factor was thus a danger; in spite of undiscriminating statements that this mill afforded a manufacturing tradition to the community, it really lost all public character.

[18] Suggested by Mr. Charles E. Johnson in an interview, Raleigh, N. C., Sept. 16, 1916. For a clear distinction between first establishments in Philadelphia and New England and genuine factory development, cf. Wright, in U. S. Census of Manufactures, 1880, "Factory System of U. S.," p. 6; Clark, in South in Building of Nation, vol. v, p. 319.

[19] For a careful narrative of the establishments of the settlers who moved into the South from New England about 1816, with details of the factories of the Hills, Shelden, Clark, Bates, Hutchings, Stack, the Weavers, McBee, Bivings, etc., cf. Kohn, Cotton Mills of S. C., and The Water Powers of South Carolina. For those in

There was little localization of the industry. There was a good deal of moving about from one water-power to another, the machinery being hauled from place to place with apparent convenience.[20]   A founder would sell an enterprise, build another and sell it and build a third.[21]   It was difficult to convey machinery to the factory when purchased at a distance.[22]   Much machinery was made in local blacksmith shops, and must have been crude even for that period.[23]   While elaboration of the point falls elsewhere, it is worth notice here that there is a difference between the old and the later mills in the character of their promoters and managers.   In the earlier period men came to cotton manufacturing in the South by more normal channels than at the outset of the subsequent development.   Like Michael Schenck, they had foreign industrial habits and traditions back of them, and they set up mills in communities populated by Swiss, Scotch-Irish and Germans.   Or like William Bates and probably the Hills, Clark, Henry, and the Weavers, they came from the industrial atmosphere of New England, then particularly stimulated by the encouragement lent to textile manufacturing by the embargo laid on English goods by the War of 1812.[24]

Or through collateral business connections or marriage they were brought into the business.   Simply private invest-

North Carolina, Holland Thompson is useful; cf. also Southern Cotton Spinners' Association, Proceedings 7th Annual Convention, p. 41 ff., and Tompkins, Cotton Mill, Commercial Features, pp. 301-302.

[20] Wood for the boiler of the Mount Hecla Mills growing scarce, the machinery was taken to Mountain Island and there run by water (Thompson, pp. 48-49).

[21] Kohn, Cotton Mills of S. C., p. 14.

[22] That for the Mount Hecla Mills about 1830 was shipped from Philadelphia to Wilmington, N. C., up the Cape Fear River to Fayetteville, and then across country by wagon to Greensboro. The equipment of six or seven hundred spindles for the Hill factory in Spartanburg County fifteen years earlier was brought by wagon from Charleston (Kohn, Cotton Mills of S. C., p. 14). Cf. Charlotte News, Textile Ed., 1917, with reference to Rocky Mount Mill, and Thompson, p. 45 ff.

[23] The Bivingsville mill (J. B. Cleveland, int., Spartanburg, S. C., Sept. 8, 1916), and Shenck mill (Thompson, p. 45 ff.) are cases in point. Cf. Thompson, pp. 42-43.

[24] W. J. Thackston, int., Greenville, S. C., Sept. 12, 1916.

2

ment enlisted participation of men in various callings. Of course these same forces operated afterwards, but in the earlier time there was no response to a public enthusiasm or a social demand that acted like a magnet in drawing into the industry men who otherwise would never have entered it, certainly not as entrepreneurs.

A plant turning out iron products was operated in connection with the Schenck mill.[25] Cotton factories conjoined with gins and saw mills are not unknown in the South to-day, but in whatever instance this occurs there is indicated a lack of specialization.

Perhaps the most striking confirmation of the view here taken of the restricted and semi-domestic character of the old mills is found in the facts relating to the marketing and consumption of their products. A commercial nature is ascribed to the establishment of General David R. Williams on his plantation in Darlington County, South Carolina, which "in 1828 . . . was turning his cotton crop, of 200 bales annually, into what was said to be the best yarn in the United States. He marketed part of his crop in New York and wove part of it into negro cloth for home use," and twenty years later distant and local demands were being supplied. Evidence hardly supports the suggestion that the product of such small Southern mills as this "controlled the Northern yarn market."[26]

On the other hand, local consumption and the link with domestic industry, noted in the above instance, were prevalent. How closely these old mills were joined with the countryside is seen in the fact that into their coarse, homely fabrics went hand-spun linen warp. The domestic char-

---

[25] Ibid.
[26] Clark, in South in Building of Nation, vol. v, p. 321; cf. Kohn, Cotton Mills of S. C., pp. 18–19, giving quotation from Columbia Telescope. Contrast, however, William Gregg, Essays on Domestic Industry (1845), p. 11: "Limited as our manufactures are in South-Carolina, we can now, more than supply the State with Coarse Cotton Fabrics. Many of the Fabrics now manufactured here are exported to New-York, and, for aught I know, find their way to the East-Indies."

acter was thus ingrained.[27]   The yarn of the Batesville Factory, before the Columbia and Greenville railroad came to Greenville about 1852, passed current almost like money, in ten pound "bunches" covered with blue paper, and although "mountain schooners" carried it sometimes a hundred and fifty miles into North Carolina and Tennessee, it was given in barter for meat and rags.[28]

A banker intimately connected with the textile industry in one of the oldest industrial communities and a member of a family to which many writers are quick to point as founders of cotton manufacture in the South through con-

[27] Clark, in South in Building of Nation, vol. v, p. 321. Of the Rocky Mount mill in North Carolina it is said that "For some years prior to and during the Civil War, the mill was a general supply station for warps which the women of the South wove into cloth on the old hand looms." So beneficial did this prove during the War that a cavalry troop of Federals was sent up from New Bern in 1863 and burned the mill (Charlotte News, Textile Ed., 1917). It is remarked that making only twelve to fifteen hundred pounds, of 4s to 12s daily, the mill could not get a steady market for its wares (Thompson, pp. 48–49). Until 1851 slaves and a few free negroes were worked in this mill. This distinguishing difference between the old mills and those of the later development, when the labor of negroes was far from the thoughts of builders and managers, will be dwelt upon in another place. The McDonald Mill at Concord, during the Civil War, dealt in barter. A gentleman in a nearby town said he remembered as a boy trading a load of corn for yarn to be woven by the women at home (Theodore Klutz, int., Salisbury, N. C., Sept. 1, 1916). In 1862 the Confederate Government commandeered the Batesville factory, in South Carolina, and took nearly all of the product. That portion allowed to private purchasers was always sold by 10 o'clock in the morning (W. J. Thackston, int., Greenville). Of the three small plants running in Spartanburg County before the War, one was on Tyger River, spinning yarns on half a dozen frames, and people drove twenty to twenty-five miles to the door of the mill for the product, although it was sold, also, in the country stores (Walter Montgomery, int., Spartanburg, S. C., Sept. 5, 1916). The first woolen mill of Francis Fries at Salem, N. C., had a little fulling and dyeing plant for finishing cloth woven by the farmers' wives and daughters (Tompkins, Cotton Mill, Commercial Features, pp. 183–184). Cf. Thompson, p. 31.

[28] W. J. Thackston, int., Greenville. The old mills were "able to barter for the small quantities of local raw cotton which they used. The standard of exchange, the par, was one yard of three-yard sheeting for a pound of raw cotton, which was a third of a pound, made into cloth, for a pound in the raw state. But this was a retail and not strictly a manufacturing profit" (John W. Fries, int., Winston-Salem, N. C., Aug. 31, 1916).

spicuous participation in the business since the early thirties, said:

The mills built after the war were not the result of pre-bellum mills. This is trying to ascribe one cause for a condition which probably had many causes. The industrial awakening in the South was a natural reaction from the War and Reconstruction. Before the War there was first the domestic industry proper. Then came such small mills about Winston-Salem as Cedar Falls and Franklinsville. These little mills were themselves, however, hardly more than domestic manufactures. When, after the War, competition came from the North and from the larger Southern mills, the little mills which had operated before and had survived the war lost their advantage, which consisted in their possession of the local field. . . . The ante-bellum domestic-factory system did not produce the post-bellum mills.[29]

It must be obvious from foregoing considerations that a census enumeration of mills of the period cannot show internal characteristics which are all-important. But even the census returns, counting one plant like another, display the Southern industry at this stage as being feeble. Some primary descriptive factors are lacking in the earliest reports of the census which are at all useful, but taking the four Southern States which were farthest advanced in the years 1840 and 1850—Virginia, North and South Carolina and Georgia—and comparing the whole of the South with New England, the showing may be summed up thus:[30]

---

[29] John W. Fries, ibid. It is not to be forgotten that lack of transportation facilities necessarily cramped the old mills, and that this operated also to keep out competing product, but their essential character was independent of this consideration. The superior trend of capital into agriculture limited ante-bellum cotton mills by preventing profitable extension of plant and embarrassing advantageous marketing of product which might require some waiting. Cf. Edward Ingle, Southern Sidelights, pp. 70-71. Another with a broad view of the history of the industry was willing to include the Graniteville enterprise, about which some controversy has clustered, in his judgment: " The cotton mills in the South before the War were third-rate affairs. I speak of Graniteville and Batesville and such plants as these. I remember my mother's telling me that the warp . . . used to be supplied by the mills for use in the homes of the housewives. They were not regular cotton mills as the plants of later establishments have come to be " (W. W. Ball, int., Columbia, S. C., Jan. 1, 1917). " The mills built in the eighties were a part of a new spirit from the ante-bellum mills. The old mills—Bivingsville, Valley Falls, Crawfordsville, in Spartanburg County—were small and insignificant affairs. They lived from hand to mouth " (Cleveland, int., Spartanburg).

[30] U. S. Census of Manufactures, 1900, " Cotton Manufactures," p.

	Census	Plants	Capital	Ops.	Spin.	Bales Consumption
Virginia	1840	22	$1,299,020	1,816	42,262	17,785
	1850	27	1,908,900	2,963		
N. Carolina....	1840	25	995,300	1,219	47,934	(a)
	1850	28	1,058,800	1,619	531,903	13,617
S. Carolina	1840	15	617,450	570	16,353	
	1850	18	857,200	1,119		9,929
Georgia........	1840	19	573,835	779	42,589	
	1850	35	1,736,156	2,272		20,230
So. States......	1840	248	4,331,078	6,642	180,927[b]	
	1850	166	7,256,056	10,043		78,140
New England..	1840	674	34,931,399	46,834	1,497,394	
	1850	564	53,832,430	61,893		430,603

Many single mills in the South today represent more than the extent of the whole industry in the most forward Southern State in 1850.[31]

Some writers have pointed to evidences of industrial activity in the period to 1840 as presaging the later development. A localizing tendency in the textile manufacture along the fall line of rivers in the decade following 1830, has been called a "slow and unconscious development."[32] George Tucker in 1843 first pointed out that slavery was showing signs of decay from economic causes and as a system would finally lapse of its own accord.[33] A study of

---

54 ff. (a) Thompson gives 700 looms and 7000 bales consumed (p. 49 ff. (b) An obviously incomplete summary.

[31] Cf. Thompson, p. 49 ff. "The number of small carding and fulling mills and of little water-driven yarn factories, in this section [the South] before 1850, may have approached the number of textile factories in the same region today; . . . but few of these establishments became commercial producers" (Clark, in South in Building of Nation, vol. v, pp. 319–320). A map showing distribution of cotton spindles in 1839 indicates a good representation for all the Southern States except Mississippi, Louisiana, Arkansas and Florida, as to mills of small size, but the localization both as to plants and spindles in New England is marked (Clark, History of Manufactures, pp. 533–560). See the whole section for an excellent discussion of both historical and economic phases). "Few mills south of Virginia had power looms prior to 1840" (ibid., in South in Building of Nation, vol. v, p. 321). Notice omission of looms for Southern States in census returns referred to above.

[32] Clark, in South in Building of Nation, vol. v, p. 322.

[33] "Progress of the United States in Population and Wealth in Fifty Years," referred to by William E. Dodd, in South in Building of Nation, vol. v, pp. 566–567.

North Carolina industrial history of the period has led to
the conclusion that "The people of the state became interested and soon a class of small manufacturers . . . came
into prominence and continued to thrive down to 1860."[34]

It is questionable, however, whether it may be truly said
that "the people of the state became interested"; certainly
there was nothing like the sweep of public sentiment that
appeared in 1880, and the suggestions relied upon in making the inference show as much against as for the likelihood
of their taking effect.[35]

The foregoing paragraphs lead up to a more important
judgment of Mr. Clark that "In the South the most striking feature of this period [1840–1860] was the gradual
breaking down of a traditional antipathy to manufactures.
This hostility was opposed to the obvious interests of a
region where idle white labor, abundant raw materials, and
ever-present water-power seemed to unite conditions so

---

[34] Pleasants.   Reference is had especially to items in State papers
and in Niles' Register.   The Tarboro Free Press declared that
should a tariff measure of the time meet with success, the people of
the Carolinas would have to "join in the scuffle for the benefit
anticipated from this new American system, and they will have to
bear a portion of its burdens and buffet the Northern manufacturer
with his own weapons."   It is noticed that a report to the North
Carolina legislature in the late twenties, looking back upon the dis-
integrating process of the preceding two decades, said: "There must
be a change.   But how is this important revolution to be accomplished?   We unhesitatingly answer—by introducing the manufacturing system into our own state and fabricating at least to the
extent of our wants. . . . Our habits and prejudices are against
manufacturing, but we must yield to the force of things and profit
by the indications of nature.   The policy that resists the change is
unwise and suicidal.   Nothing else can restore us."

[35] With preemption of land into large estates and consequent injury to small farming, discovery of gold, agitation for railroads and
improvements in cotton manufacturing machinery, the people of
Mecklenburg County, North Carolina, "many years before the war
were beginning to realize the importance of diversified industries.
. . . An industrial crisis was imminent, and the problem would have
solved itself by natural agencies within a few more years, had not
sectional differences brought on the war" (Tompkins, History of
Mecklenburg, vol. i, p. 124).   Cf. ibid., pp. 126–127; Kohn, Cotton
Mills of S. C., pp. 18–19.   That the war did come to render such an
industrial impulse impossible of effects shows the relative weakness
of the spirit at this time.   The preoccupation with intersectional differences was of greater potency than the intrasectional change of
mind, if such there were.

favorable to textile industries. Cotton planting engaged
the labor and the thought and capital of a directing white
class, but the natural operative of the South remained unemployed, and the capital of the North and of Europe was
mobile enough to flow to the point of maximum profit without regard to sectional or national lines, were such a profit
known to be assured by Southern factories. Slavery as a
system probably had less direct influence upon manufactures
than is commonly supposed, but the presence of the negro
through slavery was important."

It is frankly recognized that white immigration from Europe, which at this time supplied the most considerable mechanical skill, avoided districts heavily populated with negroes; that plantation self-sufficiency meant isolation with
small need for good communicating roads; that the market
for middle-grade goods was restricted by the servile character
of the colored inhabitants; that the credit system, by which
factors controlled the directioning of productive capital,
rested upon cotton culture by negro labor; that while the
corn laws held in England, reciprocity between the Southern States and the mother country tended to discourage
manufactures in this section while the conditions of commerce favored manufacture in the North. "These business
interests, supported by social traditions and political sectionalism, were strengthened in their opposition to new
industries by a widespread popular prejudice against organized manufactures. . . . Nevertheless the South chafed
continually under the discomfort of an ill-balanced system
of production. . . ." Mention is made of the canal at Augusta and of cotton mills at Charleston, Mobile, Columbus,
New Orleans and Memphis directly following the writings
and object lesson of William Gregg in his Graniteville factory, and it is concluded that "modern cotton manufacturing in the South dates from the founding of Graniteville
rather than from the post-bellum period. . . . However,
viewed in comparison with the cotton manufactures of the
North, those of the South were still insignificant. . . .

Nevertheless, the present attainment of the industry assured its definite future growth, and ultimate national importance."[36]

It is not hard to justify disagreement with this view. The basis of probable industrial development before the War appears in hindsight only if the pervasive numbing influence of slavery, made more powerful in the last years through the frantic effort at its maintenance through extension, is forgotten. Well enough to assert that the capital of the North and of Europe was mobile enough to flow across the Atlantic and across Mason and Dixon's line were a profit in manufacture in the South known to be assured, but the fact is that capital did not come in for industrial purposes because bright prospects had not been proved, and this largely because home enterprise was a laggard while slavery claimed the section's capital resources for cotton cultivation.[37] It is difficult to see the distinction which Mr. Clark desires to draw between the effect of the presence of the negro and the presence of slavery. While it is true that for long years after emancipation, and continuing to this day, the influence of the negro's presence in restraining inflow of immigrants is evident, the lessening of this deterrent and the removal of nearly equal drawbacks could not proceed or commence while slavery existed. From the point of

---

[36] Clark, History of Manufactures, p. 553 ff. Cf. ibid. in South in Building of Nation, vol. v, pp. 213–214, and p. 316 ff. Cf. Kohn (Cotton Mills of S. C., p. 16) : "The real and the lasting development of cotton mills in South Carolina might be started with the Graniteville Cotton Mill. . . ." Cf. Gregg, Domestic Industry, pp. 24–25.

[37] "Cheapness of cotton, abundance of water-power, the resources of the coal-fields, when steam began to supplant the dam, the other mineral resources, and the wealth of forests . . . did not even attract from other parts sufficient capital to develop the section to anything like its full extent. No artificial expedients were necessary there. But capital did not come" (Ingle, p. 73). A propagandist of the early eighties, desiring to organize small cotton mills in the South, quoted with approval a correspondent of the Morning News of Savannah, declaring that before the War the planters saw the advantage for such establishments but were deterred from manufacturing because "slavery and the factory were declared to be incompatible institutions. They could not exist together" (W. H. Gannon, The Landowners of the South, and the Industrial Classes of the North, p. 9 ff.).

view of the independent white workman the presence of the negro in slavery held as a far more forcible objection than the presence of the negro in freedom. His killing economic competition and radiated social poison were beyond dispute and beyond prospect of remedy until he was made at least a free producer. Any prospect of immigration for the South has taken its rise from the Civil War.

It was slavery that made plantation self-sufficiency in primitive needs universal, that made isolation and physical barriers to intercourse. The credit system in its heyday rested in large degree upon supply by the factor of all industrial products, which needs must be sustained so long as every local energy was foredoomed for absorption into cotton growing.

It cannot rightly be said that the traditional antipathy to manufactures was "opposed to the obvious interests of a region where idle white labor, abundant raw materials, and ever-present water-power seemed to unite conditions so favorable to textile industries," if it is meant that these interests, clear enough to us now, were obvious to Southern consciousness and purpose then. This applies particularly to the labor factor. It will be seen later that in the period before the War the mills often employed slaves as the exclusive operatives; in some cases negroes were employed with whites, and finally and more importantly, through Reconstruction years and at the very outset of the cotton mill era the inclination of establishers of factories was frequently to engage negro hands and to induce operatives to come from the North and even from England and the Continent —overlooking the native white population as a useful supply of workers as though it had not been there. Before the War the presence of raw cotton was certainly thought of rather as a guarantee of economic independence than as a stimulus to produce within the section those products of manufacturing which the staple was potent to purchase from outside.

It is not implied that conspicuous promulgators and exemplars of the need for a change in economic activity, such as William Gregg and some others, were not products of a reaction that showed itself from the long continuance of slavery, but they stand out, impotent as they are striking, against a dull and motionless background of prevalent system. They cried in a wilderness.

Materials and viewpoint are both too well understood to require further demonstration of the preventive influence which slavery and cotton had upon industry in the South. Yet a few observations of Southern men are interesting just at this point. Henry Watterson has said: " The South! The South! It is no problem at all. The story of the South may be summed up in a sentence: she was rich, she lost her riches; she was poor and in bondage; she was set free, and she had to go to work; she went to work, and she is richer than ever before. You see it was a groundhog case. The soil was here, the climate was here, but along with them was a curse, the curse of slavery."[38] Probably not over-induced by bitter animus is Helper's direct charge:

In our opinion, an opinion which has been formed . . . from assiduous researches, . . . the causes which have impeded the progress and prosperity of the South, which have dwindled our commerce . . . into the most contemptible insignificance; sunk a large majority of our people in galling poverty and ignorance, rendered a small minority conceited and tyrannical . . .; entailed upon us a humiliating dependence upon the Free States; disgraced us in the recesses of our own souls, and brought us under reproach in the eyes of all civilized and enlightened nations—may all be traced to one common source, and there find solution in the most hateful and horrible word that was ever incorporated into the vocabulary of human economy—*Slavery!* [39]

Tompkins saw clearly and in effect said again and again, " the result of the introduction and growth of the system of slavery was revolutionary; it turned the energies of the people almost wholly to the cultivation of cotton; it practically destroyed all other industries. . . ."[40]

---

[38] Quoted by A. B. Hart, The Southern South, pp. 231–232.
[39] Helper, p. 25.
[40] Tompkins, History of Mecklenburg, vol. i, p. 100. " There were no industries requiring skill or thought, and there was no necessity for scientific farming or anything else scientific. . . . Slavery not only demonstrated that people will not think unless it is necessary,

Not only did slavery hold the South down to supplying the raw material, but while its baneful influence lasted few improvements were made in the methods or appliances even for the growing and preparation of cotton for the market. As in India and China today, the cheapness of labor made ingenuity, enterprise and machinery unnecessary. Except in size and superficial appearance there was no change in the ante-bellum gin, gin-house and screw from 1820 to 1860. But after the War came a feeder, a condenser, a hand-press in the lint room, and cotton elevators.[41]

If Cotton was King, the monarch was an imperious and

but also that they will not work unless it is necessary (ibid., pp. 98–99). This statement is strongly influenced by Tench Coxe. It has been said of the Irish people by Lord Dufferin that "the entire nation flung itself back upon the land, with as fatal an impulse as when a river, whose current is suddenly impeded, rolls back and drowns the valley which it once fertilized." Sir Horace Plunkett comments: "The energies, the hopes, nay, the very existence of the race, became thus intimately bound up with agriculture" (Sir Horace Plunkett, Ireland in the New Century, p. 20). "By the influence of the negro the South lost its manufactures and largely its commerce, and became practically a purely agricultural section of the nation" (Tompkins, ibid., vol. ii, pp. 200–201; cf. ibid., Cotton Growing, pp. 3–4). As to the usefulness of negroes in latter-day cotton mills, this manufacturer advised: "Dependence upon the negro as a laborer has done infinite injury to the South. In the past it brought about a condition which drove the white laborer from the South or into enforced idleness. It is important to reestablish as quickly as possible respectability for white labor" (ibid., Cotton Mill, Commercial Features, pp. 109–110). Cf. ibid., Building and Loan Associations, p. 43; The Cultivation, Picking, Baling and Manufacturing of Cotton, from the Southern Standpoint, pp. 5–6; F. T. Carlton, History and Problems of Organized Labor, pp. 19–20.

[41] "The cotton was packed by hand, carried into the gin-house in baskets by laborers, carried to the gin by laborers, pushed into the lint rooms, carried to the screw, packed in the box of the screw and bound with ropes, all by hand," but since the abolition of slavery "all the machinery and appliances for preparing cotton for the market have been revolutionized" (Tompkins, Cultivation, Picking, etc., of Cotton, pp. 5–6). See others of his writings for a full discussion of this point. Cf. M. B. Hammond, The Cotton Industry, pp. 77–78, and, for a detailed account of bad preparation of cotton down to 1880, Edward Atkinson, in U. S. Census of Manufactures, 1880, "The Cotton Manufacture," p. 4 ff. "No slave-holding people ever were an inventive people. In a slave-holding community the upper classes may become luxurious and polished; but never inventive. Whatever degrades the laborer and robs him of the fruits of his toil stifles the spirit of invention and forbids the utilization of inventions and discoveries even when made" (Henry George, Progress and Poverty, twenty-fifth anniversary ed., p. 523).

narrow-minded tyrant, who cramped the development and put blinders to the vision of the country. Said William Gregg in 1845:

> Since the discovery that cotton would mature in South-Carolina, she has reaped a golden harvest; but it is feared it has proved a curse rather than a blessing, and I believe that she would at this day be in a far better condition, had the discovery never been made. . . . Let us begin at once, before it is too late, to bring about a change in our industrial pursuits. . . . let croakers against enterprise be silenced. . . . Even Mr. Calhoun, our great oracle . . . is against us in this matter; he will tell you, that no mechanical enterprise can succeed in South-Carolina . . . that to thrive in cotton spinning, one should go to Rhode Island. . . .[42]

"The invention of the cotton gin," wrote Tompkins, ". . . before 1860 . . . was nearer anything else than a blessing. It was primarily responsible for the system of slavery. . . . Cotton . . . in its manufacture . . . is the life of the South, but we could probably have done as well without it until we began to manufacture it."[43]

---

[42] Domestic Industry, pp. 18–19.

[43] History of Mecklenburg, vol. i, p. 194. For a careful description of the circumstances surrounding the invention of the cotton gin, and the legal documents in the dispute over the rights to it, cf. ibid., Cotton and Cotton Oil, pp. 19–31, and appendix. "We abandoned a once leading factory system; we imported slaves; we let all public highways become quagmires; we destroyed every possibility for the farmer except cotton and by cutthroat competition amongst ourselves we reduced the price to where there was not a living in it for the cotton producer. We made cotton in a quantity and at a price to clothe all the world excepting ourselves" (ibid., Road Building, p. 24). "The economic history of the South from the Revolution to the Civil War is a record of the development of one natural advantage to the neglect of several others. Fitted by nature to support a large population engaged in a variety of pursuits based upon agriculture, it had a small population occupied in the production of raw material that contributed to the maintenance of a dense population in regions where artifice contended against harsh climate and a stubborn soil" (Ingle, p. 47). Cf. Burkett and Poe, Cotton, pp. 312 and 313; E. C. Brooks, The Story of Cotton, p. 157; Thompson, pp. 44; Miller and Millwright, quoted in Manufacturers' Record, Baltimore, Feb. 22, 1883. Gregg showed that cotton, the great god, drove agricultural enterprise from South Carolina, for, with the returns to its cultivation under ordinary management amounting to only 3 or 4 and in some instances only 2 per cent, the inclination for planters to remove with their slave capital to the richer Southwest was strong, thus keeping the population of the State at a standstill (Domestic Industry, p. 18). "Perhaps the most striking economic change that the new industry [cotton culture] effected in the South

The old South had much in common with mercantilist feeling. Though coin for coffers was not precisely the aim, there was the settled ambition for exportation of a money crop that involved self-exploitation and left no room for sectional introspection. The economic system was full of inhibitions, the all-pervading effect of which cannot be calculated. In accounting in 1856 for the stagnation of Virginia as compared with the industrial activity of New England and Old England, Olmsted wrote:

> It is the old, fettered, barbarian labor-system, in connection with which they [Virginians] have been brought up, against which all their enterprise must struggle, and with the chains of which all their ambition must be bound. This conviction . . . is forced upon one more strongly than it is possible to make you comprehend by a mere statement of isolated facts. You could as well convey an idea of the effect of mist on a landscape, by enumerating the number of particles of vapor that obscure it.[44]

Duping of the people through charlatan guidance of political leaders is too evident in the South of today to require description of its operation in an earlier period.[45] A re-

---

after the reintroduction of slavery was the speedy abandonment of manufactures. . . . What was the use of nerve-racking investment in elaborate and costly machinery when a land-owner could reap ten per cent net profit from a few negroes and mules and a bushel or two of the magical cotton seed? And yet the South had unusual manufacturing facilities. . . ." (Scherer, p. 168 ff.; cf. ibid., pp. 243, 254; Ingle, pp. 49, 139; New York Herald, quoted in News and Courier, Charleston, March 9, 1881; F. L. Olmsted, Seaboard Slave States, p. 138). The social difference between North and South before the War, so often remarked as existing of itself apart, is accounted for by slavery, which arrested development on Southern soil of the industrial type of American civilization (A. D. Mayo, in The Social Economist, Oct., 1893, pp. 203–204).

[44] Olmsted, pp. 140–141, cf. ibid., p. 185; pp. 213–214. "The amount of it, then, is this: Improvement and progress in South Carolina is forbidden by its present system" (ibid., pp. 522–523). And for his general philosophy of the subject, see ibid., pp. 490–491). He took as an average expression of the views " of the majority of those whose monopoly of wealth and knowledge has a governing influence on a majority of the people," the statement of a newspaper in 1854: "African slavery . . . is a thing that we cannot do without, that is *righteous, profitable,* and permanent, and that belongs to Southern society as inherently, intricately, and durably as the white race itself" (ibid., pp. 298–299).

[45] There are many instances similar to that of a famous election speech in Virginia in the fifties, in which the aspirant declared to his audience: "Commerce has long ago spread her sails, and sailed

flection as sorrowful, however, as the confirmed bias of the people shown in applause to such guidance, is the blindness of the leaders who, no doubt with strong elements of trickery, gave even stronger signs of being themselves duped by a situation. Not that the crowd was believing, but that spokesmen were so largely sincere, was most melancholy. The drug had ceased to lead to remorse, and began to bring hallucinations.[46] Approaches to rational statesmanship and reasonable moves toward balanced economic activity, found especially in the border States, could be nothing more than

---

away from you . . . you have set no tilt-hammer of Vulcan to strike blows worthy of the gods in your iron-foundries; you have not yet spun more than coarse cotton enough, in the way of manufacture to clothe your own slaves. . . . You have rallied alone on the single power of agriculture—and such agriculture! . . . Instead of having to feed cattle on a thousand hills, you have had to chase the stump-tailed steer through the sedge-patches to procure a tough beef-steak (laughter and applause). . . . The landlord has skinned the tenant, and the tenant has skinned the land, until all have grown poor together." "And how," asks Olmsted, "does the fiddling Negro propose, it will be wondered, to remedy this so very amusing stupidity, poverty, and debility? Very simply and pleasantly. By building railroads and canals, ships and mills; by establishing manufactories, opening mines. . . . And, 'Hurrah!' shout the tickled electors; 'that's exactly what we want.'" And then he showed that it was much like the quack telling the confirmed paralytic to live generously, take vigorous exercise and grow well; that with the disease of slavery in its vitals the South could not do else than languish; that in promising wholesome measures which contemplated everything but the attacking of slavery the politicians were just laughing at the people (Olmsted, p. 288 ff.; cf. ibid., pp. 179–180).

[46] A passage of Sir Horace Plunkett in comment upon Irish politics is much to the point: "Deeply as I have felt for the past sufferings of the Irish people and their heritage of disability and distress, I could not bring myself to believe that, where misgovernment had continued so long, and in such an immense variety of circumstances and conditions, the governors could have been alone to blame. I envied those leaders of popular thought whose confidence in themselves and in their fellows was shaken by no such reflections. But the more I listened to them, the more the conviction was borne in upon me that they were seeking to build an impossible future upon an imaginary past" (Ireland in New Century, p. 147). Cf. Tompkins, Cotton Mill, Commercial Features, preface to appendix, for an incident related of William Gregg and an opponent in an election campaign, which, despite its incidental happening, shows aptly just the point of preoccupation with politics to which the Southern mind came, the degree of trifling with which the most sober proposals were met, the hopelessness of change from this state of affairs by anything short of a fundamental moral awakening.

ineffectual stirrings while slavery persisted, and were less likely of success because the last years before the War, in which they emerged, were given over to such passionate, defiant advocacy of the " Southern institution."[47]

The deterrent effect of slavery upon immigration has been noticed above. In 1860 only 6 per cent of the white population of the South was foreign-born, but immigrants made up nearly 20 per cent of that of the North. In the decade 1850–1860 the South's quota of foreign-born in the whole country dropped from 14 to 13 per cent.[48]

Independent white artizans, so important in the industrial history of the North in this period, avoided competition with slave labor; if this drawback to coming to the South was removed by their acquiring slaves themselves where a few had the means, they must then leave mechanical pursuits; many disapproved of slavery anyway.[49] Completer evidence of the damage wrought by slavery is the actual emigration of natives from the section when slaves were crowding; a portion of the population which under other circumstances might have taken root in industrial enterprise within the South was thus driven off.

---

[47] " With the line around slavery being drawn more closely . . . the cotton South lagged in the industrial race, and the border States were hampered by the institution that they felt to be a burden, but which they could see no safe way to abolish. Compassed as it was by political compromises, slavery must ultimately have toppled through its own overweight; but in 1860 it was so valuable for the plantation that it was not only not readily converted into the factory, but was an obstacle in the way of the employment of capital and of other labor in that direction " (Ingle, pp. 68–69).

[48] Ingle, p. 11.

[49] Clark, in South in Building of Nation, vol. v, pp. 213–214. Southern whites were indisposed to welcome those who could not or refused to grow into the slavery system. A newspaper in the fifties betrayed this: " A large proportion of the mechanical force that migrate to the South, are a curse instead of a blessing; they are generally a worthless, unprincipled class—enemies to our peculiar institutions . . . pests to society, dangerous among the slave population, and ever ready to form combinations against the interest of the slaveholder, against the laws of the country, and against the peace of the Commonwealth." But slave-acquiring merchants were cordially received (quoted in Olmsted, p. 511). For interesting facts as to immigration to North Carolina, cf. Tompkins, History of Mecklenburg, vol. ii, p. 204; vol. i, p. 153.

Communities with strong foreign infusion and slight or no reliance upon slavery, showed a vigor before the War which has been to them a continuing advantage into the present.[50]   It was observed that competition of the slave was almost matched in hurtfulness by the example of the prosperous white man with whom acquisition of the comforts and dignities of life did not proceed from daily toil.[51]

The dependence of the ante-bellum South upon the North and upon Europe for the most substantial and trivial appurtenances of civilization was spectacular.   It might be argued in apology for the total one-sidedness of the old South, that the section was responding to the principle of comparative economic advantage.   Certainly the most absolute adherence to the territorial division of labor could not require a more exclusive devotion to the making of cotton and fuller reliance upon less peculiarly favored districts for manufactured goods and certain foodstuffs and materials, than the South displayed.   But however strict in its conformity to superficial dictates of this policy, the program was ruinous to the section and the country, and was hurtful to the economic welfare of the world.   Easy yield-

---

[50] In the fifties it was declared that the most prosperous community in South Carolina was a settlement of Germans in the western part of the State.   Here had been founded an educational institution, varied manufactures, farming was successful and capital was invested in a railroad venture.   Slavery bore small part (Olmsted, p. 511).   In 1865 the northwestern counties of Georgia, strongly opposed to secession and which furnished soldiers to the federal armies, were held to be better disposed toward the national government than any other part of the State; slaves had constituted less than a fourth of the population.   Though cruder than those from the seaboard, delegates from this section to the constitutional convention of 1865 were said to have a well-informed outlook for the Commonwealth (Sidney Andrews, The South Since the War, pp. 342-343).   Study of the conventions of other States immediately succeeding the War shows "up-country" representatives, as contrasted with those of the "low country," more easily adjusting themselves to the new condition and readier to go ahead with a changed program.   It was said that at a time when the average wage of female operatives in Georgia cotton mills was half that paid in Massachusetts, New England factory girls were induced by high wages to go to the Southern State, but returned North because their position was unpleasant in "the general degradation of the laboring class" (Olmsted, p. 543).

[51] Ibid., p. 201.

ing to the principle did not suggest to statesmen that the South after all was in only partial compliance—that even for the most efficient production of cotton as such there needed to be a wholesome admixture of manufacturing and of other agricultural interests.   Post-bellum industry brought not a less but a more economical and larger output of the staple.

The very humor of many passages in the literature of the economic history of the South, describing the need of the section to go to the North for a thousand and one essentials of daily existence, shows the seriousness of the situation. Gregg, too lonely in his advocacy of home industry to treat the subject in other than its fundamental aspects, declared: " A change in our habits and industrial pursuits is a far greater desideratum than any change in the laws of our government . . . ," and " if we continue in our present habits, it would not be unreasonable to predict, that when the Raleigh Rail-Road is extended to Columbia, our members of the Legislature would be fed on Yankee baker's bread. Pardon me for repeating the call on South Carolina to go to work." His own city of Charleston, than which there was no greater sinner, had regulations against the employment of steam engines that stand in striking con- trast to the arguments for the comparative advantage of steam as against water power at a later date when the city centered attention upon building a cotton factory.[52]

---

[52] " God speed the day when her [South Carolina's] politicians will be exhorting the people to domestic industry, instead of State resistance; when our Clay Clubs and Democratic Associations will be turned into societies for the advancement of scientific agriculture and the promotion of mechanic art; when our capitalists will be found following the example of Boston and other Northern cities, in making such investments of their capital as will give employment to the poor, and make them producers, instead of burthensome con- sumers; when our City Council may become so enlightened as to see the propriety of following the example of every other city in the civilized world, in removing the restrictions on the use of the Steam Engine, now indispensable to every department of Manufacturing. . . ." And again: " He who has possessed himself of the notion that we have the industry, and are wronged out of our hard earnings by a lazy set of scheming Yankees, to get rid of this delusion, needs only seat himself on the Charleston wharves for a few days, and

A decade later Helper reproached a South that had not given heed to Gregg: "It is a fact well known to every intelligent Southerner that we are compelled to go to the North for almost every article of utilty and adornment, from matches, shoepegs and paintings up to cotton-mills, steamships and statuary. . . . All the world sees, or ought to see, that in a commercial, mechanical, manufactural, fiancial and literary point of view, we are as helpless as babes. . . ."[53] Gregg remarked the supply by the North not only of the articles of major manufacture, but of those adjuncts of agriculture which would naturally be made within the South—axe, hoe and broom handles, pitchforks, rakes, hand-spikes, shingles and pine boards.[54]

A newspaper in Richmond chronicled the sale to Northern interests of a large coal field in the State, and in unconscious irony placed in juxtaposition to the notice this confident exhortation:

---

behold ship after ship arrive laden down with the various articles produced by Yankee industry" (Domestic Industry, p. 9 ff.). "The labor of negroes and blind horses can never supply the place of *steam,* and this power is withheld lest the smoke of an engine should disturb the delicate nerves of an agriculturist; or the noise of a mechanic's hammer should break in upon the slumber of a real estate holder, or importing merchant, while he is indulging in fanciful dreams, or building on paper, *the Queen City of the South. . . .*" (ibid., p. 23).

[53] Helper, pp. 21, 23. Cf. for other interesting illustrations of dependence upon the North, some of which influenced Henry W. Grady. An orator at the Southern Commercial Convention, New Orleans, 1855, adapted for the occasion the famous speech in the British Parliament on taxes, and beginning, in the Southern version: "It is time that we should look about us, and see in what relation we stand to the North. From the rattle with which the nurse tickles the ear of the child born in the South, to the shroud that covers the cold form of the dead, everything comes to us from the North. We rise from between sheets made in Northern looms, and pillows of northern feathers, to wash in basins made in the North . . . ," and continuing in the strain which was a favorite with platform and pen, and many examples of which may be found (Olmsted, p. 544). Cf. Grady, New South, (ed. 1890), p. 188 ff.

[54] Domestic Industry, p. 8; cf. ibid., p. 11. Olmsted instances a case, probably common enough, where a North Carolina planter was buying hay grown in New York or New England with very large charges for carriage (pp. 378–379). Cf. ibid., p. 175. When Southern industrial resources were exploited, the total benefit might not come to the locality. Thus shipwrights at Mobile were from the North (Olmsted, p. 567).

It is plain that a new and glorious destiny awaits the South, and beckons us onward to a career of independence. Shall we train and discipline our energies for the coming crisis, or *shall we continue the tributary and dependent vassals of Northern brokers and money-changers?* Now is the time for the South to begin in earnest the work of self-development! Now is the time to break asunder the fetters of commercial subjection, and to prepare for that more complete independence that awaits us.[55]

Other appeals to domestic industry were as clearly inspired by sectional animosity; they were incidental to political ambition, and are to be contrasted with the generous, wholesome rallying-cries of the cotton mill campaign twenty-five years later, when economic sanity had gotten the better of partisan futilities. Another Virginia paper, wiser than that just quoted, urging manufacturing in the State and particularly textile mills for Richmond, anticipated with different mind the event invited by its contemporary, and foretold what was later too patent: " It must be plain in the South that if our relations with the North should ever be severed—and how soon they may be, none can know (may God avert it long!)—we would, in all the South, not be able to clothe ourselves. We could not fell our forests, plow our fields, nor mow our meadows. . . . And yet, with all these things staring us in the face, we shut our eyes, and go on blindfold."[56]

In addition to the barrier to manufactures formed by

---

[55] Olmsted, p. 363.

[56] Ibid., p. 166. An " Address to the Farmers of Virginia," read at a convention for the formation of a State Agricultural Society in 1852, adopted, reconsidered and readopted with amendments, and finally reconsidered again and rejected on the ground that it contained admissions, however true, which would be useful to abolitionists, contained the words: ". . . thus we, who once swayed the councils of the Union, find our power gone, and our influence on the wane, at a time when both are of vital importance to our prosperity, if not to our safety. As other States accumulate the means of material greatness, and glide past us on the road to wealth and empire, we slight the warnings of dull statistics, and drive lazily along the field of ancient customs, or stop the *plow* to speed the *politician—* should we not, in too many cases, say . . . the *demagogue?* . . . With a wide-spread domain, with a kindly soil, with a climate whose sun radiates fertility, and whose very dews distill abundance, we find our inheritance so wasted that the eye aches to behold the prospect " (ibid., p. 169).

cotton cultivation under slave labor, and the silent opposition which the prevalent system engendered, were not in-
frequent outspoken declarations against industry. William
Gregg was one of the few in the South to rise superior to
Calhoun's sway, and asserting that there were some who
were better able to speak of the propriety of factories than
even that statesman, faced him squarely, but tactfully:
" The known zeal with which this gentleman has always
engaged in every thing relating to the interest of South-
Carolina, forbids the idea that he is not a friend to domestic
manufactures, fairly brought about, and, knowing, as he
must know, the influence which he exerts, he should be
more guarded in expressing opinions adverse to so good a
cause."[57]   And again, speaking of manufactures, he was
regretful of the fact that " our great men are not to be found
in the ranks of those who are willing to lend their aid, in
promoting this good cause. Are we to commence another
ten years' crusade, to prepare the minds of the people of
this State for revolution; thus unhinging every department
of industry, and paralyzing the best efforts to promote the
welfare of our country? "[58]

---

[57] Domestic Industry, p. 20.

[58] Ibid., p. 14. "Lamentable, indeed, is it to see so wise and so pure
a man as Langdon Cheves, putting forth the doctrine, to South-
Carolina, that manufactures should be the last resort of a country.
With the greatest possible respect for the opinions of this truly
great man, and the humblest pretensions on my part, I will venture
the assertion, that a greater error was never committed by a statesman " (ibid). The Southern Quarterly Review in 1845, the same
year as Gregg's publication, quoted Cheves: "Manufactures should
be the last resort of industry in every country, for one forced as
with us, they serve no interests but those of the capitalists who set
them in motion, and their immediate localities." And Mr. Kohn
remarks, "This expression was not peculiar to any one class of
leaders in South Carolina at that time," and instances other examples (Cotton Mills of S. C., p. 13). Tompkins comments: ". . .
as slavery grew, . . . there was a period from 1840 to 1860, when
the interest of the South sorely needed manufacturing as well as
agricultural development. Only those men who appreciated this
condition undertook to go counter to the growing sentiment in
favor of agriculture and slave labor. Those who did continue to
manufacture, were necessarily men of broad views and great abilities," and he speaks of some of the notable few—Gregg, Fries, Holt,
Leak, Morehead, Hammett (Cotton Mill, Commercial Features, p.
180). Cf. also references to Burkett and Poe and to Brooks, n. 42.

In public-mindedness, in breadth of view, in qualities of imagination, in sanity of judgment that did not sacrifice understanding of his misguided contemporaries, in power of analysis of the confronting situation, William Gregg stood head and shoulders above other Southerners of his time. And only now, seventy-five years later, can his wisdom be thoroughly appreciated. The Lancashire opposition, which, despite the cotton famine, hated slavery and led to British disaffection when the warring South two decades afterwards most needed an ally, brilliantly vindicated his warning to his antagonists that even their selfish ambitions could only be served by attention to such reasoning as he advanced. Gregg said:

> Those who are disposed to agitate the State and prepare the minds of the people for resisting the laws of Congress, and particularly those who look for so direful a calamity as the dissolution of our Union, should, above all others, be most anxious so to diversify the industrial pursuits of South-Carolina, as to render her independent of all other countries; for as sure as this greatest of calamities befalls us, we shall find the same causes that produced it, making enemies of the nations which are at present the best customers of our agricultural productions.[59]

Because of the striking reversal of front of the city at a later date, which will be of central importance in subsequent chapters of this study, Gregg's advice to Charleston's capitalists in 1856 is interesting. Condemning, as a member of the legislature, a proposed subsidy to a railroad to link Charleston and Cincinnati, put forward in furtherance of commercial policies selfishly followed by " wealthy gentlemen, some of whom have ships floating in every sea," he declared that Charleston's destiny was " fixed and indissoluble with the State of South-Carolina, and . . . mainly her great investment in Internal Improvements should be made with a view to developing the resources of the immediate country around her . . . cheap modes of transporta-

---

Cf. Gregg, Domestic Industry, pp. 19–20. For a very fine passage refuting Cheves' position and defining what the writer meant by " domestic manufactures "—not household industry, but cotton factories throughout the State and craftsmen at every cross-roads—see ibid., pp. 14–16.

[59] Domestic Industry, p. 14; cf. ibid., p. 52.

tion from all quarters of the State could not fail to re-act on the general prosperity of the city . . . the dormant wealth of Charleston might be so directed as to be felt in the remotest parts of the State, in stimulating agriculture, draining our . . . swamps and putting into renewed culture our worn-out and waste lands; diversified industry, stimulating the mechanic arts and increasing the population and wealth of the State." Instead of this he found that "there is no city in the Union which has accumulated more wealth, to its size, than Charleston—none that has shown so little inclination to develop the resources of the State. Her millionaires die in New York. There is scarcely a day that passes that does not send forth Charleston capital to add to the growth and wealth of that great city."[60]

The characteristic inclination toward the individual rather than the corporate form of enterprise which was noticed as showing itself in the South of the Revolutionary Period, was still strong up to the Civil War. In 1845 Gregg inveighed against it, particularly as crystallized in legislative refusal to grant charters of incorporation; he was quick to hold up New England as a business model to the South. Those who have sought to magnify the industrial activities of the old South have frequently failed to take into account the differences in organization which distinguished enterprises then from those of post-bellum years. The textile industry could not be a movement in economic society, sinking its roots deep and extending them broadly, so long as investment participation sprang from and ended with individual initiative. Until the widespread emergence of the joint-stock form, the mills could not claim and embrace the generality of the community's resources. And in a period when this device was not largely turned to, it is plain that industrial stirrings were comparatively feeble.[61]

---

[60] Speech on Blue Ridge Railroad, p. 67. Cf. ibid., p. 29.
[61] Gregg hoped that dangers to be apprehended from indiscriminate granting of charters to banking institutions would "not be confounded with, and brought injuriously to bear against the charters which are necessary to develope [sic] the resources of our country, and give an impetus to all industrial pursuits. . . . The

The individualism of the old South, the inability to co-operate was due no less to physical than social isolation between portions of the population. Not only was there self-satisfaction coupled with dependence upon the North for manufactured commodities in the low-country, but the up-country, the frugal population of which was better disposed for manufacturing development, was so segregated as to be kept in mean state, or actually dependent itself upon the coastal districts. Between the Piedmont and the sea was the barrier of plantations; between the Piedmont and the industrial North were no transportation facilities. Concentration of capital, especially in the corporate form of industrial enterprise, is a mark of economic integration; in the ante-bellum South many other facts besides the absence of capital concentration show the lack of team work, of conditions making for unity of thought or action.[62]

---

practice of operating by associated capital gives a wonderful stimulus to enterprise. . . . Why is it that the Bostonians are able in a day, or a week, to raise millions at one stroke, to purchase the land on both sides of a river, for miles, to secure a great water power and the erection of a manufacturing city? . . . The divine, lawyer, doctor, schoolmaster, guardian, widow, farmer, merchant, mechanic, common labourer, in fact, the whole community is made tributary to these great enterprises. The utility and safety of such institutions is no longer problematical. . . . If we shut the door against associated capital and place reliance upon individual exertion, we may talk over the matter and grow poorer for fifty years to come, without effecting the change in our industrial pursuits, necessary to renovate the fortunes of our State. . . . About three-fourths of the manufacturing of the United States, is carried on by joint-stock companies; . . . we shall certainly have to look to such companies to introduce the business with us." He showed, by South Carolina examples, the perpetuity of the corporate form as contrasted with the frequently limited life of the personal enterprise (An Enquiry into the Propriety of Granting Charters of Incorporation for Manufacturing and Other Purposes, in South Carolina, pp. 4–11).

[62] "Isolation gave birth to individualism, as marked upon the mountain-clearing as upon the plantation; and beginnings of the co-operative spirit were dwarfed by nature and by human inclination . . ." (Ingle, p. 32 ff.). Cf. Clark, in South in Building of Nation, vol. v, pp. 314–315. Olmsted found mountain wagons coming sometimes two hundred miles to the head of navigation in North Carolina (p. 361 and pp. 358–359). The division of capital among small mills rather than its investment in larger factories is paralleled by the relatively larger number of church buildings in the South than in the North, with, however, relatively small seating capacity (Ingle, p. 32 ff.). The same tendency may be seen in respect to poorhouses,

The non-industrial character of the old South may be seen not only in internal fact, but in external reflection equally conclusive. Of external evidences, the political perhaps most readily occurs to one. Pervasive economic conditions come certainly to the surface in political pretensions; economic transitions are registered in alterations of political front. The protective tariff of 1816 was introduced and defended, respectively, by two South Carolinians—Lowndes and Calhoun. The signature of a Virginia president—Madison—made it a law. This tariff was opposed by New England in the person of Webster. In 1828, in the debate over the "Tariff of Abominations," the situation was just the reverse—Calhoun opposed protection, Webster championed it. In swapping sides, both men were answering to the changed economic interests of their respective sections. No clearer picture is needed of the trend of the South in ante-bellum years than the spectacle of Calhoun transformed from nationalist to sectionalist.[63]

Cotton, nearly exclusively in the South, and to a notable degree in New England, was responsible underneath for the alterations which were displayed in the superficial play of politics. It was the disintegration of manufactures brought about by more and more extensive embracing of cotton cultivation that turned the South from protection to free trade; it was the growing absorption in industry, especially cotton manufacture, and relative relinquishing of commerce, that made New England protectionist instead of, as before, the champion of free trade.[64]

asylums, hospitals and jails (Dodd, Expansion and Conflict, p. 231; cf. industrial map for 1860, p. 188, showing few plants of an output of $250,000 south of Maryland).

[63] Upon this whole matter, see Scherer, p. 179 ff. "In 1816, when Webster opposed protection, there was a capital of only about $52,000,000 invested in textile manufacture, of which much still lay in the South. In 1828, when he reversed his position, this capital had probably doubled, and had become localized in and about New England" (ibid., p. 181). Cf. ibid., p. 234.

[64] Ibid., p. 152. Slavery added to cotton brought the extra confusion of purely political animosities. "At the beginning of the nineteenth century the tariff was not a matter which was exclusively political. . . . The subject ceased to be an economic one and became

This is not the place to remark at length how economic interests are changing the South back, in partial measure, to the first position. Cotton is again central. Cotton factories are largely responsible for the little leaven that is working in a large loaf, producing in the heart of the Solid South Republican adherents and voices for protection. " Slavery has been abolished. The South has reestablished manufactures. Its interests in free trade and protection are changed from what they were in 1860. We need not only domestic trade, but foreign markets. We need, apparently, protection and free trade at the same time. . . . The South is as much interested in protection to home markets as New England is. New England is as much interested in export markets as the South is. In this situation we ought to get together . . . for 'Protection and Reciprocity.' "[65]

It is interesting to examine a summary of the industrial history of the South in the fifty years preceding the Civil War, given by an important writer:

Between 1810 and 1860 three periods of progress marked the factory development of the cotton states. During our last war with England. . . . mill builders from the North migrated to the Southern highlands, and with local cooperation established small yarn factories at several places in the Carolinas, Georgia, Tennessee, and Kentucky. . . . During the decade ending with 1833, when hostility to the tariff made the Southern people bitterly resent economic dependence on the North, there was a second movement towards manufactures, especially in South Carolina and Georgia, directed mainly towards the erection of larger and more complete factories. This agitation bore fruit in some corporate enterprises, most of which had but qualified success. Finally, in the late forties real factory development began simultaneously at several points, and had not two financial crises and a war checked its progress, we should probably date from this time the beginning of the modern epoch of cotton manufacturing in the South.[66]

---

a political one in proportion as slavery grew in the South and diminished in the North, and in inverse proportion as manufactures dried up in the South and became of greater importance in the North " (Tompkins, The Tariff and Reciprocity).

[65] Tompkins, Tariff and Protection.

[66] Clark, in South in Building of Nation, vol. v, p. 316 ff.; Cf. ibid., pp. 330–331. Contrast Tompkins, History of Mecklenburg, vol. i, pp. 133–137.

Two objections against this view have pertinence. In the first place, these three periods of comparative interest in manufactures can hardly be called "movements" in any social or economic sense. That of the twenties and running into the thirties may claim more color of this than the other two.[67] The plants set up by New Englanders earlier were in response to individual enterprise, and that enterprise born out of the boundaries of the South. Cooperation with the newcomers was not of the sort that marks the considerable interest of a community. To the extent that mills were built in the forties as a result of public agitation, William

[67] But some of the agitation for industries in these, as in other years, had a flavor not symptomatic of healthy desire for improvement. Conventions looking to railroad development were held in North Carolina and Tennessee in the middle thirties. Of the advantages which it was agreed would flow from the building of the Charleston and Cincinnati Railroad, it was declared that "it will form a bond of union between the States [i.e., Southern States] which will give safety to our property and security to our institutions" (Tompkins, History of Mecklenburg, vol. i, p. 125). Of more positive character was the utterance of a Southerner who viewed with concern the danger that the North would crush slavery and place the South under complete submission to tariff aggressions, congressional representation for the latter section finding a stop in the limit of slave territory. "Under these circumstances, the true policy of the South is distinct and clearly marked. She must resort to the same means by which power is accumulated at the north, to secure it for herself." If the South should manufacture a large portion of its cotton crop "we reduce the quantity for export, and the competition for that remainder will add greatly to our wealth, while it will place us in a position to dictate our own terms. The manufactories will increase our population; increased population and wealth will enable us to chain the southern states proudly and indissolubly together by railroads and other internal improvements; and these works by affording a speedy communication from point to point, will prove our surest defense against either foreign aggression or domestic revolt. . . . If the evil day shall ever come when the south shall be satisfied that she cannot remain in the Union with safety to her institutions, it [i.e., industrial self-sufficiency] will place her in a condition to maintain her separate nationality" (E. Steadman, of Tennessee, quoted in J. D. B. DeBow, Industrial Resources of the South and Southwest, vol. ii, p. 127). Objection to massing poor whites in mills was combatted by a Charlestonian with the reflection that small farming with slave labor brought discontent that might mean social upheaval, whereas the factory opened a door of opportunity making for stability; when poor whites should have the chance of owning a slave "they would increase the demand for that kind of property, and would become firm and uncompromising supporters of Southern institutions" (Ingle, pp. 25–26).

Gregg was almost wholly responsible. It has been pointed out above that Gregg was a missionary who preached an unaccepted faith. He was not a social exponent. In the second place, it is gratuitous to count upon what would have been the case had not the war broken in upon declared industrial beginnings. The Civil War was not a fortuitous event. It had to come. It was the disastrous evidence of the dominance in the South of a system which gave no room to widespread industrial enterprise. Could the war be regarded simply as an occurrence, an unfortunate happening, there would perhaps be ground for assuming that industrial enterprise might have been built into, and finally changed wholesomely, the economic regime of the ante-bellum South, but facts show that it was a case where mastery between mutually exclusive plans had to be tried on the basis of comparative strength. The spirit for manufactures had not sufficient force to avert the war, but only enough life to show, in expiring, that it had begun to be born.

The decade 1850–1860 has been reserved for specific treatment at this point because two Southern writers have sought, rather dogmatically, to invest it with a character of industrialism superior to that of ante-bellum years generally and to show that it fathered later growth. Mr. Edmonds has said: " A study of the facts . . . should convince anyone that the South in its early days gave close attention to manufacturing development, and that while later on the great profits in cultivation caused a contraction of the capital and energy of that section in farming operations, yet, after 1850, there came renewed interest in industrial matters, resulting in an astonishing advance in railroad construction and in manufactures."[68]

---

[68] Edmonds, p. 13. It is shown how the course of cotton prices affected industry; from 1800 to 1839 cotton averaged a fraction over 17 cents; in 1840 the price dropped to 9 cents, continuing to decline to the 1846 average of 5.63 cents, when, after a short crop, there was a sharp rise in 1847, only to be followed by a fall to 8 cents and less. " These excessively low prices brought about a revival of public interest in other pursuits than cotton cultivation. . . ." It is said that from 1850 to 1860 the South quadrupled its railroad mi-

It is stated that "Cotton manufacturing had commenced to attract increased attention, and nearly $12,000,000 were invested in Southern cotton mills. In Georgia especially this industry was thriving, and between 1850 and 1860 the capital so invested in that State nearly doubled."[69]

The assertion that in 1860 the South had in all 24,590 industrial establishments with an investment of $175,000,000 loses force when, by a simple division, it is seen that on an average this made the investment in each only $7,144.37, which is surely not indicative of considerable importance. Many of the establishments must have been much smaller than would be represented by this average, and the few which were a great deal larger were rare exceptions. The very disparity in size of enterprises points away from any concerted movement toward manufacturing. As to the railroads, many of them were narrow-gauge, and all the facts tend to show that railroads were looked upon as facilitating commerce rather than manufactures.[70]

In vaunting property figures of the South of 1860 as compared with those of the North, Mr. Edmonds has given himself to the most obvious and serious error of including slaves.[71] Slaves, though in the legal sense agreed to belong

leage, in the latter year being 387 miles in advance of New England (ibid., p. 10 ff.). For an account of late colonial and Revolutionary development, see ibid., p. 3 ff. Cf. DeBow, vol, iii, p. 76 ff.

[69] Edmonds, Facts about South, p. 10 ff. Judging by the United States census of manufactures, these figures are grossly inaccurate. In 1860 the Southern States had $9,840,221 invested in cotton manufacturing, and in Georgia the investment increased from $1,736,156 in 1850 to $2,126,103 in 1860, or less than 30 per cent (United States Census of Manufactures, 1900, Cotton Manufactures, p. 56).

[70] Even after the war the pet scheme to build a railroad over the mountains gathered sentiment in the long-cherished desire to link Charleston with "the producing interior" typified in Cincinnati; as rails were laid, piece-meal, through the Piedmont, advantages thus afforded for the erection of factories were seldom mentioned. The easier transport of cotton and the development of the South Atlantic ports were the thoughts uppermost. See above, p. 37. In the case of North Carolina, it is said that the railroads by bringing in manufactures cheaper than local plants could supply them, actually hurt the advance of individual enterprise (Thompson, p. 31).

[71] "Blot out of existence in one night every manufacturing enterprise in the whole country, with all the capital employed [he was writing in 1894], and the loss would not equal that sustained by the

to certain persons, were, socially and economically considered, no more property and wealth than were their masters.
In their emancipation the South did not lose, but gained, if
their labor in freedom may be thought to be more productive than when they were chattels.[72]

Mr. Edmonds makes such over-zealous statements as that
" The energy and enterprise displayed by the South in the
extension of its agricultural interests was fully as great as
the energy displayed in the development of New England's
manufactures or that of the pioneers who opened up the
West to civilization," and greatly overreaches in his disap-
proval of the phrase " The New South," " a term which is
so popular everywhere except in the South, . . . supposed
to represent a country of different ideas and different business methods from those which prevailed in the old ante-
bellum days. . . . Its use . . . as intended to convey the
meaning that the South of late years is something entirely
new and foreign to this section . . . is wholly unjust to
the South of the past and present. It needs but little investigation to show that prior to the war the South was fully
abreast of the times in all business interests."[73]   His real
purpose, which does not require ill-considered harking

South as a result of the war. . . . New England and the Middle
States, having grown rich by the war, almost trebled their property
[from 1860 to 1870] while the South drops from the first place to
the third. In 1860 it outranked the Northern section by $750,000,-
000." Mr. Edmonds does not note the inclusion of the slaves in his
"property" figures (p. 18 ff.). In reference to the false idea ot prosperity in the ante-bellum South, it has been said: " A delusion of
great wealth was created in the listing as taxable property of slaves
to the amount of at least two thousand millions" (Hart, p. 218).

[72] " As commonly used the word ' wealth ' is applied to anything
having an exchange value. But when used as a term of political
economy it must be limited to a much more definite meaning, because
many things are commonly spoken of as wealth which in taking
account of collective or general wealth cannot be considered as
wealth at all. . . . Such are slaves, whose value represents merely
the power of one class to appropriate the earnings of another. . . .
All this relative wealth, which, in common thought and speech, in
legislation and law, is undistinguished from actual wealth, could,
without the destruction or consumption of anything more than a few
drops of ink and a piece of paper, be utterly annihilated " (George,
pp. 38–39).

[73] Edmonds, pp. 1–2.

back to ante-bellum years, is to show that "the wonderful industrial growth which has come since 1880 has been due mainly to Southern men and Southern money," and it is well to rest his exposition with the proper statement that "Since 1880" the people of the South "have turned to manufacturing with a facility that not only shows that they are in no way lacking in capability to compete in manufacturing pursuits, but, considering the limited capital, this section has exhibited remarkable gains in developing its resources under adverse conditions. In a little more than a decade from the time the work of development may be said to have begun . . . nobody . . . doubts that the South can compete with New England in the manufacture of cotton goods, but many do doubt whether New England can compete with the South. . . ."[74]

Edgar Garner Murphy embraced the viewpoint and made more categorical the statements of Mr. Edmonds respecting Southern industrial history. "The present industrial development of the South," he wrote, "is not a new creation. It is chiefly a revival. . . . Instead of industrial inaction we find from the beginnings of Southern history an industrial movement, characteristic and sometimes even provincial in its methods, but presenting a consistent and creditable development up to the very hour of the Civil War. The issue of this war meant no mere economic reversal. It meant economic catastrophe, drastic, desolate. . . . Thus the later story of the industrial South is but a story of reëmergence."[75] The steps of Mr. Edmond's argu-

---

[74] Ibid., p. 21. Cf. ibid., pp. 19–20.
[75] E. G. Murphy, The Present South, p. 97. With modifications prompted by deeper study, Clark has presented about the same interpretation of the decade of the fifties as that of Edmonds and Murphy: "The South resented economic dependence, yet lacked the population, the experience, the capital and the habits that foster manufactures and diversify industries. It was topheavy with cotton, and slave agriculture unbalanced its economic life. . . . Yet had the war not intervened, manufactures would have revived and increased as settlement became denser, railways more numerous, and capital more abundant in proportion to resources, until these states by their own potency would have remoulded their industrial economy" (in South in Building of Nation, vol. v, pp. 330–331). For statements

ment are then repeated, except that Mr. Murphy failed to see the almost total lapse of industrial activity by 1840.

The incentive to discover an industrial past for the section, which Mr. Edmonds found in the desire to establish the South as the magician of her post-bellum awakening, was matched in Mr. Murphy's motive by a more penetrating purpose. In commenting upon the growing importance of manufactures as contrasted with agriculture, which was the most distinctive economic movement after 1880, he declared that "it is but one reassertion of the genius of the old South." Though his words boldly invite such a construction, it was outside of his object to mean by this that a genius for industrialism had run through the earlier history of the section. His true desire was to assert that "The old South was the real nucleus of the new nationalism," the old South in the sense of "the South of responsibility, the men of family, the planter class, the official soldiery, or (if you please) the aristocracy,—the South that had had power, and to whom power had taught those truths of life, those dignities and fidelities of temper, which power always teaches men. . . ." He regretted that this old South was not able to come into force until after Reconstruction because "a doubt was put upon its word given at Appomattox. . . . Power was struck from its hands. Its sense of responsibility was wounded and confused."[76]

This is a fine statement of a primary truth in the development of the South that began about the year 1880. The old South did draw breath with the new. The permanent character of the South, the forces resident in the South of earlier as of later years, were those which largely made possible a complete change in viewpoint, which carried through the measure of, if not indeed giving birth to, a reversed program. But, as Mr. Murphy did not see, there is a radical distinction between the continuity of this quality in the

probably influenced by Edmonds or Murphy, or both, see St. George L. Sioussat, in The History Teacher's Magazine, Sept., 1916, p. 224, and J. J. Spalding, in Proceedings, Fourth Annual Convention, Georgia Industrial Association, pp. 44–45.

[76] Murphy, pp. 10–11.

South and any continuity of its evidences in industrial pursuits. The new South did not receive from the old South
a heritage of industrial tradition; what it received was an
ingrained and living social morality, not marred in its essential characteristics, and very likely, strange as it may
appear, even assisted, by the institution of slavery.[77]

Against some suggestions of an industrial character for
the fifties,[78] may be placed much evidence of an opposite
nature. Thus Hammond, of South Carolina, in the United
States Senate on March 4, 1858, goaded, perhaps, by the
assaults of Helper and Seward, is found setting up figures
of supposed per capita surplus production of the South as
superior to those of the rest of the world, and forgetting
that not wealth but economic power is the measure of the
strength of a people.[79]

The obsession with cotton, and the crazy confidence which
the staple engendered, come out in the defiant valedictory
which this spokesman flung to the North: ". . . would any
sane nation make war on cotton? Without firing a gun,
without drawing a sword, should they make war on us we
could bring the whole world to our feet. . . . What would

---

[77] "This sense of responsibility, deepened rather than destroyed
by the burden of slavery, was the noble and fruitful gift of the old
South to the new, a gift born of the conditions of an aristocracy, but
responsive and operative under every challenge in the changing conditions of the later order" (ibid., p. 21).

[78] A list of cotton factories in Alabama in 1852, the largest of
which had only 3,080 spindles, is contained in DeBow, vol. i, p. 233.
For a similar list for South Carolina in 1847, see Kohn, Cotton Mills
of S. C., pp. 17–18; cf. Gregg, Domestic Industry, pp. 24–25. As to
railroads, see DeBow, vol. iii, p. 76 ff. Where cotton mills were
urged, the tone of the press might be casual as compared with that
characterizing the later period of the eighties when advocacy was
passionate; e.g.: "We are glad to learn that our men of enterprise
and capital are at length waking up on the subject. This is the
best business that they could turn their attention to with the view
of realizing profits . . . while at the same time it gives new life and
energy to the surrounding community" (North Carolina Standard,
Feb. 27, 1850, quoted in Pleasants MS.).

[79] Scherer, p. 235 ff. Cf. Friedrich List, National System of Political Economy. Hammond indulged largely in estimates; as to
untrustworthiness of census figures of wealth in these years, see
Olmsted, pp. 512–513, and M. T. Copeland, The Cotton Manufacturing Industry of the United States, p. 18, note.

happen if no cotton were furnished for three years? . . . England would topple headlong and carry the whole civilized world with her, save the South. No, you do not dare to make war on cotton. No power on earth dares to make war upon it. Cotton *is* King."[80]

Propaganda toward sweeping in Mexico and the Spanish West Indies to the Southern slavery system, when it became apparent by 1856 that further expansion in the West was impossible, paralleled the academic instruction given throughout his whole career by Professor Dew in the College of William and Mary.[81]

Ship-building, often urged because of superior advantages for the industry, did not take hold in the South.[82] In capital investment, presumption was against everything but cotton cultivation. Those who in the later period invested in manufactures were before the war slave holders. Fear that the presence of manufactures might undermine free trade tenets of the South had some influence against industry.[83] Only inhibitions against manufacturing as pervasive and unconsicous as they were effective can explain the surprise with which Southerners contemplated the failure of cotton mills set in the midst of cotton fields.[84] The pro-

---

[80] Quoted in Scherer, p. 235 ff. How little thought had been given to the South's economic self-sufficiency appears in this warning to the North: " The South have (sic) sustained you in a great measure. You are our factors. . . . Suppose we were to discharge you; suppose we were to take our business out of your hands; we would consign you to anarchy and poverty " (quoted in Scherer, p. 241). Cf. the spirited dissent from such thinking by Cassius M. Clay, as quoted in Helper, pp. 206–207. Hammond's views are readily amplified by reference to proslavery writings, especially those of Christy, Bledsoe, Stringfellow, Harper, Dew.

[81] Dodd, in South in Building of Nation, vol. v, p. 573.

[82] Cf. Olmsted, p. 539, note, and table on p. 541; Ingle, pp. 70–71.

[83] Cf. Ingle, pp. 70–71. "Of the twenty millions of dollars annually realized from the sales of the cotton crop of Alabama, nearly all not expended in supporting the producers is reinvested in lands and negroes," and from this proceeded " senility and decay " (Hon. C. C. Clay, Jr., speaking to a horticultural society in 1855, quoted in Olmsted, p. 577). Cf. B. F. Perry, in address before S. C. Institute, 1855, quoted in Helper, pp. 229–230.

[84] Cf. Sparta, Ga., dispatch to Charleston News, July, 1855, in Olmsted, pp. 543–544. The decade 1850–1860 was the most prosperous for the cotton industry in the country up to that time (Cope-

portion of slaves in the ten cotton States was greater in
1860 than in 1850,[85] the border States showed a positive increase in number of slaves, cotton planters of the older sections gave themselves to breeding slaves for the Texas
market,[86] and the amount of cultivated land increased 16.4
per cent.[87]   The cotton crop of 1859–1860 was the largest
to that time, being in excess of two billion bales.[88]

No distincter picture of the growing trend in the South
away from balanced economic development can be wished
than that presented by the series of commercial conventions
held in the fifteen years preceding the Civil War.   The
1845 meeting, in Memphis, did not allow the recording of
a proposition that the seat of government be removed to a
place west of the Alleghanies, and passed a resolution af-
firming that the convention " far from desiring to engender
sectional prejudice . . . regard the North and the South,
the East and the West, as one people, in sympathy and in
interest, as in government and country "; in accordance
with the purpose to build up the South, the questions
brought before the convention were at first of a practical
nature, concerning commerce, manufactures and education.
Gradually, however, border States ceased to send delegates, and the conventions were dominated by the political
aims of the cotton belt, with politicians, rather than men of
affairs, as spokesmen.   Such practical measures as were
discussed were on lines too broad to be capable of realization.   They were such proposals as made resolutions rather
than results.   The South, so far as she sought industrial
advancement, was in a maze, a novice not knowing to what
projects to lend strength, never thinking of looking inward
and never willing to start with homely enterprises that are
suggested by genuine recognition of economic needs.   It

---

land, pp. 73–74). Following opening of railway communication after
1850, which brought in outside manufactures, " the home industry
was, as a whole, distinctly less successful" (Thompson, p. 31).
  [85] Hammond, pp. 60–61.
  [86] Ibid., p. 59.
  [87] Ibid., p. 102, note 1. See table in ibid., p. 129.
  [88] Ibid., pp. 73–74.

was sought to secure the free navigation of the Amazon, to make passage of the Isthmus at Tehuantepec, to build a railroad from the Mississippi to the Pacific, to secure the introduction of slavery into Central America, to remove obstacles to filibustering plans in Nicaragua. Through the discussions in successive years at Charleston, New Orleans, Richmond, Savannah, Knoxville, Montgomery and Vicksburg the tendency toward politics grew; rather forced pronouncements of belief in the Union carried implication against their sincerity, and were mocked by speedy development of wrangles over the tariff into open use of the word "secession." "Hail Columbia" might be played at a banquet, but response was given to a toast, "The District of Columbia, the battleground for Southern institutions." Washington, and not the Southern States, drew the eye of all.[89]

---

[89] See Ingle, p. 221 ff. ". . . in all that they said there was an undertone of disappointment and apprehension. They wished to take part, but could not, in what was going forward in the rest of the country. They spoke hopefully of national enterprise, but it was evident that the nation of which they were thinking . . . was not the same nation that the Northern man had in mind when he thought of the future of industry" (Woodrow Wilson, Division and Reunion, p. 164). Cf. Scherer, p. 204. Cassius M. Clay in a speech in 1856 relentlessly pointed out the futility of all the plans proposed: "If there are not manufactures, there is no commerce. In vain do the slaveholders go to Knoxville, to Nashville, to Memphis and to Charleston, and resolve that they will have nothing to do with these abolition eighteen millions of Northern people; that they will build their own vessels, manufacture their own goods, ship their own products to foreign countries, and break down New-York, Philadelphia and Boston! Again they resolve and resolve, and yet there is not a single more ton shipped and not a single article added to the wealth of the South. But . . . they never invite such men as I am to attend their Conventions. They know that I would tell them that slavery is the cause of their poverty, and that I will tell them that what they are aiming at is the dissolution of the Union. . . . They well know that by slave labor the very propositions which they make can never be realized; yet when we show these things, they cry out, 'Oh, Cotton is King!'" (quoted in Helper, pp. 206–207). An observation of Sir Horace Plunkett with respect to Irish leaders is peculiarly applicable here, if Irish nationalism be understood as paralleling true Southern economic needs:" . . . I always felt that an Irish night in the House of Commons was one of the strangest and most pathetic of spectacles. There were the veterans of the Irish party hardened by a hundred fights, ranging from Venezuela to the Soudan in search of battlefields, making allies of every kind

The bias of these last ante-bellum years, lashed to passion by a guilty sectional conscience, or made more wild by the lack of any connected thinking, precluded even the possibility of industrialism. When a gambler on the verge of ruin is desperately playing his last cards he has no time to reflect on past errors of judgment, and no inclination to think of better methods than the fortunes of chance by which to repair a pocket that likely momentarily will be emptied.[90] What did not occur to the leaders did not rise in the thoughts of the people.[91]

Industrialism and the growth of cities are closely connected, yet in the decade of the fifties the advance in population of representative Southern cities was tardy as contrasted with the North and West.[92]

It has been noticed earlier that before the war even agriculture was carried on with the roughest, least efficient tools, such as the " scooter," the " bull-tongue," the scraper, the sweep and hoe.[93] It is found that as late as 1880 patents issued to Southerners were for devices to be employed on

of foreign potentate, from President Cleveland to the Mahdi, from Mr. Kruder, to the Akhoom of Swat, but looking with suspicion upon every symptom of an independent national movement in Ireland; masters of the language of hate and scorn, yet mocked by inevitable and eternal failure; winners of victories that turn to dust and ashes, devoted to their country, yet, from ignorance of the real source of the malady, ever widening the gaping wound through which its life-blood flows. . . . Irishmen have been long in realizing that . . . there are battles for Ireland to be fought and won in Ireland " (p. 91 ff.).

[90] " . . . the Irish mind has been in regard to economics, politics, and even some phases of religious influence, a mind warped and diseased, deprived of good nutrition and fed on fancies or fictions, out of which no genuine growth, industrial or other was possible " (Plunkett, pp. 122–123).

[91] At the height of this period Helper wrote: " . . . the stupid and sequacious masses, the white victims of slavery . . . believe, whatever the slaveholders tell them; and thus it is that they are cajoled into the notion that they are the freest, happiest and most intelligent people in the world, and are taught to look with prejudice and disapprobation upon every new principle or progressive movement. Thus it is that the South, woefully inert and inventionless, has lagged behind the North, and is now weltering in the cesspool of ignorance and degradation " (pp. 44–45. Cf. Page, pp. 22–23).

[92] Ingle, pp. 14–15.

[93] Cf. Hammond, pp. 77–78. Cf. George, pp. 522–523.

the farm or in the home rather than in mechanical pursuits, thus arguing against any considerable industrial tradition or stirrings before that date.[94]

Gregg warned the South that as surely as she separated from the Union, she would find herself economically unequipped to maintain her position. His words were realized with bitter force. The trial of the war showed how far industry had been neglected. It tore away in an instant a veil of fiction, and showed deplorable fact beneath. Not even the immediate needs of an army, in munitions and ordnance, could be met within the South. Clothing for soldiery and people was lacking, shipyards were small; transportation was insufficient. When cotton could no longer bring in the manufactures of others, the South was left without essentials.[95]

It has been seen how lacking was the ante-bellum South in any industrial character, and how some tendencies in this direction, showing themselves in the years just before the outbreak of conflict, were choked off or perverted by political motive in the rapidly growing hostility to the North. The Civil War, which brought into glaring view the absence of Southern economic self-sufficiency, cleared the

---

[94] Under date of Nov. 14, 1882, the patent for a loom shuttle was issued to D. A. Willbanks, High Shoals, Ga., but this is the only invention connected with cotton manufacturing revealed by a search of patent lists for many weeks (Baltimore Journal of Commerce and Manufacturers' Record, Nov. 18, 1882). Typical lists of patents issued in the same year to Southerners show: cultivator, saw gin filing machine, vehicle wheel, quilting attachment for sewing machines, rotary engine, couch, combined cotton-planter and fertilizer-distributor, grate feeder, paint, devices for holding the fingers in writing, hoe, animal trap, bottle washer, automatic fly can, spoke socket, cotton chopper, coffee roaster, revolving plow, bread cutter, etc. (ibid., Sept. 26, 1882, and Nov. 4, 1882).

[95] " The story of manufactures in the South from 1860 to 1865 is a record of the efforts of a people, deprived in large measure of the materials that satisfy their needs, to supply themselves without previous preparation with the equipment of war and the resources of peace" (Clark, in South in Building of Nation, vol. v, pp. 330–331). Cf. Scherer, p. 260, note; R. D. Stewart, "Firearms of the Confederacy," in Magazine of Antique Firearms, Dec., 1911; Tompkins, Tariff, p. 5; Thompson, p. 55; ibid., p. 44. It is significant that the exigency was met only by leaning heavily upon domestic household production. See above, p. 35.

fevered, suffocating atmosphere like an electric storm. Misconceived sectional political ambition and fierce protest had ridden to a fall; talent and energy theretofore absorbed to such ends were freed for wholesome introspection and material upbuilding. The Civil War set at rest the political inconclusiveness of the Union, which had operated so harmfully for the South. The political bee, which had been encouraged to buzz in the Southern bonnet by the planter particularism, was silenced.[96] This was the first condition of economic advance. Besides the negative effect of the war, through the issue of the struggle the South was drawn into the national life, and thus was given positive stimulus through the industrial example of the North and East.[97]

With the removal of political obsession vanished its cohort, slavery; slavery gone, it not only became apparent that the South had to change tactics, but that it could change tactics. Thus practical pointings were not more powerful than mental consequents—not just the slaves, but the South as a whole was emancipated.[98]

---

[96] Southerners "now renewed once and for all time their allegiance to the Union which had up to that time been an experiment, a government of uncertain powers" (Dodd, Expansion and Conflict, p. 328).

[97] "The planter culture, the semi-feudalism of the 'old South' was annihilated, while the industrial and financial system of the East was triumphant. . . . the east was the mistress of the United States, and the social and economic ideals of that section were to be stamped permanently upon the country" (ibid., p. 328. On the nonindustrial quality of the ante-bellum South, see also ibid., pp. 214-215). After emancipation, "the Southern people felt themselves in the throes of an economic revolution leading to a future of diversified industries. The old sentiment in favor of agriculture survived; but faith in it as the sole support of a nation was disappearing. The wealth and power which the North had derived from manufactures was better appreciated" (Clark, in South in Building of Nation, vol. vi, p. 254).

[98] As will be seen later, new opportunities and duties did not break on the South with full force at first. What the war made possible, however, is seen in the following striking statement of a Southern periodical some years afterward: ". . . it has been a very common thing . . . we all know, for one generation after another in southern cities . . . to beguile the monotony of their humdrum life with rosy day-dreams of a far-off greatness that has been always coming but has never come. At last, however, since the annihilation of the institution of slavery, the new awakening of the world under

It will be seen in a later chapter, in examining the wide-spread building of cotton mills, how completely the South was altered in economic outlook after the Civil War. Not the least satisfactory evidence of this changed character is in the frank avowal of it by Southerners on every hand. The war was in Southern economic history a watershed. In 1882 a publisher in the heart of the South could say: "The old sectional spirit is dying out. You can find few men now who hold the narrow views of former years."[99]

The newness of cotton manufacture, as of industry generally, to the post-bellum South is evidenced in the type of enterprisers who entered the field when its opportunities were understood. There were few experienced men upon whom to rely; it is safe to say that after the war more of the men projecting cotton mills came from any one of the accustomed callings of agriculture, commerce and the professions than from industry.[100] Before the war such propa-

the intelligent energies of an age of unprecedented progress, the delusive mirage now disappears; and the desert of hope in the South begins truly to grow green with . . . a harvest that is really ripening before the impoverished people who have so long been looking for it and have been so drearily disappointed. . . . At last we know that the South need no longer be nodding, and dreaming, and drooping, over the faded hopes that have for ages attended her traditions; but, under the auspices of a new order of things, that her people have to go on only a little further with the same heroic endurance and the same brave energies now characterizing them, to realize in all its fullness and all its force the great established and imperishable fact that the old Slave States of the Union—themselves emancipated from the industrial incubus of an institution which contracted their spirit of enterprise, enfeebled their energies, and smothered all their industries except that of agriculture,—are now at last standing straight and strong, with a cheering consciousness of their native power in the bounties God has given them. . . ." (Industrial South, Richmond, quoted in Baltimore Journal of Commerce and Mfgrs. Record, June 17, 1882). Cf. Clark, in South in Building of Nation, vol. vi, p. 254, and Grady, p. 270. Tompkins said of one community now noted for its manufactures, "The effect of emancipation upon all classes of industrial life was immediate and revolutionary," and attributed the interest in factories chiefly to abolition of slavery (History of Mecklenburg, vol. i, p. 150. Cf. ibid., pp. 151, 194–196).

[99] Patrick Walsh, of Augusta Chronicle, quoted in Journal of Commerce and Manufacturers' Record, Baltimore, Sept. 30, 1882.

[100] See Goldsmith, pp. 7–8; Clark, in South in Building of Nation, vol. vi, pp. 266–267; Tompkins, Cotton Mill, Commercial Features, p. 180; and the present writer, in Manufacturers' Record, Baltimore, May 10, 1917.

gandists as DeBow, hammering away in his Review for railways, cotton manufactures and direct trade with Europe, were pitifully in the minority. After the war, such adherents of the old order as Bledsoe ridiculed industrialism in vain; warnings against making the "New South" only another North made small appeal to thinking men who cherished precisely this ambition.[101]

How great is the temptation to conceive and attempt to carry through political and social reforms which are really contingent upon economic reorganization, is nowhere more clearly seen than in the period of Reconstruction in the South. These years, filled with the clamor of jealousy and vindictiveness and hurt and passion and greed needed so much of wisdom and patience and, above all, work. Fortunately, economic processes by some magic can usually, however uncertainly, go forward in spite of every political hindrance; the South, if hearing with one ear insults from without, listened with the other to voices from within. The degree of distraction and torment of Reconstruction testifies to the strength of purpose with which the South attended to her own best promptings. It may even be held, perhaps, that Reconstruction, in a certain point of view, was of positive assistance in nurturing the mind for industrial beginnings. There was no question but that the South was exhausted and was being drained of all but self-respect; she was humbled beyond compassion. Former slaves were apparently becoming masters. As a participant in nationality, in appreciation of broad social policies, the South knew that she had made a terrible failure. The fierce pride of the first war years had waned into the hopeless, dogged resistance of the days before Appomattox and flickered out in the degradation that followed. During Reconstruction the South, like a man thrown into prison, had time to reflect on past sins. Though perhaps it was not admitted in word,

---

[101] See Dodd, in South in Building of Nation, vol. vi, p. 546. For an excellent account of post-bellum activity as contrasted with ante-bellum quiescence, see Tompkins, History of Mecklenburg, vol. i, pp. 150–151, 194–196; Clark, in South in Building of Nation, vol. vi, pp. 262–263.

it was soon to be shown in deed that the South understood the part that slavery had played. A new course must surely thenceforth be adopted. In Reconstruction the South found itself. Not without the material assistance and more generous view that came through agency of Northern men who in this period learned to know the industrial opportunities of the section and were willing to contribute toward its development, it was still primarily a change of heart which the South experienced. In the face of a freed negro population, the idea of work first seriously presented itself to the Southern white mind.

Lack of tangible evidences of this psychological change should not hinder understanding of its presence. During Reconstruction little that was practical could be done, but how earnestly the South had been introspecting and planning is splendidly apparent in the suddenness and vigor with which industrial development commenced once impediments were removed.[102]

It will be seen later that no agency bore a larger part in the rise of cotton mills in the South than the News and Courier, of Charleston. It is therefore important to know that, according to a statement made by the paper in 1880, on the very eve of the great development, its philosophy of

---

[102] Mr. Clark has well called Reconstruction "a germinal period for manufactures." For a sympathetic interpretation of the meaning of Reconstruction years, see Clark, in South in Building of Nation, vol. vi, pp. 254–255, 262–263, 265–266. Grady wrote in 1889, speaking principally of the period of Reconstruction: "For twenty-five years the industrial forces of the South have been at work under the surface. Making little show, experimenting, working out new ways, peering about with the lamp of experience barely lit, digging, delving, struggling, until at last the day has come, and independence is proclaimed. Now watch the change take place with almost comical swiftness" (p. 270). One cannot but second the appeal of Professor Sioussat: "The political history of reconstruction has been narrated from many points of view, . . . but the vast social and economic changes, which beginning in the reconstruction time are still in progress, usually receive in our text-books less attention. Our girls and boys study carefully the work of the Gracchi, the organization of the medieval manor . . . and the condition of the peasants in France before the revolution. Is it not possible to awaken an intelligent interest in the tasks with which emancipation and the industrial revolution have confronted the people of the South?" (p. 223).

manufactures had been conceived in the thick of Reconstruction. "Ten years ago," it was said, "The News and Courier formulated what is now an accepted truth, in declaring
that the remedy for commercial distress in the North and
the secret of sure fortune in the South was to bring the mills
to the cotton." The thought was not balked by the small
success of ante-bellum factories, one of which, established
in Charleston long before the war, was at the date of this
writing "in the irony of fate, the City Alms-House"; nor
was it unassisted by the presence of men in the State "who
understood that large profits could be made by well-managed cotton factories." There were at the close of the conflict such mills as Graniteville and Batesville which were
gaining reputation, and another important venture was being
projected. Around these a body of thought, favorable to
manufactures, and new to the South, grew up, and "the
expectation of profit, which in those days had something of
a theoretical basis," was by 1880 able to stand upon "a
solid foundation, supported by . . . indisputable and convincing facts. . . ."[103]

---

[103] Feb. 10, 1880. A South Carolinian, reminded of the cotton
mill boom of the early eighties, led by the press, said "the South
had begun to develop and revive before 1880. The papers probably
stressed a program which they had already seen started" (M. L.
Bonham, interview, Anderson, S. C., Sept. 10, 1916). "No appre-
ciable break occurred in the continuity of cotton manufactures in
the South, in spite of the mills destroyed or closed by the war. Before 1870 several of the ruined factories had been rebuilt, and long
prior to that others had resumed operations. . . . In 1868 . . . there
were sixty-nine mills . . . in operation south of the Ohio and Po-
tomac. . . . By 1870 Southern mill owners were confident they could
make yarn five cents a pound cheaper than the Northern factories"
(Clark, in South in Building of Nation, vol. vi, pp. 254–255). Cf.
ibid., pp. 262–263. The News and Courier declared that "nothing
did more to show the practical advantages of a cotton producing
State in this matter than the calculation made and published a number of years ago by the President of the Saluda Factory, which
showed by actual figures that South Carolina mills could sell ordinary yarns in New York at the price which it cost the mills in New
England to make these yarns, and still realize a considerable profit"
(ibid.). See a list of mills in operation in South Carolina two
years after the war, published in an almanac of Joseph Walker,
Charleston, quoted in Kohn, Cotton Mills of South Carolina, p. 19.
With reference to the fifteen years following the war, see Thompson, p. 59 ff. For a sketch of the career of H. P. Hammett, typical

We may leave now the period of Reconstruction, with its formative influences, and come to the evidence bespeaking material proof of industrial beginnings after political hindrances were removed, economic strength was being regained and the South could concentrate on its task of manufactures.[104] The Southern States, though regaining self-government generally about 1876, did not get economic freedom of action with political rights. Later, in another connection, it will be shown how the issue of the Hayes-Tilden presidential election helped to delay for four years industrial beginnings. But aside from this, waving the wand of civic independence could not produce cotton mills immediately from a magic hat. Additional years of recovery were necessary, years far from idle, but not marked by widespread activity. The war saw a fevered South completely stricken; during radical rule the victim lay on a bed of torture; while convalescent after 1876, the patient did not comence to sit up and take solid food until about 1880.

There is every reason for selecting the year 1880 as the beginning of cotton manufacturing development in the South. Negatively, foregoing pages have shown that it did not exist, in a proper sense, earlier. Remaining parts of this study will exhibit very positive evidences of alertness and progress after that date. Though there are material bases for grounding the genesis in the year 1880, it is not meant to insist dogmatically upon this precise point of time.

---

of the South Carolinians who after the war understood that a profit could be made from well-managed cotton mills, and who in the sixties and seventies was mayor of Greenville, a member of the House of Representatives, a railroad president and mill builder, see Tompkins, Cotton Mill, Commercial Features, pp. 189–190. Renewal of cotton manufacturing in the South closely following disappearance of slavery was generally on old lines and with old machinery, but Hammett's Piedmont Factory was " designed, built and equipped after strictly modern plans " (ibid.).

104 " While some retrospect is necessary [in studying the history of the New South] the period . . . covered is principally that which began with the close of the reconstruction era, at the time when the South was permitted once more to exercise self-government, and when some progress had been made toward repairing the economic losses of the war " (Sioussat, pp. 223, 228). Cf. Tompkins, Tariff, p. 3.

Certainly, however, much in the way of convenience would be sacrificed by choosing 1879 or 1881. Writers touching the subject, whether careful students or casual commentators, have very generally selected this date as the initiation of the cotton mill era.[105]

---

[105] "The scope of the history of Southern progress along industrial lines is embraced mostly within the last twenty-five years" (T. C. Guthrie, in Proceedings, 7th Annual Convention, Southern Cotton Spinners' Assn., 1903, p. 44). See this and following pages for an extraordinarily good interpretation of stages antecedent to the rise of the mills. The suddenness with which development began is indicated: "If some soothsayer . . . twenty-five years ago . . . had essayed to predict what the South would accomplish in industrial development . . . and particularly in cotton manufacturing; if he had foretold the hundreds of millions of capital that would be invested; the number of mills; the number of spindles; . . . the quantity of cotton consumed each year; the number of operatives; the value of the annual output—if he had prophesied concerning the meeting here today, the capital, labor, values and territory represented here, he would have been set down as a dreamer of dreams." Another speaker at the same convention referred to slavery as turning back the clock of progress, which, however, started ticking off industrial advance after 1880 (Averill, ibid., pp. 123–124). Noticing the decrease in price of cotton from 1870 to 1879 from 23 to 10 cents, the growing impatience with unreliable freed negroes, the movement of people of means to the cities and willingness to invest in other things than mortgages, Mr. Thompson assumed the same date of commencement (p. 59 ff.). Cf. E. C. Brooks, Story of Cotton, p. 215. Professor Brooks prefers 1880 as the date of the Southern economic renaissance (interview, Durham, N. C., Sept. 18, 1916), and his Story of Cotton shows this clearly, as, e.g., "It was in 1880 . . . that the Southern states turned seriously to manufacturing cotton" (p. 261); he gives a table from which he says "It is apparent . . . that the real factory life in the South dates from 1880 . . . ;" " . . . a new era started in the South about 1880 . . ." (p. 257); "The whole civilization of the South had been overturned, . . . a new era in regard to the value of skilled labor and personal worth was taking the place of the old notions . . . and we have the beginning of the factory system in the South" (pp. 255–256). Mr. Goldsmith calls the year 1880 "epoch-marking" and declares it "marks the turning point in the development of modern cotton factories in the South. . . . A new era dawned" (pp. 4–5). Tompkins related the third period in Southern population history to "the industrial expansion which grew from the business revival . . . following the war," and quoted figures from 1880 (History of Mecklenburg, vol. I, p. 197). Murphy put stress upon a psychological reversal which argued industrialism: "About the year 1880 the long-waited change begins. By 1890 the industrial revival is in evident progress. By 1900 the South had entered upon one of the most remarkable periods of economic development to be found in the history of the modern industrial world" (pp. 101–102). "From the ashes and ruins left by the war a 'new South' has emerged. Between the cessation of

Innumerable evidences of the newness of the South to cotton manufacture in 1880 crop out, making it clear that united building of mills cannot be placed before that date.

hostilities and the beginning of this development, a period of fifteen years, the South had slowly recovered from the losses which it had suffered. . . . The cotton manufacturing industry has grown up in the South . . . since 1880" (Copeland, pp. 32, 34). "The revolution, . . . the evolution on the 'double quick,' began about 1880 in South Carolina. . . ." (Kohn, Cotton Mills of S. C., p. 20). Cf. ibid., pp. 18-19. "One of the most remarkable features in the industrial history of the Southern States has been the phenomenal growth of cotton manufactures there . . .; from 1880-1890 the number of spindles increased twofold . . . whilst in the following decade the growth was still greater. . . ." (T. W. Uttley, Cotton Spinning and Manufacturing in the United States of America, p. 43). This selection of 1880 is by an English student. Some references far from studied are especially confirmatory; often a painter will half close his eyes to discern tone values: "United States Census figures show that since 1880 the consumption of cotton in mills in the cotton growing states has increased 1,502 per cent. . . ." (Advertisement of Southern Railway in Textile Manufacturer, Charlotte, N. C., Aug. 19, 1915). "In other words, since 1880 the investment in Southern cotton mills has increased from less than fifteen million dollars to more than three hundred and fifty million dollars" (John A. Law, in Proceedings, Robert Morris Club, National Association of Credit Men, 1916, pp. 18-19). Cf. Henry D. Phillips, in The South Mobilizing for Social Service, p. 566; Hart, pp. 224, 232, 242. "It will be seen that the South has been taking stock since 1880, and that economic forces and influences are now better understood than ever before . . ." (Dodd, in South in Building of Nation, vol. vi, p. 550). "Mills were established in Spartanburg County first in 1879 and 1880 in numbers. About these years was the first great activity. The County was crushed before 1879. Before 1876 there was no capital, and the domination of the carpet bag government" (Cleveland, int., Spartanburg). For a looser statement, hardly to be taken in contradiction, see Tompkins, Cotton Mill, Commercial Features, preface. The year 1880 marks not only the beginnings of cotton manufacturing, but was signalized by recovery or new enterprise in other directions. Ante-bellum cotton production of over 5,000,000 bales had been reached again (Sioussat, p. 227, and News and Observer, Raleigh, N. C., Sept. 15, 1880); Tennessee and Alabama boom towns, resting on hopes of iron and steel manufacture, came a little later (Sioussat, ibid.); railroad development took its rise (Hart, p. 227); ". . . it was not until amost 1880 that the public-school idea was accepted as the best solution of the educational problem" (U. S. Bureau of Education, Negro Education, 1917); furniture and vehicle factories appeared in the upland, hardwood sections (Brooks, p. 217); agricultural method and rural life began undergoing reorganization and betterment (ibid., pp. 221-222); public interest in cotton seed oil manufacture started with 1882 (Tompkins, Cotton and Cotton Oil, pp. 210, 214); right of suffrage was withdrawn from illiterate whites and negroes (ibid., p. 64); as to good roads, see Tompkins, History of Mecklenburg, vol. ii, p. 213; the speculation

In this year only one establishment in South Carolina was located within the corporate limits of a city.[106] Descriptions of cotton manufacturing processes had to be of the most primary sort, without technical language.[107] Lack of specialization and even the link with domestic industry showed in at least one conspicuous instance as late as 1880.[108] How largely thought of industrial matters was delayed until 1880 by the issue of the Hayes-Tilden contest will be seen in detail later.[109] Contributing to the lateness of the economic awakening was the fact that South Carolina, which proved so strong in leadership when the movement commenced, was one of the last States to be freed from carpet-bag rule.

The panic of 1873 and the following depression may be considered alone sufficient cause for the failure of these years to show more industrial progress in the South.

From the combined causes of war, paper money, and scarcity of cotton, the price of the staple and of manufacturing machinery soared to monstrous figures, and did not return again to the level of 1860 until about 1880.[110]

In a list of the thirty cities having the largest gross manu-

---

of 1879 was held to have set in motion European and American spindles (Commercial and Financial Chronicle, quoted in News and Courier, Charleston, Sept. 12, 1881) ; "The cotton-manufacturing industry in almost every part of the world has continued to prosper during the past twelve months" (Financial and Commercial Chronicle, quoted in Baltimore Journal of Commerce and Manufacturers' Record, Sept. 9, 1882) ; ". . . the sudden and wonderful revival of business which took place in the republic during the last half of 1879 . . . had the effect of withdrawing us from the foreign markets to supply our home demands" (American Rail and Export Journal, quoted in ibid., Aug. 26, 1882).

[106] J. K. Blackman, The Cotton Mills of South Carolina, p. 13.

[107] See as to Clement Attachment, Daily Constitution, Atlanta, Jan. 23, 1880.

[108] In connection with the Glendale Factory, D. E. Converse & Co. operated a flouring mill, several gins, a saw and planing mill, and a wool carding mill in which upwards of 10,000 pounds of wool was prepared for the country people (Blackman, p. 10).

[109] See especially, however, correspondence signed "Local," in News and Observer, Raleigh, N. C., Nov. 21, 1880, and quotations from New York Herald and Washington Post in News and Courier, Charleston, March 8, 1881.

[110] U. S. Census of Manufactures, 1880, "Cotton Manufacture," p. 8.

facturing product, the census of 1880 enumerated none in the South, unless Baltimore and St. Louis be counted, and in neither of these did cotton manufacture rank with their six principal industries.[111]

Census figures, inconclusive when examined for particular aspects of the history of the cotton manufacture, show strikingly, when taken for a considerable period, that the Southern industry had its rise in 1880. The following table, covering the years 1850 to 1900 inclusive, gives the course of the mills of the South as exhibited in the most salient features:[112]

Year	Estab.	Capital	Opera-tives	Spin.	Looms	Lbs. Cotton
1900	401	$124,596,874	97,559	4,299,988	110,015	707,842,111
1890	239	53,821,303	36,415	1,554,000	36,266	250,837,646
1880	161	17,375,897	16,741	542,048	11,898	84,528,757
1870	151	11,088,315	10,173	327,871	6,256	34,351,195
1860	165	9,840,221	10,152	298,551	8,789	45,786,510
1850	166	7,256,056	10,043	—	—	—

That 1880 was the date of commencement, clearly seen in this tabulation, is also interestingly apparent in interpretations of the figures brought out in successive census reports. No better picture of the way in which the Southern development broke on the national consciousness can be had than by a glance at some of these comments seriatim.

As has been said, up to 1880 the Southern industry had evidenced no extraordinary or convincing advance. It is natural, therefore, to find the census of this year remarking on the degree of Southern growth merely as an extension of the manufacture, and classing the Southern mills with some new ones in the West.[113]

[111] " Remarks on the Statistics of Manufactures," p. xxvii.
[112] U. S. Census of Manufactures, 1900, " Cotton Manufactures," p. 57. These figures, strictly taken, indicate the decade, rather than the year, of commencement of striking growth. Comments in the census and other evidence, however, fill in the outline here presented.
[113] " The cotton manufacture is almost monopolized by New England, Massachusetts alone producing to the value of $74,780,835. The other New England states produce in the aggregate about as

As will be seen later, Edward Atkinson, of Boston, had much to do with rousing the South to economic activity. However, he admitted Southern industrial prospects only when he could not urge a superior advantage in New England or when he knew that to do otherwise would be futile. His comments in the census of 1880 are interestingly indicative of his frame of mind. Dwelling on the new through rail connections in this country, he computed in pound-cents the saving of New England over Lancashire in raw cotton; recognizing that this argument of relative proximity to cotton fields proved too much, applying with greater force to the Southern States, he was obliged to say that "If Georgia has twice the advantage over Lancashire that New England now possesses, it will only be the fault of the people of Georgia if they do not reap the benefit of it."[114] He went on to assert, somewhat contradictorily, that "The charge for moving cotton is becoming less year by year, and it will soon matter little where the cotton factory is placed, so far as distance between the field and the factory is concerned," and suggested that this allowed location of mills so as to utilize assets in climate, labor, and repair facilities

---

much more. . . ." And in the list of States producing in excess of $2,000,000 each are mentioned Georgia, Maryland, New Jersey, New York, North Carolina, Pennsylvania, South Carolina (U. S. Census of Manufactures, 1880, "Remarks on the Statistics of Manufactures," by Francis A. Walker, pp. xix–xx). Two obvious advantages of Southern mills seemed to be sufficient cause for greater percentage of increase in that section than in other sections. ". . . tables indicate the rapid extension of the cotton manufacture to the southern states, where the cotton is at hand and labor is much cheaper than at the north." Southern spindles increased from 1870 to 1880 by 65 + per cent, in New England 57 per cent, in the Middle States 11 + per cent, in the Western States 46 + per cent, and in the whole country 49 + per cent. "It will be seen that the states of Michigan, Wisconsin, and Minnesota have been added to the list of cotton manufacturing states since 1870" (ibid., "The Factory System of the United States," by Carroll D. Wright, p. 16). "After the success of the power loom the cotton manufacture took rapid strides. . . . Factories sprung up on all the streams of Yorkshire and Lanca-shire, . . . while in this country the activity of the promoters . . . won cities from barren pastures. They erected Lowell, Lawrence, Holyoke, Fall River . . . and now in this generation the industry is taking root upon the banks of Southern streams" (ibid., p. 8).

[114] U. S. Census of Manufactures, 1880, "The Cotton Manufacture," p. 12. Cf. p. 13.

which were possessed by New England; that the lowest cost of production existed where wages were highest.[115]

He was fond of trying to center the attention of the South on the "preparation" of cotton rather than on its manufacture. Thus he declared that ginning, which must be carried on among the plantations, "is the most important department in the whole series of operations to which the cotton fiber must be subjected; and as yet there has been less of science and art . . . applied to this department than to any other." He exhibited in much detail, on the basis of a private investigation made before the census year, the careless and wasteful way in which cotton was handled in the Southern gins and "screws," but was obliged to admit that by 1883, when his report was transmitted, "the old methods, by which the cotton has been depreciated after it had been picked, are rapidly going out of use." This was partly by agency of the Atlanta cotton exposition of 1881, in which he had been a prime mover, and which it is clear he hoped might direct efforts increasingly to the growing of the staple in the uplands, and the utilization of seed for its oil and food substances.[116]

The position taken in this study, that the Southern cotton manufacturing development really began in 1880, receives striking justification in the comments on the statistics of the industry by Edward Stanwood in the census of 1890. In the figures collected in this year the Southern development since 1880, as contrasted with the previous record of the section, and as compared with the proportionate advance of other seats of the manufacture, was too apparent to be accorded other than frank avowal, leading to speculation as to chances of the rest of the country in maintaining accustomed superiority. "The geographical distribution of the cotton manufacturing industry is an interesting study," Stanwood said, "and it is more especially so at the present time by the fact that during the last ten years a change has been taking place, which, if it should continue, will become

---

[115] Ibid., p. 14.
[116] Ibid., p. 4 ff.

5

highly important." He recited that from the beginning
New England had been chief in the industry, in 1840 having
70 per cent of the spinning machinery, in 1860 (spindles
were not taken in 1850) 74 per cent, 77 per cent in 1870,
and 81 per cent in 1880. The 1890 census, however, showed
for New England a drop to 76 per cent. In the face of this
decrease, he enlarged on the steadiness of concentration in
certain New England districts and the success with which
Massachusetts alone had maintained its percentage of spindleage increase. But, in spite of having added 2,000,000
spindles, New England was a relative loser by nearly 5 per
cent, and for the first time in the census occurs the heading
" Growth in the South." And it is declared:

> In considering the geographical distribution of the cotton manu-
> facturing industry the most important fact is the extraordinary rate
> of its growth in the South during the past decade. For a great
> many years, probably ever since the cultivation of the cotton plant
> in the South Atlantic states had a beginning, domestic spinning and
> weaving of coarse cotton fabrics has been a common fact in the
> household economy of that part of the country. Here and there
> small factories were established for the production of heavy fabrics.
> It is only in the period since the close of the civil war that mills have
> been erected in the South for the purpose of entering the general
> market of the country with their merchandise, and almost all the
> progress made in this direction has been effected since 1880.

It was remarked that the 1880 census showed for all the
States south of the District of Columbia, only 542,048 spindles, and that had all these been concentrated in one State
it would have raised that State only to seventh place in point
of production capacity. " A remarkable development of
manufacturing enterprise in the South, based on the nearness of supplies of raw material, which began ten years ago,
had no more reasonable field in which to exercise itself than
that of cotton spinning. New mills sprang up all over the
region, but particularly in the states of North Carolina,
South Carolina, and Georgia." In 1890 these three States
reported 75 more establishments than in 1880, but even this
did not indicate the increase, because some antiquated mills
had ceased operation forever, and the average number of
spindles to the mill had advanced nearly 73 per cent.

Quite as large proportionate increase had taken place in other Southern States; markets previously in exclusive possession of Northern mills had been occupied by Southern products, finer goods were being manufactured and the new mills were "for the most part equipped with the latest and most improved machinery." Outstanding Southern advantages were partially offset by disadvantages, "some of which time and experience will cause to disappear," and, in place of Atkinson's determined preference for New England, it was declared that "It can not be doubted that the development of this industry in the cotton-raising states is based upon sound commercial reasons, and that it is destined to continue." Increase of manufacturing in the Middle States had been at a slower rate than in any other part of the country, and the development in the West, while exhibiting a good rate of advance, was too small to call for extended notice. While it was recognized that the future growth of the industry, considered geographically, depended upon a variety of factors—cheapness of transportation of raw cotton, nearness to markets for finished goods, economy of power, supply of adaptable labor, spirit of State laws, and, perhaps, degree of humidity—the South was not held to be militated against in any of these respects.[117]

By the time Stanwood came to analyze the figures of cotton manufacture for the 1900 census, events had further

---

[117] U. S. Census of Manufactures, 1890, "Cotton Manufacture," by Edward Stanwood, pp. 171–172. As will later appear, a good deal had been made of the alleged disadvantage of the South in not having a sufficiently humid climate, but Stanwood showed that the superiority possessed in this particular by the British Isles had been overcome in American mills through use of artificial humidifiers. The whole of his estimate in this census report is interesting as indicating how the southern development was breaking on the national consciousness; special New England localities were given praise, but the rise of the South as a cotton manufacturing section held prominent place in the writer's thought. In addition to the percentage increases in spindles, it is important to notice that in looms, representing completer commencement of capture of the industry, the percentage advance in the United States was 43, in the Middle States 28, Western States 85, New England 35, and in the Southern States was 204 (ibid., p. 171).

clarified his thought.[118]   Covered apology for New England in stress laid upon records of special localities, such as that of Providence County, Rhode Island, which had more spindles than any Southern States except South Carolina, had to give way to the frank assertion that "the percentage of New England as a whole has suffered a considerable decline," from 81 in 1880 to 76 in 1890 to 67.6 in 1900.[119]

"The growth of the industry in the South is the one great fact in its history during the past ten years." From 1880 to 1890 the number of establishments advanced 48.4 per cent, from the latter date to 1900 the increase was 67.4 per cent, and the size of mills had easily kept pace. The interpretation of the growth of the Southern industry represents one of the earliest conscious attempts at scrutiny with desire to analyze—Southern cotton manufacture had become not only a fact, but a fact to be studied, appreciated, understood.[120]

Comments on returns in the 1910 census showed the per-

---

[118] U. S. Census of Manufactures, 1900, Cotton Manufactures, pp. 28–29.

[119] Decrease in number of establishments in New England and the Middle States was said to be more apparent than real, by reason of consolidation of plants and changes in census classification. The Western States were shown to work under disadvantages which dismissed them from further solicitude. Cf. ibid., p. 48.

[120] " Speaking broadly, the cotton manufacturing industry did not exist in the South before the Civil War, and it existed on only the most restricted scale before 1880. . . . It is probably not an exaggeration to say that prior to 1880 there was not a mill south of the latitude of Washington that would be classed as an efficient modern cotton factory, even according to the standard of that time. Before the Civil War the people of the South were almost exclusively engaged in agricultural pursuits. After the war closed it was some years before the people had recovered sufficiently from the disaster to undertake manufacturing." Extended reference to the effects of the Atlanta cotton exposition, the character of the cotton mill campaign, and the lessons learned in matters of machinery will be noticed in another place. It was remarked that the South was making experiments of value to the whole industry, the first and, for some time, the only electrically operated factory being in that section. Instead of the former speculation as to the permanence of Southern mills, it was declared that " The fact that after a phenomenal growth during more than twenty years the expansion of old mills and the erection of new ones are still going on in the South is ample proof of the success of the enterprise," and the steady increase in spindles is given by years.

centages of increase in the leading Southern States to be
decidedly greater than those in Northern States, but South
was merged with North as going to make up the nearly
exclusive seat of the industry, the East. Records of individual Southern States are intermixed with those of States
of New England, the former having come into proper comparison with the latter in point of absolute importance.[121]

Census reports uncovered fully, after a period of time,
facts which were in part contemporaneously recognized.
The following chapter will exhibit this proclaiming of a new
day in the South of 1880 in detail; but the whole study
really is a justification of the assertion that this date ushered
in industrialism. The consciousness of a new economic era,
arising in the mind of a theretofore sluggish and perverse
South, is the best evidence of the beginning of manufacturing for the very good reason, as will presently appear, that
expression of this consciousness went far to create the development.

Preliminary notice of a Charleston newspaper's trade
review covering months in 1880 and 1881 said: " In the Annual Review will be exhibited the course and strength of
the manufacturing revival in South Carolina, with especial
reference, of course, to the progress of manufactures in
Charleston."[122]   And the summary itself declared: " The
industrial feature of the year is the rapid extension of cotton manufacturing in South Carolina in common with other
Southern States. . . . diversified industries are taking the
place of the exclusive cultivation of cotton. . . ."[123]

Another paper commented on the desire of a Northern
contemporary that New England should take steps to progress into the manufacture of finer grades of cotton goods,
since it recognized " the great advance we are about to make
at the South."[124]   How certainly this was a change in Southern experience is shown in the assurance with which altera-

[121] U. S. Census of Manufactures, " Cotton Manufactures," pp.
38–39.
[122] News and Courier, Aug. 16, 1881.
[123] Ibid., Sept. 1, 1881.
[124] The Observer, Raleigh, March 26, 1880.

tion for the better was sensed. Thus, " The cities of the South are rapidly learning to appreciate the great value of manufacturing industries, and the great development of the last year or two is only a beginning of what may be expected when that whole section throbs with industrial life and activity in the near future."[125]

By 1884 the new turn in events was so evident that, in brief retrospect, the date of genesis could be discerned. Of South Carolina it was said: " The State has now recovered the ground that was lost by emancipation, by negro suffrage, by political misrule and official corruption. And the most significant circumstance is that the industrial triumph now proclaimed is mainly the result of the work of four or five years." And a significant point was touched in the observation that "agricultural operations could be carried on with reasonable success, in even the darkest days of strife and misrule, but the undertakings which were dependent on the concentration of capital for their development remained torpid, if not dead, until the return of confidence breathed into them new life and vigor."[126]

By 1880 one of the oldest Southern cotton manufacturing towns had recovered. In 1865 the Federal army burned 60,000 bales of cotton and all the mills of Columbus. " The very heart of the city was burned out. . . . Within fifteen years the waste places have been rebuilt and industry revived from its very ashes."[127]

---

[125] Baltimore Journal of Commerce and Mfgrs. Record, Aug. 26, 1882. ". . . too little heed is given by manufacturers and mechanics to the immediate prospects opened up by what is termed the new departure of the South; . . . there is no possibility that the South can immediately become a section of great manufacturing centres; but it is unquestionable that a combination of present efforts will in time yield important results " (American Machinist, quoted in ibid., July 15, 1882). Cf. ibid., July 15, and, in connection with buying by Southern merchants, Aug. 26, 1882.

[126] News and Courier, Charleston, Feb. 4, 1884. Giving figures of cotton manufacture, it was said: " In a little more than three years . . . the increase in production was a third more than in the ten years ending in 1880, and the whole production in 1883 was ten times as great as the product in 1860 " (ibid.). As to the process of agricultural recuperation, cf. Hammond, p. 166.

[127] Observer, Raleigh, Sept. 10, 1880.

Newspaper notice of organization of the Charleston Manufacturing Company in 1881 was headed, "The dawn of a new era," and the same paper, which did so much to bring about cotton manufacturing, often showed how sharply defined was the movement's beginning.[128]

The 1880 census enabled the South to take stock of its industrial condition as a section and as part of the nation, and furnished a definite basis on which to calculate improvement. Speaking of the increase in manufacture in Augusta, a cotton manufacturer of that city summed up what had been done since the census of 1880, as follows:

Well, to particularize, the Sibley Mill has been completed; the King and Goodrich Mills built up entirely since that time. The Summerville, McCoy, Globe and Sterling Mills have all been increased largely, and the Enterprise Factory more than doubled. These increments since the meagre census reports were sent in mean 63,000 new spindles, 2,200 additional looms and about 2,200 fresh hands . . . the increase in cotton manufacturing property alone since the census amounts in Augusta to $300,000.[129]

It will presently be shown that the Atlanta Exposition of 1881 had much to do with stimulating interest in cotton manufacturing in the South, and in accelerating and broad-

---

[128] News and Courier, Charleston, Aug. 1, 1881. Commenting on an address of H. P. Hammett, "Cotton Mills in the South," which was in itself a full exposition which indicated widespread popular inquiry into the subject, it was said that the speaker's own factory "was projected and built before the opening of the Cotton Mill Campaign in the South, and Major Hammett ranks, therefore, as one of the pioneers . . ." (ibid.).

[129] Manufacturers' Record, Baltimore, Feb. 15, 1883. Nine months earlier a Georgia paper could read in the progress since the census the promise of a time when the South might "spin every pound of cotton made upon her fields" (Columbus Chronicle, quoted in Baltimore Journal of Commerce and Manufacturers' Record, Oct. 14, 1882). Cf. Atlanta correspondence of Augusta Chronicle and Constitutionalist, quoted in Manufacturers' Record, Baltimore, Feb. 8, 1883, and Augusta Trade Review, Oct., 1884. A special issue of the Baltimore Journal of Commerce and Manufacturers' Record, Sept. 2, 1882, denominated "an exponent of the new South," gave statistics of the important features of cotton manufacturing in the South, by States, at that date, indicating that from $15,000,000 to $18,000,000 had been invested in the business since 1880. Cf. Manufacturers' Record, Baltimore, March 8, 1883; Baltimore Journal of Commerce and Manufacturers' Record, July 29, 1882.

ening and lending confidence to the "cotton mill campaign." But it was result as well as cause. The rapidity with which the exposition was planned and opened in a small town in the heart of a section unaccustomed to such ventures, and the readiness of response to its appeal cannot be explained except in recognizing that the Southern thought for industry had gone far toward crystallizing. A few years earlier it would have been impossible because the suggestion of such a scheme would have been unmeaning.[130]

After Atlanta had had the faith to act host to the first exposition predicated upon belief in the South's industrial future, other places, by entering eagerly into plans for similar undertakings, testified to the awakening. It was even proposed to duplicate the Atlanta Exposition in Boston; this was perhaps a sophisticated suggestion intended to lessen the enthusiasm for the manufacturing of cotton in the South that had been the rather unexpected outcome of the original exhibit.[131] Baltimore in 1882 tried to launch an exposition that would allow the city to spring into leadership of a movement of proved success, and it was even said that the future of Baltimore would depend upon the way in which the proposal was met.[132] The next year Louisville and Nashville actively entered into rivalry for another

---

[130] "The Atlanta Exposition, in 1881, was the hopeful and conscious expression of the opening of a new era for Southern industry; . . . consequently, wonderful as has been the growth of this quarter century, it is but the realization of what was even then practically assured by existing attainments and conditions" (Clark, in South in Building of Nation, vol. vi, p. 280). See editorial giving a summary of Atlanta's prosperity in The Daily Constitution, Jan. 2, 1880. ". . . it was all the work of merely ten months from the time the project was conceived until the exposition was thrown open to the people. It was impossible in that short time, at that remote distance, and in that small city, to do the whole South complete justice. But a knowledge of the South's resources was demanded . . ." (J. W. Ryckman, secretary of the exposition, in Baltimore Journal of Commerce and Manufacturers' Record, June 24, 1882). "The visitors to this [exposition] were convinced that 'an industrial revolution had actually been effected in the South . . .'" (Hammond, pp. 328-329).
[131] See Philadelphia Industrial Review, quoted in Baltimore Journal of Commerce and Manufacturers' Record, June 10, 1882.
[132] See ibid., June 10, Sept. 23, Oct. 7, 21, 1882.

exhibition.[133]   In 1883 the board of agriculture of North Carolina, aroused to the possibilities of the State, paid a visit to Boston, and the next year occurred the Raleigh exposition.   The New Orleans undertaking followed in 1885.

The detailed description of the condition of the cotton manufacture in South Carolina, published by the News and Courier in 1880, was evidence of the same consciousness of industrial stirrings as was the Atlanta Exposition.[134]

There was abundant recognition outside of the South of the industrial awakening that occurred about 1880 and was made manifest in the Atlanta Exposition.   Agreement among Philadelphia cotton manufacturers to shorten production of coarser fabrics was held to be as wise as it was significant, for "the time can not be far distant when all our coarse cottons will be supplied from the cotton belt; and the child is born who will see the great mass of cotton manufacturing in all its diversified branches, carried on where the fleecy staple is cultivated."[135]

It naturally took a little time for the reality of the Southern awakening to break upon observers who had hardly expected industrialism from that section.[136]

---

[133] Manufacturers' Record, Baltimore, Feb. 22, 1883.

[134] "Attempts have been made at different times to show the extent of the cotton manufactures in South Carolina, but until to-day no thorough and complete statement upon that subject has been given to the public" (Blackman, p. 3).   Cf. Kohn, Cotton Mills of S. C., p. 20.

[135] Chicago Herald, quoted in Baltimore Journal of Commerce and Manufacturers' Record, July 29, 1882.   A Boston journal struck a generous note that differed from some emanating from New England in an article, "The Drift of Manufacturing": "Another Pittsburgh is growing at Birmingham, Alabama; another Lowell at Augusta; another Lawrence at Columbus. . . . The East has no sole right to the term 'manufacturing'; the drift is Westward and Southward, and is already a larger one than is generally supposed. . . . The time is not far distant when the breeders of domestic strife will be relegated to another clime, or at least to where they will cease attempting to array one set of industries in this great country against another set" (Commercial Bulletin, quoted in ibid., Sept. 23, 1882).

[136] "Progress has been made with considerable acceleration as the wisdom of the new order of things became apparent, until now, when it appears that a new state of things has become established" (Miller and Millwright, quoted in Manufacturers' Record, Feb. 22, 1883). After speaking of the local character of ante-bellum mills, the Dry

Space only remains for bare mention of some objective evidences recommending 1880 as the date to be chosen as that marking the South's industrial awakening. The return to specie payments, bringing confidence to enterprise, showed itself in the veritable boom of the fall of 1879, precipitating events in the South as all over the nation.[137] In 1880 Southern railway building took on new life, roads in financial difficulties being reorganized and narrow gauge being changed to broad gauge.[138] Southerners were accumulating a little surplus cash, as was indicated by their ability to go again to Saratoga and other watering places.[139]

Charleston shipbuilders were busy.[140] Plans for a cotton mill in Charlotte, though going the full length of organization of a company in the middle seventies, did not mature until 1881.[141] Something of the changed impulse back of cotton manufacturing about 1880 may be indicated in the fact that little was heard of extensions of woolen mills, though there had been many small ones in the South. The Clement Attachment, coordinating the work of ginning and spinning cotton, apparently did not cause pilgrimages and attract discussion until 1880.[142]

Goods Economist, in 1896, said: " Whatever the expansion of the cotton industries of the South in the years following close upon the war, . . . such progress pales into insignificance when compared with what has taken place almost within the last decade" (Jubilee number, p. 78). Cf. Baltimore Journal of Commerce and Manufacturers' Record, July 29, 1882; Sept. 23, 1882; News and Observer, Raleigh, Oct. 10, 1880; early suggestion of English interest is seen in a quotation from Iron, Philadelphia, in Manufacturers' Record, Feb. 8, 1883; cf. ibid., Dec. 21, 1882.

[137] See Commercial and Financial Chronicle, Jan. 10, 1880; Copeland, p. 266; Clark, in South in Building of Nation, vol. vi, pp. 264–265.

[138] See Observer, Raleigh, Jan. 15, 1880, quotation from Railway Age; ibid., Jan. 8; Baltimore Sun, Jan. 22, 26, Feb. 2, 20, 1880.

[139] News and Courier, Charleston, May 30, 1881.

[140] News and Courier, April 13, 1881.

[141] Tompkins, History of Mecklenburg, vol. i, pp. 181–182. Agitation for a special school tax, bringing several unsuccessful elections, during which time the school was suspended, resulted in an overwhelmingly favorable vote only in 1880 (ibid., p. 168). The streets of Charlotte began to be paved (Tompkins, Road Building and Broad Tires, p. 6).

[142] See Blackman, pp. 18–19, and many other references in this pamphlet.

The economic South was coming rapidly to a national point of view, strikingly signalized in the invitation of business men to Edward Atkinson to address them in the Senate chamber of Georgia in October of 1880.[143]

Cotton goods in 1880 were in brisk demand, their price advancing more rapidly than that of the raw material; in this benefit Southern mills shared.[144]

Production of cotton in the South had gradually increased by 1880–1881 to three times the number of bales of 1865–1866,[145] and exports of the staple from the section to foreign countries regained 1860 figures by 1880.[146] The abundance of cotton in the section where factories would be likely to start,[147] coupled with the price (on the average about 11 cents), which had resulted through a general fall in the fifteen previous years,[148] was of consequence.

Shortly after 1880 the manufacturing development of the South required special spokesmen and interpreters, and brought publications with such an aim, as the Manufacturers' Record of Baltimore, the Industrial South, of Richmond, and Southern Industries, of Nashville, into existence.[149]

---

[143] On this occasion, called by him (proceed. Southern Cotton Spinners' Assn., 1903) " The first opportunity ever given to a Northern anti-slavery man to speak words of truth and soberness to Southern men," Mr. Atkinson said: " Malignant conditions [of disunion] have passed away. The active and vigorous men born of the new South refuse to be controlled any longer by the Bourbons of that section, and the 'stalwarts' of the North, who dare not trust the principle of liberty to work its first results, are being themselves classed as Bourbons incapable of guiding or directing the true union that now exists in this Nation" (Address at Atlanta, p. 8). See also ibid., p. 12, and John W. Ryckman in author's preface of ibid.

[144] See Commercial and Financial Chronicle, Jan. 3, 1880; Baltimore Sun, Jan. 8, 20, 28, 1880; Blackman, p. 15.

[145] Quotation from Bradstreet's, in Baltimore Journal of Commerce and Manufacturers' Record, Nov. 4, 1882.

[146] Brooks, p. 209.

[147] Blackman, p. 7.

[148] Quotation from Bradstreet's, in Baltimore Journal of Commerce and Manufacturers' Record, Nov. 4, 1882. As to improvements in agricultural implements in the South by 1880, see Tompkins, History of Mecklenburg, vol. i, p. 181; a Georgia community wanted an agricultural implement factory; steam engines were sold for farm use (Manufacturers' Record, Baltimore, Nov. 30, 1880).

Managers of the New England Manufacturers' and Mechanics' Institute announced in March of 1883 that space in the exhibition to take place in the fall had been applied for by Southern exhibitors.[150]

Suggesting something as to the date of commencement of cotton manufacture is the fact that in 1886 South Carolina repealed an act of 1872 exempting from state, county and municipal taxes for ten years capital invested in cotton, woolen and paper mills.[151]

In the next chapter it will be seen what positive bearing the defeat of the Democratic candidate in the presidential election of 1880 had upon the Southern cotton manufacturing industry. In this place it is only necessary to note that after 1880 Southern political animus never gave itself again to such bitterness against the North, and thus one undoubted obstacle to economic advance was removed.[152]

---

[149] See Baltimore Journal of Commerce and Manufacturers' Record, Aug. 5, Nov. 18, 1882; Manufacturers' Record, Baltimore, Nov. 23, 1882, Jan. 25, 1883.

[150] Manufacturers' Record, Baltimore, March 29, 1883.

[151] Clark, in South in Building of Nation, p. 282.

[152] See statement of executive committee of Columbia and Lexington Water-Power Company, in News and Courier, Charleston, March 25, 1881.

CHAPTER II

THE RISE OF THE MILLS

It has been seen how cotton for long years had been hurtful to the South; how it had joined with slavery and secession to bring the disaster of the Civil War; how after humiliating but sobering Reconstruction years the curtain was ready to lift on a new act in which the characters should be chastened in spirit, clarified in thought, and quick to discharge changed rôles. The South by 1880 was ready to be no longer negative, but affirmative; not just the passive resultant of its past, but the conscious builder of its future. From a consequence, the South was to become a cause.[1]

The determination with which the South entered the War was to hold over to receive new application. " The fortitude of the march, the courage of the charge, the heroism of the retreat, the touching sacrifices of the ill-paid and ill-equipped soldier-life—these were to be emphasized and prolonged, when the tattered flag no longer flew, the quick roll of the drum had ceased, and the comradeship of the camp and march was dissolved. From defeat and utter poverty were to be wrought victory and plenty."[2]

The South suffered a change of heart. An altered purpose animated its leaders, and gradually but certainly seized upon its rank and file. President Baldwin, of the Louis-

---

[1] " There are scores of turning-points " in the history of cotton in America " where, if wisdom had taken the skeins from the hands of prejudice and passion, a righteous and peaceful pattern might have been the result " (Scherer, p. 296). This was a juncture where judgment was to prevail.

[2] Grady, The New South, p. 166. On the Confederate monument in the busy little city of Anderson, South Carolina, are the words: " And above all let him [the truthful historian] tell with what sublime endurance they met defeat, and how in poverty and want, broken in health, but not in spirit, they have recreated the greatness, and made it again the sweetest land on earth. In grateful acknowledgment of their prowess in war, and of their achievements in peace, this monument is erected."

77

ville and Nashville Railroad, born in Maryland and for many years resident in New York, and so competent to speak for both sections, declared with force:

> The commercial men of the cotton States fully appreciate the situation. . . . They now see clearly how very little politics have done for them, and seriously turn toward the real "reconstruction" which active trade will inaugurate. . . . All the war issues are dead and buried—except to a few politicians who misrepresent their constituents and merely use the language of the past to give them, personally, . . . prominence. . . . True, we hear a great deal more about the few men who stand forth prominently as the advocates of these dead issues than we do of the thousands of young and energetic Southern men who are building cotton and woolen mills; who are opening mines and starting iron, copper and zinc furnaces, or who are relaying the roads between the Atlantic and the Ohio and the Gulf. These men don't talk, they don't write books, they don't go to the Legislature or to Congress. They speak, trumpet toned, in results. . . . Years have brought time for thought, and compulsory thinking has produced marvellous results. . . . The people of the South have suffered—it is not pertinent whether we regard their sufferings as just or unjust—but they have put aside mourning and are ready for work.[3]

A Georgian in welcoming South Carolinians to the Atlanta Exposition said of the display that "It comes at a most propitious moment, for the South, in sympathy with the quickening energies which excite the continent, is even now trembling in the initial throes of the mighty industrial revolution that surely awaits her. A great change is evidently about to come upon us. 'In the fabric of thought and of habit' which we have woven for a century we are no longer to dwell, and a new era of progressive enterprise opens before us."[4] This whole study goes to show a funda-

---

[3] Quoted from New York Herald, in News and Courier, Charleston, July 11, 1881. "Mills for the weaving of the coarser cotton fabrics are now in successful operation in Tennessee, Georgia, Kentucky and several of the Atlantic Coast States, all of which have been built by native labor, mostly with local capital and are managed by Southern men. . . . The class formerly known as 'poor whites' are . . . assimilating with their more fortunate neighbors. They are making good workers in mine and field, good operatives in factories. . . ."

[4] News and Courier, Charleston, Dec. 27, 1881. ". . . there are 213,157 spindles to Georgia's credit. . . . These are the weapons peace gave us, and right trusty ones they are. . . . The story the spindles tell is one of joy to all, and show (sic) how rapidly we are climbing the hill of prosperity" (Columbus Enquirer, quoted in Daily Constitution, Atlanta, March 9, 1880). Professor Hart has

mental distinction between the English Industrial Revolution and that in the South, namely, that the former was, certainly in its immediate causes, unanticipated, accidental, while the latter was deliberately planned.[5] This is plain in the quotation just given, and at a dinner of the Burns Charitable Association in Charleston, along with toasts to the poet and the queen, this was offered: "The State of South Carolina—A new era of prosperity is about to dawn upon her: increasing commerce, manufactures, agriculture and population, are the echoes of its coming."[6]

Reconstruction governments, under radicals, outsiders and blacks, had attempted a political display through wasteful, ruinous expenditure; it will be seen how different was the program of economic advancement embraced in the "Real Reconstruction" of Southerners come into their own.[7] Observing that "These old commonwealths were

quoted an editorial in a Southern newspaper, presumably of the early eighties, declaring that "the great South . . . is self-contained, and what is more, she is self-possessed, and she has set her face resolutely against the things which will hurt her" (p. 219).

[5] Cf. B. L. Hutchins and A. Harrison, A History of Factory Legislation, pp. 19–20.

[6] News and Courier, Charleston, Jan. 26, 1881.

[7] Cf. Dunning, Reconstruction, pp. 205–206. How much earlier reorganization might have come in the South had not the carpet-bag regime been instituted, may be guessed from the frankness with which South Carolina, which so largely led the revival in the eighties, reentered the Union in 1865. The sincerity and dignity of surrender is sufficiently apparent in the speech of Huger, the aged postmaster of Charleston, in seconding the motion nullifying secession, in the constitutional convention following the war. Of South Carolina he said: "She is my mother; I have all my life loved what she loved, and hated what she hated; everything she had I made my own, and every act of hers was my act; as I have had but one hope, to live with her, so now I have but one desire, to die on her soil and be laid in her bosom. If I am wrong in everything else, I know I am right in loving South Carolina,—know I am right in believing that, whatever glory the future may bring our reunited country, it can neither brighten nor tarnish the glory of South Carolina. She has passed through the agony and the bloody sweat; as we now return her to the Federal Union, let every man do his duty bravely before the world, trustfully before God, remembering each man for himself that he is a South-Carolinian. She has been devastated by the invader, reviled by the hireling, mocked by the weak-hearted, but she has accepted the invitation to return,—accepted it in good faith, with the assurance of a word better than a bond; and now, no matter what she gives up, no matter what there is to endure and to

arrested in their development by slavery and by war and by the double burden of a sparse population and of an ignorant alien race," Walter Page recognized that "The process that has been going on in the upland South in particular is a process of conscious and natural State-building, constructive at every important step," and working itself out through the two instruments of industry and popular education.[8] The quickness with which creativeness displaced destruction showed a purposeful people. "Eighteen years ago," it was written in 1882, "the upper bank of the Augusta canal was walled up with a chain of turretted tenements of brick . . . over which stood, in lofty suggestiveness, the smoke spire. . . . These buildings were frequented by silent men who worked in quiet and in gloom, and who sifted through their machinery the acids and minerals which go to form the explosives of war. From a hundred battle-

---

forget, let us all do our duty as becomes her children, counting it our chiefest honor to stand by her in evil report as well as in good report, honor alike to live with her and to die with her" (Andrews, The South since the War, pp. 52–53). Orr, deploring quibbles and extenuations, declared: "We must put it in the constitution that slavery is dead, and that we will never attempt to revive it. . . . We seem to forget where we stand; we forget that we made the war and have been beaten; we forget that our conquerors have the right to dictate terms to us. . . . Let us be wise men. Let us strengthen" Jackson's "hands by graceful and ready acquiescence in the results of the war. So shall we strengthen ourselves, and soon bring again to our loved State the blessings of peace and civil rule" (ibid., pp. 61–63). Cf. ibid., p. 94.

[8] Rebuilding of Old Commonwealths, p. 139. Grady's plan—"the settlement of the race problem and the development of the material resources of the South"—was nothing different (see Oliver Dyer, Sketch of Grady, in The New South, pp. 76–77). "Mr. Grady's patriotism partook of the quality of his love; although romantic and general, it was also practical and local. . . . It took hold of the . . . condition and interests of the country—of its diversified industries, its agriculture, its manufactures, its commerce, its internal development, its external relations, its education and its religion" (ibid., p. 20). He said in 1889: "The industrial growth of the South in the past ten years has been without precedent or parallel. It has been a great revolution, effected in peace" (New South, p. 191). On Professor Hart's discussion of the comparative wealth of the South and other sections, it may be commented that given the fact of huge potentialities in the South and of an awakened eagerness to develop these, status counts for little; given the loaf, and the leaven working in the loaf, and the most exacting of economists must be satisfied" (see Southern South).

fields of the civil strife, the blackened granulations of the Augusta Powder Mills flashed and thundered, and when the war was over the mills went down before the ravages of time. . . . To-day, the same spire, with extinguished craters, overlooks the same spot. The same river rolls at its feet; the same hills confront it on the other side. But in place of the scattered walls of war, a massive structure, granite and compact, is reared. In the place of musty explosives of darker days, the purest productions of peace are. fed into the present mill, and from its looms will go forth the texture to clothe the people of the land, to weave the white wings of commerce and to float the bunting of the Newer South. The old picture has rolled away—the new one has received a solid setting."[9]

One cannot view the passion with which revival was undertaken without realizing how pointed were the lessons taught the South in the war and its aftermath.[10] Convinced of old errors, the remaking of the South was emphatically in response to a moral stimulus, not less real because not always outwardly apparent. "A man who has been in the whirl of New York or in any of the brand new cities of the great West coming into Charleston might easily enough come to the conclusion that the old city was in a sad state of decadence—but our own people who have been accustomed to its quiet way of doing business, if they have their

[9] Chronicle and Constitutionalist, Augusta, Feb. 23. Though four years earlier North Carolina " would not be caught " in the " Yankee money trap " of the Philadelphia Centennial Exhibition, in 1880 it was being asked: " Shall our Commissioner of Agriculture or our State Geologist be . . . subjected to the mortifying . . . task of standing in those grand halls [of the proposed world's fair of 1883] . . . and present the ridiculous farce of representing this . . . State by showing a dump-cart load of rocks? " (News and Observer, Raleigh, Nov. 12, 1880). Cf. ibid., Dec. 2, 1880. The ten " supreme advantages " claimed by Augusta in 1884 were every one economic, the first being its superiority as " a manufacturing center " (Trade Review of Chronicle and Constitutionalist, Oct., 1884).

[10] Citing statistics of property losses to South Carolina between 1860 and 1870 and the relative gain to a state such as Rhode Island, Murphy wrote: " Beneath these cold and unresponsive figures there lie what tragedies of suffering, what deep-hidden recurrent pulses of despair, of self-repression, of patience, of silent and solemn will, of self-contest, of ultimate emancipation! " (Present South, p. 101).

6

eyes open (or hearts open would perhaps be the better expression) could not fail to see manifest improvement—progress even, if you like the word better."[11]

As the movement proceeded from introspection, the very genius of "Real Reconstruction" was self-help. It took courage to begin, but confidence rallied about every sign of genuine performance. Thus it was said that "Every true South Carolinian must rejoice at the . . . energy exhibited by the citizens of Columbia in their management of the Cotton-Mill Campaign. For years they have appeared to depend on somebody else to help them. The Legislature made liberal concessions. No effort was spared to interest Northern capitalists in the splendid water power. . . . But nothing was done. Tired of waiting a number of business men in Columbia took up the matter themselves. They soon found that the citizens generally would sustain them. . . . the city is full of life again. A handsome sum of money has been subscribed already to the capital stock of the Cotton Mill Company. . . . It will be a happy day for the whole State when the hum of a myriad spindles is heard on the banks of the historic Canal."[12]

---

[11] News and Courier, Charleston, March 24, 1881. Timrod wrote of Charleston:

> "How know they, these busy gossips, what to thee
> The ocean and its wanderers may have brought?
> How know they, in their busy vacancy,
> With what far aim thy spirit may be fraught?
> Or that thou dost not bend thee silently
> Before some great unutterable thought?"

(Henry Timrod, Poems, Memorial Ed., 1899, p. 172). Professor Sioussat has stressed the significance of the economic readjustment between 1865 and 1880, "a readjustment more fundamentally important than the political events which in large degree overshadowed the less dramatic factors" (History Teacher's Magazine, Sept., 1916, p. 224). Cf. Ingle, p. 5. Declaring right after the war that negro slavery had been hardly more debasing than white slavery, Andrews foresaw that the remaking of the South must reach down to basic tasks: "That is the best plan which proposes to do most for the common people" (pp. 387-388). Cf. Clark, in South in Building of Nation, vol. vi, p. 254.

[12] "The News and Courier busies itself with every enterprise, big and little, that will turn a dollar's worth of raw material into more than a dollar's worth of manufactures. . . . we confess to a weak-

This self-reliance never meant exclusion of assistance from the North or elsewhere; it meant a broadening, not a contracting of view. "Some of that credit which was accorded to the man who caused an additional blade of grass to grow should be given to everyone," whether home or outside enterpriser, "who affords facilities to manufacture an additional boll of cotton. . . ."[13] The South, ready to plunge into its task, took stock of itself. "All questions of domestic economy, and especially those involving the capital of our people, whether in the shape of labor or dollars, will necessarily be canvassed and scrutinized very closely in their bearings on our material progress. . . ."[14]

Even those communities most earnest in social regeneration, and most anxious to forget the past in looking to a saner future, very occasionally slipped back into old ruts, and found in material advancement the means of satisfying spitefulness. Thus an attempt to settle foreigners upon a large tract in eastern Tennessee was commended partly because it would increase congressional representation of the

ness for Columbia, which suffered so sorely at the end of the war. . . . But cotton mills will soon make amends for the vicissitudes and hopelessness of the past . . ." (News and Courier, Charleston, March 19, 1881). Another paper discouraged reliance upon the government for prosperity, and pointed to relief that had come to the West only through self-help: "That government is the best which is not required . . . to pass new laws, leaving to the people the utmost freedom, with full liberty to devote their energies to the improvement of their own condition. . . . We know of no people more favorably situated than North Carolinians are in this respect" (Observer, Raleigh, Jan. 9, 1880). As Ireland in its cooperative agricultural efforts later, the South was experiencing a "combination of economic and human reform" (see Plunkett, pp. 205–206). "There came a different viewpoint," said one informant. "The old South was done away with. The problem was to utilize the thing nearest at hand to support a large portion of our people." And so the North Carolina Board of Agriculture made an investigating trip to New England, and an industrial exhibit was held" (Henry E. Fries, int., Winston-Salem, N. C., Aug. 31, 1916).

[13] News and Courier, Charleston, June 28, 1881.

[14] News and Observer, Raleigh, Dec. 1, 1880. "South Carolina in 1884," a 60-page pamphlet published by the News and Courier after a comprehensive survey of economic conditions prevailing in each county, shows the strength of this spirit. In descriptive detail it is a valuable photograph of agriculture and industry in the State at that date.

South and enable it the better to protect itself against "adverse legislation."[15]

Once awake, how immediately the South went to work is evidenced in notices proclaiming the new order of things. " The time was when the South was exclusively agricultural in its pursuits, but the past few years have seen factories springing up all over this section. . . . The South is destined at no distant day to not only raise cotton . . . but to manufacture it . . . thus keeping at home all the profits."[16]   It was recognized that Southern economic life was becoming more diversified, in agriculture and in industry, and so communities were growing independent.[17]   The franker and more generous Northern papers joined writers at the South in encouraging the new development. It was generally held at the time that internal impulse was chiefly responsible for the change in program. It could not be said of the South as of the establishment of the factory regime in England

[15] Observer, Raleigh, Aug. 25, 1880. Virginia, never so ardently back of economic recuperation as States to the south, was perhaps hindered by internal dissension over repudiation of part of her debt; the papers at this juncture were filled with political wrangles (cf. Daily Dispatch, Richmond, Feb. 9, March 24, 1880). The proposal to exempt manufacturing plants from taxation, already bringing results further South, could raise protest from the farming interest (cf. ibid., Jan. 14, 27, 1881). Public solicitude over industrial development was far less marked than in the Carolinas and Georgia, partly because of border position of Virginia, partly, perhaps, because there was not the one chief manufacture, cotton, on which to center attention. There was less reliance on home effort, more looking to outside assistance (cf. ibid., March 29, 1880). Mississippi had time for childish vituperation over dead issues. A Wisconsin editor had asked a Mississippi contemporary, " Did you ever read of Appomattox? " He received the reply: " O, Yes! We've read of Appomattox, where a few hungry and ragged thousands surrendered to a man with a million of men under his command. . . . the whole wide world remembers that it required five of your federals to whip one of our confederates. . . . Will you fight for Grant if he should slap a golden crown on his cranium? . . . The last man of you that shoulders a shot-gun in behalf of your gory god will be hunted down like dogs . . ." (quoted in Daily Constitution, Atlanta, Feb. 1, 1880). Cf. a headline in Daily Constitution, Atlanta, April 11, 1880, and colloquies in ibid., March 14, 1880; News and Observer, Raleigh, Dec. 18, 1880; News and Courier, Charleston, June, 1881.

[16] Americus, Ga., Recorder, quoted in Baltimore Journal of Commerce and Manufacturers' Record, Oct. 14, 1882.

[17] Cf. Miller and Millwright, quoted in Manufacturers' Record, Baltimore, Feb. 22, 1883.

that "As a great fact the system originated in no preconceived plan; on the contrary, it was formed and shaped by the inevitable force of circumstance. . . . The first force which tended to create this system was that of invention. . . ."[18] After deploring "the errors of previous generations in their persistent blindness to home possibilities, while spending their money North and abroad," it was declared: "The war cost us heavily—oh! so heavily—but we bent our stout hearts patiently to our tasks, and have profited, and will profit, by its lessons."[19] Contemporary spokesmen were naturally in some instances cautious to explain that "The New South" did not imply repudiation of the best spirit of the old South.[20] An understanding interpreter has observed that Southerners, when slavery and the war were past, "began . . . to beat their swords into plow shares and their spears into pruning hooks and to enter upon the childhood of material growth . . . , to give up the old time Southern ways and ideas of life, and to blend the characteristics of that day with the new spirit of business enterprise and thrift, changing from 'hornets in war to bees in industry.' . . ."[21]

Before 1880 the South had worn a veil before her eyes, had been running a temperature that distorted economic perspective, corrupted public judgment. When the veil was torn off and the fever subsided, normal thinking brought frank avowal of the past distemper. The section had woven "rosy day-dreams of a far-off greatness," and been tortured

---

[18] Carroll D. Wright, "The Factory System of the U. S.," in U. S. Census of Manufactures, 1880, p. 1.

[19] Augusta correspondence of Savannah Morning News, July 4, 1882. Cf. News and Observer, Raleigh, Nov. 16, 1880, praising the industrial progress of Augusta.

[20] Cf. News and Courier, Charleston, Dec. 27, 1881. Mr. Edmonds' solicitude on this point has been noticed; cf. Edmonds, p. 1.

[21] W. C. Heath, in Southern Cotton Spinners' Assn., proceed., 1903, p. 49. Post-bellum activity in mill building recalled the fact that years before planters had conceived the advantage in manufacturing, but were deterred by slavery; originality, to be effective, needed to work under a new dispensation. Cf. Gannon, Landowners of South and Industrial Classes of North, p. 6 ff.; Andrews, pp. 224–226.

by a "delusive mirage,"[22] but now "The South must . . .
look out for herself, and bring her great advantages to bear
in her favor, asking only a free field and a fair fight against
all competitors. . . . It means work and not words."[23]

To appreciate the strength of the demand for social regeneration, it must be recognized that while cotton manufacturing formed its central purpose, the movement was
comprehensive, embracing, in thought if not in deed, many
departments of life. Progress along all lines was not simul-
taneous or equal. It is not hard to see why public education,
for example, did not so soon translate desire into realization as did industry. Bread and meat must first be looked
to, and the South then could turn to plans which, if more
truly fundamental, were still less instantly pressing.[24] If
the will was surely present, and it was felt that "The Southern States ought, in justice to posterity, to take this matter
of public schools in hand,"[25] it needed twenty years until
performance could follow. When the South, after 1900,
did embark on an educational campaign, the fervor previously given to industry received new expression.[26] It
was "Real Reconstruction" reaching another task.

In the English Industrial Revolution other trades borrowed stimulus from textiles;[27] in the South, where the
causal force was subjective rather than objective, this would
more certainly be the case. Improvement in farming was

---

[22] Industrial South, quoted in Baltimore Journal of Commerce
and Manufacturers' Record, June 17, 1882.
[23] Gannon, Landowners of South and Industrial Classes of North,
pp. 6–7.
[24] "I do not . . . suggest that any other agency of . . . economic
progress can be more than a very partial substitute for education;
but only that, in the peculiar circumstances of Ireland, we must have
recourse to supplementary influences which will produce a more immediate effect upon the general life of the present generation while
its young people are being educationally developed" (Plunkett, pp.
51–52).
[25] News and Observer, Raleigh, Nov. 20, 1880.
[26] Sioussat, p. 270. "Enthusiasm like that of a great religious
movement developed and the result was that in the decade 1900–
1909 the total school revenues in these States had been more than
doubled."
[27] Cf. Scherer, pp. 51–52.

especially significant. In the zeal for manufacturing, the temptation would be to neglect agriculture, the old *bête noire,* and so not keep ever in mind the higher wisdom of an economic balance.[28]   But exodus of many negroes from a South Carolina county was thought by some a blessing in disguise, in that it would stimulate diversification and rotation of crops, rest land which needed rest; crops requiring less attention than cotton, grain for example, would be raised.[29]   North Carolina farmers were encouraged to attend an agricultural meeting in far-away Connecticut.[30]

"We at the South," it was said, ". . . if we intend to turn over a new leaf and seek a new development for our section," must inaugurate shipping relations with Brazil,[31] form something like a Southern chamber of commerce,[32] form a mercantile connection with Cincinnati,[33] send cotton abroad through Southern ports,[34] promote harmony within the section.[35]   "The railroad fever is epidemic in Georgia," it was asserted.   "Every village wants a railroad to its neighbor."[36]   The next year it could be said "There are now over 20,000 men and 100,000 horses and mules employed in railroad building in Texas,"[37] and a North Carolina editor even foresaw danger of railroad domination in state politics.[38]

---

[28] A friendly adviser pointed out the danger of excessive manufacturing in England, and urged that the South seek development of agriculture beside industry (United States Economist, quoted in Baltimore Journal of Commerce and Manufacturers' Record, Sept. 30, 1882.

[29] News and Courier, Charleston, Jan. 2, 1882.

[30] News and Observer, Raleigh, Nov. 30, 1880. "Our system of agriculture is too much on the order of present enjoyment and does not have sufficient regard for future use. . . . We would gladly see all of the profits of this year's crop spent on the land itself. . . ." (ibid., Sept. 19, 1880).

[31] News and Observer, Raleigh, Nov. 17, 28, 1880.

[32] Ibid., Dec. 5, 1880.

[33] Observer, Raleigh, April 1, 1880.

[34] News and Observer, Raleigh, Nov. 13, 1880.

[35] Observer, Raleigh, July 11, 1880.

[36] Observer, Raleigh, Feb. 6, 1880. Cf. ibid., Jan. 15, Feb. 20, 1880.

[37] News and Courier, Charleston, May 30, 1881; cf. ibid., April 29, 1881.

[38] Observer, May 1, 1880.

Interest was taken in extension of telegraph and telephone lines.[39]   Temperance societies showed augmented support.[40]   Duelling was coming to be called murder in South Carolina.[41]   The section exulted in the erection of cotton seed mills and exploitation of iron ores and phosphates, cultivation of oranges and rice, and extension of cattle and sheep raising.[42]   Cries for colonization of the negro, earlier condemned,[43] had hushed.

More than a contributing cause in the growing desire for economic renovation of the South, and amounting certainly to a decisive accelerant, was the defeat of Hancock by Garfield in the presidential election of 1880. The South, emerging from the humiliation of Reconstruction, had centered hopes on a victory for Tilden over Hayes four years earlier, and when the Democratic candidate was counted out, by a likely fraud as the section was willing enough to believe it, despair gave way to resentment and the Solid South, nursing its pride and revengefulness during Hayes' administration, dedicated itself to Hancock's triumph. In the four years between elections, the South, bearing many real grievances, sought to lighten them by lashing itself to a false ambition. Hancock's success would give answer to the North and cure Southern sorrows. It was looked forward to as "the first full, and fair, and free presidential election in which the South has participated since the war. There will be no intimidation of voters by means of the army. . . . There will be no southern returning boards upon whose venality the republican leaders can rely in case of a close contest."[44]

The shock of Hancock's defeat threw the South, so to speak, back upon its haunches. The days immediately following are surcharged with interest for the student of Southern economic history.

---

[39] See News and Courier, Charleston, Jan. 1, May 4, 1881.
[40] Ibid., April 22, May 5, 28, June 13, 1881.
[41] Ibid., March 10, 1881.
[42] Observer, Raleigh, Sept. 4, 1880. Cf. Daily Constitution, Atlanta, March 30, 1880.
[43] Andrews, p. 158.
[44] Daily Constitution, Atlanta, Feb. 15, 1880.

The *News and Observer,* of Raleigh, which had been violently sectional and which for a few days after the election consoled its readers with hope of victory four years hence, within a week changed front and gave expression to a new spirit that, suddenly and with compelling force, was sweeping the people.[45] It was declared that "we have been defeated in the national contest. In the administration of the national government for the next four years we need not concern ourselves, for as far as possible our councils will be ignored. What, then, is our duty? It is to go to work earnestly to build up North Carolina. Nothing is to be gained by regrets and repinings. No people or State is better able to meet emergencies. . . . And what nobler employment could enlist the energies of a people than the developing of the great resources of our . . . State. . . . But with all its . . . splendid capabilities it is idle to talk of home independence so long as we go to the North for everything from a toothpick to a President. We may plead in vain for a higher type of manhood and womanhood among the masses, so long as we allow the children to grow up in ignorance. We may look in vain for the dawn of an era of enterprise, progress and devolpment, so long as thousands and millions of money are deposited in our banks on four per cent interest, when its judicious investment in manufacture would more than quadruple that rate, and give profitable employment to thousands of our now idle women and children.

"Out of our political defeat we must work . . . a glorious material and industrial triumph. We must have less politics and more work, fewer stump speakers and more stump pullers, less tinsel and show and boast, and more hard, earnest work. . . . Work for the material and educational advancement of North Carolina, and in this and

---

[45] In quotations from influential newspapers it will be observed that the changed view, breaking on the South so quickly, at first carried something of sectional prejudice; industrial upbuilding would be partly spitefulness against the North. But this was the whimpering of a child while drying its tears.

not in politics, will be found her refuge and her strength."[46]

Following the installation of Garfield, another editor finely said:

> But if we lost the victory, in one sense, we have won it in another. We have been taught what the South can do for itself if it wills to do it. If we have lost the victory on the field of fight we can win it back in the workshop, in the factory, in an improved agriculture and horticulture, in our mines and in our schoolhouses. There is where our fight lies now, and the only enemies before us are the prejudices of the past, the instincts of isolation, the brutal indifference and harmful social infidelity which stands up in our day with the old slave arguments at its heart and on its lips, " I object" and " You can't do it."[47]

No people less homogeneous, less one family, knit together and resolute through sufferings, could have taken instant fire, as did the South, at such appeals. Facilities for satisfying the need were not narrowly investigated. The South was shut up to such and such means—they must fit into imperative requirement.[48]

---

[46] Nov. 9, 1880. "We must make money—it is a power in this practical business age. Teach the boys and girls to work and teach them to be proud of it. . . . Demand all legislative encouragement for manufacturing that may be consistent with free political economy."

[47] Columbia Register, quoted in News and Courier, Charleston, March 18, 1881. Columbia at this time was entering upon the fervor to develop its canal and build a cotton mill. The editor of the Register had been a slaveholder. This pronouncement is purged of an earlier and unworthy jealousy which had sometimes appeared in such expressions as the following from another paper: " The South should depend upon its own virtue, its own brain, its own energy, attend to its own business, make money, build up its waste places, and thus force from the North that recognition of our worth and dignity of character to which that people will always be blind unless they can see it through the medium of material, industrial and intellectual strength. We may proclaim political theories, but it is the more potent . . . argument of the mighty dollar that secures an audience there, and the sooner we realize it the better for us" (News and Observer, Raleigh, Nov. 27, 1880).

[48] Also, as has been seen, a philosophy which had right quietly, sometimes half-consciously, been taking shape in the Southern mind, was just now becoming fully articulate. For example, some months before the election, it had been said: "While the politicians are making a great deal of noise over the states rights question, the people of the South are quietly making substantial industrial progress. . . . The cotton mills in operation have proved very profitable. New mills are projected. . . . The signs of the great industrial change now going on in the South are plainly visible everywhere.

But the South did more than receive a new economic aim. Garfield elected, it began to show further the faith that had been welcomed, and moved to renounce political separatism: " The Southern people must be National themselves, in their aspirations and conduct, if they would have the Government truly national in spirit," and Garfield president not of a section or party. " To have a government of 'the whole country,' to be entitled to it, we must think of the whole country as our own, and demand no more than we are ready to give. It must come to this."[49]

Garfield's assassination showed how ready the South was to join hands with the North. " It could not have been foreseen . . . that the outburst of sympathy and condemnation would have been universal in its manifestation, affectionate in tone and National in spirit. South Carolina does more

---

. . . The people of the South are beginning to learn that the true road to power is not through the white house, supported by a swarm of federal officials. They are learning that solid wealth is power, and that wealth is attainable only by working up their cotton and wool into fabrics and their ores into metals " (Memphis Avalanche, quoted in Daily Constitution, Atlanta, March 30, 1880). " Distinction must be made between the political talk in the papers and what the people really wanted. There was a strong but silent undercurrent for economic welfare, while the politician was still singing the old song " (E. C. Brooks, int., Durham, N. C., Sept. 18, 1916). Approval of the thought that Hancock's defeat threw the South into a reversed frame of mind was received in interviews with some men who lived through the events, but from none of the newer generation.

[49] News and Courier, Charleston, March 9, 1881. " In the near future the successful leaders, South and North, will be those whose first thought is for the Republic; men who are National in feeling and purpose; men who understand that the political and social strength and safety of each State depend not on isolation and separation, but on combination and union." Cf. ibid., May 7, 1881. A New Orleans editor said: " The bitterness, prejudice and hostility to the changes wrought by the war which were so marked a few years ago are disappearing. There is now a very noticeable . . . disposition to accept the situation as it is, and on this basis to build a new South which shall surpass in wealth, glory and greatness the old South. . . . before another National campaign opens this element will control the political and material affairs of the South " (Times-Democrat, quoted in ibid., Feb. 4, 1881). Cf. A. K. McClure, The South: Industrial, Financial, Political, p. 53; Dunning, p. 198. Not all leaders were so sensible; Senator Vance, of North Carolina, looking forward to Garfield's term, was belying his professions by asserting " The thing that has been is the thing that shall be " (News and Courier, Charleston, Feb. 23, 1881).

than reprobate assassination. The . . . whole people, resent the deed because the victim is the President of the
United States. . . . The forces of reunion had gone on
with a rapidity which few appreciated. All the elements of
cordial friendship and of national good-will were there. It
needed only the threat of a common misfortune to give
shape and voice to the recreate [sic] but sturdy love of the
Republic."[50]

It is clear that the pressing task of the South, from the
day of Appomattox, was truly an economic and social and
not a political one.[51]   By 1880 this was publicly apparent,
and no later expression of this view[52] has been plainer than
contemporary exhortations that the people shut ears to
politicians and open sympathies to constructive action.

"So long as we have sectional enmity in politics in the

---

[50] News and Courier, Charleston, July 13, 1881. " . . . the President's desperate illness . . . has done more than years of ordinary
events in bringing the North and South together. . . . Vainly will
the politicians flourish the 'bloody flag.' The people will not rally
on the ensanguined colors again " (ibid., July 18, 1881). Cf. ibid.,
July 14, giving interview with Jefferson Davis, and Sept. 20, 1881;
William A. Harden, A History of Savannah and South Georgia, p.
485. The cordiality with which the First Connecticut Regiment was
received in Charleston the month following Garfield's death was
believed an outgrowth of the city's sorrow at the national tragedy.
The first column of the News and Courier bore the flags of Connecticut and South Carolina crossed, with the legends, "Yankee
Doodle Come to Town," and "A Welcome Invasion." An editorial
spoke of the war as a "grand lesson to the South," and declared:
"We have learned that we cannot stand alone, that our fight must
be made within the Union . . ." (Oct. 24, 1881).

[51] Cf. Sioussat, p. 223.

[52] "The greatest statesman of the South in recent times was Sea-
man A. Knapp, who believed that the demonstration farm was of
more value to society than the noisiest political convention . . .; that
a boy's corn club would do more to enrich materially the life of the
people than the fattest office won on the hustings. . . . The unselfish
servants of the people, working in humble ways to improve the farm,
the road, the factory, the home, the school, and the church are the
true statesmen of the South " (Samuel C. Mitchell, "The Challenge
of the South for a Better Nation," in The South Mobilizing for
Social Service, p. 46). Cf. ibid., p. 45. "Back of the patriotism of
arms, back of the patriotism of our political and civic life, there lies,
like a new and commanding social motive, the patriotism of efficiency.
. . . It is not merely the patriotism of industrial power. It is the
patriotism of social fitness and of economic value. It is the passion
of usefulness " (Murphy, Present South, p. 148). Cf. ibid., p. 316.

South its material prosperity will be checked and an absolute injury will be sustained . . . by exciting distrust of
capital and prejudices of immigration. The Southern people, outside of the professional politicians, care very little
about Federal politics. They are endeavoring to develop
the resources of the South and regain the broken-down fortunes left by the desolation of civil war."[53] Asserting that
the South should welcome outside enterprisers, bid for government appropriations and hold to the party that could
insure peace in which to follow economic pursuits, a South
Carolinian wrote that " The object of our politics should be
the development of our resources. . . . In this State we
need capital and less party and politics."[54] It was not until

[53] Sumpter, S. C., Southron, quoted in News and Courier, Charleston, May 14, 1881. " So taking the past and the present as indices
for the future, it is plain to see that a dissolution of the Solid South
will cut at the very roots of all these wrangles between the North
and the South in which sectionalism is involved." Cf. Observer,
Raleigh, Jan. 29, 1880, in comment on an editorial of Financial
Chronicle.

[54] " Brutus " in News and Courier, Charleston, May 25, 1881. For
a list of Federal appropriations for North Carolina in the rivers and
harbors bill the year previous, see Observer, Raleigh, May 6, 1880.
It was said, apropos of the approaching meeting of the Southern
Press Association, that the Associated Press in its selection of news
did not always contribute sufficiently to the business progress of the
South. " The commercial prosperity of the South is of far greater
consequence to the Southern press than any mere political object.
. . . Any association, therefore, that will aid in . . . dissemination
of truthful information about the social, business and industrial life
of the Southern States, should be encouraged by those who control
the Southern press " (News and Courier, Charleston, March 29,
1881). " It is time to stop impeaching the South's development, for
. . . business is driving sentimental politics to the woods " (Springfield Republican, quoted in News and Observer, Raleigh, Dec. 31,
1880). Years earlier Gregg took McDuffie severely to task for his
half-hearted entrance into cotton manufacturing: " Had you . . .
mixed a little more patriotism with your efforts, you would have
taken the pains to ascertain why your Vaucluse establishment did
not realize . . . sanguine expectations. . . . You would have put
your own shoulders to the wheel. . . ." Instead of political opposition to protection (Gregg did not favor a tariff), McDuffie should
have advocated turning it to economic advantage (Domestic Industry, p. 8). " It would indeed be well for us, if we were not so re-
fined in politics—if the talent, which has been, for years past, and is
now engaged in embittering our indolent people against their industrious neighbors of the North, had been . . . engaged in . . . the
encouragement of the mechanical arts " (ibid., pp. 7-8). Cf. Ingle,

1880 that men like Gregg, pleading that "politicians, instead of teaching us to hate our Northern brethren, endeavor to get up a good feeling for domestic industry,"[55] and who were overborne by such followers of Dew as Calhoun, Simms, Hammond, Rhett, Davis, Yancey, and Cheves,[56] could be justified in the public judgment as expressed by Grady when he said: "Every man within the sound of my voice, under the deeper consecration he offers to the Union, will consecrate himself to the South. Have no ambition but to be first at her feet and last at her service. . . ."[57]

Nearly every stage of this study testifies to the large extent to which such economic publicists as these, by conscious teaching and by example, were responsible for industrial growth. It is a nice matter to strike a balance between the force of their inner promptings and the external influences operating upon them. It has been seen that their identical philosophy, held by earlier Southerners, could not bear fruit before 1880, and certainly from this date forward moral stimulus gathered strength from the constantly more apparent physical advantages for manufacturing. As to whether desire for industry uncovered facilities, or facilities for industry suggested their employment, a careful thinker said: "My answer is for the ideas, the internal stimulus, but subject to the qualification that in a longer time we would have had the mills by force of external influence. So far as the period from 1880 to 1900 was concerned, it

---

Southern Sidelights, p. 40; Andrews, South since the War, p. 96). The "old dislike of the peddling, money-making Yankee is being replaced by admiration for his thrift, and desire to adopt the means by which he has left his impress upon the nation's life" (Springfield Republican, quoted in News and Courier, Charleston, April 7, 1881). One who now feels this view has been overemphasized said, speaking of the lack of strong men in politics in South Carolina, "they have gone into this great economic movement, and let most other things go to the dogs" (Mrs. M. P. Gridley, int., Greenville, Sept. 9, 1916).

[55] See Domestic Industry, pp. 14–16; 11, 24; Olmsted, Seaboard Slave States, p. 363.

[56] Dodd, in South in Building of Nation, vol. v, p. 568 ff.; Kohn, Cotton Mills of S. C., p. 13.

[57] Dyer, in New South, p. 90.

was as nearly the immediate result of internal agitation as any industrial growth could be." It is probably correct to conclude that "the social and economic influences cooperated with the human purpose."[58]

Enough has been said to make it apparent that at the outset the employment of children in the mills, if not absolutely necessary, was practically so, and never excited the least question. Search has failed to reveal one instance of protest against their working, but, on the other hand, cotton manufacturing was hailed as a boon especially because it gave means of livelihood to women and children. Poverty-stricken, the South was mustering every resource to stagger to its feet. All labor power was empirically seized upon; response was eager. At that critical juncture, later results of the employment of children could not be looked to. The great morality then was to go to work. The use of children was not avarice then, but philanthropy; not exploitation, but generosity and cooperation and social-mindedness.[59]

---

[58] W. W. Ball, int., Columbia, Jan. 3, 1917. "The building of the Pelzer Mill was the germination of the idea implanted by The News and Courier." A competent student wrote: "The growth of cotton manufacturing . . . is significant of a change in Southern ideals . . . a change from a social system in which work was held to be degrading, to one in which great interest is taken in industrial enterprise" (Copeland, pp. 32–33). Sir Horace Plunkett said unhesitatingly of a development not far different: "The story of the new movement . . . begins in the year 1889, when a few Irishmen . . . set themselves the task of bringing home to the rural population . . . the fact that their prosperity was in their own hands . . . to arouse and apply the latent capacities of the . . . people . . ." (cf. pp. 178–179). An objective judgment is: "Other industrial conditions beside the nearness to the cotton crop produced this growth, chief of which has been the general industrial awakening experienced by the South" (New International Encyclopaedia, article on "Cotton," p. 159). Mr. Brooks leans toward environment when he says: "In . . . natural resources the South has found the basis of . . . new economic policy, a new social order . . ." (p. 214).

[59] Between 1880 and 1890 the number of children was doubled, and between 1890 and 1900 trebled (cf. U. S. Census of Manufactures, 1890, "Cotton Manufacture," by Stanwood, p. 173; ibid., 1900, p. 33). "Manufacturers took whom they could get for operatives in the new mills. The employment of children was not a matter of choice but of necessity. . . ." Cf. Edmonds, p. 20. It must be remembered, too, that whole families were transferred from farms to mill villages, which alone, in the then condition of the South, would have required that the children work. Of course, the use of chil-

Understanding that the South, from inner impulse, environmental suggestion and the union of these two, was determined for manufacturing, the immediate reasons for the building of mills may now be considered. It must be remembered that there is a distinction between industrial advantages believed to be present, and facilities as they were afterwards proved out. In the next pages the effort is to discover the thought back of the erection of factories, rather than the evaluation of supposed advantages as revealed in actual operation.

It is clear, first, that there could be no single proximate cause. A mill president said: "You cannot find any uniformity in the reasons for establishment of mills. There were a thousand reasons. Sometimes it was salaries that were wanted; sometimes commission houses that were after the charges; sometimes it was to build up the community; sometimes the profits of one mill that brought another into being; sometimes the machinery men; sometimes it was just because they were . . . fools."[60]

When Mr. Edmonds declared that "What the South has done . . . has been without any special stimulus," he meant there were few demonstrated aids to manufacturing in the

---

dren has long since become unnecessary, and has been as cruelly unjust as at first it was natural. Cf. the writer's "Some Factors in the Future of Cotton Manufacture in the South," in Manufacturers' Record, Baltimore, May 10, 1917, and "The End of Child Labor," in Survey, Aug. 23, 1919. Some of Murphy's eloquent pleas for abolition of child labor, while courageous and fitting when he wrote, did not, perhaps, recognize sufficiently the facts of the inception of the system. Cf. Present South, pp. 114, 142-143, 147; George T. Winston, "Child Labor in North Carolina," in Pamphlet 262 of National Child Labor Committee, p. 1 ff. For a statement true for the eighties but not for 1916, see Hearings before Committee on Labor, House of Representatives, January, 1916, p. 12.

[60] Landon A. Thomas, int., Augusta, Ga., Dec. 29, 1916. Others gave similar medleys: "I think the chief advantages observed were the possession of ample raw material and cheap motive power. . . . Also, cheaper common labor, and . . . the fact that the climate . . . is . . . a good one . . ." (S. S. Broadus, Decatur, Ala., letter, Jan. 27, 1915). "Mills were located about Spartanburg because they had cotton to grow to their doors, water power, tax exemption, encouragement in railroads giving two-thirds rate on machinery and material hauled, and willingness of supply men to take stock" (J. B. Cleveland, int., Spartanburg).

beginning; he neglected to take account of the subjective factor of popular resolve which flourished just because of the surrounding poverty.[61] "To help the city of Charleston and the people was the simple reason for starting the Charleston Manufacturing Company. The projectors thought the time had come for Charleston to do its part; they had been sending a good deal of money to the Piedmont mills and they thought they would build one at home."[62]

It is not hard to discern several specific influences making for the industrial development, and these may be examined separately, bearing in mind that all of them, in varying degree, doubtless bore a part.

Some, especially in North Carolina, have found a cause in manufacturing made necessary during the Civil War. The State, urged by Governor Ellis and Governor Clark, became a workhouse for the production of war supplies and goods no longer obtainable from outside. It is said that a vision of what lay in manufactures was firmly imbedded in the North Carolina mind, and that after Reconstruction the people went back to industry.[63]

---

[61] Facts about South, pp. 20, 22. Contrast R. M. R. Dehn, The German Cotton Industry, pp. 13, 16.

[62] George W. Williams, int., Charleston, S. C., Dec. 27, 1916. Cf. a statement respecting development of English economic thought, in Edwin Cannan, Theories of Production and Distribution, ed. of 1894, pp. 147–148.

[63] D. H. Hill, int., Raleigh, N. C., Sept. 16, 1916. Governor Clark, in his message to the Legislature, August 16, 1861, stated the situation: "First, that in our commercial relations we have been dependent on the North for almost every article that we use connected with machinery, farming, merchandise, food and clothing . . . including almost every article we need for our defence. The second and more important fact is now established, that we have the means and material for supplying all these wants within our own borders. Necessity is developing these resources and *driving* us to *the use of them.* The continuance of this war and blockade for two or three years may inflict much personal suffering, but it will surely accomplish our national and *commercial* independence." Many cotton mills were chartered in North Carolina during the war. "War changes the habits of a people. After the Revolutionary War and the second war with England America relied less on England and became self-supporting. The Civil War changed the habits of the Southern people and made them rely on their own skill and energy for every necessity of life. Where there was no skill, attempts were made to

7

Conveniently mentioned, too, in connection with North Carolina is the thought that certain groups of immigrants had planted their manufacturing tradition. This has been referred to in the previous chapter, and it will be remembered that slavery and agriculture forbade these foreigners making a lasting public impression. By maintaining an occupation in particular families, however, late members of which came to bear in the industrial awakening, they did a service.[64]

Entertaining a synthetic rather than analytic viewpoint, it has been sometimes said, with empirical reasoning, that industry in the South grew out of a natural recovery following the war. While not accounting very well for a change of mind that was certainly present, this argument has point. A survey of South Carolina in 1884 asserted: "The State has now recovered the ground . . . lost by emancipation, by negro suffrage, by political misrule and official corruption. . . . Since the redemption and regeneration of the State, in 1877, the growth of manufactures has been astonishing in its rapidity and volume. Agricultural operations could be carried on with reasonable success, in even the darkest days of strife and misrule, but the undertakings which were dependent on the concentration of capital for their development remained torpid, if not dead, until the

---

develop it" (Brooks, pp. 199–200). That "a new form of expression of patriotism took the place of military service" after the Revolution,—encouragement of home industry—is clear; it may be held that such economic patriotism was delayed in the South by Reconstruction following the Civil War, and that industrial progress was thus "the result of both moral and economical forces" (cf. U. S. Census of Manufactures, 1880, "Factory System of U. S.," by Carroll D. Wright, p. 6).

[64] Cf. Clark, in South in Building of Nation, vol. v, pp. 313–314. In a few instances, it is true, local communities were given an industrial character that resisted an enervating economic environment. Germans at Wachovia, in North Carolina, within a year after settlement had in operation a flour mill, carpenter, shoe and blacksmith shops, pottery, tannery and cooperage establishments (M. R. Pleasants, unpublished MS., "Manufacturing in N. C.," p. 5). Cf. Tompkins, History of Mecklenburg, vol. i, pp. 24–25; Olmsted, p. 511. Winston-Salem, N. C., owes much to its Moravian settlers.

return of confidence breathed into them new life and vigor."[65]

A similar account was given twenty years afterward:

The war destroyed the capital and property of the South . . . and left in its wake a grinding poverty. . . . The problem of procuring wherewithal to feed and clothe themselves, the fight for a mere subsistence, employed all the energies . . . of the people. This poverty and the struggle to get rid of the carpet-bag government, left no time for anything else. But there came a time when the people could pull themselves together and take an inventory of what they had accomplished . . . they had a little time to look about them, and to take some thought of the morrow. It required no particular wisdom to see that here where the raw material was produced, where natural resources abounded, and where there was . . . the steadiest and most intelligent class of labor, that in this favored land was the essential home of cotton manufacturing. So it became merely a question of providing capital with which to buy some machinery, the transfer of labor from the farm to the mill, and the South's career as a manufacturing people was fairly begun.[66]

The war and Reconstruction took one generation of activity; by 1880 the South had convalesced. "We took our minds off the war, and began thinking about home affairs." Before 1880 there was a great social pressure that prevented attention to constructive measures.[67]

---

[65] News and Courier, South Carolina in 1884. "We shall see how the people of this section, reduced to poverty by . . . war, . . . bestirred themselves cheerfully, amid the ashes and waste of their homes; how they met new and adverse conditions with unquailing courage; how they gave themselves cordially to unaccustomed work; with what patience they bore misfortune, and endured wrongs put upon them through the surviving passions of the war. . . . How . . . at last controlling with their own hands their local affairs, they began, in ragged and torn battalions, that march of restoration and development that has challenged universal admiration. We shall see how . . . things despised in the old days of prosperity, in adversity won unexpected value. How frugality came with misfortune, fortitude with sorrow, and with necessity invention" (Grady, pp. 142–143).

[66] Southern Cotton Spinners' Assn., proceed. 7th Annual Convention, address of T. C. Guthrie, p. 44 ff.

[67] E. C. Brooks, int., Durham, N. C., Sept. 18, 1916. The night of the Hayes-Tilden election the informant's father and uncle sat up all night with their shotguns, expecting trouble with the negroes. A representative of the old South said: "From the close of the war, all through Reconstruction time, we had it pretty hot. Politics took up the time of all of us. The effect of Reconstruction, even after we got rid of it, lasted us six or seven years. When that blew away, everything took on new life. We began to build up all sorts of

Mr. Clark has pointed out that with restoration of confidence in political conditions in the reconstructed States, outside capitalists no longer feared disorders that threatened safety of investments; and when work became a necessity, opportunities for diversifying work were seized upon.[68]   The South, of course, shared in the country's revival from the depression that followed the panic of 1873. The recovery symbolized in the return to specie payments in 1879, in its influence on Southern industry, will be spoken of later.[69]

One is quite ready to agree to the suggestion, also, that "there was in the South a quiet element of business and professional men who did not approve the course of the leaders of the section, and who, smothered under, so far as public attention was concerned, kept up activity and stood forth when a liberal industrial and commercial program became the order of the day," and that the revulsion of feeling was not really so quick as study of public expressions might indicate.[70]

The high price of cotton right after the war and a belief that this condition would continue because cotton could be

enterprises" (James Morehead, int., Greensboro, N. C., Aug. 30, 1916). "After they got straightened out, with their State governments in their own hands, people began to feel there was a future for them" (Summerfield Baldwin, Sr., int., Baltimore, Md., June, 1917). Cf. Tompkins, Cotton and Cotton Oil, p. 64; Copeland, pp. 32-33.

[68] In South in Building of Nation, vol. vi, pp. 265-266. This statement is one of the best-considered by this writer.

[69] Cf. Clark, in ibid., pp. 262-263, 258 ff. "The growth of population, the building of railways, the accumulation of capital, the slow perfection of commercial finance, the spread of popular education, each assisted the imperative trend toward industrial diversification and expansion. In spite of the panic and depression . . . between 1870 and 1880 every important Southern manufacture was completely rehabilitated . . ." (ibid.).

[70] Walter S. McNeill, int., Richmond, Va., Aug. 29, 1916; M. L. Bonham, Anderson, Sept. 10, 1916. Another said there is nothing esoteric in the cotton mill campaign, that the South was looking about for something to lay its hand to and naturally fell upon the omnipresent staple; the cables that moored the South to its past had worn thin, and it needed only some lucky accidents about 1880 to part the last strands and set the ship free on her course (J. L. Hartsell, int., Concord, N. C., Sept. 2, 1916). Cf. Clark, in South in Building of Nation, vol. vi, pp. 254-255.

only scantily raised with free labor, focused attention again
upon the staple; the local merchant was given credit at the
North, and he in turn gave credit to the farmer, who pledged
his land to cotton. This temporary restoration of King
Cotton saddled the farmer with debt and delayed agricultural diversification and industrial beginnings.[71]

In coming to the directly personal factor, the part of promoters and projectors in the building of the mills, it is well
to bear in mind the caution that " it is . . . not unnatural
that most of us should fall into the error of attributing to
the influence of prominent individuals or organizations the
events and conditions which the superficial observer regards
as the creation of the hour, but which are in reality the outcome of a slow and continuous process of evolution."[72]

In certain cases where it would seem plain that mills were
due exclusively to one man, it is necessary only to ask where
and why he received his impulse, to show that he was really
an exponent of a prevailing tendency, just as the community upon which he relied for assistance, in its response to
his appeal, answered a little later to the same social stirring.[73]

---

[71] Cf. Grady, p. 175 ff. For other references, see Tompkins, Cultivation, Picking, Baling and Manufacturing of Cotton, pp. 5–6;
History of Mecklenburg, vol. i, pp. 150–151; Thompson, p. 59 ff.

[72] Plunkett, p. 27. The mistake has often been made: " You might
write volumes, but you would never be able to get beyond the fact
that the cotton mill development in Gastonia, Gaston County, North
Carolina, and the whole South, is the result of the fact that a few
men had a vision" (Joseph H. Separk, int., Gastonia, N. C., Sept.
14, 1916). Cf. Southern Cotton Spinners' Assn., proceed. 7th Annual Convention, address of Edward Atkinson, p. 89; Cannan, p. 23.

[73] One of the sincerest men talked with said: " The Gaffney people
never thought of having a mill before I came back from the Clifton
village, where I was putting up buildings, and got them stirred up.
You get an idea in another place where you happen to be, and you
say to yourself: 'Why won't that work in our little town?' Well,
you've got to do a lot of talking after you get home with the idea,
but they'll catch on in the end. The people of Union asked some
Gaffney men to come there and tell them about the business. The
professor at the high school and I went down to Union, and I recol-
lect I made them a right smart good talk down there, and they
caught on to it and built the mills they've got now. And that was a
dead town" (L. Baker, int., Gaffney, S. C., Sept. 13, 1916). An
interview with a mill official whom Mr. Baker persuaded to come
to Gaffney showed that he had acted so completely under Mr. Baker's
enthusiasm that he accepted the factory as a matter of course. In

It has been seen how Murphy pointed out that the New South was the child of the Old South, fathered in large degree by the same leaders who in less happy days had bred only economic deformities. "The old South was the real nucleus of the new nationalism. The old South . . . was the true basis of an enduring peace between the sections. . . ." And everyone must share his regret that "a doubt was put upon its word given at Appomattox. . . . Power was struck from its hands. Its sense of responsibility was wounded and confused."[74]

Nothing stands out more prominently than that the Southern mills were conceived and brought into existence by Southerners. The impulse was furnished almost exclusively from within the South, against much discouragement from selfish interests at the North, and capital was supplied by the South to the limit of its ability.[75]

Coming now to the part of ex-Confederates in the industrial regeneration of their people, it is apparent with what speed they embraced their new duty and how the promise of their participation was welcomed by the wisest heads in

no instance did one personality stand out as an almost exclusive influence more than in the development of mills at Columbia through Mr. Whaley (Washington Clark, William Banks, W. W. Ball, interviews, Columbia, S. C., Jan. 1, 2, 3, respectively, 1917). " If I had at my disposal the history of Major Thos. L. Emry, who was the founder and father of Roanoke Rapids, I would simply tear a few pages from it and spread them across this space and you would have the whole story of the pioneering of this wonderful industrial . . . center " (Charlotte News, Textile Ed., 1917).

[74] Present South, pp. 10-11. Such men as E. M. Holt, Francis Fries, J. M. Morehead and William Gregg, who years before had seen the wisdom of industrial development along with agriculture and, besides the usual activities of farmer and legislator, were engaged in building railroads and mills, could not have their way with the South. Men of opposite faith, later converted to new courses, did no more than adopt a program which earlier had been spurned. On these unfollowed leaders, see South in Building of Nation, vols. xi and xii; Cyclopedia of Eminent and Representative Men of the Carolinas; Jerome Dowd, Sketches of Prominent Living North Carolinians (1888); Biographical History of North Carolina; Tompkins, Cotton Mill, Commercial Features, pp. 181, 185, 187-188; Clark, in South in Building of Nation, vol. v, p. 323; Copeland, pp. 32-33; Goldsmith, p. 4; Southern Cotton Spinners' Assn., proceed. 7th Annual Convention, p. 168.

[75] Cf. Grady, pp. 182-184, 197-198; Edmonds, p. 32; Charlotte News, Textile Ed., 1917.

the North. It has been observed that just as citizens of Salem, Massachusetts, established a club where descendants of the witches and of those who hanged them toast one another, so "the same people that turn out, by the city-full, to build Lee's monument and to bury Davis, are taxing themselves for the schooling of negro children. . . ." Each of these Southerners, "devoutly remembering the old; understanding as no one else can why he remembers it; but all the time looking for something not only better and larger than he has known, but grander than any one ever dared to hope for this side of heaven," showed a divine versatility that is the very stuff of civilization.[76]

James L. Orr, soon to be governor of his State, was a type man, and he appeared with others of the same persuasion in South Carolina as early as the constitutional convention of 1865. There was nothing sullen about him; what he did, he did whole-heartedly. "He was considered one of the coolest-headed men in the State five years ago this summer; but, for all that, he was one of the leading members in the Secession Convention, and in the Rebel Senate during the whole existence of the Confederate government. Now he is one of the leading reconstructionists. . . . He . . . carries himself with a very democratic air."[77]

Often reprobated at the North, this was as normal as it was fortunate; Southerners would choose those in whom they had rested old confidences because people and spokesmen had made a mental readjustment which, however unbelievable to enemies, was easy and natural.[78] A Northern observer not over-disposed to find good in the beaten South, disagreed with those who wished to antagonize and hinder

---

[76] A. D. Mayo, "Is There a New South?", in Social Economist, Oct., 1893, pp. 201–202; cf. ibid., p. 207.

[77] Andrews, p. 50. The promptness with which distinguished participants in the Confederate cause came forward after the war was an indication of the consistency of Southern leadership. Lee was as much the general at the head of a college as at the head of an army.

[78] Cf. Dunning, pp. 44–45. Twelve members of the South Carolina constitutional convention of 1865 had been members of the secession convention (Andrews, pp. 38–39). Cf. Thompson, pp. 57–58.

rather than help these inevitable leaders. "For my part," said Sidney Andrews, "I wish every office in the State [South Carolina] could be filled with ex-Confederate soldiers. It is the universal testimony of every officer of our own troops . . . that the late Rebel soldiers are of better disposition toward the government, toward Northerners, toward progression, than any other class of citizens."[79]

The year 1880 was reached before these men could really assert themselves. Their training in politics stood them in good stead when they came to organize public sentiment in a new campaign, that of industrial awakening.[80] Their old mastery, with even increased power, sprang forward to the evident task. The pity is that they had not longer time left them in which to work for the South.[81]

When the student of Southern industry meets one of the few surviving members of this company, he at once feels himself in touch with the spirit that was the South's salvation. Far-seeing, public-minded, generous-natured leaders because lovers and servers, these have proved themselves true patriots.[82]

---

[79] South since the War, p. 95; cf. ibid., pp. 393, 371-372; Dunning, pp. 185-186; Tompkins, History of Mecklenburg, vol. i, pp. 151-152. Andrews had more faith in a "conquered Rebel" than in "most of these North Carolina Unionists" (ibid., p. 167).

[80] Cf. Punkett, pp. 72-73.

[81] The Industrial South, of Richmond, in 1882 was asking "when will . . . prosperity come" and declared this especially "the impatient utterance of the surviving veterans of the war . . .—the men who were crushed to the earth by the loss of all their worldly possessions, who have ever since been struggling for a footing in life again, and who are looking longingly for some assurance . . . that their children and their children's children will have large opportunities for improvement of their fortunes through the exercise of energy in utilizing the bounties of nature around them" (quoted in Baltimore Journal of Commerce and Manufacturers' Record, June 17, 1882).

[82] It is worth while setting down impressions of one or two. A ruddy, white-haired old gentleman, cordial, cultivated, and a little shyly if gladly reminiscent, received me in the office of his ship chandlering store in Bay Street, Charleston. He showed by look and phrase and occasionally by direct remark that he had been nicely familiar with all the details of the important mill project in which he had taken a chief part, and that they had been obscured, never obliterated, by the years. Almost with a child's embarrassment he explained he did not know why he had kept a packet of

It was natural, at the opening of the period, that many cotton factors should head mill enterprises. They had some money, business connections and a knowledge of the staple that was important. Frequently they had been buyers for, and stockholders and directors in, some of the first enterprises. Charleston cotton merchants played a leading rôle. Captain F. T. Pelzer is a case in point; he made money in cotton right after the war, was a director in Hammett's Piedmont Factory, became interested in several other ventures and ended by founding the mill bearing his name.[83] Sometimes factors were already executives of mills established before 1880, and went into manufacturing more deeply when industrial development became a fixed policy.[84] A cotton buyer for Hammett's Piedmont mill,

---

intimate memoranda concerning a devoted but unsuccessful venture, and handed them over to me with charges for their safe return. Another, nearly ninety-eight years old when interviewed, sat in the office of the mill which he built and of which he had long been president. He wore a greenish-black, threadbare overcoat, and clutched a bulging umbrella of the same sort. Clear-brained, almost excessively direct, of dominating personality, one felt he had always been equal to the tasks confronting him. As he looked about at the bookkeepers, he spoke with much emphasis, to soften the too pitifully evident chagrin at being dispossessed. His successor, exulting in what has been called "juvenile capitalism," had little of the affection of the old man for the enterprise. Here was the South of slavery, agriculture and aristocracy, that made the South of free labor, industry and democracy. A writer on the mills has said: "These little personal things will creep into my story and break the continuity of dry developments, but the human element pulsates so frequently through the proposition that I must be excused if I fly off at a tangent at almost any word and mix up the material and the psychological" (Charlotte News, Textile Ed., 1917, concerning Roanoke Mills). Cf. ibid., concerning Edenton Cotton Mill; Southern Cotton Spinners' Assn., proceed. 7th Annual Convention, p. 44 ff.

[83] Frank Pelzer and William Banks, interviews, Charleston, Dec. 28, 1916, and Columbia, Jan. 2, 1917. Col. W. G. Smith was a cotton buyer in Orangeburg County, S. C., before organizing a mill there. Leroy Springs, in his mercantile business at Lancaster, took cotton in exchange for goods. A little later it will be noticed how he became a cotton manufacturer (Banks, ibid.). The same is true of John H. Montgomery (cf. Columbia Record, Textile Ed., Oct., 1916).

[84] Thus "William C. Sibley, the president of this company, has had a long experience in cotton, and is one of the largest cotton buyers of the Southern States. . . . He is at present handling, and has for many years . . . efficiently handled, the corporate affairs of the Langley mills . . ." (Boston Journal of Commerce, July 29, 1882).

after plans to invite him to Anderson had fallen through, started a factory on his own account.

By no means all of the mill builders had direct or even indirect connection with cotton. How thoroughly local most enterprises were and how general in communities was the desire for mills, is seen in the callings from which men came to cotton manufacturing. Lawyers, bankers, farmers, merchants, teachers, preachers, doctors, public officials—any man who stood out among his neighbors, or whose economic position allowed him a little freedom of action, was likely to be requisitioned into service or to venture for himself.[85] Neither did the South rely only upon those socially prominent, or upon intellectuals. There was no authoritative leading exposition of the problems facing the section. Measures were hit upon by intuition, by force of circumstance, because of pressing necessity and first-apparent opportunity. It was a movement of the whole South.[86]

Especially did merchants become mill builders. When large plantations broke down into small farms and tenant holdings, factors at the ports could no longer market the whole cotton crop or supply needed credit, because they did not have knowledge of local conditions. Merchants, many of them mere country storekeepers, found themselves more than ever drawn into the buying and selling of the staple, and lending money on growing crops. Supplying every material want of the farmer and taking his incoming cotton in surety, the merchant was the pivot of the economic system. These merchants, more than anyone else in their communities, had credit relations at the North, the importance of which in their manufacturing enterprises will be observed in the chapter on capital.[87] They had an interest

---

[85] Cf. Goldsmith, pp. 7–8. "All that was necessary was that the promoter of the mill should have succeeded in the business in which he had been formerly engaged."

[86] Cf. Plunkett, p. 133 ff.

[87] Cf. Hammond, p. 144 ff. The description of usury in sales on "time" applies over much of the South today. I heard of a North Carolina farmer who, in 1920, with cotton prices unprecedentedly high, was asked half of his crop in payment for fertilizer.

in the prosperity of their localities that was none the less effective because not always academic or sentimental.[88]

The man who later had capital to head cotton mills at Clinton, South Carolina, set up the only store in the place immediately following the War. The town was then in a poor way, and not being helped by several barrooms.[89] Leroy Springs operated a general mercantile business in Lancaster, South Carolina. A new railway came through the town, but some thriving young places sprang up along it and drew business from Lancaster, which came to a standstill, was "dead." Realizing that something must be done to keep business going in Lancaster, the merchant, with a small capital, built a cotton mill. It had the desired effect.[90] In a conspicuous instance a mercantile firm outside of the South entered the industry in a similar way. Appealed to by Southern customers to take stock in local mill undertakings, a Baltimore groceries house came to have large manufacturing interests, and ultimately changed over to making and selling cotton goods.

The moving man in the Charleston Manufacturing Company was half merchant as head of the ice company.[91]

Saying that Massachusetts mills created only in quantity values that Rhode Island manufacturers produced through quality of goods, William Gregg years before saw that the Massachusetts method would first be introduced in the South, and said: "Cotton manufacturing will not, probably, be speedily introduced into this State [South Carolina], unless our business men of capital take hold of it. Merchants and retired men of capital may erect factories, . . .

---

[88] Mr. Clark is hardly justified in asserting that "The conditions were no longer those that attract a few hardy adventurers into a new field of business, but such as draw conservative capital, in large units and in the hands of trained administrators, to assured spheres of enterprise" (cf. in South in Building of Nation, vol. vi, pp. 266–267). Administrators were rarely trained and large investments of capital were rarely for dividends only.

[89] Columbia Record, Textile Ed., 1916. Cf. ibid. respecting John R. Barron's Manchester Cotton Mills.

[90] Columbia Record, Textile Ed., 1916.

[91] Cf. advertisement of Alva Gage & Co., Deutsche Zeitung, Charleston, 1881.

our wealthy planters may engage in this business . . . but it will be long before the Southern States shall have a set of manufacturers similar to those in Rhode Island; they must grow up among us. . . ."[92] When at length Gregg's advice was being followed, and entrepreneurs had to be recruited quickly, it is surprising how few failures appeared. True, they were not manufacturers in Gregg's sense, but they worked under natural advantages which well-nigh insured success.[93]

Mr. Estes' entry into manufacturing was typical. "I was first in the dry goods business, then the grocery business. I was mayor here for six years. I was successful. They got me to get up the mill. Old Judge King took first $50,000 and then $100,000 of stock, with the idea that I was to be president."[94]

---

[92] Domestic Industry, p. 27.

[93] Some mistakes there were bound to be, when an industry was being built overnight. "Gen. Irving Walker, a stationery man, was the first president of the Charleston Manufacturing Company. He was a nice man, but he knew nothing about the business. That was at the bottom of nine-tenths of the failures of cotton mills in this State—the presidents were popular, you know, everybody liked them, but they were incompetent, with no technical knowledge." The founder of one mill, mayor of his city, was denominated "a hot air politician." The type of man who could succeed in the eighties usually fails now. Mills at Bessemer City, North Carolina, are illustrative. There is no longer the leeway. Cf. Thompson, p. 272. "Looking back on them," one informant said, "I can see that the first mill men were a set of blundering children, some a little more apt than others." Cf. Ga. Indus. Assn., proceed. 4th Annual Convention, address of J. J. Spalding, pp. 46–47, and the writer's "Some Factors in Future of Cotton Manufacture in South," in Manufacturers' Record, Baltimore, May 10, 1917. Newer manufacturers, though still bearing marks of neglected training, are supplementing "a deep desire to succeed, faith in the soundness of the task and in one's own self, and business and social imagination" with intimate knowledge of detail. Cf. Charlotte News, Textile Ed., 1917, for many instances, especially that of C. B. Armstrong.

[94] Charles Estes, int., Augusta, Ga., Dec. 29, 1916. "When this enterprise was inaugurated there were those who doubted whether the mill would ever be built, but with Mr. Charles Estes, to whom, by universal consent, the work of organizing the company was intrusted, there is no such word as fail . . ." (newspaper clipping in Raworth Scrapbook). "Mr. A. Scheurman, a leading merchant of Griffin, Ga., is now closing out his business with the intention of engaging in cotton manufacturing . . . (Manufacturers' Record, Baltimore, Dec. 14, 1882). Cf. Grady, p. 181; Southern Cotton Spinners' Assn., proceed. 7th Annual Convention, pp. 111–112.

If space permitted, a review of the histories of H. P. Hammett, G. A. Gray, R. C. G. Love, Daniel Rhyne, and others would show interestingly the channels by which chief leaders came to build mills. Hammett and Gray were both linked with the ante-bellum industry. The former grew up on a farm, taught school, married the daughter of William Bates and was taken into his cotton manufacturing company; he entered the Civil War and was given duty in the Confederate tax office. After the war he represented his native county in the State legislature, was mayor of Greenville, made president of a rundown railroad and, knowing men of influence and being acquainted with an excellent water power, built his mill in the seventies.[95] Gray at the age of eight entered the old Stowe Mill, at Pinhook, Gaston County, N. C., as a doffer boy, at ten cents a day. He attended school hardly at all. He became an overseer in this mill and later was in charge of the installation of machinery in various new plants. He was superintendent of several factories, and moved to Gastonia with a small capital and built the first mill in the place. At the time of his death the town had eleven mills, nine of which he had been largely instrumental in projecting.[96]

D. A. Tompkins, less than thirty at the opening of the cotton mill era, was late enough to profit by the pioneering work of others. There was enough industry in the South to make the mill engineer's profession profitable. Tompkins was one of the first men in whose career it was evident that the South was becoming a real seat of the cotton manu-

---

[95] Cf. Tompkins, Cotton Mill, Commercial Features, pp. 189–190.

[96] Cf. Gastonia Gazette, Feb. 9, 1912, and C. W. Patman in Knit Goods, N. Y., March, 1912. Men drawn into the business as a result, directly or indirectly, of Gray's influence, had been teachers, public officials, bankers and farmers. Cf. Patman, ibid. One of the most successful manufacturers in Gastonia was raised on a farm and ran away from home when a young man and went through the country peddling clocks and quilts. He said that as a boy he believed the treasurer of a cotton mill the biggest man in the country, and that he thought this over while tramping about later with his wares. He finally set up an instalment furniture business in Gastonia, was made sheriff and was elected to the vice-presidency of a cotton mill. He is now president of many factories (C. B. Armstrong, int., Gastonia, N. C., Sept. 14, 1916).

facture, with facilities for machine design and repair and all that general guidance which new companies needed. Tompkins, unlike his predecessors, had technical training. Partly in furtherance of his engineering business, partly from the broadest social motives, he almost raised by hand many cotton mills—inspiring the idea, supervising construction, assisting first steps in production.[97]

"When manufactures have become well established a new mill is sometimes organized by a number of men who perceive that some one man is a promising manufacturer."[98] Though frequently exemplified at present, notably at Gastonia, this was rarely true in the early years. Where an executive was not himself the projector of a mill, the thought that created it was not dependent upon any individual. Thus a nearby manufacturer was persuaded to become president of a factory at Albemarle, North Carolina; but the enterprise had its root in the local pride of an old farmer of the place.[99]

There has been an erroneous notion that many promoters of mills in the South in the eighties were Northern men and firms. In the beginning cotton manufacturers of New England did much to discourage establishment of the industry at the South, and have never sought to realize Southern advantages in a large way. In later days there was never such an incoming of Northerners as that of the Hills, Bates,

---

[97] As an exhibit in Southern economic history, his two little offices in Charlotte ought really to be moved intact to a place where they would be kept for the public. Glimpses revealing Tompkins' personality may be found in his own writings: Nursing and Nurses, p. 3; History of Mecklenburg, vol, i, p. vii; Cotton and Cotton Oil, preface; Road Building and Repairs, p. 26; Building and Loan Associations, preface; a notion of the character of his service may be gained from: Water Power on the Catawba River, p. 20 ff.; A Plan to Raise Capital for Manufacturing, p. 18 ff.; the backs of some of his many pamphlets give the plan of organization of his company.

[98] Tompkins, Coton Mill, Commercial Features, p. 30.

[99] J. L. Hartsell, int., Concord. This was true of other mills headed by the same man. A merchant fathered a mill at China Grove quite irrespective of its later foster parent (W. R. Odell, int., Concord, N. C., Sept. 2, 1916). At Salisbury the matter of an executive was an afterthought.

Shelden, Clark and Weaver.[100]   The Cotton Mill Campaign,
so far from showing any of the antagonism of former years
toward Northern men and money,[101] developed the most
enthusiastic desire for the cooperation of any outsiders.
This led to delighted acclamation of any reported design of
Northerners to set up manufacturing in the South, but
there were undoubtedly more reports than performances.
The Northern observer who said of Charleston directly
after the war that the city had not sufficient recuperative
power for its own rebuilding, and that New Englanders, if
anyone, must make it over, would have been surprised fifteen years later to see Charlestonians supplying impulse to
their own city and really to the whole South.[102]

A Southern writer in 1882 said: "Capital and skill are
the only things needed to make the South preëminently a
manufacturing country and shrewd, energetic men from the
East and from Europe are rapidly supplying the defi-
ciency."[103]   The Southern Land, Emigration and Improvement Company, a New York organization, had as one of its
purposes bringing investment opportunities to the attention
of Northern capitalists.[104]   The leading railroads travers-
ing the South Atlantic States combined on a similar plan in

[100] Cf. J. B. O. Landrum, History of Spartanburg County, p. 58.
Cf. Dehn, German Cotton Industry, pp. 4-5.

[101] Andrews, p. 378.

[102] Ibid., p. 3.

[103] Baltimore Journal of Commerce and Manufacturers' Record,
June 3, 1882. "The Barnett Shoals have at last been purchased by
Davenport, Johnson & Co., of New York, for $22,000, and it is
thought that work will begin here in a short time. Athens is yet
destined to be the Lowell of the South" (Athens Banner, quoted in
ibid., June 24, 1882). "A party of New York capitalists . . . visited
the Peach Stone Shoals in Henry County, Ga., a few days ago, and
were so much pleased with the property . . . that they purchased it
with the intention of at once erecting a cotton mill, to rank as one
of the largest and best equipped in the South" (Manufacturers'
Record, Baltimore, March 1, 1883). Cf. Fredericksburg correspondence in Daily Dispatch, Richmond, Feb. 23, 1880; Charlotte News,
Textile Ed., 1917, concerning Wayne Mill. The considerable Northern participation in Southern mill development, as in the Chadwick-
Hoskins group and the Pacific Mills, came much later. Cf. Charlotte News, ibid.

[104] Baltimore Journal of Commerce and Manufacturers' Record,
Aug. 5, 1882.

1880.[105] Not a few of the Northerners that undertook industry in the South did so at directly Southern solicitation. A mill man of Alabama in 1881 was consummating a contract "by which a New England company of capitalists will revive cotton manufacturing in a factory building at Corinth, Miss.," and he expected to induce a Connecticut spinner who wished to come South to remove to Huntsville, Alabama.[106]

The pages of this study bear ample testimony to the power of a different group of promoters from those here mentioned, namely, the editors of Southern newspapers. Being peculiarly a public movement, the cotton mill development sprang in large part from the activity of the press. The "Federalist" did not fight harder for union than Southern papers, big and little, strove for industrial awakening in the eighties. By 1880 most editors knew that they were to follow DeBow and not Bledsoe, working for understanding between the sections and not separatism, for diversity and not narrowness of economic pursuit.[107] County weeklies were stout followers in a campaign in which city dailies were leaders. No paper was more influential than the News and Courier, of Charleston. The philosophy of Gregg's "Essays on Domestic Industry," published in the Charleston Courier in 1845, was made concrete in the News and Courier's exhortation, "Bring the mills to the cotton," which rang throughout the South and was taken up as the rallying cry of every mover for industry.[108]

---

[105] Ibid., July 15, 1882.

[106] Huntsville Democrat, quoted in News and Courier, Charleston, July 30, 1881. Similar bidding for location of a business designed to be set up in the South has been seen later in the case of a Philadelphia carpet manufacturer being brought to Gaffney, S. C.

[107] Cf. Dodd, in South in Building of Nation, vol. vi, p. 546.

[108] Mr. Hemphill declares this sentence "resulted in the conversion of South Carolina in less than the life of a generation into the second cotton manufacturing state of the nation. . . ." It is "by its statesmanship and largely through the work of its press" that the South has achieved progress since the war (James C. Hemphill, "The Influence of the Press in Southern Economic Development," in South in Building of Nation, vol. v, pp. 548–549. See this whole paper for interesting material). In 1880, in presenting a survey of

The very genius of the News and Courier was its editor, F. W. Dawson. The power he exerted could never be duplicated under any other circumstances than those of the South in the eighties. His inspiriting force can scarcely be overestimated. Born in England in 1840, he was drawn to the Southern cause and enlisted as a sailor on the Confederate vessel *Nashville* at Southampton the opening year of the Civil War. He entered the army and was promoted to the rank of captain. After the war he worked on Richmond newspapers before becoming one of the proprietors of the Charleston News; his editorship came to full strength when this paper was consolidated with the Courier.[109] He saw the truth of the South's problem and saw it whole; that the people must drop conceits and go to work. Besides his major effort for cotton manufactures, he effectively urged tobacco cultivation in South Carolina and preached against duelling. Doubtless his foreign birth and knowledge of English industrialism was of great assistance to him. Of fine physique, handsome, imperious, brilliant, level-headed, " he had full confidence in himself, with good reason. He was a godsend to South Carolina—the leader in bringing the State back into its own."[110] He met a tragic

the mills of South Carolina, Dawson wrote: " Ten years ago The News and Courier formulated what is now an accepted truth, in declaring that the remedy for commercial distress in the North and the secret of sure fortune in the South was to bring the mills to the cotton. . . . The belief was that the manufacture of cotton in a cotton producing State must necessarily pay well, by reason of the saving in the cost of the raw material, by the saving in commissions, and charges for transportation, by the saving in waste, in the rental of land . . . and in the wages to be paid to operatives . . ." (Leading article, published in Blackman). For an instance of how this idea was acted upon in Texas, see Manufacturers' Record, Baltimore, Nov. 23, 1882. Dawson stressed the slogan " Bring the cotton mills to the cotton fields " and associated ideas, " and kept hammering them, until some fellows caught the point and began to build mills " (W. W. Ball, int., Columbia, Jan. 1, 1917). Interviews with Messrs. James Simons and F. Q. O'Neill of Charleston and Tracy I. Hickman, of Augusta, bore out the same point. Cf. Kohn, Cotton Mills of S. C., p. 20.

[109] Cf. South in Building of Nation, vol. xi, p. 271.

[110] Yates Snowden, int., Columbia, S. C., Jan. 1, 1917. I am indebted to Professor Snowden, of Columbia, and to Messrs. W. H. Parker, W. P. Carrington, F. W. Wagener and William M. Bird, of

8

death, being murdered in 1889 by a physician whose office Dawson entered, it is said, in order to resent an affront to an Irish servant girl in his home.[111]

Dawson was not an orator, and had none of the flourish of Grady. Also because his attack was more direct and concentrated than that of his Georgia contemporary, he is not so well known now. Of Dawson as of Grady it may be said: "His influence in exciting hope and inspiring confidence in the ability of the South to cope successfully with her difficulties was immeasurable. . . . 'He did not tamely promote enterprise and encourage industry; he vehemently fomented enterprise and provoked industry until they stalked through the land. . . .' "[112]

The old Baltimore Journal of Commerce in February, 1882, began to devote some pages to industrial development in the South, changing its name to the Journal of Commerce and Manufacturers' Record. In November of the same year the Manufacturers' Record became a separate paper, because "it has been demonstrated that there was an actual need for a paper which would adequately represent the

---

Charleston, for descriptions of Dawson. His picture shows rather curly dark hair, fine, searching eyes, fullish lips, long, somewhat irregular nose and a strong jaw—the face of a thoroughbred.

[111] If Professor Hart has reason for a late statement that the News and Courier "has for its stock-in-trade, ultra and Bourbon sentiments" and "represents an age that is past," such a comment would not apply to the paper's earlier history (p. 70). As a single illustration of its position in the South's critical years, articles written by a member of its staff and reprinted under the title "The Cotton Mills of South Carolina," in this study referred to as "Blackman," with a striking editorial from Dawson, should be examined. How dynamic was the paper's advocacy of industry comes out in the complaint of a manufacturer opposed to the use of the Clement Attachment (a machine which represented the extreme of the doctrine of "Bring Mills to Cotton" in that it accomplished both ginning and spinning), that "the newspapers are assuming a great deal of responsibility in giving it so much notoriety" (Blackman, p. 12).

[112] Dyer, in The New South, pp. 78–79; cf. ibid., p. 128. Grady gave as the text of the Atlanta Constitution: "If the South can keep at home the $400,000,000 it gets annually for its cotton crop, it will soon be rich beyond comprehension. As long as she sends it out for the supplies that make the crop, she will remain poor" (pp. 219–220). In this thinking, however, the News and Courier preceded the Constitution by ten years.

manufacturing interests and would keep abreast of the rapid improvement in the material affairs of the South."[113]

The Manufacturers' Record caught a spirit which had its birth in the heart of the South; as its own words show, it was to "represent" and "keep abreast of" industrial development in the South rather than originate this in the first instance. In its best years it was a useful popularizer of Southern opportunities.[114]

A fundamental cause of the building of cotton mills in the South, really self-evident, was an awakening to the advantage of adding the profits of manufacture to those of production of raw material.[115] Dawson in 1880 put the matter in simple terms:

The point on which we lay the most stress is that, to the extent in which cotton . . . produced in South Carolina is manufactured in the State, the whole of the profit upon that cotton, from the first stage to the last, remains in some form within the State for the benefit of its people. Where the cotton is produced here and manu-

[113] Cf. Baltimore Journal of Commerce and Manufacturers' Record, Nov. 18, 23, 1882.

[114] Cf. Hemphill, in South in Building of Nation, vol. vi, p. 539.

[115] This primary consideration had been explained to an earlier unheeding generation. Gregg said that coarse goods mills in Massachusetts presented "a fact that cannot but strike a cotton planter with great force, viz: *that 174 hands in 12 months, convert 4,329 bales of cotton . . . into cloth . . . thus adding over $40 to the value of each bale*" (Domestic Industry, p. 27 ff.). "Have we not the raw material on the spot, thus saving the freight of a double transportation?" (cf. ibid., pp. 21, 24–25). It was shown a little later that Tennessee cotton planters made only 11½ per cent profit, while manufacturers of the same crop made 24 per cent, and it was asked: "Are there any so blind as not to see the advantages of the system?" (DeBow, vol. i, p. 126). A writer in 1866 quoted an advocate of the "cotton-field system" of manufacture of seventeen years before, who declared that "the spindles and looms must be brought to the cotton fields. This is the true location of this powerful assistant to the grower," and that to bring mills to cotton "is but one move, whilst sending the cotton to the mills is a heavy annual, perpetual tax," and proceeded to estimate how this could be cheaply accomplished (Barbee, The Cotton Question, p. 138 ff.). In 1878 total costs of manufacture in Lowell, Mass., and Augusta, Ga., were shown, leading to the conclusion that in freight, commissions, insurance and exchange the Augusta manufacturer saved $6.62 per bale over his New England competitor on goods shipped to New York, and $10.23 on those sent direct to the West. For Montgomery to double the value of its cotton in this way "is our right, and our duty . . ." (Berney, Handbook of Alabama, p. 271).

factured elsewhere South Carolina is in the position of furnishing the elements which make other communities rich; . . . we know that the wealth of New England is due to the profit made upon the manufacture of the raw material which the South supplies, and which the South . . . buys back from New England at a high price in its manufactured state.[116]

A Southerner speaking at the Atlanta Exposition asked "by what rule of political economy should the Southern people send their cotton at an expense always deducted from its price, to distant sections and foreign countries to the spun and woven . . . ," and told his listeners that "Here the cotton grows up to the doorsteps of your mills, and supply and demand clasp hands. . . ."[117]

---

[116] Leading article, in Blackman. Besides many collateral benefits, the eighteen mills of the State converted cotton worth $1,631,820 into manufactured goods worth $3,932,150. An editorial headed "The Gold in Cotton," said: "At present Charleston does nothing to increase the value of the cotton which comes here for sale. It leaves us as it finds us. The city lives on the pickings and scrapings. . . . Cotton mills change all this. A bale of raw cotton, worth forty dollars, is spun into yarns or cloth worth eighty dollars. There is the usual profit in buying and selling the cotton, and, in addition to this, Charleston gets forty dollars a bale, which goes into our purses and comes out of the pockets of the persons who consume the goods" (News and Courier, Charleston, Feb. 2, 1881).

[117] Ibid., Oct. 10, 1881. " . . . every Southern man is sure to prove to you that it is a dead waste to ship raw cotton to a mill 1,500 miles away when it could be made into yarns and fabrics much cheaper in factories distant from the cotton field only a short half-day's journey for a mule" (Atlanta correspondence of New York Times, quoted in ibid., Nov. 5, 1881). Cf. Richmond Dispatch, quoted in ibid., March 25, 1881. "We have the raw material—New England takes it and augments its value by her labor . . . we, too, must endeavor to mix skill and labor with our raw material before letting it pass from our hands . . ." (Observer, Raleigh, March 2, 1880). Cf. ibid., June 6, 1880; News and Courier, Charleston, April 25, 1881. "Freights were high then; it was a great argument that we saved by manufacturing the cotton here and shipping the goods to the North for just what it cost to send the cotton there" (Charles Estes, int., Augusta). Hammett told a meeting of the South Carolina Agricultural and Mechanical Society: "The South is fitted for the cotton manufacture, which adds profits and value of labor to value of raw material," showed that the South had an advantage of 10 to 20 per cent over New England in the business, and counted the benefit to Southern communities through establishment of mills (News and Courier, Charleston, Aug. 1, 1881). "There is no reason why the South should lose the entire profit upon manufacturing cotton and be content to gain only the beggarly profit of producing it, while England and the North grow rich upon handling it . . ." (Baltimore Journal of Commerce and Manufacturers' Record, Sept.

No one did more to impress this idea upon the South than Tompkins; he presented it in primer-like plainness and from every angle. It is difficult to realize how far this was from a truism to the South even by the time he wrote and spoke.[118]

The question whether the South should manufacture cotton or be content with cultivation of the raw material was made vivid by the opposition to Southern mills on the part of Edward Atkinson, of Boston. It may almost be said that he conducted a propaganda to show that the South should devote itself to raising, ginning and preparing the staple to be spun and woven elsewhere. A talented organizer of business, a not unkindly egotist, officious without being patronizing, gifted in social imagination, and one of the first New Englanders to concern himself actively in a public way with Southern economic affairs after Reconstruction, Atkinson sought, sometimes with semi-private purpose, to mirror the South to itself. The image he furnished, by its very distortion, assisted Southerners to a clearer view of their task. At that peculiar juncture in the South he was listened to attentively, and negatively and positively exerted a striking influence.[119]

2, 1882). Cf. ibid. for quotation of an expressive illustration of this thought; a labored explanation is given in ibid., June 3, 1882.

[118] An ordinary county producing 10,000 bales would get, at 6 cents a pound, $300,000 for its cotton; if sold as cloth at 18 cents, this cotton would bring $900,000. "Assume that this cloth was shipped to China instead of shipping the raw cotton to England and it becomes evident that the English cotton buyer sends here $300,000 while the Chinaman would send $900,000," and he showed how this $600,000 increment would be distributed; that, also, factories would bring other benefits by increasing the value of raw cotton and of farms, creating a market for perishable produce and affording diversity of employment to members of the community (Cotton Mill, Commercial Features, p. 16 ff.). Cf. Observer, Raleigh, May 19, 1880, in comment upon Winston and Durham. Cf. Tompkins, ibid., pp. 23–24, 177–178; History of Mecklenburg, vol. i, p. 24. Tompkins' ingenious little book, "Cotton Values in Textile Fabrics," is an object lesson on this point.

[119] See Who's Who in America, 1906–1907, p. 54. The range of his writings, from the science of nutrition to the cost of war, indicates his ready versatility. He was frequently disingenuous, understanding more than he expressed, but his blunt force compelled notice.

He enters this story when, at the invitation of leading men of city and State, he delivered an address in the senate chamber of the capitol in Atlanta in October, 1880, especially to explain his proposal for the holding of a cotton exposition.[120]   Shortly before he had expressed himself as unable to recommend to the North investments in Southern cotton mills, but entered into no details. This had roused a storm of protest and discussion.[121]   The incident showed, with many others, that Atkinson interested himself in the South a little too late to suit his purpose; the people had already formed a desire for cotton mills that was not easily dispelled. In the speech he had to advert to this, and in its printed form more references were included. He was frank to say, however, that if he were wrong, the proposed exhibition could have no more urgent reason than to demonstrate him mistaken.

In judging his statements it must be remembered that as head of factory mutual fire insurance companies, he was constructively representing New England cotton manufacturers. He said at Atlanta: "The true diversity of employment which makes self-sustaining communities consists of occupations that do not appeal to the imagination like the great cotton factory; but the artisans . . . who work in iron or wood, the stove-maker and the like, the furniture-maker and the tinman, the house-wright, the wagon-builder, the blacksmith, and the whitesmith are the most valuable citizens. The hundred arts that require but little capital and support many men are the ones that, next to the farmer, form the bone and sinew of society. When these are established, the textile factory may well follow, but ought not to precede in any large degree."[122]   Rather than cotton mills, the South should put up shops to make implements, and the manufacture of clothing would give work to women in their own homes. "On the other hand, the most impor-

---

[120] Cf. Address at Atlanta, preface, p. 3.

[121] Ibid., p. 27, and preface, p. 4.

[122] Ibid., p. 28. If factories there must be, then shoe factories required only one-third as much capital per operative as cotton mills.

tant branch of the cotton manufacture—that of ginning, packing, and pressing cotton for the use of the factory— must continue to be done in the South, and every million dollars spent in the right manner in this department will . . . do more to build up the cotton States than any million expended in cotton factories. It is in order that these opportunities for immediate profit may be made apparent that the cotton exhibition should be held."[123] The cotton crop, he declared, was depreciated 10 per cent by careless handling in preparation for shipment to the spinner at the North or abroad. The cotton manufacture is a unit, beginning in the field and ending in the cloth room of the factory, and "if the South desires to enter upon the safest, surest, and most profitable branch of cotton manufacturing" it should confine itself to the initial processes.[124]

He said that Southern spindles could not keep pace with Southern demand, and so Northern manufacturers did not fear Southern competition; he did not see that this demand constituted an encouragement to establishment of Southern mills. He tried to scare the South by enlarging on the supremacy of the New England manufacture and contemplated extensions that were imminent.[125]

---

[123] Ibid., preface, p. 5 ff. Interdependence was the foundation of union between the sections. "The railroad has almost eliminated distance; and each section that serves the other best, serves itself also " (ibid., p. 8).

[124] Ibid., appendix, p. 34 ff.

[125] Ibid., preface, p. 7 ff. He naïvely said it would be greatly to the advantage of New England manufactures "to have a solid body of men in the South interested like themselves in promoting better ginning, baling, and handling cotton as it comes from the field" (ibid.). He made suggestive allusions to possible unsuitableness of Southern climate for cotton spinning (ibid., p. 4 ff.). One would like to attribute to Atkinson nothing less than a national viewpoint in advocating Atlanta as the place for the exposition because it was in the cotton country where the preparation of the staple could best be urged; manufacturing machinery needed no encouragement (ibid., pp. 9–10). He tried to interest the South in the use of ensilage (ibid., p. 28), was working on employment of then wasted by-products of the cotton plant (Bradstreet's, quoted in Baltimore Journal of Commerce and Manufacturers' Record, June 3, 1882), carried attention to the soya bean (Southern Cotton Spinners' Assn., proceed. 7th Annual Convention, p. 102), said there would not be sufficient labor for cotton mills, and that people would prefer out-

When Edward Atkinson and a committee from the New England Cotton Manufacturers' Association visited the Atlanta Exposition the next year, an official statement of their impressions showed that they appreciated most those exhibits having to do with "ginning and preparing" the cotton, and declared the identity of interest between cotton grower and manufacturer were here demonstrated.[126]   In an interview with press representatives he led away from manufacturing, and sought to arouse enthusiasm over the roller as opposed to the saw gin.[127]   In a set address in the exposition building he reiterated these points, feared the real reason why cotton manufactures would not succeed in the South was that most enterprisers did not know how to work on a close margin, did not "know the difference between a cent and a nickel."[128]   He urged rather the building of railroads, the opening of schools and savings banks, development of dairying, and even the importation of Pongee, Tussah or Cheefoo silk worms.[129]

But the purpose of the South had solidified too much to be dissolved by such discouragement or neglect, and, as will presently be seen, an exhibit which was planned by Mr. Atkinson to be primarily agricultural, gave tremendous impetus to the manufacturing of cotton.   Commenting on his

door employment anyway (Address at Atlanta, preface, p. 5 ff.), and that even coarse yarn mills involved risks the South could not take (ibid., pp. 27–28).   He asserted that the approaching exposition "should be rather with a view to the development of tools and implements for the cultivation and for conversion of the plant into its primary forms of fibre, seed, oil, oil-cake, paper stock, and wool, than with a view to the manufacture of cotton fabrics" (ibid., p. 22).   Cf. Southern Cotton Spinner's Assn., proceed. 7th Annual Convention, p. 85 ff.   The seal of the exposition bore a cotton boll but no spindle.

[126] News and Courier, Charleston, Nov. 1, 1881.   The advantage of sending cotton north in the raw state was implied in frequent assertions of Atkinson (cf. Address at Second Annual Fair of New England Manufacturers' and Mechanics' Institute, Boston, 1882, pp. 2, 27–28).

[127] News and Courier, Charleston, Nov. 8, 1881.   Cf. Tompkins, Storing and Manufacturing of Cotton, p. 14.

[128] News and Courier, Charleston, Dec. 5, 1881.   Cf. the writer's "Factors in Future of Cotton Manufacture in South," in Manufacturers' Record, Baltimore, May 10, 1917.

[129] News and Courier, Charleston, Dec. 5, 1881.

exposition speech, an editor said: "Mr. Atkinson is mis-
leading only when invincible prejudice keeps him from seeing clearly, and even Northern newspapers admit that he is
wrong in his belief that cotton manufacturing, on a large
scale, will not pay in the South."[130] H. P. Hammett had
observed a few months earlier: "It is said the South should
plant and prepare the cotton for market, and increase its
value by improved cleaning and ginning appliances (which
in themselves are proper and commendable), and then send
it to the North to be manufactured there, to be returned to
us in goods. . . . I do not impute any . . . selfish motives
to the parties who have thus . . . given their advice, but
. . . I am of opinion that good earned dividends by Southern mills are much more convincing arguments to stockholders than fine spun theories. . . ."[131]

---

[130] News and Courier, Charleston, Dec. 5, 1881.
[131] Ibid., Aug. 1, 1881. It is said that in connection with the founding of Hammett's Piedmont Factory, Atkinson wrote a notice showing how cotton manufacturing in the South could never pay. This
came under the eye of Hammett, who pinned to the clipping his
annual balance sheet, showing a profit of 20 per cent, and sent them
to Atkinson (W. J. Thackston, int., Greenville). Atkinson never
did really give up his campaign. In the section on cotton manufactures of the United States census of manufactures of 1880, written
by him, and transmitted not until 1883, he devoted 6 of the 16 pages
to the preparation of the staple, inveighed against bad ginning and
urged upon the South opportunities for improvement. Twenty years
later he was still on the subject of ginning in talking to the Southern
Cotton Spinners' convention, but the revival of one of his Atlanta
ideas (Address, pp. 18–25), namely, the folding of sheep upon worn-
out cotton uplands, met now with the retort: "Let Massachusetts
successfully grow our 'fleecy staple' in her New England meadows
before she advises us to raise Northern sheep in a Southern cotton
patch" (proceed. 7th Annual Convention, remarks of B. W. Hunt).
Some Southern manufacturers remember well Atkinson's position.
"Edward Atkinson?" rejoined one of these, "He was the man that
didn't believe in Southern cotton mills. He was one of the most
prominent authorities on cotton in his day. He made himself very
obnoxious to our folks by the way he opposed cotton manufacturing
in the South. He just took the wrong turn on it" (W. R. Odell,
int., Concord). And another, who had heard the Bostonian in Atlanta: "Edward Atkinson tried to have an influence in deterring
Southerners from founding cotton mills, but we had our own ideas.
When he talked to a reporter here against Southern mills, I replied
to him in the paper" (Charles Estes, int., Augusta). The very
exposition building, which Atkinson suggested might be taken away
in sections to be used for ginneries or oil mills, was used on the

The International Cotton Exposition, held in Atlanta in the closing months of 1881, occupies a significant place in the history of Southern cotton mills. It accomplished two things: first, it drew together the South's apostles of a new industrial order into confirmatory exchange of views and plans, and afforded concrete, tangible encouragement to already forming aspirations; second, it opened the eyes of the North to the field of investment that lay in the South, breaking down intersectional economic and political barriers of prejudice. From commencement of practical organization of the exposition in December, 1880, it was apparent, in prospectus and executive personnel, that it was to be a more comprehensive undertaking than Edward Atkinson had suggested. Having origin in his mind, it expanded and developed in the hands of others. New England cotton manufacturing machinery makers and mill engineers were included with Southern industrialists and publicists in choice of officials. Not only raising and preparing of raw cotton, but production of cotton goods, was to receive emphasis. The secretary said: "Machinery of all the classes demanded in cultivation . . . and . . . in ginning, baling, packing, and compressing raw cotton, belongs to the first division of machinery exhibits. The machinery requisite for manufacture of cotton, with the best form of mills, the most economical applications of power, and all the details of subsequent manufacture, constitute a great department in which there is a world of interest." The exposition would demonstrate generally that the South had a great future before it, and that, with assistance, it would become "prosperous in its own right through a liberal development of its own resources."[132]

---

spot as a cotton factory. On the gratuitous advice offered to the South "by those interested in preventing manufacturing development," of which Atkinson's must serve here as typical, cf. Thompson, pp. 62–63.

[132] John W. Ryckman, in author's preface of Atkinson's Address at Atlanta, p. 4. Another connected with the exposition gave as part of its purpose: "To exhibit to the Southern people and to visitors from America and Europe the different processes in the manufacture of cotton from the boll to the complete fabric, and by the

That South and North were both ripe for the undertaking is shown by the rapidity with which it was accomplished. The exposition was opened in less than a year after first mention of it, in less than six months after real steps began to be made toward it, and in just 108 days after actual work of erection was begun.[133]

The Atlanta Exposition was not the inception of the industrial idea in the South, but rather its manifestation. It augmented rather than initiated a purpose. Had the South not known its own mind already, Atkinson's attitude might easily have narrowed the exhibits and diminished their usefulness.[134]

The timeliness of the exposition being apparent all along, its influence in stimulating cotton manufacturing and all

---

friction of competition ascertain the best methods and find the best machinery. . . . We people of the South should embrace every opportunity which . . . will bring among us intelligent and interested observers of our industrial condition, resources and aptitudes. We have in the midst of us the raw material . . . of a magnificent prosperity. We lack knowledge, population and capital. These may be slowly accumulated in the course of years, or they may be rapidly by well directed efforts to obtain them from beyond our own borders. We advocate the latter plan" (News and Courier, Charleston, March 14, 1881).

[133] News and Courier, Charleston, Dec. 5, 1881. An Atlanta cotton manufacturer headed the executive committee, a Vermont engineer was made chief of machinery, and agents made tours of investigation through the North and Europe. Subscriptions came simultaneously from North and South; General Sherman started Northern subscriptions with $2000 (ibid., March 8, May 3, 1881). On the opening day, Daniel W. Voorhees, of Indiana, spoke against free trade (ibid., Oct. 6, 1881).

[134] A correspondent in a new mill community wrote: "It is to be hoped the Atlanta Exposition will not take all the enthusiasm out of our capitalists and enterprising men, but that it will only tend to a greater and more speedy development of our resources" (ibid., Oct. 21, 1881). "A good work has been done, the benefits of which will be felt in every part of the country. The New South takes a fresh start at the Atlanta Exposition" (ibid., Oct. 7, 1881). The secretary declared the exposition was pushed through hurriedly because "a knowledge of the South's resources was demanded . . ." (Baltimore Journal of Commerce and Manufacturers' Record, June 24, 1882). Cf. ibid., Oct. 7, 1882. "The Atlanta Exposition . . . was the hopeful and conscious expression of the opening of a new era for Southern industry . . ." (see Clark, in South in Building of Nation, vol. vi, pp. 280–281). Visitors to the exposition "were convinced that 'an industrial revolution had actually been effected in the South . . .'" (see Hammond, pp. 328–329). Cf. Copeland, pp. 32–33; Goldsmith, pp. 4–5.

industrial development was quickly evidenced.[135]   The new statesmen of the South, industrially and not politically minded, found voice.[136]   Hints and hopes became certainties. "When the Atlanta Exposition closed . . . it began to be realized that the South was awakened to a new life. . . . Intelligence was to take the place of ignorance in methods of cultivation; machinery was to take the place of hand labor; manufacturing was to take the place of exporting raw material and bringing back the manufactured article. . . . Capital began to see the rich rewards waiting to be won, and prepared to occupy the vantage ground."[137]

Many of the exhibits were sold during the exposition, and orders taken to the amount of $2,000,000.[138]   When

[135] A manufacturer remembers that operatives from his mill who visited the exposition brought back small-pox, four hundred cases resulting. But Atlanta spread other and more salutary infection as well. Another's dominant recollection is that "they had a great deal of eastern machinery there, with men sent along to operate it" (Charles Estes, int., Augusta).

[136] Cf. letter of A. J. Russell in Baltimore Journal of Commerce and Manufacturers' Record, July 15, 1882.

[137] "W. B. C.," in Baltimore Journal of Commerce and Manufacturers' Record, Oct. 7, 1882. David R. Francis ("The Influence of Agricultural and Industrial Fairs and Expositions on the Economic Development of the South since 1865," in South in Building of Nation, vol. vi, p. 568 ff.), does not mention the Atlanta Exposition of 1881, and apparently is unacquainted with its meaning. He attributes to the New Orleans Exposition of 1884–1885 a significance that belongs to the earlier effort. "Not all the books and papers and speeches that man can produce would do the South as much good in half a century as the single event of the Atlanta Exposition did last year. . . . The cotton spindles of the south will increase year by year until the river cities will resound with the music . . . and the old battle-fields are the scenes of a great industrial revival" (Boston Economist, quoted in Baltimore Journal of Commerce and Manufacturers' Record, Sept. 30, 1882). The whole lesson of the exposition was expressed when "the governor of Georgia appeared on the grounds dressed in a comfortable suit of cottonade manufactured on the premises from cotton picked from the bolls the same day in sight of the spectators." Cf. Goldsmith, pp. 4–5, on this episode and the influence of the exposition generally; U. S. Census of Manufactures, 1890, "Cotton Manufactures," by Edward Stanwood, pp. 28–29.

[138] Baltimore Journal of Commerce and Manufacturers' Record, Sept. 23, 1882. In Atlanta itself in the year following the exposition two cotton mills began operations, one in the exposition building itself; plow works were greatly enlarged; a cotton seed cleaner company increased output; bridge builders extended their business; a cotton compress was erected; a company to manufacture a cotton

the Atlanta Exposition closed, some of its exhibits were moved to Charleston and formed the nucleus of an industrial display there.[139] Other fairs were projected more widely than achieved, but the North Carolina industrial exhibit, at Raleigh, in 1884, carried on the Atlanta spirit and made it local to the State in a way that assisted cotton mill growth. Northern machinery manufactures sent equipment that was manned by North Carolina operatives.[140] An exposition unsuccessfully urged for Baltimore, to have been held the same year, borrowed incentive from benefits derived by the city of Atlanta; there was the idea of capturing leadership of an advance which had been born to the South in a more generous impulse.[141] William Gregg in 1845 had instanced for Charleston the appropriate lesson of the way in which leading propertyholders of Newburyport, Massachusetts, when the shipping of the place deserted in favor of Boston and the town was going to ruin, determined to make an effort to resuscitate its prosperity by establishing cotton manufactures with steam power. "It acted like a charm. The three or four establishments put in operation, have all done well and produced a new state of things." So it might be, he showed, not only with Charleston, but with Augusta, Columbia and

---

planter commenced building; a cotton seed oil mill was erected and other enterprises went forward (ibid., Sept. 30, 1882). "In six months after the exhibition closed, $2,000,000 had been invested in manufacturing enterprises in that city of only 40,000 inhabitants, all of which was directly traceable to the exhibition" (ibid., Oct. 21, 1882). Cf. ibid., June 24, 1882.

[139] Cf. News and Courier, Charleston, Jan. 1, and for month of February, 1882.

[140] W. R. Odell, int., Concord.

[141] "The rapid development of the South in all her material interests has been the wonder of the age, and yet the past is but the harbinger of the future. Baltimore now has the opportunity of placing herself at the head of this grand Southern movement, and thus so closely allying herself with the South as to be ever afterwards the recognized centre of the commercial and manufacturing affairs of that section. Will she do it? The answer must come from our business community and upon it will depend the future of Baltimore" (Baltimore Journal of Commerce and Manufacturers' Record, Sept. 23, 1882). Cf. ibid., June 10, 17, July 1, 22, Oct. 1, 14, Nov. 11, 1882; Feb. 1, 1883.

other points at the South.[142]   More than any other man of
his time, he understood the public benefits resulting from
industry, especially cotton manufactures, and held these to
constitute a prime reason for building mills.[143]   An advocate of rural cooperative credit associations in the South,
believed that prosperous men, though not themselves needing aid, would take hold of the scheme from "philanthropic
motives which always animate the minds of a large proportion of the well-to-do citizens of any country, stimulating
them to efforts in behalf of the community in which they
live."[144]   And one who knew the South said of Southerners

---

[142] Domestic Industry, p. 30.   He lamented that Charleston's large
surplus of dormant wealth was not directed to internal improvements in South Carolina instead of seeking Wall Street (Speech on
Blue Ridge Railroad, pp. 6–7, 29), and urged that limited liability
be granted to industrial corporations which might thus lay small
investors under tribute for the building up of the State (Propriety
of Granting Charters of Incorporation, pp. 4–11).

[143] An earlier manifestation has been alluded to. "About 1833,
following the agitation against the tariff, several companies for
manufacturing cotton were organized from patriotic and political
rather than from purely commercial motives" (see Clark, in South
in Building of Nation, vol. v, pp. 321–322).

[144] Hammond, pp. 203–204. "Probably no better field for the
exercise of such motives could be found than among the large
planters of the South.   Long accustomed to leadership in all the
political, business and social affairs of the community, imbued with
a spirit of helpfulness which their control over the . . . earthly
destiny of others taught them to exercise during slavery days, taught
finally by their own discouragements during the years of reconstruction how bitter is the curse of poverty, these men would not lack
. . . the willingness to help their poorer neighbors along the road
to . . . industrial independence."   Murphy wrote that the Old South
in the New South "chiefly . . . has maintained . . . the old sense
of responsibility toward the unprivileged," and that it is this "quick
sense of social obligation," this "local conscience," which has given
"distinction and beauty to the allegiance between the aristocracy
and the common people" (p. 16 ff.).   "Coöperation . . . is the very
spirit of democracy—concern for the common good, not only feeling
that I am my brother's keeper, but more—I am my brother's brother.
We have at last awakened to the fact that the whole is greater than
the part.   Too often heretofore we have thought of a social class, a
segment of interests. . . . But a better day is dawning when we are
alike embracing in our affections the whole people, the lowly no less
than the lofty . . ." (S. C. Mitchell, in South Mobilizing for Social
Service, pp. 50–51).   Sir Horace Plunkett has recognized that the
pioneers of England's industrial preeminence "have been often
actuated as much by patriotic motives as by the desire for gain"
(pp. 153–154).

that "they are not only demonstrative; they really care for one another in most affectionate ways. Helpfulness is not an act of conscience: it is an impulse."[145]

Understanding the straits of the South at the opening of the cotton mill era, the readiness of Southern men to realize and assume responsibility in public matters, and the spirit of social service which characterized the awakening to a program of "Real Reconstruction," one accepts as natural the fact that cotton manufactories were frequently motivated by the desire to help a community to its feet. Often this wish was joined, and very properly so, with usual commercial promptings, but sometimes it controlled alone.

The organization of the Charleston Manufacturing Company with a purpose to give work to poor people of the city will be spoken of presently; this company gives admirable illustration of conception of a cotton mill with a plan of general civic betterment. It typified the concern of Charleston for the welfare of the whole State, a concern which, when finally manifest, answered to Gregg's utmost solicitude.[146] A notice supplementing an advertisement of the Charleston Manufacturing Company at the time it was soliciting subscriptions concluded: "The advantages, direct and incidental, accruing to every citizen of Charleston from this industry about to be started in our city are so manifest that those who have inaugurated the enterprise have every reason to feel confident of a ready response to the call for capital and of abundant success."[147]

---

[145] Page, pp. 111–112. Cf. John Skelton Williams, The Billion Arrives, pp. 16–17; Manufacturers' Record, Baltimore, April 19, 1917, suggestion for non-interest-bearing bonds to meet war expenditure.

[146] Such cities, in "the heroism with which they meet the daily and the extraordinary crises that time brings . . . leaven the nation of which they are a part" Hemphill, quoted in Kohn, Charleston: Condensation of Jubilee Industrial Edition of News and Courier, p. 15). Charleston invested in South Carolina cotton mills that surplus of bank capital which Gregg had seen going to other quarters, and was largely responsible for incitement to an industrial movement that witnessed the purchase of used machinery from mills at Newburyport, Mass., perhaps the very spindles that Gregg had pointed to as building up the New England city.

[147] News and Courier, Charleston, Jan. 27, 1881; cf. ibid., Jan. 28,

In 1868, Messrs. Sprague, Rhode Island manufacturers, undertook to develop the water power at Columbia, but failed; the property passed to the State Canal commission, and some Columbians contributed to the employment of an engineer to push the work. In February, 1880, the development was taken over by a firm of Providence engineers with a liberal State franchise, but this scheme also failed. When capitalists of Columbia bought the rights they set forth that " The work . . . is one of great magnitude and involves expenditure beyond the ability of this community. Nor is the interest merely local, but reaches out to every part of the State. We call, therefore, upon all . . . to take part in this . . . central development. . . ."[148]

The inception of the first mill at Gaffney has been mentioned. This was distinctly a community enterprise, inspired and pushed through principally by one man with the object of the good of the little town. A Tennessee mountaineer, he had come to Gaffney working on the railroad, and stayed. There was little enough in the place to attract anyone, but he held high hopes for its development. His spirituel face with fine eyes, a dreaminess in his easy movements, a vigor that resides nowhere and everywhere in him, indicate how in spite of the most restricted resources, he possesses capacity that built cotton mills out of hand. As a contractor he was working in a mill village near his town. " At Clifton I'd see the hands paid off, the amount of money they spent. I was convinced that stockholders wouldn't go into

---

1881. One of the chief movers in this mill, when it had failed and manufacturing was to be revived in the old plant by a new company, received from a fellow citizen a note thanking him " in the name of the public generally, for being instrumental . . . in directing Mr. Montgomery's attention to the Mill. It means much for Charleston, and is only another of your constant and inspiring efforts for the public material advancement of our city. A hundred men like yourself would ' save the city.' "

[148] News and Courier, Charleston, March 25, 1881. Cf. ibid., March 18, 1881; Blackman, p. 9. " The capital, *because it was the capital*, was laid in ashes by Sherman's troops. In the person of Columbia, all South Carolina was ravaged. . . . The city which suffered so sorely may reasonably expect the just assistance of the State . . ." (News and Courier, Jan. 25, 1882).

such a large thing unless it paid them to. The first week-end I could get away, I went back to Gaffney and had a talk with some of the leading citizens, and tried to and finally did persuade them that to establish a mill here would build up the town and pay good dividends." He was not discouraged that Gaffney had no water power like Clifton, and resolved to make steam answer. The head of a little bank was elected president of the mill company, $50,000 was subscribed to stock and a charter applied for. The local banker visited a New York bank to ask for cooperation, but returned deeply discouraged. Others lost interest, but the original promoter would not. He sought to interest the president of the mill at Clifton in the Gaffney enterprise, and received confirmation of his beliefs that he could succeed, but no active support. He next attacked the superintendent of the mill at Clifton, sat with him many nights to persuade him to come to Gaffney with money and experience and head the venture, and finally succeeded.[149]

Notices of ceremonies held when a mill commenced operation convey sometimes touchingly the pride of a community in the plant and the public character of the enterprise. Townspeople were like children with a very precious new toy; newspapers described the arrangement of the machinery in the factory with the keenest interest.[150]

The potency of associative effort, so marked in Southern cotton mill building in this period, overcame timidity that might have been prompted by a frank and individual canvass of attending economic facilities. "The mill at Albemarle, North Carolina, had its origin in the desire of the Efirds to have a mill at the town. Whether there existed real advantages or not, the people would make it appear that there were advantages for that particular location. Many mills were located at places where there was the spirit for them, rather than where they would be, economically,

[149] L. Baker, int., Gaffney.
[150] Cf. Chronicle and Constitutionalist, Augusta, Feb. 23, 1882; Chronicle, Augusta, Nov. 11, 1883.

9

most successful."[151]   A Marylander knowing the industry thoroughly said there was little community interest in his State, but that "down South the community interest was very strong. Every little town wanted a mill. If it couldn't get a big one, it would take a small one; if not a sheeting, then a spinning mill."[152]

[151] J. L. Hartsell, int., Concord. "But with any kind of management in the first years of their rise they made money, because there was no competition to require close figuring." Cf. Plunkett, p. 186.

[152] Summerfield Baldwin, Sr., int., Baltimore. A mill investor of long experience believes that "usually community good played a larger part than monetary gain in the founding of a cotton mill" (Theodore Klutz, int., Salisbury). "One mill would encourage another, but the greatest factor in the growth of cotton mills in the South was community pride" (C. S. Morris, int., Salisbury, N. C., Sept. 1, 1916). The story of the building of a mill in South Carolina, told by a participant, is typical. "The town had a population of about 2500. It was stagnant, on no trunk line of railroad. Perhaps only one man in the place was worth as much as $100,000. There had been talk of building a mill; a retired business man, with no manufacturing experience, had tried and failed. Mr. X., living in Spartanburg, had been in charge of a small iron concern. He was an experienced cotton buyer and, though not wealthy, had great ability. He came to our town and announced to gentlemen there that if the local people would take $75,000 in stock he would get up the rest of the money for a 15,000-spindle mill. This offered a ray of hope. This was throwing out a rope to us. Many men saw a chance of getting a job out of it. But in the town and county generally a tremendous effort was made. The largest subscription was $2000. By raking with a fine-tooth comb they got the pledges for $75,000. The average man at first didn't give a thought to dividends. He was thinking of building up the town. I was running a country newspaper, and took $300 in stock because I thought it would give me increased circulation and job work. Every merchant thought he would get some trade by it. There were some who hadn't even an indirect motive, who just wanted to see the town grow." And again, another said: "Captain S. E. White was about as near the type of the old plantation head as South Carolina has had since the war. He had 4000 acres under cultivation, under his direct supervision. Fort Mill was just a hamlet in 1887. He wanted to see it become a town, so he started a cotton mill in it" (William Banks, int., Columbia, S. C., Jan. 2, 1917). "Colonel R. L. Mc-Caughril, a banker in Newberry, was the leading spirit in the town. He wanted to see the place grow, so he started a mill" (ibid.). The same was true of the Orr Mill at Anderson. Cf. Charlotte News, Textile Ed., 1917, respecting McAden Mills. "Town pride played an important rôle. The cotton mill was looked upon as a dynamo to effect changes in all departments of life in a community" (Sterling Graydon, int., Charlotte, N. C., Sept. 4, 1916). A commission merchant said: "As a rule the starters of mills got all classes of people to take stock. Usually eight or ten of the leading men of

"A good deal of patriotism developed," said a not impressionable mill man, "and every town would vie with others in building mills. Some people took stock and sold it at a discount when it was apparent that the mill would be operated. They were willing to give so much to secure the mill for the town."[153] There is no stronger indication of the different spirit characterizing the building of mills in the eighties as contrasted with earlier periods than the fact that after 1880 many plants were located within the corporate limits of towns and cities. In the earlier enterprises community spirit had not counted, and even the mills of the seventies, such as Piedmont, were taken to the water powers.[154] Eager discussion as to the comparative advantages of water and steam power marked this transition. From being an excuse for the town, the cotton mill came to be erected to invigorate a place that was languishing. It has been said that at least half the South Carolina mills were community enterprises. Later, when the commercial spirit was more pronounced, factories were built just outside the corporation to escape town taxes.[155]

In the case of some investors with whom assistance to the town was an indirect motive, the creation of a payroll,

---

the town could be got to serve on the board—doctors, merchants, lawyers, planters. There would be one leading man who would take the thing up and push it through. He would come to see us. Everybody would want the mill" (Summerfield Baldwin, Sr., int., Baltimore). "What did the lawyer, doctor or fertilizer man know about running a mill? Yet it got to the point where, if he were prominent in the town and did not become a cotton mill president, he lost his social position. Of course, he couldn't do that" (W. J. Thackston, int., Greenville). George A. Gray, as a mill expert, organized and built some factories and managed them only until they were running smoothly, having been drawn in by an inexperienced community (G. A. Gray, Jr., and J. Lander Gray, int., Gastonia, N. C., Sept. 14, 1916).

[153] E. A. Smyth, int., Greenville, S. C., Sept. 12, 1916.
[154] In 1880 Camperdown was the only factory in South Carolina within the corporate limits of a city (Blackman, p. 13). But this, like the Enterprise Factory at Augusta, was on a water power (Augusta Trade Review, Oct., 1884).
[155] Cf. News and Courier, Charleston, Jan. 28, 1881. For the pros and cons of county versus town location, cf. Tompkins, Cotton Mill, Commercial Features, pp. 34-35. The building of cotton mills to help towns was entirely sincere; contrast Clark, in South in Building of Nation, vol. vi, pp. 273-274.

putting more money in circulation, was the causal stimulus.
An editorial recommended the Charleston Manufacturing
Company "as a means of enlarging the common income.
. . . The employment given to hundreds of persons . . .
will increase the value of house-property at once. They
who earn nothing can't spend much. It was calculated last
year that every $228 invested in cotton manufactures in
South Carolina supported one person. . . . It is evident that
the building of half-a-dozen cotton factories would revolu-
tionize Charleston. Two or three million dollars additional
poured annually into the pockets of the shopkeepers . . .
would make them think that the commercial millennium
had come."[156]

To give employment to the necessitous masses of poor
whites, for the sake of the people themselves, was an object
animating the minds of many mill builders. One does not
have to go outside the ranks of cotton manufacturers to
find denials of this, but a study of the facts shows how frequent and normal was the philanthropic incentive.[157]   It

---

[156] News and Courier, Charleston, Jan. 28, 1881. Leroy Springs
wanted a payroll at Lancaster, so built a mill (William Banks, int.,
Columbia). "The thing that built most mills was the fact that the
business men of the town wanted the increased payroll. There is
an annual payroll of $2,000,000 in Greenville today, and it was
this result to which the town looked in the establishment of mills"
(W. J. Thackston, int., Greenville). A textile editor went so far
as to say that "the principal cause of the cotton mills of the South
was that the people had to be given something to do; it was desired
to create a payroll" (David Clark, int., Charlotte).

[157] The genuineness of altruism as a motive in the Cotton Mill
Campaign is supported by observation of Southern character in
other particulars and especially as operative in this period. "It is
only when a people, united by a common suffering and bearing a
common burden, are overheard in their converse with one another,
it is only when the South speaks freely to the South, that one may
catch that real spirit of *noblesse oblige* which has so largely dominated the development of Southern life" (Murphy, p. 7). Answering the statement that North Carolinians were very conservative, an
acquainted speaker recalled how one enthusiastic New England
woman induced the State to spend for an asylum for the insane at
one time a larger sum than the whole annual resources of the Commonwealth. "Our whole history is full of such incidents. Almost
every noteworthy thing that we have done has been done in obe-
dience to an impulse. Conservative? We are the most impulsive
people imaginable" (Page, pp. 9–10). The South had recently gone

will be noticed in another chapter how important with Gregg had been the plan to afford work to natives desperately needing support.[158] The South might have learned its duty, too, from the kindly admonitions of a Rhode Islander, Senator James. He was thirty years in advance of the section when he wrote:

But it is not only the benefit to be derived in a direct manner to the individual manufacturer, that holds out a strong inducement to the South to go largely into the business—nor yet, alone, the prospect of enriching a community as a body. Motives of philanthropy and humanity enter into the calculation, and these should not be disregarded. This is a subject on which, though it demands attention, we would speak with delicacy. It is not to be disguised . . . that a degree and extent of poverty and destitution exist in the southern states, among a certain class of people, almost unknown in the manufacturing districts of the North. . . . The writer has no disposition to reproach the wealthy for the existence of such a state of things. He is well aware that it is the result of circumstances which have to them been unavoidable. But he cannot resist the conviction that, when a fitting opportunity presents itself to the wealthy men of the South to obviate these evils . . . and that even in a way to benefit themselves, they can hardly be held guiltless in case of refusal or neglect to apply the remedy.[159]

Hammett, in his Piedmont mill of the seventies, very regardful of his responsibility toward his unfortunate fellows, anticipated by a few years the action of many factory projectors.[160] Sentiment must be strong to find place in an

---

through so much misery that the body politic was closely knit; calculations of commerce were for the time relaxed, and leaders were thinking for the whole people. Cf. Lewis G. Janes, "The Economic Value of Altruism," in Social Economist, July, 1893, p. 16. As to the effect of the Civil War in rousing the South to extraordinary measures, cf. Andrews, pp. 340–341.

[158] To the stockholders of his Graniteville Mill he said: "We may really regard ourselves as the pioneers in developing the character of the poor people of South Carolina," and he called the factory village an asylum for widows and orphans and families brought to ruin (see Kohn, Cotton Mills of S. C., p. 21).

[159] "I . . . appeal to the planter of the South, as well as to every other capitalist. Let your attachment to your interest and the interests of the community, united with love for your species, combine to stimulate you to enter, with resolution, this field of enterprise . . ." (quoted in DeBow, vol. i, p. 241).

[160] Samuel Stradley, int., Greenville, S. C., Sept. 12, 1916. It has been pertinently said of the years following 1880: "There was no thought . . . in those times, with regard to who should work or how many hours they should work. The problem was not one of seeking

advertisement soliciting subscriptions to stock, yet the Charleston Manufacturing Company frankly said: "The necessity of establishing manufactures in our city, not only as a profitable means of utilizing capital, but more especially for furnishing employment to many in our midst, has been long felt. To put this matter into practical operation, a few gentlemen applied to the last Legislature and obtained a most favorable charter. . . ."[161]   A committee of the State Agricultural Society of Georgia recommended the Clement Attachment to planters with capital as "furnishing means of support to needy and worthy people, to wit, women and children principally," and as keeping at home money "to give comfort and support to the planting community."[162]

No undertaking was born more emphatically in the impulse to furnish work than the Salisbury Cotton Mills. All the circumstances of the founding of this factory were

---

or creating wealth; it was essentially one of employment, of human welfare in the sense of providing instrumentalities by the use of which men, women and children could earn a livelihood. The exigent demand for the bare necessaries of life, which could be gotten in the cotton mills of that period only by the combined toil of the whole family, overshadowed all other considerations. Literally it was a question of 'bread and meat,' and the mills provided work for thousands who could not otherwise subsist" (R. Charlton Wright, in Columbia Record, Textile Ed., 1917). Cf. the writer's "End of Child Labor," in Survey, Aug. 23, 1919. "There was much in the humanitarian movement. People saw that the cotton mill man was a benefactor. Unlike the profit of the bank, his money went to feed the poor people. This contagion spread and had a great deal to do with the building of mills" (G. W. Ragan, int., Gastonia, N. C., Sept. 14, 1916).

[161] News and Courier, Charleston, Jan. 27, 1881. One inquiring among surviving incorporators of this enterprise is told today that "our idea in starting the company was that there were many people here who wanted work, needed it" (W. P. Carrington, int., Charleston, Dec. 27, 1916).

[162] Observer, Raleigh, Aug. 24, 1880. "Aside from purely mercenary considerations," said an appeal to Charlestonians to take stock in mills at Columbia, ". . . is the incalculable benefit to be derived from the employment of thousands of unwilling idlers . . . in the State, the women and girls for whom it is so hard to find healthful and profitable work" (News and Courier, Charleston, April 13, 1881). It must be remembered that whites, particularly women, could not compete with negroes in certain occupations, and in "servile" ones would not.

singularly in keeping with the philanthropic prompting. The town of Salisbury, North Carolina, in 1887 had done nothing to recover from the war. It was full of saloons, wretched, unkempt. It happened that an evangelistic campaign was conducted; Mr. Pearson, remembered as a lean, intense Tennesseean, preached powerfully. A tabernacle was erected for the meeting, which lasted a month and, being undenominational, drew from the whole town and countryside. The evangelist declared that the great morality in Salisbury was to go to work, and that corruption, idleness and misery could not be dispelled until the poor people were given an opportunity to become productive. The establishment of a cotton mill would be the most Christian act his hearers could perform. "He gave Salisbury a moral dredging which made the people feel their responsibilities as they had not before, and made them do something for these folks. There had been little talk of manufacturing before Pearson came; there had been some tobacco factories in the town, but they had failed. The Salisbury Cotton Mills grew out of a moral movement to help the lower classes, largely inspired by this campaign. Without the moral issue, the financial interest would have come out in the long run, but the moral considerations brought the matter to a focus."[163]

---

[163] O. D. Davis, int., Salisbury, N. C., Sept. 1, 1916. Cf. Page, p. 12 ff.; U. S. Census of Manufactures, 1880, "Factory System," by Carroll D. Wright, pp. 4–5. The spirit of that evangelistic campaign still rests upon those all along connected with the enterprise. Mr. Davis remarked the fact that three ministers of Salisbury were prominently connected with the inception of the mill. One of them, Mr. Murdock, was its secretary and treasurer and later president. The first minute-book shows how closely connected were preacher and manufacturer, even in point of time. An account copied into it from the North Carolina Herald (the local paper) of Nov. 9, 1887, headed "The Cotton Factory," says: "Mr. Pearson, in a lecture yesterday afternoon, dwelt upon the fact that the great many poor . . . people we have here ought to be and must be helped not by gifts and alms but by a chance to make an honest living. That a cotton factory would be the remedy. Pursuant to these urgent appeals a large number of citizens gathered this morning in the Warehouse and organized by calling upon Rev. F. J. Murdock to act as chairman. . . . Mr. Murdock, in strong, eloquent, and earnest words pointed out that it had almost become a necessity to build a

Mr. Murdock seems to have been the chief local inspirator of the mill at Salisbury; before the factory was built he had established a building and loan association. A very similar case is that of Dr. Jacobs at Clinton, South Carolina. He found that the sodden little town needed to have industry preached to it. He inspired a merchant to build a cotton mill, took the lead in urging improvements for the community, and succeeded in founding an orphanage, funds of which were invested in manufactories of Clinton.

On the whole, North Carolina was probably later in responding to the philanthropic impulse than South Carolina. The local Democratic press censured a North Carolina congressman, an Independent, in 1886 for a speech urging mills as means of employment of poor people, because this was opposed to the interest of the farmer.[164] Yet a factory was built in the suburbs of Raleigh the next year partly with this purpose.[165]

As late as 1902 a representative manufacturer declared that although negro labor was feasible, abundant, and would be cheapest, the managements " have recognized the

---

cotton mill here to help the poor whites, quoting the Hon. J. S. Henderson's words—that next to religion Salisbury needed a cotton factory. Rev. J. Rumple, D.D., seconded Mr. Murdock's appeal. He said that he knew so well the appealing condition of the poor whites of our town and that a cotton factory would be a sufficient remedy. Mr. I. H. Faust urged three reasons for the building of a mill. 1. Increased general prosperity of the town. 2. Benevolence and charity in giving the poor a chance to earn a living. 3. Cotton mills pay a handsome interest to investors." Others spoke of the profits of all Southern mills, of the health of Salisbury as an asset, and " Maj. S. W. Cole, the veteran advocate of cotton mills, spoke earnestly and fervently in favor of the undertaking." A committee appointed to solicit subscriptions met the same afternoon. Subsequent items show that by Dec. 15 organization was complete, some $60,000 having been locally subscribed, and a successful manufacturer in Concord, nearby, who was consulted in the enterprise, being elected president.

One director was a minister; the others were pillars in Salisbury churches. " The mill was religion-pervaded from the outset." It was decided at the start not to have a company store, thrift has been consistently encouraged in the operatives, the mill has never run at night (Theodore Klutz, int., Salisbury). Especially through Mr. Murdock's influence, several boys growing up in the mill have become ministers (Charlotte News, Textile Ed., 1917).

164 John Nichols, int., Raleigh.
165 A. A. Thompson, int., Raleigh.

fact that the mill life is the only avenue open today to our poor whites, and we have with earnestness and practically without exception kept that avenue open to the white man alone" to provide an escape from competition with the blacks.[166]

It has been seen that the spirit for manufacture in the South was born pretty much irrespective of the direction which activity was to take. Bearing this in mind, if one were asked what inspirited cotton mills, he would probably answer first, "Presence of the raw material." There is everything to commend this reply. In the beginning Southerners did not reason out all the implications of their thus setting up cotton factories in cotton fields. If success attended the pressing present, this was enough. Moreover, New Englanders, as noticed in the case of Edward Atkinson, more able to calculate upon the future, sought often to discourage a movement which they realized portended danger for their section as the principal American seat of the industry, and in this way the outlook of the South was clouded. Ten years after the opening of the period, however, a writer could put the matter plainly, justifying the South's best hopes and rebuking New England's dissimulation by saying: "The ultimate transfer of the cotton industry from New England to the South may be regarded as an inevitable consequence of industrial development, which should be neither feared nor prevented. . . . There is no more reason why cotton cloth should be manufactured in Lancashire than why cucumbers should be raised in Iceland."[167]

---

[166] See testimony of Lewis W. Parker, Hearing before Committee of Judiciary, House of Representatives, April 29, 1902, p. 11 ff. This statement would bear some modification today. Perhaps at the outset some saw in the cotton mills not just the means of immediate employment, but the first step toward a better grade of work. Until the present these have been disappointed (W. W. Ball, int., Columbia, Jan. 1, 1917). These well-wishers of the operatives have not been willing to accept continued evidences of philanthropy in welfare work for the more wholesome self-help to be gained when Southern mill hands, like successive generations in New England, assisted by a greater diversity of industry in the section, reach out to more skilled employments.

[167] Social Economist, May, 1891, p. 152 ff. On the purpose of

From the outset, though, convinced of the strength of its position, the South put by hypocritical gratuities: "Sir, it matters not what anyone may say to the contrary, common sense tells us that other things—machinery, skilled labor, motive power, and facilities of shipment—being equal, a cotton factory in the midst of cotton fields must prove more profitable than the same concern a thousand miles from the base of supply could possibly be."[168]   "Leave it to the North to make the finer, lighter and fancy goods," Hammett counselled. "Their manufacture will come South in due time if it should be desirable to make them. . . . We need have no fear of competition in making the heavy goods from the North. They will never build another mill there to make them."[169]

English manufacturers to build mills at the South, cf. C. C. Baldwin, quoted in News and Courier, Charleston, July 11, 1881. The South was not entirely without similar penetration much earlier. Of E. M. Holt, manufacturing in North Carolina long before the war, it is said that "To him it seemed a geographical and economical inconsistency and perversity that this staple should be carried thousands of miles from the place of its growth to be made into cloth, much of which was to be brought back . . . to clothe the very people who had produced it; . . . he foresaw that not Manchester, not New England, but the South was to control the cotton industry of the world" (Martin H. Holt, in Biographical Hist. of N. C., vol. vii, pp. 182–183). A New Englander said of the South, also before the war: "As respects all raw materials, especially that of a bulky character, economy dictates that, all other things being equal, they should be wrought on the spot on which they are produced. . . . There may be some exceptions to this rule, but . . . there is none in favor of the transportation of cotton to a distant market" (Charles T. James, in DeBow, vol. ii, p. 236 ff.). Cf. Olmsted, pp. 165, 542–543. Atkinson in 1880, though speaking especially for New England, really put the case for the South when he said that "the supremacy in the art of converting cotton into cloth must ultimately fall to that country or section which possesses . . . proximity to the source of raw material" (U. S. Census of Manufactures, Cotton Manufacture, p. 8). For clear statements in the South in 1880, cf. Blackman, p. 14, and prefactory leading article.

[168] See Gannon, p. 6 ff. Later, Grady declared. "The industries of other sections—distant from the source of supply—may be based on artificial conditions that may in time be broken. But the industrial system of the South is built on a rock—and it cannot be shaken!" (pp. 206–207). Cf. ibid., p. 80 ff.

[169] Quoted in Manufacturers' Record, Baltimore, Feb. 1, 1883. "The water powers are located in the midst of the cotton fields, from which a large part of the cotton consumed may be purchased direct from the producer and delivered at the mills. . . . A very

Nor did some Northern papers at this time fail to recognize the superiority of Southern manufactories in possession of the raw material. "They have the advantage of cotton location, and, when they have secured new and improved machinery, will do an unrivalled business."[170] The pertinence of such recognition was admitted by New England manufacturers in deed if not in word. Their appeal for lower freight rates " on account of the growing opposition of Southern cotton mills . . . was a plea of weakness. . . . The manufacturers of New England would do well to heed the advice of the New York Times . . . and give up the attempt to compete with Southern mills on coarse goods."[171]

Many factories were built right in the cotton fields, just

---

material advantage is that it comes direct from the gins, is clean, has not been compressed for shipment . . . and as a consequence works here infinitely . . . easier . . ." (ibid., quoted in News and Courier, Charleston, Aug. 1, 1881). " Among the public enterprises which have been started in Memphis during the past twelve months none have attracted more . . . interest than the ' Pioneer Cotton Mill.' . . . . With the great staple at our doors it does seem strange that it should be sent to the Eastern States or to Europe to be manufactured into goods that will be sent back here for sale at a handsome profit" (Memphis Avalanche, quoted in Manufacturers' Record, Baltimore, Dec. 28, 1882). Cf. ibid., Dec. 14, 1882, March 8, 1883.

[170] Manufacturer and Industrial Gazette, Springfield, Mass., quoted in News and Courier, Charleston, Feb. 3, 1881. " They can save freights, buy cheaper and hire cheaper labor. They save buyer's commission, and warehouse delivery and cartage, sampling, classing, pressing, shipping, marine risks, and freight and carriage to interior towns, which amounts in all to some seven dollars per bale. . . . This makes a tax of eighteen per cent which Fall River pays in competition with Columbus. . . . As yet the South manufactures principally coarser goods . . . but the time is not far distant when it will come to make prints, cambrics, laces, and all the finer qualities of staple goods." Cf. Philadelphia Record, quoted in News and Observer, Raleigh, Dec. 16, 1880. By 1882 it was being said that Northern mills must make fabrics of higher grade or go out of existence. " Much invested capital will have to be sunk, much good machinery cast aside, and much acquired skill regarded as useless; but there can be no wisdom in hesitating to make the sacrifice when the refusal to make it means ruin at any rate" (Textile Record, Philadelphia, quoted in Baltimore Journal of Commerce and Manufacturers' Record, Oct. 28, 1882). Cf. Boston Commercial Bulletin, quoted in ibid., Sept. 23, 1882; April 5, 1883.

[171] Manufacturers' Record, Baltimore, March 29, 1883. Cf. a reference to a protest to the Massachusetts legislature against a 58-hour bill in 1890, in Social Economist, May, 1891, p. 159.

as saw mills are placed in the woods. The Woodlawn and Lawrence mills, at Lowell, North Carolina, even conducted their own cotton plantation.[172]   Although a water power mill at Cedar Falls, in the same State, had the disadvantage that its product must be hauled twenty-seven miles to High Point, most of the raw cotton was bought loose from the field.[173]   A cotton planter built a factory at Enterprise, Mississippi, which took cotton loose from the gin.[174]

Founders of the industry and others expressed the pre-eminence in the mind of mill builders of proximity to cotton.   "There seemed nothing else in the South for manufacturing to turn to but cotton."[175]   "Their whole purpose and idea was to build mills right in the heart of the cotton fields."[176]   "In establishing cotton mills the chief advantage, in the minds of Southern people, was proximity to the raw cotton."[177]

[172] Baltimore Journal of Commerce and Manufacturers' Record, June 3, 1882.   Several mills owned cotton lands.

[173] W. R. Odell, int., Concord.   Tompkins built a plant at Edgefield, S. C., for which cotton was secured unpacked from the field (J. H. M. Beatty, int., Jan. 3, 1917, Columbia).   Many mills are to be seen today standing in cotton fields (cf. Columbia Record, Textile Ed., 1916.   Cf. ibid., as to Lancaster Mills).   The Proximity mill, Greensboro, was named with reference to nearness to raw material (cf. James A. Greer, in Textile Manufacturer, Charlotte, Aug. 19, 1915).   The treasurer of the company thinks proximity to cotton was the prime cause of the Southern industry (Bernard Cone, int., Greensboro, N. C., Aug. 30, 1916).   Cf. Charlotte News, Textile Ed., 1917, advertisement recommending Monroe, North Carolina, as a location for mills because of excellent and abundant cotton of Union County; cf. advertisement of P. H. Hanes Knitting Co., in Every Week, Nov. 12, 1917, p. 15.

[174] Mississippi Beacon, quoted in News and Courier, Charleston, June 18, 1881.

[175] James W. Cannon, int., Concord, N. C., Jan. 6, 1917.

[176] Tracy I. Hickman, int., Augusta, Ga., Dec. 27, 1916.

[177] Theodore Klutz, int., Salisbury.   "The whole development was the result of the desire of the people to use their raw product" (William Banks, int., Columbia).   "They had in mind all over the South the fact that the cotton was on the ground" (James Simons, int., Charleston, S. C., Dec. 27, 1916).   "There came a different viewpoint.   The old South was done away with.   The problem was to utilize the thing nearest at hand to support a large portion of our people" (Henry E. Fries, int., Winston-Salem).   "Other things were side issues.   Proximity to raw cotton was the great advantage, as it appeared to us" (A. B. Murray, int., Charleston, S. C., Dec. 28, 1916).   Some helps to development through this proximity were not

The causes of manufacturing development reviewed and others to be touched upon, sometimes exerted a secondary influence through example of factories already in operation, or even of old mills which had gone out of existence. The stimulus lent by the older establishments, those founded before 1870, was largely through individuals or families, was personal, not inspiring new erections at the hands of men not in some way connected with the original ventures; on the other hand, a mill built after 1880 often had a social bearing, attracting to the industry enterprisers and communities with no manufacturing tradition. Of course, there

---

foreseen by the first mill builders. Actual spinning tests of the staple may be made, instead of relying upon conventional grading (cf. Tompkins, Cotton Mill Processes and Calculations, pp. 4–5). Atkinson did not realize that in this way only mills in the fields could improve preparation of cotton for manufacture. Southern mills, moreover, may rely upon a reserve in the hands of farmers, and not stock up in the picking season as heavily as Northern factories. A few smaller mills even buy cotton as they receive orders for goods (cf. Copeland, pp. 182–183). Nor did the founders guess that supposed benefits of contiguity to cotton would vanish and actually turn out as hindrances. Where mills have concentrated, local cotton does not satisfy the demand. The local price is sometimes driven above that of spot in New York. Cotton brought from the Delta or other distant points bears a relatively or absolutely higher freight charge than staple shipped to New England or Liverpool. Also, the product must be sent north to market and, in most cases, to be finished. Any saving in purchase of raw material locally, amounting hardly ever to more than half a cent a pound, is about counterbalanced by freight on goods. When Southern mills were few and small, presence of cotton was a real asset, and product was often sold locally. Unless all forecasts are futile, the present is a "period of transition" for the Southern mills which will give way to more widespread distribution of plants (overcoming the singular disadvantage of some factories, such as those at Gastonia which can use no local cotton for their manufacture of fine yarns), to finishing of product at the South and the development of a Southern goods market, when old superiorities of location will reappear and prove greater than ever. (These points were substantiated by interviews with John W. Fries, Winston-Salem; George W. Williams, Charleston; Charles Estes and Tracy I. Hickman, Augusta; J. B. Cleveland, Spartanburg; Benjamin Gossett, Anderson; Joseph H. Separk, Gastonia. For fuller discussions see Copeland, pp. 36–37; Uttley, p. 39 ff.; Thompson, p. 271; the writer's Factors in Future of Cotton Manufacture in South, in Manufacturers' Record, Baltimore, May 10, 1917; an excellently detailed illustration of drawbacks in regard to freight charges is contained in the petition of certain up-country South Carolina mills to the State Railroad Commission, Feb. 24, 1903).

were exceptions in both cases. Graniteville, more than other ante-bellum manufactories, possessed public significance; it is difficult to tell how far promoters of mills at Augusta and elsewhere knew Gregg or were trained in his factory, and how far they were inspired simply by the example of Graniteville.[178]

The factory is said to have had a fifty-year record of dividends.[179] It is likely very true that its success had an influence in the Cotton Mill Campaign of the eighties through Dawson of The News and Courier, who frequently referred to it.[180]

Other old factories furnished more exclusively personal incentive. George Makepeace founded little mills on Deep River in North Carolina. Others, such as the Fries family at Salem, learned from him. Ante-bellum manufacturing of the Fries' was the forerunner of their post-bellum activities. The Pattersons at Roanoke Rapids were connected with the Fries family. The grandfather of a mill president of Raleigh had been a stockholder in two small mills at Cedar Falls, and knew Makepeace. The pioneer cotton manufacturer of Durham had clerked in the store at Cedar Falls.[181]

William Bates, who came from Slater's mill at Pawtucket, Rhode Island, was important because he influenced his son-in-law, Hammett, as has been noticed earlier. William Entwistle, an Englishman with textile training in Lancashire, worked in Lawrence, Massachusetts. He came South with the intention of farming, but entered Granite-

---

[178] Cf. Clark, History of Manufactures, p. 553 ff. The influence of Graniteville has been discussed more fully in the first chapter.

[179] Tracy I. Hickman, int., Augusta.

[180] H. R. Buist, int., Charleston, S. C., Dec. 28, 1916. Local advocates of mills sometimes harked back to successes at Graniteville and Augusta (cf. Society Hill correspondence, News and Courier, Charleston, Feb. 23, 1881). Graniteville had personal ties with many later establishments. The grandfather of LeRoy Springs, pioneer manufacturer of Lancaster, was one of the organizers of Gregg's company (Columbia Record, Textile Ed., 1916). The projector of the Rock Hill Factory was the son of a Graniteville founder (William Banks, int., Columbia).

[181] A. A. Thompson, int., Raleigh.

ville as a section hand in 1869, then was at Langley and removed to the Great Falls mill at Rockingham, North Carolina, to become overseer of weaving. Great Falls was itself built on the site of the much older Richmond Manufacturing Company's factory. Mr. Entwistle has been responsible for much mill building at Rockingham and has given technical advice to other projectors, such as Mr. Cooper at Henderson. The Leak family, owning mills at Rockingham, two generations ago had the Richmond Manufacturing Company.[182]

Coming to mills which were patterns to communities rather than individual enterprisers, it is clear that Hammett's Piedmont Factory, projected in 1873 but delayed in commencing operation until 1876, was "a crucial experiment "; that in a real sense "the success of the mills of the South depended upon Piedmont, the initial business."[183] It may almost be said that Hammett belonged to the development of the eighties; he anticipated the South's duty and opportunity by seven years. His mill was so excellent and complete, he was so able an advocate of manufactures and his public attitude was so constructive that his venture was really "the kindergarten for the industry in the up-country for twenty years."[184]

---

[182] William Entwistle and T. C. Leak, int., Rockingham, N. C., Aug. 14, 1920. The Holt mills in Alamance represent distinctly a family development. Gray's apprenticeship served in the old " Pinhook Factory" has been remarked. The industry at Columbus owes much to the fact that before and during the war the place was "a miniature Lowell" (Observer, Raleigh, Sept. 10, 1880). The Lawrence (1878) and enlarged Woodlawn (1880) mills, at Lowell, N. C., grew out of the original plant of the company built in 1851 (Baltimore Journal of Commerce and Manufacturers' Record, June 3, 1882). Clifton was descended from the older Bivingsville and Glendale factories (Blackman, pp. 10-11; William Banks, int., Columbia).

[183] W. J. Thackston, int., Greenville.

[184] " The mills built in this locality about 1880–1885 were simply results of the great success made by the Piedmont Manufacturing Company. The projectors of these mills used no arguments different from those of H. P. Hammett" (James D. Hammett, int., Anderson, S. C., Sept. 11, 1916). Pelzer was an outgrowth of Piedmont, its founder driving over to look at the water power after an annual meeting at Piedmont (W. J. Thackston, int., Greenville). Following Hammett, Charlestonians had built mills in the Piedmont dis-

When mills were erected in numbers, experience in these was shared with intending projectors. "In the Trenton mill we made a big success. It got into the papers, and I had letters from all over the country, even from Texas, inquiring about it."[185] It seems plain that "the success of the Salisbury mill built the Advance mill. A good many who had held back from the first venture went into the second."[186]

Most extensions of plants were of course outgrowths of successful experience.[187]

Depressed condition of agriculture during and preceding the early eighties was in a large way a cause of cotton manufacture. Unremunerative farming led to industry in two main ways: by putting those able to initiate enterprise on the search for new investments, and by throwing out of a livelihood those unable to make new opportunities for themselves. In North Carolina, a poor agricultural State anyway, the process was especially clear. Water powers were more profitable than land.[188] The same was true of the upper part of South Carolina. Before the war there was little fertilizer used, and this district could not grow cotton. "The State was forced to appropriate $5000 one year to enable Spartanburg County to meet expenses. There was simply not enough property in the county of value."[189] This agricultural poverty reflected itself in a

---

trict. Explaining the causes back of the Charleston Manufacturing Company, one of its incorporators said: "We thought that if a mill could pay in the up-country, it would pay to build a mill in a large center like Charleston" (William M. Bird, int., Charleston, S. C., Dec. 28, 1916). And speaking of this enterprise, a local paper urged: "Let us realize that what is good for Charleston in this respect, is better for us" (Kershaw Gazette, quoted in News and Courier, Charleston, Jan. 31, 1881). Cf. ibid., Feb. 26, 1881, regarding mills at Augusta.

[185] G. W. Ragan, int., Gastonia.

[186] Theodore F. Klutz, int., Salisbury. "The Salisbury mill showed what could be done in the field" (O. D. Davis, int., Salisbury). Cf. Daily Constitution, Atlanta, Jan. 2, 1880, editorial "Atlanta's New Year."

[187] Cf. Charlotte News, Textile Ed., 1917, respecting Erwin Cotton Mill Company.

[188] John Nichols, int., Raleigh.

[189] J. B. Cleveland, int., Spartanburg, Cf. Hammond, p. 80.

supply of surplus labor that had been of long standing.

Low ebb of agriculture was inevitably expressed in low price of cotton, which directly and indirectly encouraged manufacture of the staple. Generally speaking, the number of mills erected has varied inversely with the price of the raw material.[190]

Just before the war a bale of cotton was worth $40 to $50, and the cost of constructing an average spinning and weaving mill was $16 to $20 per spindle. With war, paper money and scarcity of cotton, the value of the bale went to $900, and soon afterwards mills were costing $30 to $40 per spindle. By 1880 cotton and mill construction had returned to the 1860 levels.[191]

With crops constantly larger, it was seen that the South had reached the maximum quantity of cotton that could be produced profitably until world demand increased,[192] and that American manufacturers needd to expand and extend their export trade.[193] "For a few years after the war, when the price of cotton was so high that anyone could live by a small amount of farming, the land was cultivated extensively; but when the cultivation reached its limit, and the price of cotton became lower, the farmers and home capitalists realized that the only way their condition could

---

[190] "Low cotton meant an increase in the number of failed white farmers. This meant an enlarged labor supply. Low cotton also increased the feeling in the community that the town should be kept going by something else than bankrupt cotton farmers" (W. W. Ball, int.. Columbia, Jan. 3, 1917). Cf. Columbia Record, Textile Ed., 1916, regarding Oakland Mills.

[191] U. S. Census of Manufactures, 1880, "Cotton Manufacture," by Edward Atkinson, p. 8. The average annual price for middling upland cotton at New York, gold value, was 30.76 cents in 1865–1866, and fell, with irregular recoveries, to 11.24 in 1880–1881. Though bales were increasingly heavier, production of bales trebled in these years (cf. table from Bradstreet's, quoted in Baltimore Journal of Commerce and Manufacturers' Record, Nov. 4, 1882). As to alleged serious turning to manufactures in the South consequent upon low prices of cotton from 1839–1844, see Brooks, pp. 148–149; on the increase of spindles in the country in the twenties, similarly caused, see Hammond, p. 246.

[192] Baltimore Journal of Commerce and Manufacturers' Record, Nov. 4, 1882.

[193] News and Courier, Charleston, Sept. 12, 1881. Cf. Observer, Raleigh, June 12, 24; Aug. 3, 14, 1880.

10

be bettered was by manufacturing the raw product at home."[194]

Not only were cotton manufactures made a likely field of investment by low price of material through increased production, but mills rose with the wave of recuperation of business after the panic of 1873 and its following years of depression. Return to specie payments lent assurance, and the demand for cotton goods was brisk. The year 1880 opened very hopefully.[195] The testimony of the president of Graniteville was matched by that of South Carolina manufacturers generally: "We have . . . been running

[194] See Tompkins, History of Mecklenburg, vol. i, pp. 181–182. Another writer "remembers seeing five bales of cotton bring the owner only $104. Then the cry went up, 'Take the mills to the cotton fields,' and the people from the farms flocked to tend the machinery" (L. P. Hollis, in Columbia Record, Textile Ed., 1916). Cf. Brooks, p. 203 ff. An old ledger of the Sibley mill at Augusta contains memoranda of cotton bought at 4 cents a pound. For the benefits conferred on the cotton farmer, see an illustrative but not quite accurate statement in Tompkins, "Marketing Cotton," in Textile World Record, Boston, Sept., 1908. Cf. Sioussat, p. 228.

[195] For the country it was said that "following the resumption of specie payments, which inspired confidence on all sides, and after the last of the United States called bonds matured . . . and when the out-turn of the harvest was pretty well ascertained, the whole scene changed: gold began to pour into the country, business increased with wonderful rapidity, prices of bonds, stocks and merchandise advanced by jumps, and the whole field of commercial and financial transactions was marked by a great rebound from former depression, which will be remembered . . . as the great 'boom' of the Fall of 1879. In 1877 the country appeared as an insolvent debtor . . .; in October, 1879, it appeared as the same party with every matured obligation paid up in full, and with abundant capital in hand, rousing himself to engage in a new career of industrial prosperity" (Commercial and Financial Chronicle, Jan. 10, 1880). Cf. Baltimore Journal of Commerce and Manufacturers' Record, Sept. 9, 1882. For the South it was stated: "The year that is just finished will be to the present generation a red-letter one; for it brought to an end the long and weary period of enforced economy and restricted business that followed the panic of 1873, and put every branch of industry at work. Agriculture was encouraged in the west and south . . . the factories received more orders than they could fill, the railroads were blocked with freight, the mines were pushed to a greater extent than ever, and all other interests were quickened towards the end of the old year in a way that was full of promise" (Daily Constitution, Atlanta, Jan. 7, 1880). Cf. Observer, Raleigh, Jan. 2, 8, 15, April 24; Daily Dispatch, Richmond, Jan. 1, 1880; for a similar statement for 1882, cf. Manufacturers' Record, Baltimore, Dec. 7, 1882.

since 1873 between two fires, but we seem to have emerged from that trouble now, and we are at present making handsome profits. If this condition of affairs continues for five years . . . we will make a heap of money. Everything has conspired during the last twelve months to help this country."[196]

It is scarcely necessary to say that expectation of profits stimulated the erection of mills. While always considered, the prospect of money gain in dividends was not always most important in the minds of factory builders. Sometimes projectors were able to estimate from proven experience of mills running in the South, but more often profits were argued from believed advantages of the section for textile manufacture. Most advocates shared their hopes openly with community or State; few followed a course of communicating a secret to hand-picked investors. Profits realized in these years will be discussed in a later chapter. Dividends of mills were regularly brought to public attention and calculations were printed to show how any properly managed mill could make money.[197] The demand for goods in 1880 allowed sale ahead at value; prices of product advanced faster in proportion than those of raw material; mills could not fill their orders; some Southern factories ran day and night. All of this tended to draw the attention of the North and of the world to Southern mills, helped up their standards, enlarged their outlook, gave established and prospective plants a springboard for the great impending leap forward.[198] Charleston, the only lending community

---

[196] See Blackman, pp. 4–5; cf. ibid., p. 10. Some foresaw New England seizing fine goods manufacture from England to protect itself against Southern coarse product, but ultimately surrendering the whole industry more and more to the factories in the fields (ibid., p. 14, and leading article). Hammett was resolutely hopeful when leaner times began to be feared (cf. Daily Constitution, Atlanta, quoted in Manufacturers' Record, Baltimore, Feb. 1, 1883). As to gain of American exports to China at the expense of English mills, cf. Observer, Raleigh, Feb. 14, June 19, July 25, 1880.

[197] Cf. News and Courier, Charleston, Sept. 13, 1881; Observer, Raleigh, Aug. 26, 1880; Daily Constitution, Atlanta, March 18, 1880.

[198] Cf. Baltimore Sun, Jan. 8, 20, 28; Observer, Raleigh, March 6, April 24, 1880; Blackman, p. 15. By the end of 1884 less favorable

in South Carolina, putting money in mills at a distance, showed more investment primarily for profit than did local districts.

In some instances, ten years and more after the cotton manufacturing development commenced, mills were established partly to take advantage of cheap labor. This motive of exploitation was very different from the earlier desire to give the people supporting employment. It has been pointed out that there is a distinction between arguments used in promoting factories and the factors which have contributed to the success of the industry. When commentators on the mills say that their rise has been chiefly due to inexpensive labor, it is usually meant that this has turned out to be their chief asset.[199] In estimating the influence of water powers in mill building it must be remembered that while representative plants were located on streams right at first, there came a time when communities without this facility wanted factories and utilized steam. So far as they go, statements explaining the causal character of water powers are proper. The industry at Augusta and Columbus prior to 1880 was attributable chiefly to falls in the Chattahoochee and Savannah rivers, and plants erected after this date owed much to the presence of this asset.[200]

conditions were at hand, but the Southern industry had received its impetus by this time.

[199] Cf. Copeland, pp. 143-144; Murphy, p. 103; and the writer's "End of Child Labor," in Survey, Aug. 23, 1919. Of course, proposals by Northerners to erect factories in the South considered from the outset the advantage in, not any advantage to, labor. Cf. Manufacturers' Record, Baltimore, Feb. 1, 1883; Baltimore Journal of Commerce and Manufacturers' Record, July 15, 1882.

[200] Cf. ibid., Sept. 9, 1882, as to Columbus; Manufacturers' Record, Baltimore, Jan. 4, 1883, as to Augusta. When it is said that "Without the canal Columbia would have had no mills" (Washington Clark, int., Columbia, Jan. 1, 1917), correction must be inserted that without the desire for mills there would have been no canal; it was constructed in the main after 1880. Communities wishing outside assistance frequently advertised their water powers (cf. News and Courier, Charleston, Aug. 17, 1880, assets of Oconee County). Comparatively late in the development, as in the case of labor, exploitation of water powers came to a leading place. Cf. Charlotte News, Textile Ed., 1917, regarding Roanoke Rapids; Columbia Record, ibid., 1916, regarding Ware Shoals. Speaking broadly, railroads have been responsible for the extension of the industry and the

Like some other causes, purpose of promoters to provide themselves with salaries did not appear in the beginning. Later, the practice is said to have been common, applying particularly to extensions with accompanying salary increases, or to projection of plants in new communities by an established manufacturer who wished money to come principally from local investors. The man who subscribed heavily to make positions for himself and members of his family had little in common with the founders of the Southern industry.[201]

A few mills were started because of desire to use idle land and buildings. Commencement of manufacturing in the building of the Atlanta Exposition is a case in point.[202] Mills were regularly erected to help stagnant towns; it was exceedingly rare that one was proposed to create a town or to benefit land speculation.[203]

Exemption of factories or of new machinery from State or local taxation made more appeal to the investor as such than to promoters and shareholders participating in community enterprises; it was believed to encourage assistance from the North and counted with Southern founders who owned most of the stock in their ventures.[204]

From time to time reference has been made to reported

---

location of plants rather than for the inception of mills (cf. Columbia Record, Textile Ed., 1916, regarding Glenn-Lowry mill).

[201] A. N. Wood, Gaffney, Sept. 13; Clement F. Haynsworth, Greenville, Sept. 9, 1916; August Kohn, Columbia, S. C., Jan. 5, 1917, interviews.

[202] See News and Courier, Charleston, Jan. 14, 1882. The Arista mill at Winston-Salem put idle land in use (John W. Fries, int., Winston-Salem). Cf. Baltimore Journal of Commerce and Manufacturers' Record, Nov. 11, 1882, as to a project at Gainesville, Ga. When the development was well begun, plants of various sorts were converted for cotton manufacture.

[203] The case of the Region of the Savannah Colonization Assn. is noticed elsewhere. Bessemer City, North Carolina, was an instance (S. N. Boyce and J. Lee Robinson, int., Gastonia, N. C., Sept. 14, 1916).

[204] Cf. quotation from Bradstreet's in Baltimore Journal of Commerce and Manufacturers' Record, Nov. 4, 1882; Observer, Raleigh, Feb. 13, 1880; Clark, in South in Building of Nation, vol. vi, p. 282; Blackman, pp. 6–7; Manufacturers' Record, Baltimore, Dec. 7, 1882; Baltimore Sun, March 4, 1880; News and Observer, Raleigh, Nov. 2, 1880; Kohn, Cotton Mills of S. C., pp. 99, 101.

intent of English enterprisers to exploit Southern cotton manufacturing facilities. An Englishman who, from being an operative in Lancashire, Massachusetts, and South Carolina, has become important in the Southern industry, said that while there has always been much talk of this, nothing ever resulted.[205] As will be seen in another chapter, Northern participation was principally by commission and machinery firms and through investment. Before the cotton mill era properly opened some Northern manufacturers came to the South, and after the movement had demonstrated its success New England companies opened branch plants.[206]

It is said that in Lancashire machinery manufacturers, commission houses and supply men have established mills with speculative purpose.[207] Equipment firms may even teach operatives in English and Japanese mills to run the machinery. Dull times in the American textile machinery manufacture have prompted makers to encourage erection and enlargement of factories by several means.[208] It is doubtful whether their motive in this policy followed in the South has been in any large degree speculative. It was not such in the eighties; their desire was to profit from sale of machinery, not from sale of stock taken in payment for machinery. They furnished a facility rather than supply-

---

[205] William Entwistle, int., Rockingham.

[206] George Putnam, a member of a commission firm in Boston, established Camperdown at Greenville in 1873; through its example this mill had some influence, and, with Batesville, taken over by Putnam in 1879, had only Northern capital (Mrs. M. P. Gridley, int., Greenville, S. C., Sept. 9, 1916). Converse came from New England to join the Confederate forces and was assigned to operation of the Glendale Factory; after the war, he continued to manage the mill, and conceived the idea of the influential Clifton enterprise (J. A. Chapman, int., Spartanburg, S. C., Sept. 5, 1916). Makepeace and Entwistle are other cases in point (A. A. Thompson, int., Raleigh). It is proper, also, to consider the services of A. D. Lockwood, mill engineer of Providence, who was employed by enterprises at the opening of the period. Cf. Clark, in South in Building of Nation, vol. vi, pp. 264–265.

[207] Copeland, pp. 317–318.

[208] J. L. Hartsell, int., Concord.

ing an impulse.[209]   Tompkins, as mill engineer, as head of a repair and supply firm and as Southern agent of machinery manufacturers, was instrumental in building many factories, but he was motivated by desire for legitimate profit and by public spirit.[210]

Following the war much new machinery was installed in New England.   Southern mills with more than a local market, many of them overworked during the war and run down during Reconstruction, had to reequip or build new plants.   This circumstance assisted the spirit for cotton manufactures.[211]

These, and others, were reasons why the industry came into being.   In the subsequent chapters on Labor and on Capital it will be shown how the South carried out its purpose.   The present pages deal with the actual rise of factories and aim to exhibit attending public interest as it expressed itself in the "Cotton Mill Campaign."   The movement, it has been seen, had a definite beginning about 1880.   The whole South not joining in right at first, it is difficult to say when the "drive" ended.   Certainly by 1895, if not earlier, it had been demonstrated that the industry carried its own excuse for being, and nothing more than economic motives were necessary to its encouragement.[212]

---

[209] It is charged, however, that an industrial journal represented machinery manufacturers in more than simply an advertising capacity.

[210] He would be invited to speak to citizens of a town contemplating erection of a mill, explaining the broad benefits the factory would bring them and imparting as much technical information as they needed for organization (Sterling Graydon, int., Charlotte). Cf. Tompkins, Cotton Mill, Commercial Features, p. 25 ff.; Plan to Raise Capital, pp. 13-14.

[211] Henry E. Fries, int., Winston-Salem.

[212] Better argument than the first appearance of the term is the clear implication of the News and Courier that, economically, the Cotton Mill Campaign began with 1880. It was said that Hammett ranked as one of the pioneers in the Southern industry because his Piedmont Factory was built before the opening of the Cotton Mill Campaign, and, in seconding his authoritative judgment, the paper took satisfaction in the practical undertaking of a program which it had long urged, and exulted that "seen in the cold light of accomplished facts, the enthusiasm of which some of our friends have

152

Hammett, in 1883, to allay discouragement that had arisen in some quarters, made an explanation that exhibits the Cotton Mill Campaign: "A state of things has developed which many of us expected to see, and which was inevitable. Too many yarn mills have been built in the last two or three years all over the South from Virginia to Mexico, and as a consequence the market for coarse yarn is overstocked. . . . They were built for the most part by inexperienced men, taken from other pursuits, without any experience or knowledge of the business, badly built, the cheapest machinery put into them, with no scientific system for doing the work intended, many of them without sufficient capital to pay for them when they were completed."[213] It is plain here how suddenly, under what social pressure, the movement was born. "Once the opportunity had been presented to them the chance was eagerly seized, and all who were able to do so contributed to make the new enterprise successful. The press urged it upon those who had capital to invest, hailed joyfully every manufacturing project, and made much of every successful establishment. . . . As is commonly the case with enterprises of this nature, it has been attended with not a little public excitement. . . ."[214]

complained, as carrying us too far, has not taken us a hair's breadth beyond the confines of solid business truth" (Aug. 1, 1881). Cf. ibid., April 25, 1881. Something as to the closing date may be drawn from the fact that in 1886 South Carolina repealed an act exempting cotton mills from taxation (cf. Clark, in South in Building of Nation, vol. vi, p. 282).

[213] "They made poor yarn, which they pledged for the money to operate them, which was of course sold to realize, for such prices as were offered, and when the yarn was thus slaughtered it made a price for them and others to sell by, and it is not strange that they made little money." Most of them made more, however, than Northern mills (quoted from Atlanta Constitution, in Manufacturers' Record, Baltimore, Feb. 1, 1883).

[214] ". . . more mills have been projected than have been built; more have been erected which their projectors would not have erected had they studied the matter carefully before entering upon the experiment. But the failures have been few, and upon the whole the return upon investment in Southern cotton mills has exceeded that upon factories in the North" (see U. S. Census of Manufactures, 1900, "Cotton Manufacture," by Edward Stanwood, pp. 28-29). An instructive table shows that Southern spindles increased from 610,000 in 1880 to 1,756,000 in 1890, reached more than 2,000,000

An impressive interpretation of the English industrial revolution has shown that while it began through invention, invention alone would have taken generations to establish the different regime. The philosophy of Adam Smith and the moral impulses imparted by the Wesleys and Hannah More joined with the work of Watt to speed the process. " It required all the forms—physical, mental, commercial, and philanthropical—working in separate yet convergent lines, to lay the foundation of an entirely new system of manufactures. . . ."[215] In the South all sorts of forces, more directly and consciously applied than in the case of England, headed up in the Cotton Mill Campaign; regret for the past, resolution for the future, expressed themselves here. Economic inertia was overcome with moral incitement,[216] industrial activity was lent momentum by a " passion for rehabilitation" which made erection of cotton mills, as twenty years later of schools, "a form of civic piety."[217] Leaders were mindful of the psychological qual-

by 1892 and more than 4,000,000 by 1900. From 1880 to 1883, 450,000 new spindles were put into operation. Taking 10,000 for the average-sized mill, this means that three years saw 45 factories opened (ibid.). Cf. Baltimore Journal of Commerce and Manufacturers' Record, June 10, 1882, introduction to column headed " Manufacturing." On Aug. 26, eight items out of thirty-six dealing with manufactures were about cotton mills; this was typical. Cf. ibid., Sept. 2, 9, 1882; Manufacturers' Record, Baltimore, Jan. 11, Feb. 8, 1883; News and Courier, Charleston, July 30, 1881; Augusta Trade Review, Oct., 1884; Thompson, p. 73. " The South burst into the development; mills grew up like mushrooms" (Summerfield Baldwin, Jr., int., Baltimore, Md., Jan. 8, 1917).

[215] See U. S. Census of Manufactures, 1880, Factory System of U. S., pp. 4-5.

[216] Cf. Ingle, pp. 72-73.

[217] Cf. Murphy, pp. 17-18. The volitional quality of the campaign appears in contemporary references to it as an " experiment." Cf. Plunkett, p. 170. Industrial advantage. arguing from the past, seemed to be on the side of water power; the wish was sometimes father to the thought in reasonings for steam power to be used at towns not on streams but which wanted mills. Cf. News and Courier, Charleston, March 26, April 25, 29, 1881. In many ways the Cotton Mill Campaign was a romantic movement, resulting in spindles instead of sonnets. There had been intense public interest in the Pacific railway, stretching across a desert to guarantee the Union's integrity (cf. Dunning, pp. 144-145). The South felt a homogeneity in making cotton mills rise from an industrial wilderness.

ity of the movement and were jealous that it should have no backsets. "The State cannot afford a single failure in her cotton mill campaign . . . ,"[218] said one, and another: "A few disasters amongst new mills would be a calamity, the extent and effect of which it would be difficult to estimate or realize, for while one successful mill inspires confidence, the failure of one to succeed would have directly the opposite effect. The people should not allow themselves to be carried into it too rapidly by popular enthusiasm, which now prevails to some extent throughout the South. . . ."[219]

Few episodes are more illustrative of the wholeheartedness and wisdom with which the South entered upon the Cotton Mill Campaign than that of the Clement Attachment. This was a device that combined ginning and spinning in one process; it was small, cheap, and made a limited amount of yarn. Recommended for the use of planters, its employment would represent the first step from agriculture into industry. When Southerners were beginning to think of cotton manufacturing there was eager, widespread inquiry as to this equipment, and it was put into operation in some places. But it was not tarried over long—it was recognized as a makeshift, a partial solution which did not satisfy the purpose for a real industrial development.[220]

The spirit of the movement for factories may best be

---

[218] "Enquirer," in News and Courier, Charleston, April 29, 1881.

[219] Hammett, in ibid., Aug. 1, 1881.

[220] An enthusiastic forecast missed fire in asserting "we shall have in a half century some scribbling journalist of the future writing the gossips of the invention of the Clement Attachment—which will by that time have worked greater revolutions in the South than the cotton gin has done in the past half century!" (Daily Constitution, Atlanta, Feb. 6, 1880). Cf. ibid., Jan. 2, Feb. 20, 1880. Blackman solicited many opinions about it, and received generally unfavorable replies; cf. especially pp. 17–18, showing to what pains enterprisers from all parts of the South went to examine the machine; cf. News and Courier, Charleston, Feb. 26, May 26, 1881; Observer, Raleigh, Jan. 31, 1880. Nor was the South, when the Cotton Mill Campaign began to gather momentum, greatly regardful of outside comment; answerable to the faith that was in them, papers printed onlookers' discouraging and heartening references with like composure. Cf. letter of Robert P. Parker to New York Sun, quoted in Daily Constitution, Atlanta, Feb. 13, 1880, and quotation of Detroit Free Press in Observer, Raleigh, Aug. 31, 1880.

caught in newspaper items. These appeared constantly and in numbers, in county and city papers, and there was a lively exchange of such information between publications. Any news bearing upon industry, particularly cotton manufacture, was put to service. The following is a characteristic heading: "The Straws that Show! Indications of the Way the Wind is Blowing. The Latest Movements in the Cotton-Mill Campaign." And there follow notices of the receipt of machinery by Clifton mill and praise from Boston of the efficiency and profitableness of factories at Columbus.[221] Correspondence from a little place since become a manufacturing point of consequence gave a typical instance: "In conclusion let me say a few words in regard to the 'Pet' of the town, the Rock Hill Cotton Factory. This factory is owned and controlled by the citizens of the town (except $15,000 in stock owned in Charleston). It has a capital of $100,000, has over 6,000 spindles with 1,500 more to be added in a few days. The best evidence of its success is that not one dollar of its stock can be bought. It is the intention of the company . . . to run the factory day and night . . . to keep up with its orders."[222] It was reported that "strenuous efforts are being made in Greensboro to establish a cotton factory in that city."[223] In an article on railroads occurred this paragraph: "It is rumored that the Columbia and Greenville railroad car shops at Helena will be removed to Columbia. . . . In case the removal is made

---

[221] News and Courier, Charleston, March 22, 1881.
[222] News and Courier, Charleston, Jan. 12, 1882. News of mills from a distance, too, was frequent; it was noticed that enterprises at Wesson, Miss., were paying handsomely, that a mill building was constructing at Natchez, that companies were organizing at Vicksburg and New Orleans; when a mill at Nashville declared a 14 per cent dividend another was built; mills at Pulaski, Tenn., were anxious to double their capacity; $50,000 was subscribed for a plant at Jackson, Tenn.; Dallas was starting a $200,000 factory and Sherman wanted a $75,000 mill (ibid., Aug. 12, 1881).
[223] Winston Leader, quoted in Observer, Raleigh, June 17, 1880. "The Statesville Landmark, with its characteristic level-headedness, calls for the building of manufactures. With this would come commercial strength for our beloved South" (News and Observer, Raleigh, Dec. 12, 1880)

the Newberry *News* suggests that the buildings at Helena might be easily converted into a cotton factory."[224]

It was reported that "the 'Cotton Mill Campaign' is progressing satisfactorily in Yorkville. We heard an old citizen remark some days ago that he had never seen the town so thoroughly aroused and united. . . . Yorkville to all appearances is moving forward with a determined purpose to put into successful operation a cotton mill. . . . The shares have been placed at $500 each, and up to this writing about $25,000 have been subscribed. I would state that this amount has been raised within the limits of the town."[225] It was advertised that "We will give to a Cotton Manufacturing Company that will organize and locate at Landsford, S. C., with a capital of $300,000, a site, 20 acres of land and 300 horse water power."[226] There were many items like the following: "The project for establishing a manufactory for cotton near Walhalla is being mooted. An informal meeting of some of the citizens of that place was held last week with this view and stock to the amount of nearly $10,000 was subscribed by the few present. It is believed strongly that as much as $25,000 will be subscribed in that neighborhood, and if the people of the county will join in the enterprise as much as $50,000 might be made available."[227]

Town pride expressed itself in keen rivalry. "One little place would have a mill, and its neighbors would say: 'Here,

---

[224] News and Courier, Charleston, March 22, 1881.

[225] News and Courier, Charleston, March 25, 1881. "The signers to the prospectus of the mill are among the most reliable and responsible men in York County " (ibid., March 31, 1881).

[226] News and Courier, Charleston, Feb. 23, 1881. "One gentleman at Griffin, Ga., offers to subscribe one-fourth the amount necessary to build a cotton factory " (ibid., March 25, 1881).

[227] News and Courier, Charleston, Feb. 26, 1881. Cf. ibid., Jan. 9, 1882, as to Fort Mill. From Marion came this notice: "Our wants: A bank, an academy, a cotton factory, a comfortable room for passengers at the depot, an iron foundry . . ." (ibid., Feb. 22, 1881). "There is not a cotton factory at Raleigh, but there are not less than five large planing mills, two foundries, two boiler factories . . . ," and newspapers and schools are mentioned (ibid., Jan. 26, 1881). Cf. as to Henderson, Baltimore Journal of Commerce and Manufacturers' Record, Oct. 14, 1882.

we can't let that town get ahead of us. We must start a cotton mill.' "[228] "If Belton got a mill, Williamston would want one. The townspeople would go to their leading citizen. It made no difference what a man was, so long as he was the leading citizen he had to become a mill president."[229]

It has been said that the Charleston Manufacturing Company, in all but its ill success, was the type enterprise of the Cotton Mill Campaign. It was peculiarly the child of the slogan, "Bring the Mills to the Cotton."[230] Though never really prospering itself, this factory had much to do with encouraging others, not least because it showed that the city practiced what it preached.[231] In Charleston every detail

---

[228] Henry E. Litchford, int., Richmond, Va., Aug. 29, 1916.

[229] Benjamin Gossett, int., Anderson, S. C., Sept. 11, 1916. A promoter, by visiting other mills, assured himself of the profitableness of an enterprise in his town: "Will a mill pay in Sumter? Why not? Every mill I visited had to pay $2 per cord for wood—it will cost less here in Sumter. . . . Every one of the mills received their cotton in bales . . . at a loss of $1.90 to $2 per bale on bagging and ties. A factory in Sumter can use at least one-third of cotton without being packed . . ." (quoted from Sumter Southron, in News and Courier, Charleston, March 31, 1881). Many out of the way places came into notice through erection of cotton mills that would never otherwise have been heard of; ventures in every part of the South, small and large, visionary or likely to mature, were not only chronicled, but were watched in their development from week to week. Interesting references, similar to those given already, may be found in News and Courier, Charleston, Jan. 4, 6, 21, 26, Feb. 3, 24, 26, March 23, April 6, May 21, Sept. 1, Oct. 21, 1881; Deutsche Zeitung, Charleston, Feb. 28, 1881; Baltimore Journal of Commerce and Manufacturers' Record, June 3, Aug. 26, Sept. 2, 23, 30, Nov. 18, 1882; Observer, Raleigh, Jan. 2, Feb. 20, 1880; News and Observer, Raleigh, March 18, Sept. 15, 18, Oct. 12, Dec. 24, 1800; Baltimore Sun, Jan. 20, 1880.

[230] Little memorandum books informally kept by officers of the company covering organization, building and operation, show with what inexperience and yet with what genuinely affectionate solicitude this project was undertaken and followed through the seven years of its luckless career. A flyleaf gives: "Facts & Figures relating to the Charleston Mfg. Co. Born March, 1881; died Feby., 1888, leaving a large circle of disconsolate stockholders to mourn their loss. 'Requiescat in Pace,' " and there is the significant addition: " ' Bring the Mills to the Cotton.'—News and Courier " (Punctuation is the writer's). Dawson, editor of the paper, was one of the incorporators.

[231] " Charleston is in a fair way to have two large cotton factories in a short while. . . . Camden is preparing for a cotton factory. Hodges . . . is preparing for a cotton factory. Rock Hill has a

of the taking of subscriptions and of erection of the plant was watched with the most absorbed interest.[232]

The speed with which companies were organized and plants erected was significant of impatience to be at the task that invited. The company that erected the Huguenot Mill at Greenville formed February 10, 1881; a charter was obtained March 13; a lot was bought in the heart of the city and the first brick was laid March 23, the last June 2; by July 22 the machinery was in place and the mill was weaving cloth.[233]

At the same time that new enterprises outright were being undertaken, old mills were being greatly enlarged or

---

cotton factory. Greenville has several cotton factories. Newberry, the best location for a factory in the State, and the place most needing one, is not preparing for a cotton factory, and there is no present likelihood that she ever will. . . . There are numbers of people ready to aid in the enterprise . . . but there is nobody to take the lead" (Newberry Herald, quoted in News and Courier, Charleston, Feb. 8, 1881). It was not long before a citizen of Newberry did take the lead in erecting a cotton mill. "Why does not Fairfield make the experiment? It is said that fifteen thousand dollars will set in motion over five hundred spindles, and continual additions can be made. . . . The way to begin the new era is to erect a small factory in every county, and then to improve as facilities increase. Imagine Fairfield converting her eighteen or twenty thousand bales of cotton into yarn or cloth each year, and realizing a double price. If we can do no better let us spin a hundred bales at first. . . . Shall the effort be made, or shall other counties, once far behind us in wealth, take the lead and rapidly outstrip us?" (Winnsboro News, quoted in ibid.). The Barnwell Sentinel approved Charleston's course, and the Keowee Courier said Charleston had set the entire state an example (ibid.).

[232] Cf. News and Courier, Charleston, Feb. 1, March 16, 28, April 9, July 6, Sept. 2, 1881; Jan. 14, 1882; Deutsche Zeitung, Charleston, March 21, 1881. At the same time a movement among German citizens of Charleston to establish a cotton mill with $100,000 capitalization got as far as application for a charter, but apparently no farther. Cf. News and Courier, Charleston, Jan. 27, March 30, May 4, 23, 1881, Deutsche Zeitung, Charleston, March 31, April 21, 1881.

[233] Baltimore Journal of Commerce and Manufacturers' Record, Oct. 28, 1882. "Inside of four months from the commencement of the building, the mill was in operation and the capital invested yielding returns to its owners." A mill at Rome, Ga., the cornerstone of which was laid in June, was to be in operation in November (ibid., June 17, 1882). From the organization of Pelzer to completion of the initial plant, including development of the water power for two later factories, required fourteen months (E. A. Smyth, int., Greenville, Sept. 12, 1916). Cf. News and Courier, Charleston, March 25, May 18, Sept. 10, 1881.

equipped with new machinery, plants were changing hands, those that chanced to burn were promptly rebuilt, factory projects that had lapsed were revived and pushed to completion, buildings were converted from other uses to be cotton manufactories, places which had previously had mills reestablished them. Low prices brought by some factories early in 1880 contrasted with the profitableness of the industry a few months later and indicate how suddenly cotton manufacturing burst upon the South; small ventures which had had a chequered career, doing a small business and frequently failing, were taken by progressive managements that made them over and put new life into them.[234]

[234] Cf. Daily Constitution, Atlanta, Jan. 20, Feb. 29, 1880; Baltimore Journal of Commerce and Manufacturers' Record, July 15, Sept. 16, 1882; News and Courier, Charleston, Feb. 18, March 4, Aug. 19, Dec. 14, 1881; Augusta Trade Review, Oct., 1884; Kohn and Berry, Descriptive Sketch of Orangeburg, 1888, p. 12.

CHAPTER III

THE LABOR FACTOR

The story of the rise of cotton mills in the South is a human story. Loyalty, love, purpose, charity, hope and faith are so intertwined with the specifically economic motive as to be inseparable from it. This is true of the narrative in all of its aspects. England may be said to have launched upon her Industrial Revolution unawares. With the South the movement was conscious, distinctly marked in its commencement in the minds and hearts of the people. In Britain the human problems came as a consequence of the development; in the South they emerged with it and remained, for a long period at least, coeval with the industrial advance.

In this view, one would naturally expect the business impulse to be less dominant in the labor factor than in other particulars, but it is singularly characteristic of the inception of the Southern cotton mills that other phases of the history, as for example the activities of entrepreneurs and the securing of capital, were as much bound up with the essential aspirations of the section as was the participation of men, women and children as operatives. Even machinery was wrapped with idealism and devotion. As the industry has succeeded, with the passing of years there has been a separation of the economic and humanistic elements so intermixed at its beginning; the opaque solution has been clarified by precipitation. Forces that were unified at the outset have developed contrary directions and have shown unequal power.

The story of the workpeople has become less and less the story of the employers. Just as the erection of plants, once the object of close concern on the part of a whole community, has changed to a technical problem, and just as the monetary operations of the companies, forty years ago part

and parcel of the public life, have narrowed to their purely
financial qualities, so divergent interests of capital and labor
have emerged. In a region as newly industrial as the South,
this has brought questions broadly and acutely social. In
this study of the infancy of the manufacture, it is not attempted, except sketchily, to trace the lines of later development.

The part played by labor in the rise of the mills cannot
be understood unless it is recognized that the white population of the South is homogeneous and has always been so.
There is no distinction in blood between employers and employees. The inauguration of the industry, in point of
capital and labor alike, took place within the Southern family. It made for an intimacy which at first rendered impossible and which continues to retard division between factory owners and workers according to economic interest.
The settlers of the South were of the same strains and possessed the same characteristics. For an initial period they
moved along the same occupational lines. The invention of
the cotton gin placed slavery in the ascendant. Cotton cultivation became dominant. The healthy industrial impulse
which had shown itself gave way before agriculture. The
gin, slavery and cotton formed the wedge that pried a unified population apart. Landowners stood separated from
the propertyless; as industry could not compete with agriculture, so those without farming land could not compete
with slave labor.

The "poor whites" were dispossessed, not only of progressive occupation, but of participation in the larger life
of the section. From the time that cotton began to control
until after the period of Reconstruction, these people lapsed
into the background.[1]

---

[1] Cf. Tompkins, in South in Building of Nation, vol. vi, p. 58.
"There is no difference in blood or heritage between them [the
operatives] and the mill managements. . . ." It is interesting to
see how a writer in 1809, regretting the exclusion of propertyless
whites through the cultivation of indigo and rice, welcomed the new
cotton farming as bringing these people back to economic participation, little knowing how cotton itself would soon work their vaster

When the "poor whites" entered the mills, they reentered the life of the South. As cotton culture had blocked progress, so cotton mills, while not dispelling the certainty of painful readjustments, opened the way to a rational economic future.

The settlers of the South were mainly English, German, Swiss, French Huguenot and Scotch-Irish. They were able pioneers—hardy, industrious, independent, self-sufficient. They desired to have their own religions and to maintain their political and economic freedom. Whether from the Barbadoes, from New England, Pennsylvania, Virginia; whether Moravians setting up their churches and industries; whether Highlanders loyal to the Stuarts and fleeing Scotland by shiploads after the battle of Culloden, they blended to make a stock which has no superior.[2]

The term "poor white" is not easily defined, although every Southerner knows pretty accurately what it means. Writers, some through carelessness and others after better

ruin: "By the introduction of the new staple the poor became of value, for they generally were or at least might be elevated to this middle grade of society. Land suitable for cotton was easily attained. . . . The culture of it might be carried on profitably by individuals or white families without slaves, and afforded employment for children whose labor was of little or no account on rice or indigo plantations. . . . The poor having the means of acquiring property without the degradation of working with slaves, had new and strong incitements to industry. From the acquisition of property the transition was easy to that decent pride of character which secures from low vice, and stimulates to seek distinction by deserving it. . . . In estimating the value of cotton, its capacity to incite industry among the lower classes of people, and to fill the country with an independent industrious yeomanry, is of high importance. It has had a large share in moralizing the poor white people of the country" (Ramsay, History of South Carolina, quoted in Scherer, pp. 170–171). As it turned out, cotton in another phase, in manufacture, as William Gregg observed nearly fifty years later, was the means of "developing the character of the poor people of South Carolina." The mills, however, have dangers of being harmful in their evolution as they were helpful in their inception, if they are allowed to be an economic pressure instead of stimulus.

[2] Material as to the blood-strains in the Southern white population is plentiful. The following references are convenient ones, and in several instances give illustration of the character and early life of the people: Tompkins, ibid., and History of Mecklenburg, vol. i, pp. 4–6, 14–15, 18–19, 97–98; Thompson, pp. 17–18, 20–22; Hart, p. 32. County and State histories are helpful in this connection.

consideration, are mainly at variance on three points. The first is whether there was and continues to be a difference in essential character between the indigent classes in the mountains and foothills and in the low country; second, whether the name "poor whites" is applicable to both of these groups; third, whether there was a middle class in the South, at and before the period of mill building, which was to be distinguished from the lowest stratum of population.

Fortunately for purposes of illustration, observations of writers anywhere from about 1840 forward can be used, because the character of the people from whom factory hands were recruited did not change materially from the time that cotton became king until their ranks had become greatly thinned by influx to the mills.

One who employed broad terms spoke of the "non-slaveholding white men . . . outside the essential councils of the South," who "stood aloof; they were supposed to follow where others led,"[3] and said it was from this "vague multitude of the unlettered and unskilled . . . from the great army of the non-participants that the population of the factory is chiefly drawn."[4]

Mr. Thompson asserts a difference between the indigent whites of the mountains and those nearer the middle portion of North Carolina, saying that in the extreme west the inhabitants in 1860 lived the same primitive lives as their grandfathers, while unpropertied whites in the Piedmont were not socially distinguished from their more fortunate neighbors until a late date. White men would often assist a landowner whose slaves were insufficient, at such times sleeping in his house and eating at his table. "Indeed, it is not too much to say that the Piedmont section of North Carolina was more nearly a social democracy after 1840 than were the manufacturing sections of New England, where by that date there was a well-defined manufacturing aristocracy." The Civil War, however, marked the com-

---

[3] Murphy, pp. 14–15.
[4] Ibid., pp. 104–105. Cf. ibid., p. 103, and Phillips, in South Mobilizing for Social Service, p. 567.

mencement of the increase of tenant farmers and share-
croppers with consequent class cleavage. Those afterwards in very poor circumstances had been closely associated
in general estimation with the small traders and professional men.[5]

The common origin of mountain whites and tenant whites
and the applicability of the term "poor whites" to both
groups is noticed by Mr. Hammond, who calls them all
quite properly, in view of circumstances in which they
found themselves, "parasitic."[6] Along with his characteristic bias and exaggeration is the usual portion of truth in
this observation of a Northern newspaper correspondent
who traveled through the South in the autumn following
Lee's surrender: "Whether the North Carolina 'dirt eater,'
or the South Carolina 'sand-hiller,' or the Georgia
'cracker,' is lowest in the scale of human existence would
be difficult to say. The ordinary plantation negro seemed
to me, when I first saw him in any numbers, at the very
bottom of not only probabilities, but also possibilities, so
far as they affect human relations; but these specimens of

---

[5] Thompson, p. 99 ff. Early title deeds show the settlers in the
Piedmont of North Carolina to have been weavers, joiners, coopers,
wheelwrights, wagon makers, tailors, teachers, blacksmiths, hatters,
merchants, wine makers, surveyors, fullers and "gentlemen" (Tompkins, History of Mecklenburg, vol. i, pp. 24–25). Slavery and cotton
had worked their change by 1856, when Olmsted wrote that "the
slaveholders have . . . secured the best circumstances for the employment of that slave-labor which is the most valuable part of their
capital. They need no assistance from the poor white man; his
presence near them is disagreeable and unprofitable. Condemned
to the poorest land, and restricted to the labor of merely providing
for themselves the simple necessities of life, they are equally indifferent and incompetent to materially improve their minds or their
wealth" (p. 515). Cf. ibid., p. 296; Tompkins, ibid., p. 88.

[6] Speaking of cotton culture before the War, "the majority of the
white laborers were of the class of 'poor whites,' many of them
descendants of the 'redemptioners.' . . . these people . . . had become the parasites of Southern society. Some of them were forced
into the mountain region of eastern Tennessee and Kentucky and
western North Carolina, and others were left on the abandoned cotton and tobacco lands of the sand hill region of South Carolina and
Georgia" (Hammond, p. 97).

the white race must have reached a yet lower depth of squalid and beastly wretchedness."[7]

That the poor whites were the victims of the economic regime and that their laziness was to be attributed in large measure to this prime fact, has been made clear by a keen and sympathetic student of Southern economic history. "All whites who were poor were not 'poor whites,' but many embraced in that term of contempt and pity were poor . . . in the ambition to contend against what seemed to be the inevitable." He thinks that, corresponding to the countryman in New England, there were very moderately circumstanced whites in the South that might be taken as constituting a "yeomanry," but that below these were "the neglected people who . . . were but little removed from the status of the settled Indian. . . . They were the degenerates, the children of ancient poverty and wrong, with little or no opportunity to better their condition among surroundings of a corrective character. . . . Had they not been too lazy to wander far from their apologies for home, they would have become American gypsies. . . . The victims of heredity and of institutions in which they had no interest, placed under laws made for them rather than by them, they were happily removed from the pressure of population that would undoubtedly have reduced them to the criminal or the dependent class."[8]

---

[7] Andrews, pp. 335–336. "The Georgia 'Cracker' . . . seems to me to lack not only all that the negro does, but also even the desire for a better condition and the vague longing for the enlargement of his liberties and his rights."

[8] Ingle, p. 22 ff. "John Forsythe of Mobile hit off some of their traits in contrasting the unadulterated 'Cracker' and an unadulterated Yankee, born and bred in the country. 'One is slow . . . and the other quick; one takes a minute to rise from his seat, the other never sits at all except in pursuance of a calculation; one is not without faculties, but they seem to be all asleep, the other with all his wits alive with sagacity, curiosity, invention. The one content to doze away life with as little labor as possible and all the enjoyment compassable; his log hut, wool hat, homespun suit, and corn and bacon the limits of his desires . . .; loving his gun and his horse, addicted to tobacco and strong drink, quick to anger, a dangerous enemy, and a fast friend. The other instinct with life . . . never satisfied with the present wellbeing while anything better

Governor Hammond, of South Carolina, was moderate when he said: "According to the best calculations which, in the absence of statistic facts, can be made, it is believed that, of the 300,000 *white* inhabitants of South Carolina, there are not less than 50,000, whose industry, such as it is, and compensated as it is, is not, in the present condition of things, and does not promise, hereafter, to be, adequate to procure them, honestly, such a support as every white person in this country is and feels himself entitled to."[9]

Professor Hart believes that the term "poor whites" means lowlanders, and that the mountaineers belong in a different category. His reason is chiefly that the mountain whites do not have to contend with the universal presence of the Negro. It is to be remembered that this distinction is of later emergence, and that slavery was responsible for

---

is beyond to tempt his longings and his wits.' " A South Carolinian who seemed to be informed gave Olmsted his opinion that communities of poor whites on the banks of the Congaree River were in more hopeless plight than the degraded peons of Mexico, and a rice planter described similar people living in the pine barrens nearest the coast: "They seldom have any meat . . . except they steal hogs, which belong to the planters, or their negroes, and their chief diet is rice and milk. They are small, gaunt, and cadaverous, and their skin is just the color of the sandhills they live on. They are quite incapable of applying themselves steadily to any labor, and their habits are very much like those of the old Indians" (p. 505 ff.). A Northerner told Olmsted of stopping once at a sand-hiller's cabin. One of the four grown daughters was weaving, the others seeming to have nothing to do. " 'I asked the girl at the loom how much she could make a day by her work. She did not know, but I ascertained that the stuff she wove was bought at a factory in the vicinity, to be used for bagging yarn; and she was paid in yarn. . . . She traded off the yarn at a store for what she had to buy. . . . If she worked steadily from daylight to dark . . . her wages . . . were less than sixteen cents a day, boarding herself. . . . These people are regarded by the better class with as little respect as slaves . . .' " (ibid., p. 507). This was in South Carolina. Twenty-five or thirty years later such establishments as this bagging mill had largely disappeared, the bartering of yarn was no longer practiced, and such a family of girls as here described was in all likelihood working immediately in a cotton factory for money wages.

[9] Quoted in Olmsted, p. 514. Here again is the thought that they were crowded out of occupations: "Some cannot be said to work at all. They obtain a precarious subsistence by occasional jobs, by hunting, by fishing, sometimes by plundering fields or folds, and, too often, by . . . trading with slaves, or seducing them to plunder for their benefit."

the history of the class of unfortunate whites, whether they were left in the low-country, stranded upon the sandhills between coastal plain and Piedmont, or driven into the hills.[10]

The pertinence of recent accounts of the poorer mountain and tenant whites in their native surroundings is illustrated by the fact that the mills very recently were receiving families in just as destitute condition as those which first entered the factory communities.[11] They regularly came with empty hands. An episode recited of a mill at Spartanburg is typical, where "one day a covered wagon or mountain schooner drove up to the . . . office. It was full of family and that was about all. 'You could put upon a small table all the earthly possessions of that family,' said Mr. Montgomery. The man asked for work. Mr. Montgomery told the superintendent to find them a vacant house. 'But what about the rashuns?' inquired the new 'help.'"[12]

The most recent historian of the American industry in his description of the people who filled the mills of the South does not distinguish between Piedmont, mountain, and lowland (tenant) whites.[13]

It has been seen that while many of the Southern mill ventures were undertaken partly with the express purpose

---

[10] Southern South, p. 30. For some account of the middle-country poor whites, with a list of the disparaging names applied to them, see ibid., p. 38; a description of the mountaineers (p. 34 ff.) is most dismal.

[11] An admirable recent picture of the life of the poor whites in mountain and lowland sections is contained in a painstaking pamphlet by Frances Sage Bradley and Margaretta A. Williamson, "Rural Children in Selected Counties of North Carolina," published by the Children's Bureau of the U. S. Department of Labor.

[12] Columbia Record, Textile Ed., 1916. Of a factory at Rock Hill it is reported: "A man who moved to the mill from Union County a few years ago was so poverty stricken that he had not even a bed upon which to sleep. He was in such poverty that it was a matter of jest" (ibid.). Of another mill village it is told that "nineteen families have moved into this community within the last fourteen years, bringing their entire worldly possessions in one wagon load . . . ; none of these . . . families had a stick of furniture or a sack of flour or the means to provide for the same" (ibid.).

[13] Copeland, pp. 40–41.

of giving work to the poor whites, in a good many cases the opportunity for profitable employment of these people was entirely overlooked, this giving color to the belief that in proportion as the poor whites dropped out of participation in the economic order, they tended to drop out of the mind of the dominant class. The abolition of slavery did not bring the neglected men and women immediately back into the thought and sympathy of the South any more than into the employment of the South.[14]

It has been seen that William Gregg, the builder of the Graniteville Factory in South Carolina, was the father, in the sense that he was the anticipator, of a new economic life for the South. His keen consciousness of the poor whites stands out in striking contrast to the state of mind indicated in the preceding paragraphs. It is interesting to notice a statement of Gregg's which shows clearly the condition of the lower strata of the white population fifteen years before the war; it is to be remarked that he was combating a tendency not simply to omit the poor whites from consideration, but to place the negroes ahead of these even, as possible industrial workers. "Should we stop," he asked, "at the effort to prove the capacity of blacks for manufacturing? Shall we pass unnoticed the thousands of poor, ignorant, degraded white people among us, who, in this land of plenty, live in comparative nakedness and starvation?" And he continued:

Many a one is reared in *proud* South-Carolina, from birth to manhood, who has never passed a month in which he has not some part of the time, been stinted for meat. Many a mother is there, who will tell you that her children are but scantily supplied with bread. . . . These are startling statements, but they are nevertheless true, and if not believed in Charleston, the members of our Legislature, who have traversed the State, in electioneering campaigns, can attest their truth.

---

[14] A Virginia correspondent of the American Agriculturist before the War asserted that whites could be got to work for less price than blacks, but the slaves were preferred. Newcomers were advised, if they wished to use whites, to bring them with them, since the native white population was inferior to the black (quoted in Olmsted, pp. 211–212). A farmer in the same State who employed only free labor found Irishmen at $120 a year the best workers; native whites were declared worse than free blacks (ibid., p. 99).

It is only necessary to build a manufacturing village of shanties, in a healthy location in any part of the State, to have crowds of these poor people around you, seeking employment at half the compensation given to operatives at the North. It is indeed pitiful to be brought in contact with such ignorance and degradation; but on the other hand, it is pleasant to witness the change, which soon takes place in the condition of those who obtain employment. The emaciated, pale-faced children, soon assume the appearance of robust health. . . . It is, perhaps, not generally known, but there are *twenty-nine thousand* white persons in this State, above the age of twelve years, who can neither read nor write—this is about one in every five of the whole population.[15]

A writer already quoted refers to the poor whites of the ante-bellum South as constituting part of the last grade of a class distinguishable from both the unpropertied and the influential landowners, which might be termed a "yeomanry," but he notices their tendency to sink rather than rise in the social order.[16]

Thus again it is indicated how the pressure of slavery, if it worked to bring a small number to the surface, gave to masses an impulse ever downward.

There is very little to show the character of the white operatives in the small and scattered factories that existed in the South prior to the great rise of mills about 1880. Many were doubtless immigrants or descendants of recent immigrants. The Graniteville mill had workpeople who did not differ materially in their economic or social aspects from those in later manufacturing communities, and perhaps the same may be said of a few other establishments in the ante-bellum period. But Graniteville was not typical of

---

[15] Domestic Industry, p. 22. It is to be observed that knowledge of the plight of the poor whites gained in electioneering campaigns was passive, and did not awaken a purpose to improve conditions. Gregg himself, as a member of the legislature, was the exception that proved the rule. Despite the difficulty of travel and the absence of "statistic facts," as Governor Hammond said, public ignorance of a 20 per cent illiteracy in the white population is as reprehensible as the fact of the illiteracy itself. When Gregg was working out his philosophy in practice, he reported to his Graniteville stockholders in 1855 that 79 in 100 grown girls who came to the mill could neither read not write, adding that "that reproach has long since been removed" (quoted in Kohn, Cotton Mills of S. C., p. 21). Cf. statement of a colporteur in Olmsted, p. 510.

[16] Ingle, pp. 20–21.

its time. Graniteville tapped a class of labor as a class; the smaller factories, with all sorts of local limitations in situation, power, machinery and peculiarities of operation, attracted only individuals, had no labor objective. It was not recognized that any widespread condition existed that made employment in mills desirable, and no distinctive problems grew out of the collecting of persons in the little villages surrounding the factories. That many negroes were used in these enterprises, alone or with whites, helps to blur the picture of the white operatives. In the matter of labor, these early establishments corresponded roughly with grist mills and saw mills then and today. Nobody bothered about where the employees came from or why. It is probable that in most instances they had been living in the immediate localities. It may be concluded that the difference between the mills before the great period and those which followed, with respect to labor, was one of size of the manufacturing unit and of degree of standardization of the industry.[17]

The amount that had to be done for the poor whites after they came to the mills (speaking now of the large development of factories), and their too evident entire newness to the demands of progressive living, reflect a light back upon the years in which they had been pushed aside. The history of the industry since 1880, in the human phase, has been chiefly the effort at reinstatement of a great portion of the population previously neglected.[18] Sometimes the people brought with them little besides bad habits and a

---

[17] Glimpses of before-the-war operatives frequently indicate foreign birth or ancestry, and are not always inspiriting. Cf. Olmsted, pp. 356–357; Buckingham, Slave States of America, vol. i, p. 171.

[18] A recent president of the chamber of commerce of a capital city said that while in office he refused to give his especial support to projects to establish cotton mills in the place because of all the people who came to a factory, only five or six families would be composed of desirable citizens, the rest lowering the average of population. "You have to take care of these people when they are sick," he explained, "and you must give them schools and churches. Thousands of dollars, of course, were spent in eradicating the hook worm."

total dependence upon the management for moral care and physical upbuilding.[19]

However much the poor whites had failed of recognition before, instances are rare in which mill men, at the outset of the factory era in the South or later, have complained of the quality of the operatives. It may be said that the work of a cotton mill, certainly a mill on coarse goods, is scarcely skilled at all, and that in the beginning management was as unaccustomed to its task as spinner and weaver to theirs. It may be observed that labor was above all cheap, and that advantage thus conferred silenced all objection. But the fact is not altered that Southern mill owners showed a splendid faith in the capacity of their workpeople. Northern superintendents in Southern manufactories seemed unanimous in their satisfaction with the labor.

One of the most distinguished of Southern mill projectors wrote in reply to some doubting remarks of another Southern manufacturer: "I do not admit that the Northern people are any better material out of which to make cotton manufacturers and operatives than our own, and especially in the 'Piedmont belt,' of the South, is the best in the United States, and capable of being educated to as high an order of skill as any other. I have been in most of the best mills at the North . . . and have observed their operations closely, and I challenge that there is as high skill and an equal degree of expertness in the operatives of the Piedmont Mill, as far as the kind of goods made requires . . . as is to be found in any mill in New England."[20]

---

[19] The head of a large establishment told how "ninety per cent of the operatives—kids and all—used to use snuff. We would get from the loom-boxes, where they would leave them, a barrel of snuff boxes a week in cleaning. Now not fifteen per cent use snuff" (T. S. Raworth, int., Augusta, Ga., Dec. 30, 1916).

[20] Letter of H. P. Hammett to Atlanta Constitution, quoted in Manufacturers' Record, Baltimore, Feb. 1, 1883. An old man, looking back to the starting of his mill forty years ago, said to the writer with a determined look in his eye: "In a speech made in Atlanta at the Exposition [1881] Edward Atkinson told us that we couldn't manufacture goods in the Southern States because we couldn't get help down here; that we should let them manufacture the cotton and we raise the cotton. I saw the help coming in from

It has been seen that some writers would distinguish between the mountain whites, the poor whites of the Piedmont belt and the corresponding group in the coastal plain; that some question exists as to the application of the term "poor whites"; and that some believe there was a tolerably defined middle class in the South before and following the war. However these facts may be, it is chiefly important to understand that the mills drew from all these divisions of poor whites, and if there was a group between them and the upper whites, it did not work to alter the essential economic situation. Whatever technical differences existed prior to the opening of the factories, in the willingness to seek mill employment there was a general merger of types of indigent white people.[21]

Generous estimates of the capacities and promise of the poor whites in the mills and out of them are as easy to find as it is natural to give them. Anyone who sees the people in the country or in the industrial communities and who knows anything of their lives, feels a respectful warmth go out to them. With all the marks of their hindrance upon them, he must recognize that they have all the worth which the best blood in America can bestow.[22]

---

dinner at Fall River in the eighties, and it couldn't compare to ours!" (Charles Estes, int., Augusta). Another old man declared: "North Carolina has within its borders more Anglo-Saxon blood than any other State in the Union. There is no better labor in the United States than in the cotton mills of North Carolina" (Charles McDonald, int., Charlotte, N. C., Sept. 3, 1916). It has been properly observed that the term "poor white trash," common in writing about the South, is rarely used by Southern whites. "They are unprogressive, they fail to make the most of their opportunities, but they are not degraded. It is suspended or arrested development rather than degeneracy" (Thompson, p. 113).

[21] Cf. Thompson, pp. 69–70.

[22] The statement of Mr. Baldwin, principal of the Piedmont Industrial School at Charlotte, while very familiar, is worth quoting here. He is speaking especially of the operatives in his own section: "I am satisfied that they are the finest body of people on earth doing similar work. Descended from the early English, Scotch and Germans, they have been sleeping, as it were, while the procession of progress has been passing by. Serious, independent, as all hill and mountain people are; sensitive, because of that independent spirit, for the most part sober, they are a people of untold possibilities, now that they are beginning to arouse themselves from the drowsi-

The cotton mill operatives came immediately from the soil. The cotton manufacturing South sprang directly from the cotton growing South. It is probable that never before or since in economic history has an agricultural population been so suddenly drawn into industry. The sharp emergence of manufacturing from farming, the more abrupt because long delayed, is in a large way the theme of this study. The picture is one with a cotton mill in the foreground and acres of cotton plants in the background, stretching away almost to the horizon.

The relation between farm and factory was especially close in the case of labor. In the decision of individual men and families to leave the land for the manufacturing village it is possible to see, very tangibly, the working of causes that were moving the whole South. In another place the counter pull of the plough against the spindle will be mentioned, when it will be shown how now one and now the other, in the estimation of workers, has gained ascendancy. At this point it is important to notice briefly the agricultural conditions prevailing at about the time of the rise of the mills.

It has been said of North Carolina that "before 1890 the question of satisfactory labor had not been entirely solved. The better class of labor was not easily drawn from the farms to the factories." After 1890 the price of cotton, due to increased production of the domestic staple, to the size of Egyptian and Indian crops, and the depression following the panic of 1893, fell lower and lower. The crops of 1894 and 1895 brought for the most part about five cents per pound, and low prices of wheat, corn and tobacco accompanied the drop in cotton. Fertilizer bills were hard to meet, mortgages were difficult to carry. Cotton mills were running day and night and selling yarns in the markets of Philadelphia, New York, Boston and the Orient. In this

---

ness of generations and to grapple earnestly with the duties of this active, work-a-day world " (quoted in Goldsmith, p. 27). Cf. Kohn, Cotton Mills of S. C., pp. 21–22. " These people are all Americans, and hundreds could qualify as Sons or Daughters of the Revolution " (Thompson, pp. 110–111).

condition of things, farms were sold, rental arrangements were not renewed and industrious and lazy alike flocked to the mill communities.[23] In the case of other Southern States, the development came earlier and more abruptly than in North Carolina, and the abandonment of farming for the factory occupation was not so dependent upon the price of the staple at the particular time. Even in North Carolina, however, the causes back of the migration, if it may be spoken of as such, were of much longer standing than the account just given might be taken to indicate.

The condition of South Carolina in the decade before the war, in which the average value of the productive industry of the State was declared not to exceed $62 per head of the whole population, omitting the two largest cities, persisted, roughly, down to the years of the rise of the mills.[24]

The desperate, almost comical poverty of after-the-war years left on the minds of men who lived through them impressions that will not be erased. "In my county," said one of these, "the term ' farmer' applied to a man was a name something very like reproach. Every bull yearling was under chattel mortgage."[25]

---

[23] Thompson, pp. 69–70. Cf. H. J. Davenport, Economics of Enterprise, p. 201.

[24] From an article on the agriculture of South Carolina, written for The Carolinian by a resident of the State, and printed afterwards in DeBow's Review; quoted by Olmsted, pp. 518–519. "Full one-half, or more, of this amount is consumed on the plantation or farm, as necessary means of subsistence; leaving about $31 as the value of cotton and other marketable produce, per head."

[25] Henry E. Litchford, int., Richmond. The story of a family brought to a Charlotte factory when the Mountain Island mill was washed away in the summer of 1916 is illustrative of conditions prevailing forty years ago. The old woman and her three daughters had recently become operatives, and had nothing. With a fourth daughter, afterwards married, the family had tried to farm in the foothills. They made fairly good crops, the girls working in the field, but, in payment for land, stock, implements and feed, the landlord took all they made above a bare living and a dress or two a year and a pair of shoes for each occasionally. When the old woman finally left for the mill village she was able to pay herself out of debt and, so "the man" told her, she had $7.50 coming to her in cash, but this she never got. In the mill town they proved thrifty, the mother managing to keep her family going a whole week on $5 advanced by the management (Sterling Graydon, int., Charlotte).

One who has witnessed the economic awakening of Greenville County, South Carolina, from the commencement, rehearsing the evils of the system under which farmers bought on credit, paying once a year, frequently by note, much to the hurt of the agricultural community, spoke with satisfaction of the change since that time. He said that now no merchant in Greenville does a time business with farmers. The latter get small loans at the banks; one bank has for many years been lending some people regularly such small sums as thirty dollars, and it will lend as little as ten dollars. He remembers what may almost be said to have been the beginning of a local money economy. He saw the first whole bale of cotton ever brought to the Greenville market. The man who purchased it was consumed with fear as to his wisdom in putting so much money in cotton. Would the county ever need so much? This was about 1870, and gives a notion of the pettiness of farm operations in the up-country region then and later.[26]

A system of tenancy in which the farmer contributed little or nothing besides his own labor; in which, by custom, by pressure of the landlord, by dictate of his creditor merchant and by absence of initiative, the tenant raised only cotton; and by the working of which the proceeds of a crop, on which a lien was held, were consumed before they were realized, could not make agriculture promising.[27] It is re-

---

[26] W. J. Thackston, int., Greenville. The almost total absence of money in rural communities will be noticed later. Mr. Kohn, after reviewing the situation of operatives at the time they were farmers, came to the conclusion that "the attraction of the cotton mills, to those who are in them, in a word, is the cash money" (Cotton Mills of S. C., p. 26). Cf. ibid., pp. 22, 27.

[27] Some facts gathered by Mr. Kohn as to recently prevailing tenancy arrangements in South Carolina serve as a fair picture of earlier conditions. In the Pee-Dee section the landlord ordinarily paid for fertilizers, ginning, bagging and ties, and the tenant received half the crop. It was thought good for a tenant to "make" fifteen bales of cotton, his half, at $50 a bale, bringing him $375. The sale of a few bushels of corn not needed to feed the stock, and hauling and other work might net him $150 additional, a total of $525. This family might have one plough and two hoe hands. The same family in a cotton mill, at the time of writing, would have made about $900. A tenant in the Piedmont section, having to share in the cost of fer-

lated that the help for a mill built as late as 1896, picked up
on the neighboring farms, "had no money, no prospects.
Cotton was the only money crop and the price, four and
one-half cents, was such as to make a year's wages insignificant by comparison with what could be earned in the
mills. They came to the mills for employment, for relief
from the weight that pressed down upon them."[28]

Having seen something of the character of the poor
whites and the economic situation in which they were before
the building of the factories, it is natural next to examine
the experience of the mills in recruiting labor. First will
be noticed the cases, almost universal, in which applicants
for work were plentiful, and afterwards some instances in
which, for special reasons, operatives were not so readily
obtained.

The labor motive for the building of mills has been dealt
with in a previous chapter. Plentifulness of labor is an
easy conclusion from the arguments advanced that cotton
manufactories should be established in the South because
labor was cheap and because the employment would be a
benefit to large numbers who had only precarious means of
livelihood. In only a few cases in which sufficient labor for
a proposed mill was felt assured, did the anticipation prove
incorrect. There was little guessing involved; it was a
mine the veins of which lay in a net-work on the surface of
the earth. The question was whether mills could be built,
not whether they could be filled with workpeople pressing
to be admitted.

Gregg's recognition that the poor whites would make

---

tilizer, would have very little left after meeting the advances of the
merchant and fitting out his family with clothes (Cotton Mills of
S. C., pp. 27-28). Cf. News and Courier, Charleston, South Carolina in 1884; Bradley and Williamson, pp. 20-21; Charles H. Otken,
The Ills of the South, chaps. ii and iii; Hammond, pp. 144 ff., 155.

[28] Columbia Record, Textile Ed., 1916. For a good statement of
the reasons why poor whites came to the mills, see Derrick, "The
Cotton Mill Population of the South," in Bulletin of Newberry College (S. C.), vol. ii, no. 8, pp. 32-33. Cf. Thompson, p. 114 ff. on
this point and for an interesting classification of types that enter the
factories; the same classification might have been made forty years
ago with equal truth.

good cotton mill operatives is matched by the view of a Northern man made a decade before the war, that if the cotton manufacturing industry should be founded in the South, labor would be in supply. He urged that cotton planters should become cotton manufacturers, showing how the profits from industry were greater than from agriculture, and continued: "But, after having admitted all this, the cotton planters and capitalists of the South raise the inquiry: Suppose we wished to go into the manufacturing business, though we had plenty of raw material, how should we obtain the labor and skill qualified for the work, and of both of which we are deficient?" This conjectured inquiry, one coming naturally from owners of large plantations worked by negro slaves, was answered without hesitation: ". . . a fine supply may at all times be obtained, in New England, to manage and supervise . . . operations . . . and there are thousands of persons at the South, who would gladly and gratefully accept such employment to earn a livelihood, much superior to that which their present means can possibly afford; and would quickly become qualified for the work of operatives, under the charge and direction of good . . . managers. . . . In a comparatively short period, hundreds of factories might be erected and started at the South, and fully supplied with every description of skill and labor wanted."[29]

Impossible as was this proposal for widespread manufacture of cotton at the South at the time it was made, the prophesies it contained were realized, when finally the mills were built, with remarkable completeness. Thus thirty years after James wrote, the president of the Louisville and Nashville Railroad was able to say in a Northern paper: "Mills for the weaving of the coarser cotton fabrics are now in successful operation in Tennessee, Georgia, Kentucky and several of the Atlantic coast States. . . . The labor question in the South, which a few years ago presented many difficulties, is now as practically settled there

---

[29] James, in DeBow, vol. i, p. 233 ff.

as in any other portion of the land. The class formerly
known as 'poor whites' are mixing and assimilating with
their more fortunate neighbors. They are making good
workers in mine and field, good operatives in factories.
. . ."[30] It was stated in 1880 that within a few months five
hundred white North Carolinians had left the State to seek
homes in the West, and that the movement was increasing.
The number of emigrants with sufficient energy and means
to go far away did not need to be large to indicate that there
was a surplus of labor.[31]

The Atlanta correspondent of the New York Times, describing the cotton mill campaign in the South, said that
"there is an abundance of native white labor to be had at
from 50 to 60 cents a day"; explained that while negroes
had not been proved entirely unsuitable for the work,—
"there are white men and women enough for all present
demands,"—and continued: "Of the many benefits which
the community at large, as distinguished from the capitalist
and manufacturer, will enjoy from the extension of manufactures in the South, the chief one will be the opportunity
afforded for the profitable employment of thousands of
hands now idle." White labor must yield to black in cotton
growing and in the less skilled trades. "Shut out in so
many directions the whites, who now find life a bitter struggle, will gladly turn to the spindle and loom as a means of
gaining a livelihood. Manufacturing will be their deliver-
ance. . . . For girls and women who have hitherto had no
opportunity to earn money the establishment of factories in
every town and village will be an incalculable blessing."[32]

---

[30] Quoted from New York Herald in News and Courier, Charleston, July 11, 1881. By 1888 the abundant supply of labor in South
Carolina was not only recognized in the State itself as an asset, but
was advertised as such to manufacturers who might be considering
locating there, the State department of agriculture publishing that
"the manufacturer of cotton goods finds . . . a population willing
and anxious for employment, out of which can be made as intelligent, skillful and reliable operatives as are to be found anywhere"
(South Carolina Department of Agriculture, Sketch of Industrial
Resources of S. C., 1888, p. 27).

[31] Concord Sun, quoted in Observer, Raleigh, Feb. 24, 1880.

[32] Quoted in News and Courier, Charleston, Nov. 5, 1881. How

From one of the new cotton mill localities in 1881 came the following, which has the distinctive flavor of the times:

Not only should there be different kinds of crops, but we ought to have other ways of securing a livelihood besides farming. There ought to be other kinds of work furnished the girls of the State besides housekeeping. The factories that are springing up over the country will help them a great deal. Here is a factory established at Piedmont which will give employment to six hundred persons, half of whom will be girls. But we need others. There is a man here now from Edgefield who has a family of six girls and who has come here to get them work in the Piedmont factory. But he is too late. Every house in the place has been engaged and there are twenty families that have applied for positions, but have been refused because they are not needed. Four families of thirty persons have moved in since yesterday.

Many who were not idle or even, perhaps, exactly "marginal" producers, came to the mills, thus increasing the visible labor supply. It was said that "as soon as the crops are gathered all the others that have secured places will move here. The population at present is over one thousand and it will be 1,500 in two months. There are more carpenters and mechanics employed here now than at any past time. . . . 240 rooms are being plastered."[33]

---

little conditions in the South varied from one locality to another, how universal were the causes which underlay its economic plight, are instanced on every hand. Places outside the South were more likely to possess peculiar economic characteristics. Thus a Philadelphia textile journal remarked that "Baltimore . . . offers some of the best advantages for starting manufacturing establishments of any point in the United States. . . . Labor is plenty and cheap, there being a great number of females who are employed during the packing season, which lasts but a short time; the balance of which they eke out a miserable existence by sewing." Here was a purely local circumstance (Philadelphia Hosiery and Knit Goods Manufacturer, quoted in Baltimore Journal of Commerce and Manufacturers' Record, July 15, 1882).

[33] News and Courier, Charleston, Oct. 21, 1881. The son of the founder of this mill told the writer that "there was no opposition among the country people against the mills. At Piedmont in the early days it was impossible to give employment to all that offered themselves" (James D. Hammett, int., Anderson). The rush to hastily constructed mill villages, though from a local region, was much like the lightning growth of gold towns in California and Alaska, and, more recently, at munition plants. Of the Clifton mill in South Carolina it was said that "there are families coming in constantly and the cottages as fast as completed are occupied, and still they come" (News and Courier, Charleston, Oct. 21, 1881). There were many reasons for a large proportion of women and girls

Of operatives proper in Southern mills, the census of 1870 showed that women comprised 41.2 per cent. In 1880 the percentage was 49.4, but by 1890 it had receded again to 40.6. In the New England mills, on the other hand, the proportion of women in all classes of employes was a little higher in 1890 than in 1880—49.4 per cent as against 49.2 per cent. In Southern mills the percentage of children decreased slightly between 1880 and 1890—from 24.5 to 23.7, whereas in New England the proportion of children fell away greatly in the decade—from 13.9 to 6.8 per cent. In the South the percentage of men increased from 30.2 to 35.6, and in New England from 36.8 to 43.7. Thus in New England mills, decrease in the proportion of children was accompanied by an increase in percentage of men, but also by some increase in percentage of women. In the South, on the other hand, a slight reduction in proportion of children was coincident with an increase in the proportion of men and a correspondingly sharp fall in proportion of women. In New England there was a relative elimination of children, and in the South of women.[34]

---

in the ranks of those who applied to the cotton mills for employment. Elsewhere the effect of the Civil War in reducing the number of men and boys and in crippling others is noted. It was less easy for females to compete with colored labor than for males, not only from physical but from social causes. The cotton factories offered a field from which negroes were excluded. The work was light and suited to deft fingers. What applied to women and girls was true in slightly less degree of young boys.

[34] The percentage of women in Southern mills in 1880 is taken from absolute figures in U. S. Census of Manufactures, 1880 (Cotton Manufacture, by Edward Atkinson, pp. 15–16), and is higher than that given in the census of 1890 (Cotton Manufacture, by Edward Stanwood, p. 173)—45.3—in which all classes of employes, and not simply operatives, were included. Obviously, office force and "outside" help would include few women. Other percentages approximated in the fractions are from U. S. Census of Manufactures, 1890, ibid. The trend pointed out above may be seen more clearly by taking the year 1900 into consideration. Between 1890 and 1900 the number of children in New England mills increased 8.7 per cent; women 1.89; and men 23.9. In the South the number of children made a gain of 177 per cent; women 125; and men 223 per cent (percentages from absolute figures in U. S. Census of Manufactures, 1900). Of course, it must be remembered that the number of all employes in Southern mills was greatly increasing after 1880. In

In the South and in New England the cotton industry, in respect to labor, has eased itself at the points of relatively greatest strain. In the South this meant proportionate decrease in number of women employed; in New England it meant decrease in relative number of children. If it is borne in mind that in the South there was first great pressure for employment, changing gradually to insistent demand for workers, distinction in alteration of proportions of operatives in the two sections is not difficult to account for. In the South in the beginning everybody was eager for work, and women seemed better suited to take hold of an industrial task than children; later, when the fullest numbers were needed, the nature of factory work was familiar, and more children could go into the mills if mothers worked at home.[35]

Census figures are borne out roughly by many references that may be found relative to labor in the mills at the outset of the period. Thus two-thirds of the operatives at Langley were female (girls included with women) in 1880, and it was reported of Graniteville and Vaucluse that "the number of operatives employed is 775; two-thirds of whom are females and who range from 11 years up."[36] In a factory at Selma, Alabama, "the operatives number 120, mostly women and children, taken from Selma and vicinity."[37]

The prevailing low rate of wages, as also variations in wages between one mill and another, may be taken as indications that labor was in abundant supply. An examination

1850 and 1860 the number of women was about the same—6157 and 6039. In 1870 there were 4190, in 1880 there were 7587, and in 1890 there were 15,083 (ibid.).

[35] Edward Stanwood (Cotton Manufacture, p. 33, in U. S. Census of Manufactures, 1900), was mistaken in neglecting these considerations. "Whole families in that region," he said, meaning the South, "enter the factories, because in no other way can the demand for labor be satisfied. Consequently the changes in the proportion of men, women and children employed are largely fortuitous." On the face of it, his statement is unfortunate, because taking together great numbers of families entering the mills, a statistical trend would easily show itself; moreover, after a family has been in the mill a while, some members may discontinue the factory employment.

[36] Blackman, pp. 7 and 4.

[37] News and Courier, Charleston, March 31, 1881.

of newspaper files covering the opening years of the cotton mill period failed to disclose a single advertisement for operatives. When it is remembered that factories sprang in great numbers and simultaneously from an agricultural regime, this is striking.[38]

An article summarizing a newspaper correspondent's study of the South Carolina cotton mills in 1880 declared that "the difficulty in obtaining operatives is not great, it seems. Indeed no new industry has ever been adopted with less difficulty, and with fewer drawbacks and discouragement [sic], than the business of manufacturing cotton in South Carolina."[39] There appeared to be no apprehension about getting operatives for the largest plants. Thus the King mill at Augusta in 1883 began production confidently. "The first beam was taken off the slasher Wednesday morning . . . at 10.30 o'clock, and the first loom was started Wednesday afternoon at 3 o'clock. Last evening there were fifty-three looms running. Supt. Smith reports that so far he has had no trouble getting hands, and does not anticipate trouble in this direction."[40]

---

[38] It is true, of course, that newspapers were then not so widely read as now, and did not reach to very large extent the people who were attracted to the mills. Many of the first mills were from the start operated at night, which required a double force of hands. Thus more mills than were built might have sprung up and had labor to run during the day, without exhausting the labor supply, providing the conclusion reached in this study, that workers were plentiful without respect to locality, is correct. For example: "Quite a number of Mr. Cornelson's new factory hands have already arrived at Orangeburg, and the mill is now being run at night" (News and Courier, Charleston, April 9, 1881).

[39] Leading article, in Blackman. The article was probably written by F. W. Dawson, editor of the News and Courier.

[40] Chronicle, Augusta, Nov. 11, 1883. The first president of this mill told the writer that the factory "got plenty of help right here locally, all natives" (Charles Estes, int., Augusta). A factory which had its start before the cotton mill campaign was in every sense a local enterprise. Its operatives were described as being "all natives, with one exception, who have been educated to the business. This class of labor is very readily obtained from the surrounding country" (Blackman, p. 10). Speaking of the beginnings of the cotton mill South, a commission merchant who has been intimately identified with the development said that "labor was superabundant and very cheap" (Summerfield Baldwin, int., Baltimore).

The superintendent of the Langley factory stated that "labor was very plentiful and that they could get 20 per cent more than was required to run the mill. The . . . operatives are made up entirely of the people born and raised right in the vicinity."[41] An old man who saw the founding of the mills said that the availability of a labor supply did not form a strong motive in the locating of factories, for there was never any difficulty about getting operatives.[42]

A superintendent in another State gave similar testimony: "Proximity to a labor supply was not considered in the location of mills early in the period. There was plenty of labor at first." Mr. Tompkins, explaining what he considered the corrective results of manufactures protected by a tariff, gave a little picture of the South that had been familiar: "You all know that fifteen and twenty years ago we did have an army of unemployed. . . . Any town in those old days presented a street spectacle of listless loafers, white and black, leaning against the door facings, telegraph poles and sitting on boxes. Even the dogs caught the listless spirit and didn't get up to bark."[43]

---

[41] Blackman, p. 7.

[42] Charles McDonald, int., Charlotte.

[43] American Cotton Manufacture and the Tariff, p. 9. For the Arista Mills, at Winston-Salem, the attempt was made to get skilled operatives from other factory communities, but this proved expensive and unnecessary, because many in an already floating population offered experienced services and others came in sufficient numbers (John W. Fries, int., Winston-Salem). It will be seen later that labor continued in abundance for a good many years following 1880. Tompkins, whose largeness of view is not often to be interpreted as exaggeration, thought the South had enough idle people to fill factories that would drive England and Germany out of world markets (Cotton Mill, Commercial Features, p. 177). He argued that "Those who know the existing conditions will probably not dissent from the opinion that it would be easy to put 1,000,000 people to work manufacturing cotton, and never miss them from present employments. Estimating 12,000,000 out of the entire population as being white people, even from amongst these, a million could be more than easily spared" (ibid., p. 20 ff. There is much in this reference to show how cotton mills in the South took up slack in the available working force and improved conditions of urban and rural communities). In 1900 Tompkins believed night work was necessary if all of the mill people were to be kept in jobs. "The night work in cotton mills

Having seen how generally willing the people were to offer themselves for work in the cotton mills for a long period after the first establishment of the industry in the South, it may next be shown from what localities labor was drawn, what were the immediate and what the secondary regions of supply. Before speaking of the migrations to the mills from districts just surrounding them, however, incidental notice might be taken of the fact that farmers' daughters frequently embraced temporary employment in the little neighborhood mills running before the Civil War. They wanted to make money to buy trousseaux or to help their families, but they did not intend to become factory workers. They perhaps walked to and from the mill morning and evening, or, if their homes were at an inconvenient distance, might live with a friend near the factory. These conditions prevailed with respect to five mills on Deep River in a Quaker community in North Carolina prior to 1850. This was not considered menial service, and the young women often married officials in the mills. The custom was roughly that of farmers' daughters in parts of the South today, who work in canneries in their neighborhoods a few weeks in the summer.[44] This practice had nothing to do with the readiness with which an agricultural population entered factories from 1880 forward.

It is difficult, speaking for the majority of cases, to agree with the statement of Mr. Copeland relative to the smaller Southern factories that "frequently a mill was established in an out of the way place so as to employ workmen who were not willing to move but would work for low wages

---

is better than any other work the operatives can get now or they wouldn't take it. It would be a hardship to close all the mills at night and throw all these people at once out of regular employment" (Labor Legislation, p. 4). Mr. Thompson thought it necessary to state in 1906 that "the difference [in wages] in favor of the factory is so great that only the natural inertia of a rural population combined with certain social disadvantages of factory labor prevents an over-supply" of operatives (p. 274).

[44] Cf. Thompson, p. 51 ff. With reference to similar conditions in cotton mills in New England at about the same period, see Copeland, p. 12.

near their homes."[45]   There were instances in which the
proximity of a labor supply was a factor in determining the
location of a mill, but with these comparatively rare establishments, the thought was that the plant would be closer
to prospective hands than other mills, would be in the path
of an efflux of labor.   In hardly any case could the people
do otherwise than move their homes to the village provided
by the factory, or to the town in which the factory was
located.   They usually knew that they were divorcing themselves from the soil.   The mills went to the labor only in
the sense that they competed for positions convenient to a
general labor supply.   It is said that cotton manufactures
were located at Anderson, South Carolina, partly because
the place is only about thirty miles from cheap labor in the
mountains, but workers came to this mill first from the
close neighborhood, and afterwards from the mountains.[46]

It is true that sometimes the prejudices of the people and
their local ignorances assisted a mill placed near them.   A
superintendent who has had experience in soliciting labor
for a large mill in a city said that "a new operative from
the country naturally goes to a country mill.   These people
look on Spartanburg as I would look on New York City, as
a great big corrupt assemblage of humanity where folks
can't raise their children right."[47]   But the people who went
to the mills had decided to become operatives, and if country families sought country mills, these might have been at
a greater or shorter distance from their homes without considerably influencing their willingness to seek the industrial
employment.

Ordinarily, "it was possible then to locate a mill almost
anywhere and strike a labor supply."[48]   Labor was so abundant that it was an advantage, rather than an object.

It has been suggested to the writer that the cotton mill era
in the South was made possible by the pushing of railroads

[45] Cotton Manufacturing Industry of U. S. (p. 143).
[46] J. A. Brock, int., Anderson, S. C., Sept. 11, 1916.
[47] W. J. Britton, int., Spartanburg, S. C., Sept. 5, 1916.
[48] C. S. Morris, int., Salisbury, N. C., Sept. 1, 1916.

up to the mountains, thus tapping pools of labor that flowed down into the Piedmont and lower country. Perhaps three considerations have prompted the thought: first, that cheap labor certainly contributed largely to the success of the factories at the outset; second, that there was an important period of railroad building in the South Atlantic States just before and during the years in which the cotton factories were erected; third, that many operatives came from the mountains. The number of mountaineers and "hill people" in the mill population of the South is large, but the curiously prevalent impression that all factory operatives were drawn from mountainous districts is mistaken.

Labor in the years of the rise of cotton mills was scattered; it was available in nearly every part of the South; it was not dammed up in the mountains alone. It will be seen that the people came to the mills first from districts immediately surrounding the plants. Wagons carrying the entire household goods of the new help formed the means of conveyance. After a good many mills had supplied foci for the labor of their localities and some operatives had been trained, labor begun to be a little fluid. Workpeople moved from mill to mill. As more factories were established, the populations of more sections were attracted to industrial life, the total body of operatives became larger, the distance from one plant to another was less, information as to comparative conditions in mill villages was more easily obtained, and there developed what has been called "the floating element." But this mobile element, it is to be noted, was composed of cotton mill operatives, and not of people just from the land.[49]   Not until late in the history

---

[49] "Railroads to the mountains did not tap pools of labor. There was not much floating or flowing of labor until the mills had been long established" (Charles McDonald, int., Charlotte). President Baldwin, of the Louisville and Nashville Railroad, in the interview in the New York Herald already quoted, spoke of the part of the railroads in opening up a future for the South and dwelt at some length upon the poor whites and their entrance into the factories, but did not mention any assistance of railroads in forming an outlet for pent-up labor supplies. Cf. George B. Cowlan, The Undeveloped South. Search has failed to reveal a case in which, among the many

of the Southern mills, as will be pointed out in more detail presently, did establishments get fresh labor from any distance, and in these cases the stimulus to move came from the mills, not from the people. The iron filings had no greater impulse to move to the magnet than formerly; more power had to be given to the attractive force. The mills had been building a good many years before it was necessary for them to solicit labor, and it proved hard work.[50]

Labor from the mountains came a greater distance, perhaps, than that from the farming districts, but this was because there were no mills right in the mountains. It was essentially local, just as much as was the tenant labor.[51]

For the Westminster Mill, in South Carolina, a very small affair owned by cotton planters, "the operatives consisted of seven young girls of the neighborhood who had never seen a cotton factory and one skilled operator, who trained them and attended to the card."[52] So far from bringing labor to mills, railroads may rather be said to have brought mills to labor. A newspaper correspondent wrote from the Piedmont: "Six years ago the country now traversed by the Air Line Railroad was an almost unbroken wilderness. There were few people, little energy and no progress. Now there are towns and villages all along the

reasons urged for extending small up-country branch lines, that of releasing needed labor figured.

[50] Cf. U. S. Census of Manufactures, 1900, Cotton Manufacture, p. 30. Even at this time, when the industry was "growing at a wonderful rate," the report was that "the help employed is chiefly local."

[51] It is interesting to note that very recently, since hands have become scarce, a tendency to erect mills actually in the mountains has shown itself.

[52] Blackman, p. 18. In this instance the operatives must have lived at their fathers' places, but this was unusual. The local character of the labor supply is frequently indicated in the provision made for the operatives' homes and general living—poor people from the vicinity came to and snuggled up against the mills like chicks under the protecting wings of the mother hen. The villages were like medieval hamlets clustered about a fortified castle. The factory was the provider. An officer of a small establishment which commenced operation in the seventies said: "Our labor is composed entirely of natives who have been educated to the business. They are very comfortably located, and have the free use of all the wood they require" (ibid., p. 8). The same had been true of the older Graniteville factory all along (cf. ibid., p. 55).

route, and the back country is rapidly being occupied by a thrifty and industrious population. In Pickens County, at Greenville and in Spartanburg, cotton factories have been built. . . . One hundred hands are now employed in the factory [Clifton], and, when the mill is finished, this number will be increased to four hundred. The employes, with the exception of the superintendents in the various departments, are all natives; there are no others on the pay rolls of the company."[53] In an account of the Huguenot factory, in the same State, it was said that " in the operation of the mill home labor is employed, the weavers being principally native women and girls, who with application soon become proficient in the art of operating the looms."[54]

One evidence of the local origin of operatives and mill projectors alike was the mutual respect prevailing between management and workpeople. The owners of cotton mills did not look down upon their employes. They might and usually did recognize that the operatives were lacking in education, thrift, energy and property, and they applied themselves to alleviate these conditions, but always there was the knowledge that employer and employe were of the same origin, the same blood, and, not remotely, the same instincts. After-war struggles brought an intimacy through propinquity which in earlier years had been impossible. Men who were active in the opening of the cotton mill era in the South resent any suggestion, recognizing in it a slur somehow upon themselves, that the operatives were inferior people.[55]

---

[53] News and Courier, Charleston, May 21, 1881.

[54] Baltimore Journal of Commerce and Manufacturers' Record, Oct. 28, 1882.

[55] A very elderly gentleman, characteristic of the best the old South produced, had no sympathy with writers who are free in forming theories about the South, or who wish to make Southern problems seem distinctive. " Where did the first labor for the Greensboro mills come from?" he was asked. " From the mountain sections?" He replied with scorn: " That's all stuff! Magazine writers and such people, magazine writers, I say, come down here and spread such statements. The people came from right 'round here—some from this county, some from counties adjoining this. They were no paupers, either. They were the best kind of people.

The remarkable story of the Salisbury Mills, born in a religious and philanthropic impulse, has been told in a previous chapter. It goes without saying that this factory "was built for the home people," and it is interesting that the managers "never had anybody else in it."[56]

For the Kershaw mill, "the employes came from right around Kershaw and are good citizens."[57] In many mills early conditions are reflected today. The Shelby Cotton Mill, it is recently reported, "employs . . . about three hundred operatives. They are . . . in most cases native Cleveland county stock—good old Scotch-Irish and similar blood lines,"[58] and it is said of the small Indian Creek Mill: "It gives employment to about sixty operatives and these workmen are native Lincoln county people."[59]

Proximity was the chief determining factor in the source of labor. If there were not enough people in the immediate vicinity of a mill in the Piedmont to fill its needs, some operatives would be recruited from the higher country a little distance away. Thus of the Spartanburg mills:

They went into the mills because it was a new thing, you know, and looked like a good thing." Asked then, "What did they do before going into the mills," he replied: "Farmed! [with emphasis, as though anyone should know that]. Worked their farms! 'Course, many of them didn't own their places, were tenants. They helped themselves by going to the mills—got schools now and all that." This statement is mistaken in excluding the attraction of labor from the mountains, and overdraws the propertied character of the first operatives, but is significant in spirit. Though recognition was granted the poor whites belatedly, it was generous when it came (James Moorehead, int., Greensboro).

[56] O. D. Davis, int., Salisbury. Operatives came from within a radius of twenty-five miles (C. S. Morris, int., Salisbury). Cf. Charlotte News, Textile Ed., 1917, with reference to this establishment.

[57] Columbia Record, Textile Ed., 1916.

[58] Charlotte News, Textile Ed., 1917.

[59] Ibid. Instances are easily multiplied. Cf., respecting Clyde, Carolina, Great Falls, Raleigh, and Bladenboro mills, ibid.; for example, "The greater part of the employes in these mills, particularly the older ones, came to the mills from the territory surrounding Rockingham. Many of them came from tenant farms where a year's livelihood was earned by the proverbial sweat of the brow, and much of it" (ibid.). Cf. also Columbia Record, Textile Ed., 1916.

"Labor first came from this immediate section, supplemented by people from the mountains and foothills."[60]

A great many workpeople for a South Carolina mill located in the country came from the four surrounding counties, but "another big body of the new help came from the mountains of western North Carolina."[61]

A woman who had been president of the Batesville factory, in South Carolina, gave an interpretative account of the commencement of the mill period. "The section was desperately poor," she said. "The village of Greenville would have been called in the foothills. Farming returned hardly anything to put in the farmers' mouths. There were women and girls—many more women than men, because the war had taken the men—whose lives were empty. The mills opened a vista before these; it was like finding a mine, you know. Most of the mills got local labor. In 1880 Camperdown, say, could draw no labor within a radius of half a dozen miles. This was also true of Batesville a few years later, before labor came from the foothills of the mountains. . . . After ten or fifteen years the labor of the localities was exhausted, and it was necessary to send to the mountains."[62]

It will be noticed presently that the pull of the field

---

[60] J. A. Chapman, int., Spartanburg. Of a knitting mill at Union: ". . . fifty per cent of the operatives are natives of Piedmont South Carolina, the others from the mountains of North Carolina and East Tennessee" (Columbia Record, Textile Ed., 1916. Cf. ibid. with reference to the Ninety-Six Mill, and Charlotte News, Textile Ed., 1917, the account of Rhyne's establishments in Lincoln County, and such mills as Marion and Mayworth).

[61] Columbia Record, Textile Ed., 1916. A newspaper summary of a survey as late as 1917 said: " Many mills will be found where there is not a man or woman employed except North Carolinians. . . . For the most part these employes come from the territory immediately surrounding the mills with additions from the mountains of the State" (Charlotte News, Textile Ed., 1917).

[62] Mrs. M. P. Gridley, int., Greenville. Cf. Kohn, Cotton Mills of S. C., pp. 22–23. A Piedmont manufacturer said: "The labor at first was strictly local. Neighboring farm people came, probably from the same township or school district with that in which the mill was situated. Later it was necessary to send for labor from a distance—North Carolina and Tennessee. Labor at first was localized and did not move much " (J. B. Cleveland, int., Spartanburg).

against the factory has tended to make cotton mill labor in
recent years doubly difficult to secure. Not only have those
readily willing to do factory work been drawn to the mills,
but many who enter the mills return to the farms. This is
true more largely of tenant help than of mountain people.
When the family pulls up stakes in the mountains and
comes down to a mill village, the temptation to leave again
is not so strong as in the case of a family which has moved
in from a familiar farm a few miles away.[63]

In rare instances mills at considerable distance from the
mountains received their labor primarily from the mountain regions. It is said that labor did not come to the Charlotte mills to any great extent from the adjoining country,
but almost entirely from the mountains or foothills. Even
for tenants, the farming was too good in the vicinity of the
city to allow mill wages to tempt them away.[64]

Before proceeding to other topics, it is convenient to
speak of certain instances in which mills found difficulty in
securing operatives. Usually, peculiar local circumstances
were responsible for the inability of a factory to provide
itself with employes. As has been made clear, the rule was
an abundance of help.

A writer who lived in the South in the years just preceding the first years of mill building assumes that a prime
perplexity of the mills was the recruiting of operatives.
Thus, speaking of the founding of the industry in South
Carolina, he says: ". . . the money had to be raised, largely
with the assistance of the North; the companies formed,
property bought, materials secured, homes for the operatives constructed, and last and most difficult of all, employees obtained." He quotes approvingly a letter of an

---

[63] It is said that "most of the operatives at Kannapolis (at any
rate thirty miles from the mountains)—the permanent ones—come
from the mountains. A good many come in from the surrounding
farms to work a few months, and then go back to the farms" (H.
W. Owen, int., Kannapolis, N. C., Jan. 6, 1917).

[64] "If you will trace back through two or three generations, you
will find that 75 per cent of the operatives in my mill are descended
from people who came from the mountains" (Sterling Graydon, int.,
Charlotte).

Englishman who was in the State during the Civil War, written to a mill president in 1908, saying that the rise of industry from agriculture seemed "all the more extraordinary because the State possesses no coal, and there was no superfluous population out of which to evolve mill hands." Paucity of labor was spoken of as an apparently insurmountable difficulty.[65]

Probably both of these writers meant that there were no laboring people accustomed to factory employment, that there was no industrial class from which to draw.[66] It will appear later that in a good many important instances, the projectors of cotton mills in the eighties failed to see the opportunity of utilizing the labor of the poor whites, and looked for operatives from every other than this most plausible source.

Contemporary estimates of facilities for establishing a cotton mill rarely voiced any doubt on the head of labor.[67]

If any cause of scarcity of help may be termed general, it was a prejudice against factory work under bosses on the part of persons who had been, in however poor or supposititious a fashion, their own masters. It might be supposed that objection to indoor employment and life in a mill village would be frequent with people with rural traditions. It must be remembered, however, that, their farming being at lowest ebb, they needed to take desperate remedies, and, moreover, dislike of a mill community could not be very strong in the face of the barrenness of country living.

---

[65] Goldsmith, p. 7.

[66] The Englishman concluded with the question: "For how could anyone see that the water power of the Alleghanies [Blue Ridge] could be converted into electric force, or that you could turn the clay-eating Cracker into a self-respecting mill hand?" (ibid.). Perhaps this correspondent's surprise at the success of the mills is rendered plainer by recalling the devastated condition of parts of South Carolina during and right after the war. Cf. Andrews, p. 34, as to Columbia in 1865.

[67] No particular apprehension can be ascribed to the desire of a correspondent of a newspaper that, lest a single failure should occur in the development of mills in the State, all possible light should be thrown upon comparative costs of steam and water power and advantages of location with respect to freight, health and labor (News and Courier, Charleston, April 29, 1881).

Where unwillingness to accept factory employment actually operated to keep some people out of a mill, the plant was in most cases located in a city and could depend upon the urban population for its help.

But there might be difficulty even here. The President of the Atlanta Cotton Factory in 1880 was unable to get hands to run the mill at full capacity. He thought this was due to objection of women and girls to the class of work or to surroundings in the mill. A newspaper editorial, commenting on the situation, thought that the girls, when they considered the matter, did not mind factory work, but that the absence of cottages for operatives was the cause of the dearth of labor, rents in the vicinity of the mill being high, and the pay being too small to allow of a long trip from home to plant. It was pointed out that if operatives were brought from the North, as was being contemplated, the same housing problem would confront them as the natives. However, if suitable cottages were built near the mill, the president " could obtain in Atlanta and the section of country adjacent any number of women and girls who will not only gladly work, but will be eternally grateful to him for furnishing them the means of earning a comfortable and honest livelihood."[68]

It was explained that the managers of the Charlotte Cotton Mills, employing fifty-five hands, nearly all skilled workers drawn from surrounding factories, " had been anxious to obtain their operatives among home people, but some insuperable prejudice seems to exist to the business, and not more than one or two, so far, have engaged."[69]

Difficulty in getting labor was not more hindering in any

[68] Daily Constitution, Atlanta, Jan. 2, 1880. In Charleston, which has had a bad reputation on the score of availability of labor, a mill in the last two decades has solved the problem by building an excellent village around the factory. Most of the operatives, it is true, have not come from Charleston, but from other parts of South Carolina and from other States. " We have always had enough help; we could start another mill right in our village and have labor enough for it" (Julius Koester, int., Charleston, S. C., Dec. 27, 1916).

[69] Raleigh Observer, quoted in News and Courier, Charleston, Feb. 26, 1881.

13

city than in Charleston. Labor was the *bête noire* of the Charleston Manufacturing Company. And after the event transpired, it seemed that every one should have recognized that this would be the case. That a plant which was the perfect embodiment of the cotton mill campaign, as has been seen, should be built in Charleston, was natural; that it could not succeed was almost as inevitable. Founded in idealism, it was not able to prosper in fact. Born in the minds and hearts of Charleston's best, it did not proceed from the determined and more silent cooperation of the whole community in the manner of other ventures which became permanent. It must be remembered, however, that this mill stood at the commencement of the cotton mill period in the South; it in a sense marked the epoch. There were few traditions, either local, state or sectional, upon which to calculate. One of the leading projectors of the company, explaining that at the time the mill was started there were few females in cotton factories, described the unfortunate experience of this first enterprise in a large seaport: "It was considered belittling—oh! very bad! It was considered that for a girl to go into a cotton factory was just a step toward the most vulgar things. They used to talk about the girls working in mills up-country as if they were in places of grossest immorality. It was said to be the same as a bawdy house; to let a girl go into a cotton factory was to make a prostitute of her."

"How was it," he was asked, "that this was not understood by you gentlemen in launching the Charleston Manufacturing Company; that the women of the laboring class in Charleston would not go into the mill?"

The reply was undoubtedly the plain fact. "It never occurred to us," he said. "We canvassed the matter among ourselves."[70]

"Our idea in starting the Charleston Manufacturing Company," said another of the original stockholders, "was that there were many people here who wanted work, needed

---

[70] William M. Bird, int., Charleston.

it. We found out they did not want it. They were ashamed
to work in a factory. We thought it was going to help the
town immensely. We found just the reverse. Instead of
people flocking here, we had to take discarded labor from
other mills and bring it here. We thought we could get
enough people in Charleston to fill the mill, but we found
the number here willing to work was very small."[71]

Local help failing, there was difficulty in obtaining hands
from the up-country. "Some operatives from the Piedmont objected to coming to Charleston in the summer time.
They had seen many Charlestonians going through the Piedmont region to the mountains for, they said, their health.
This unfounded prejudice operated."[72] "Men were getting good pay in fertilizer works, on the wharves and in

---

[71] W. P. Carrington, int., Charleston. Another said: "Young
women looked upon factory work as lowering, and thought it was
dangerous for young men and young women to work together as
they must do. I thought this myself until I saw them working in factories at the North; every girl would have two hundred or three
hundred jealous girl eyes watching her; they were safer than in their
own homes" (it is useful to remember that country people going to
a country mill village found themselves surrounded by persons all in
the same situation—there was nothing but the industrial community. In a city, however, even if the factory has its own cottages,
operatives might feel censure of a non-industrial population. Furthermore, among city dwellers, however poor, women and girls were
less accustomed to work than was true in the country, and would be
more regardful of fancied social distinctions). The Charleston
Manufacturing Company encountered trouble in recruiting labor that
an older and smaller venture in the place did not, partly because it
had been so much discussed and stood out in the public mind, impressed with a declaratively industrial character. "The Charleston
Bagging Manufacturing Company," this informant continued, "making bagging from jute, used native labor, a hundred operatives or
so. The bagging mill had been successful with female labor, and
this encouraged us in our company." But the event as it transpired
was not a complete surprise: "Still we understood that Charleston
having had almost no factories, there would be prejudice against
females working. But we thought this would wear off. We did
not expect to get our labor force from Charleston at first. We
thought the native labor would sift in gradually, and this proved to
be true. Lockwood (the New England engineer who designed the
mill) told truly when he explained that the first expert operatives
to come to a new place were floating, and that it would require two
or three years to get a steady, experienced force. In our impatience
we looked upon the natural slowness in getting operatives, particularly women, as a terrible delay" (A. B. Murray, int., Charleston).
[72] Ibid.

industries," said another, "and women did not need to work. There was not the press of life there was in a colder climate."[73]

This story of trials seemed to be coming to a bright conclusion: "We brought the expert labor from the Piedmont, and the native population sifted in later, and took hold very nicely." But it was only passing into its final phase: "The two or three years following 1880 were bad ones for cotton mills. On August 31, 1886, the end of the company's fiscal year, the mill showed a small net profit. On the night of that day, the earthquake occurred. The railroads gave free transportation, and our operatives that had come from the up-country left. You couldn't have held them here with chains. Even the local operatives went away with the up-country operatives. We had a good working force at the time of the earthquake—after the earthquake, the only thing left was overhead charges. The officers were here, but the operatives had all disappeared." The prospects of this mill were never really promising afterwards.[74]

Until very recent years, any class consciousness among Southern cotton mill operatives was induced by the prejudice of the general community against them. The mill village, especially the company-owned town, has crystallized this sentiment, and politics and the lack of any other considerable industry in the South have made their unfortunate contributions. Dislike of the operatives' station is

---

[73] George W. Williams, int., Charleston. He meant this to apply to the Charleston Manufacturing Company and to a successor, the Vesta Mill. "We were great phosphate people down here, and the laborers were distracted. But the leaders stuck to it [the enterprise of a big mill in Charleston]. We went through three organizations" (F. Q. O'Neill, int., Charleston, S. C., Dec. 27, 1916).

[74] A. B. Murray, int., Charleston. "The ground was in a tremor for several years after the earthquake. It took two years to reorganize the plant. We had to send to the up-country for skilled operatives." And another concluded: "We thought that if a mill could pay in the up-country, it would pay to build a mill in a large center like Charleston. The labor trouble was the chief reason for the failure." He felt that had the attempt been made fifteen years later, after 10-cent stores and dry goods stores had begun to employ women, the mill might have succeeded (William M. Bird, int., Charleston).

undoubtedly greater at present than in the years when the mills were building. A just statement of the facts as they prevailed forty years ago is the following: "There was some prejudice against operatives on the part of others, but it did not show itself. So far as speaking to them cordially, etc., was concerned, they were received."[75] It has been said that mill managements in the eighties showed none of the spirit of neglect of the poor whites that had characterized the period before the Civil War, and this attitude was not persuaded merely by business motives. It is probable that no great development could have taken place, calling for enlistment of the service of thousands in the population, without some objection against workers in the new industry becoming evident. But in the case of the cotton mill operatives this was at a minimum. The South was too much in earnest in its work to question the social status of those who were factors in its accomplishment; work was too scarce to permit of a choice influenced by popular dislike or esteem; the South of the eighties was twenty years removed in time and many more years removed in experience from the older South of an idle class; and last, the poor whites by entering the mills tended to throw off the atmosphere of unnoticed destitution in which they had been enveloped before they had been given a useful outlet for their services. If their situation was not envied by some, by the majority it was not despised; if they were looked upon as a class with disfavor, this was not on the surface, and nobody had time to bother with such notions.[76]

A part of the prejudice against operatives, if it may be

---

[75] Charles McDonald, int., Charlotte. "Many of those who became operatives had owned their own land, and when misfortune overtook them, in the shape of bad crops and debt, came to the cotton mills" (M. L. Bonham, int., Anderson).

[76] The usual sentiment is illustrated by some words of Hammett: "It is clear that what the South needs more than anything else is diversified labor, and to realize that to labor is respectable, and to be idle is not respectable. With all the unemployed water power and other natural facilities one of the main industries should be to convert into goods a part of the cotton produced by the soil" (quoted in Manufacturers' Record, Baltimore, Feb. 1, 1881).

called such, perhaps took rise in objection to mills on the part of rural communities. This was a different thing from the social discrimination spoken of above. It was a conflict between occupations, not between elements in the population. "Right at first," said one informant, "there was a good deal of opposition to the mills on the part of farmers, and this made labor hard to get."[77]   Another asserted: "Our white people were accustomed to be their own masters. They had not lived in great groups or worked under bosses and that kind of thing." He remembered that this hindered the recruiting of local hands.[78]

In the same issue of a South Carolina newspaper saying that "Cedar Creek . . . affords ample water power at this point [Society Hill] for a factory," and that "there is plenty of labor," it was told that the management of the Camperdown Mills, at Greenville, was finding it impossible to get two hundred and fifty extra hands needed to run the plant at night. This was due, it was explained, to the presence of disorderly women in the neighborhood, who were proposed to be used as operatives, and who could not be got rid of. Circulars were distributed all along the line of the Atlanta and Charlotte Railroad, and in other directions. The mill offered free transportation and a dollar a day for all time lost by prospective operatives, but, after an expenditure of $500, no more workers were in the factory, and it was regretted that the mills were "receiving a large accumulation of orders it will be impossible for them to fill."[79]

The scarcity of labor which was experienced twenty-five years later was of an entirely different character from the

---

[77] Marshall Orr, int., Anderson, S. C., Sept. 10, 1916.

[78] M. L. Bonham, int., Anderson.

[79] News and Courier, Charleston, Feb. 23, 1881. Without mention of the reason for it, this fact of scarcity of help for the Camperdown Mills was recalled to Mrs. Gridley, who confirmed the report of years before: "If Camperdown sought in vain to get 250 operatives in the early eighties, it must have been because the mill had a rough class of help. The bad reputation the labor force earned kept away the mountain people the mill was trying to attract" (Mrs. M. P. Gridley, int., Greenville).

scattered instances here noted. After 1900 it became a problem of more or less general concern; many mills had been built, some of them very large, and the condition of the body of the poor whites was somewhat better than in the earlier period, not a little by agency of the cotton manufacturing industry itself. In spite of a degree of optimism, difficulty was presaged in an address before the Southern Cotton Spinners Association in 1903: "Now in regard to an insufficient supply of native-born help. This may be true in localities, but it has been the experience of all manufacturing centres that the building of the mills has eventually drawn, in close proximity, people from the country and outlying districts, and it is not worth while to consider this matter as fatal to the future increase of spindleage here." The speaker thought that "even when our native country help is exhausted . . . if it be true that cotton manufacturing may decline in our sister countries, there will be opportunities for skilled employes from those countries to be obtained. We should not cross this bridge until we come to it."[80]

It has been said that the projectors of cotton mills in the South not only welcomed the native whites as workpeople,

[80] Proceedings 7th Annual Convention, address of E. W. Thomas, p. 149 ff. Tompkins in 1900 had foreseen that the objection to night work would take care of itself, for "as mills increase labor will become scarcer until there will be no available labor for night work" (Labor Legislation, p. 4). In 1904 a Georgian speaking to Georgians said: "Why one section—a comparatively old one—is short of labor, is not my province to discuss. It is simply a question and no theory that we have confronting us." He thought that immigration agents ought to draw workers from Italy, in about the same geographical latitude with Georgia, to fill the domestic "vacuum of labor," and wanted Georgia represented at the St. Louis World's Fair by a solicitor who would operate in conjunction with real estate firms and the railroads in bringing home-seekers to the State (Georgia Industrial Assn., proceed. 4th Annual Convention, address of Hon. I. C. Wade, p. 34 ff.). The convention appointed a committee "to urge the establishment of a Department of Immigration by the State of Georgia" (proceed., p. 33). In 1907 Mr. Kohn wrote that "there is plenty of capital, energy, enthusiasm, business ability, water power and cotton for South Carolina to have very many more spindles than she now has. The one difficulty is that of securing additional labor" (Cotton Mills of S. C., p. 60). Cf. ibid., p. 63, and T. W. Uttley, p. 68.

but planned factories in many instances partly with the express purpose of affording them employment. There were some cases, however, in which the possibility of employing the poor whites was curiously overlooked, and operatives were sought or proposed to be sought outside of the South. It cannot be said for this strange neglect of the obvious opportunity of utilizing the Southern population that the poor whites were "out of sight, out of mind." They were very much in evidence everywhere, were mutely appealing for assistance and notice; even asking, if one pleases, to be exploited. The disposition to seek operatives outside of the South, so far as it showed itself, was fostered by three circumstances: first, the feeling that experienced workers must be found to start the industry; second, the desire to weaken the negro by increasing the white population; third, new and prospective cotton manufacturers fell in easily with the prevalent plans of agricultural interests to secure immigration to the section.

How earnestly Senator James, of Rhode Island, plead for the establishment of cotton mills by Southern planters, and how he urged that the needy native white people be employed in the factories, has been noticed. Eager, however, to leave no stone unturned in proving the plausibility of his proposal and in answering especially the question as to how help was to be gotten, he declared that "Even should the planter, who goes into the manufacture of cotton, find it necessary to import his operatives from Europe at his own expense, he would still be a great gainer by the transaction." He showed how, by saving one cent per pound on raw cotton—the cost of transporting the staple to a Northern mill—the Southern manufacturer would be able to defray the charges of bringing over English operatives, and have a considerable surplus to his credit.[81] This suggestion seems to have been tried in practice, for it is said that a superintendent of the Augusta Factory, probably in the seventies, brought a boatload of operatives from Scotland.

[81] Cf. DeBow, vol. i, p. 238 ff.

The mills of Augusta still have English and Scotch people in them, likely descendants of these immigrants.[82] Foreign-born operatives transplanted to Augusta supplied many of the mills throughout the South, particularly in the Carolinas, with skilled superintendents and overseers.

A writer at the close of the Civil War would have been right in including the whole South in an observation made as to Charleston, that it wished immigrants from Europe rather than newcomers from the North. "Immigration is held to be the panacea for all present evils and troubles. One of the representatives elect from this city will make strong efforts to secure legislative action at the coming session of the General Assembly in favor of a bill granting State aid to foreign immigrants. The Yankee is not wanted here, except by the enlightened few; but Germans who will consent to take a secondary position will be welcomed."[83]

The extraordinary scheme of "The Region of the Savannah Colonization Association" for bringing New England operatives to cotton mills in the South is worth mention because, with its preposterousness, it shows the thought in the minds of some. It was set forth in 1882, and never got beyond the stage of advocacy. It was a promoters' plan for combining a pastime for rich men of leisure with a health resort and an industrial community. An agency of the Association explained that the Region of the Savannah (the entire States, apparently, of Georgia and South Carolina), offered in its piney woods and mild and dry climate the only relief from pulmonary diseases. New England cotton mill operatives who, left in Northern factories, were destined to lose their ability to work or would even die, might come to this salubrious district and regain their health by coupling farm work with factory attendance. In New

[82] George T. Lynch, int., Augusta, Ga., Dec. 30, 1916. Compare the proposal of "Hanover" that English operatives be brought to Richmond (Daily Dispatch, Jan. 14, 1880).

[83] "'The only way in which we can control the labor of the free negro is to bring him in competition with the white laborer,' is the language of scores of men." By "the white laborer" the native white was not meant (Andrews, pp. 207–208).

England were found, besides the broken-down mill hands, retired business and professional men of means, for whom the Northern climate from December to May was too severe for comfort. It was proposed that some of these wealthy invalids should buy a few thousands of acres in the Region of the Savannah, build forty or fifty neat but inexpensive houses on the tract, and rent those not occupied by themselves (they would be there to give character to the project), to sick New England operatives, and to pleasure-seekers wishing a wintering place in the South. " This would give a nucleus for a permanent settlement, and in a very short time an industrial community would grow up about it." A correspondent of the Savannah Morning News was quoted approvingly, this writer proposing that each family might have a forty-acre farm and divide its labor between agriculture and a cotton mill which would be centrally situated. It was asserted by the projectors of this scheme that it would make a return of 100 per cent on the capital invested.[84]

[84] Gannon, p. 8 ff. " The Region of the Savannah Colonization Association " was built on the constitution of the defunct American Colonizing Company, founded in 1818, for the furtherance of trade, it was declared, between the South Atlantic States and the West Indies, the west coast of Africa and the Brazils, the principal American depot being at Charleston, Port Royal or Savannah; the building of small cotton mills, to be operated by a transplanted New England industrial population, would be linked with the construction of small ships to carry the product of these factories. Another inspiration to the project was President Grevy's system of cooperation; the success of the young Meaux workman who in one year built 250 houses on a tract of land of an old marquis and started his colony at a cost of 240,000 francs with considerable profit to his fellow-enterprisers—he began with only ten 5-franc pieces of his own—was instanced. The aims of the Savannah Association were to be accomplished largely through dissemination of information. The pamphlet was published as propaganda by Gannon and Mayhew, 176 Tremont Street, Boston, who were general agents for the organization. The Southern Land, Emigration and Improvement Company, a New York organization designed to encourage immigration to the South, said in its prospectus: " That the South now offers greater inducements to capital, enterprise and intelligent industry than any other quarter of the globe, is beyond question to those who are informed upon the subject. . . . The Southern people themselves are thoroughly awakened at last to the fact of the abundance of their resources. They are putting forth every energy to secure their share of the overflowing tides of population from the old

A journal which championed the South's interests, lamenting the failure of immigrants to go to that section, declared that "if the South is to be built up, her unoccupied lands turned to the uses of civilization, her streams become the seats of great manufacturing enterprises, and all her natural advantages made to bear material development, there must be a systematic effort to induce immigration. Railroads, States, private individuals, are all alike interested in this; and it behooves all to work persistently to accomplish it."[85]

It seems likely that immigrants, especially where foreigners, were not often sought by the South for industrial workers. Agricultural interests were uppermost in the minds of the people, and schemes to supplant the free negro were, for the time being, as natural as they were impracticable.[86]

Even where immigrants had been in mechanical pursuits in their own countries, their usefulness in industry might be overlooked.[87]

---

world . . ." (quoted in Baltimore Journal of Commerce and Manufacturers' Record, Aug. 5, 1882). The alliance of the South Carolina Railroad with the Georgia Railroad and the Central Railway was looked upon as bringing to Charleston "increased business, direct trade with Europe and white immigration" (News and Courier, Charleston, April 14, 1881).

[85] Baltimore Journal of Commerce and Manufacturers' Record, June 24, 1882.

[86] An editorial on the benefits of immigration to South Carolina placed the whole stress upon agriculture. Nothing was said about using immigrants in cotton mills, though Charleston's advantage in being able to get them from German ports at two-thirds of the charge if taken to New York, was mentioned (News and Courier, Charleston, May 20, 1881). A week later the same paper commended the commissioner of immigration for steering foreigners away from "towns or cities where they would be a burden to themselves and those around them" (June 17, 1881). A like omission of cotton manufacturing in stating the reasons for immigration is seen in an address of the Georgia Commissioner of Land and Immigration to the State legislature (quoted in ibid., Aug. 5, 1881). Cf. editorial in Observer, Raleigh, April 10, 1881.

[87] Sixteen families—Poles, Germans and Austrians—in 1881 passed through Charleston on their way to Columbia. "They have no property, and are uncertain of their final destination. They are generally mechanics, but claim to know something about farming, and are willing to do anything to make a good and honest living."

In conclusion of these references to advocacy of immigration as apart from the needs of cotton mills, it is interesting to notice a jeu d'esprit of "Henry LeBlank," written under date of July 13, 1893, twelve years in the future, predicting failure of plans for European immigration to South Carolina, the foreigners being unsuited to the climate, crops and mode of living, and adding in a postscript: "It would do you good to see the immense number of factories at Columbia, down by what was an old ditch, but now a splendid canal. Spartanburg has over 30,000 population, and seven railroads centre there."[88]

Instances in which immigrants were looked for as cotton mill operatives show the newness of the South to industrialism, the suddenness with which an urgent program was embraced. How foreign manufacturing was to the South's past, how novel a departure it represented in the minds of mill projectors, comes out in the rare cases in which native whites were not considered as operatives; such an opportunity might not even be debated, but it was thought that new wine was to be put into new wineskins. Thus in advocating the building of a mill near Winnsboro, South Carolina, in a county in which poor whites were plentiful, these were overlooked as industrial workers and, for that matter, as agricultural laborers. "If we can do no better let us spin a hundred bales at first. . . . We believe

---

There was no mention of directing them toward cotton mills (News and Courier, Charleston, May 10, 1881). Relatively few immigrants actually came—seventy-four persons colonized in South Carolina in a typical week—and most of them were placed with farmers (see ibid., March 23 and July 1, 1881). Despite every demonstration of failure, projects for bringing in foreigners to become cotton farmers would not die. As late as 1908 Tompkins declared: "Every condition in the cotton growing States is favorable for the European farmer who wants to emigrate. . . . Such a movement would go further than any other to insure a cotton supply adequate to the world's demand and at a reasonable price" (Cotton Growing, p. 7). And earlier he had urged that "the New England Cotton Manufacturers' Association turn itself into an emigration society pro tem. for the purpose of securing the occupation of the Southern cotton land" (The Storing and Marketing of Cotton, reprint from Transactions of New England Cotton Manufacturers' Assn., vol. 77, p. 19 ff.).

[88] News and Courier, Charleston, June 15, 1881.

there is money enough in the county, here and there, to make at least a modest beginning, so as to attract outside capital. Shall the effort be made, or shall other counties, once far behind us in wealth, take the lead and rapidly out-strip us? We want white immigrants. Bring the mills here and they will come. Colored labor will raise the cotton, and white immigrants will convert it into yarn."[89] A news-paper in another community concluded that the freed ne-groes had done little to better their condition and had, more-over, kept away skilled immigrants; ". . . remove at least half the negro labor from the State, then it [skilled immi-grant labor] will come, and with it capital which will seek investment in our manufacturing interests, and at once put us on the highway to wealth, power and happiness."[90]

Another editor, in contrast to these less thoughtful con-temporaries, expressed sanely the better judgment in op-posing wholesale immigration on the ground that there were needy people in the South to be thought for first, and because the section was in no position to invite new-comers to share in her uncertain lot: "We have many worthy native people of the more indigent classes who must be pro-vided for in some way before we talk of hurrying those here who, at the best, may take the bread out of the mouths of our own people. We are by no means opposed to legiti-mate immigration, but we are very far indeed from seeing the good sense of bringing upon ourselves or our unhappy visitors the cruel lot of being thrown into Southern com-

[89] Winnsboro News, quoted in News and Courier, Charleston, Feb. 8, 1881.

[90] Pickens Sentinel, quoted in News and Courier, Charleston, Feb. 3, 1881. An opportunity of securing skilled textile operatives among immigrants from Alsace-Lorraine was evidently received gladly. J. H. Diss DeBar, of New York, directing a movement to bring over foreigners, had written to the president of the Atlanta Factory, for facts as to the employment of any immigrants that might be sent down. Other Georgia mills were urged to communicate with this agent with information as to wages, rent and other conditions affect-ing work in the manufactories (Daily Constitution, Atlanta, March 24, 1880).

munities without bread and without any hope of employment."[91]

The futility of attempts to attract immigrants began to be
seen in South Carolina early in the eighties, a newspaper
declaring "We hope the State will abolish the office of
superintendent of immigration. It is . . . a worse than
useless expense."[92]   Twenty-five years later, following

---

[91] Columbia Register, quoted in News and Courier, Charleston,
Feb. 3, 1881. One long acquainted with the State's politics believed
the motive of supplying cotton mill operatives was not important,
that "back of the efforts of South Carolina, through Commissioner
Boykin's office, to secure immigration, was the desire to get rid of
the negro and to bring in whites to take his place." When Boykin
left office, another commissioner was appointed. "Then there were
some years when there was no commissioner of agriculture or immigration. It was largely a matter of politics" (M. L. Bonham, int.,
Anderson). As to the purpose to oust the negro, the comment of a
German-language newspaper is indicative, especially since Germans
were particularly sought: "Col. Boykin, the immigration commissioner, has returned from New York, and reports that he is able to
get in Castle Garden as many immigrants for South Carolina as are
wanted. He seems to be intent chiefly upon getting laborers who
are able to take the place of the negroes" (Deutsche Zeitung,
Charleston, April 25, 1881). Cf. Daily Constitution, Atlanta, Jan.
31, 1880. With the negro question in mind, Henry W. Grady said:
"Companies of immigrants sent down from the sturdy settlers at
the North will solve the Southern problem . . ." (Dyer, in New
South, p. 139). Cf. State of S. C., Fourth Annual Report of Commissioner of Agriculture, Commerce and Immigration, p. 4, and preceding reports; DeBow, vol. ii, p. 127. Frequently immigration to
the South from other parts of this country was in mind; cf. DeBow,
ibid., and quotation from United States Economist, in Baltimore
Journal of Commerce and Manufacturers' Record, Sept. 30, 1882.

[92] Abbeville Press and Banner, quoted in News and Courier,
Charleston, Nov. 25, 1881. Cf. State of S. C., ibid., p. 32. A pamphlet issued by the immigration commissioner was attacked as
sophomoric, unfair in claiming too much, and generally "a disgrace
to the State" (News and Courier, ibid.). In 1894 the editor of a
publication that had done much to encourage immigration admitted
that the South had been "in no condition to invite immigration. . . .
All efforts to attract settlers to this section could only prove futile.
The time was not ripe" (Edmonds, p. 29 ff.). The most famous
effort to recruit foreign immigrants as operatives for Southern mills
was the episode of the *Wittekind*, which, even without hindrance
from the federal authorities, was so unsuccessful that it would
hardly have been followed up. South Carolina planters were interested in securing farm hands by the venture, and combined with
manufacturers in a fund which was utilized through the State immigration commissioner. The North German Lloyd steamer *Wittekind*,
in two trips to Charleston, in November, 1906, and February, 1907,
brought a few hundred passengers, principally Belgians, Austrians

South Carolina's unsuccessful effort at importing immigrants, the Georgia Farmers' Union " unanimously voted against foreign immigration, because it would bring undesirable people who would compete with the Georgians for factory labor and would raise so much cotton that it would lower the price."[93]   This is a far cry from the disposition remarked in a few of the early mill projectors to overlook the opportunity, not to mention duty, to employ the native whites in the textile industry.

The Southern mills have almost no foreigners. Just occasionally a few trickle in by chance. "Once in a while," said a superintendent, " we have a spasm of French Canadians and Poles. They are not imported, nobody goes after them. They don't stay very long, and come only two or three families together."[94]

---

and Galicians. It is likely that disappointment of disingenuous prospective employers at frustration of their plans by the central government has colored judgment of the results of the experiment, but it appears all in all that the new-comers were not so well content as to form a satisfied nucleus which would automatically attract relatives in succeeding years. Mr. Gadsden, a representative of South Carolina business men, who investigated the matter in Europe, wisely reported: " Our efforts have been almost entirely expended in inducing immigrants to come to the South, and we have thought little or nothing of how the immigrant is to be treated after the immigrant has come in our midst; . . . we have entirely overlooked our industrial conditions, namely, that the wage scale throughout the South is based on negro labor . . . our attitude throughout the South toward the white labor will have to be materially altered before we can expect to have the immigrant satisfied to remain as a laborer with us " (quoted in Hart, pp. 52-53). On the whole matter see State of S. C., ibid.; a good deal of reading between the lines is necessary. Cf. also Goldsmith, p. 10, and Kohn, Cotton Mills of S. C., p. 24. The action of South Carolina was preceded by agitation in manufacturers' associations in other Southern States looking toward immigration. A speaker before the Georgia Industrial Association in 1901 asserted: " There is room in Georgia for several hundred thousand competent white foreigners." Three years later it was being urged that practical steps be taken (Proceed. Fourth Annual Convention, p. 13 ff.).

[93] Hart, p. 54. A " Southern writer " was quoted as saying that " The temptation of cheap alien labor from abroad is obvious as one of the ways in which a home population may be dispossessed. When it ceases to fill the rank and file with its own sons . . . it ceases to be master . . . of the country " (ibid., p. 55).

[94] George T. Lynch, int., Augusta. Cf. Thompson, p. 30, and Kohn, Cotton Mills of S. C., p. 24.

It has been seen that despite shortage of operatives in peculiar individual instances and ill-advised efforts to attract immigrants to compensate for an actual or anticipated scarcity of immediately available labor, the rule at the opening of the cotton mill era was an abundance of local help. The mere erection of a factory was sufficient inducement to the gathering of a working force. The problem was rather to secure the plant than the operatives. This condition lasted for about twenty years. "Labor for the early factories came from the localities—90 per cent of it. But after 1900, when there was a madness of mill building, they began to pull labor from a distance of 250 miles. Whereas people had before straggled in at will, the mills now commenced concentrated efforts to get them out of the mountains."[95] In the active years preceding the panic of 1907 this practice became more frequent. A superintendent in the up-country gave his experience: "The first labor for the Spartan Mills came from the surrounding country, and was supplemented soon by people from the mountains of North Carolina and Tennessee. In 1905–6 and 1906–7 there was a scarcity of labor. Spartanburg mills sent agents into the mountains to bring out help, the mill advancing railway fares of operatives. In this way from 1905 to 1907, 171 families were brought to this mill."[96] The advantage of the cotton mill village as contrasted with the mountain farm, which had earlier been too patent to require statement, began to be carefully explained in dodgers distributed through highland districts, or were set forth

---

[95] H. R. Buist, int., Charleston.

[96] W. J. Britton, int., Spartanburg. He was much disappointed in the results of the soliciting system, and said that of the 171 families brought to the mill village, only 10 remained. "I would rather have half a dozen families that paid their own way to the mill than fifty families brought here." Commenting on the necessity of scouting for labor, Mr. Copeland declares "The growth of the industry has taken away the advantage which was its chief asset." In the period referred to employers bid against each other for help, so that wages were raised nearly one-fourth. Almost all the mills were reported to be short of their full complement of operatives; "for the time being the South had built more mills than it had labor to operate" (p. 46 ff.).

by satisfied operatives taken along by agents as bait.[97] Ex-
haustion of the readily available supply of poor whites is
further indicated in efforts since the Great War to attract
workers from the eastern sections, which lowland tenants,
in their full knowledge of the needs and opportunities of
the mills, had already been constructively solicited, and in
the building of mills actually in the mountain districts.[98]

It has been seen how slavery was largely responsible for
crushing the early manufactures which arose in the South
and prevented recovery of industries in the section. At
first blush it seems strange that negroes, in the period
before the Civil War in which manufactures were at lowest
ebb, should have been employed in cotton mills. It might
be objected that slavery, so far from being an enemy to the
textile industry, assisted such factories as were in operation.

The point, however, is easily cleared up when it is remembered that the old mills were generally very small, scattered, unstandardized, and made the rudest products, and
when it is considered that managers of factories, many of
them planters, might naturally use slaves whom they owned
or could hire cheaply rather than whites who were less dependent and who must be better paid and differently treated.
There was less difficulty in adapting slaves to the work of
the ante-bellum cotton mills than in employing free negroes
in later years, because processes were more elementary and
because many slaves, especially women and girls, had been
taught something of the textile art in domestic industry on
the plantations. Thus the finding of negroes in mills which
anticipated the real development of cotton manufactures in
the South is to be considered rather a proof of the depressing effect of slavery upon the industry than as supporting a
contrary argument.

It may be believed that most of those who before the War
advocated the use of negroes in cotton mills held no very
hopeful or plausible economic philosophy. If they really

[97] Cf. Kohn, Cotton Mills of S. C., p. 23, and John C. Campbell,
From Mountain Cabin to Cotton Mill, especially p. 5.
[98] S. N. Boyce and J. Lee Robinson, int., Gastonia.
14

understood the situation, the proposal to employ slaves must have been acknowledged as a makeshift; if they did not, it was none the less a fanciful dream. In most cases there must have been no further thought behind the use of negroes than that it was convenient, cheap and sufficient for the limited project in hand.

Certainly William Gregg made a sound diagnosis of the South's ailments, and showed more foresight in economic matters, it may be thought, than any other Southerner of his day. Some surprise, therefore, may attach to the statement that he advocated the operation of cotton mills with negro labor. The explanation lies in two facts: first, though he had visited the Pennsylvania and New England factories, there was nothing in the South to compare with them, and it would have taken an imagination and faith superior even to his to transcend the numbing effect of his dominantly agricultural surroundings and reach beyond them to visualize the necessary conditions of industry as afterwards proved in history; and second, seeing the great difficulties in the way of his proposals, statesmanship prompted him to utilize any means that offered to make a beginning.

There is something pathetic in the tone of his appeal, born almost of exasperation:

Surely there is nothing in cotton spinning that can poison the atmosphere of South-Carolina. Why not spin as well as plant cotton? The same hand that attends a gin may work a carding machine. The girl who is capable of making thread, on a country spinning wheel, may do the same with equal facility, on the *throstle frame.* The woman who can warp the thread and weave it, on a common loom, may soon be taught to do the same, on a *power loom;* and so with all the departments, from the raw cotton to the cloth, experience has proved that any child, white or black, of ordinary capacity, may be taught, in a few weeks, to be expert in any part of a cotton factory; moreover, all overseers who have experience in the matter, give a decided preference to blacks as operatives.[99]

---

[99] Domestic Industry, p. 21. He had not only the sight of Southern mills of his time operating with negroes, but he relied upon the judgment of a well-known authority who understood the English and the American industry, quoting James Montgomery to the effect that "If the experiment of slave labor succeed in factories as is confidently expected, the cost of manufacturing the cotton into cloth

The Saluda Factory, near Columbia, was reported in the early fifties to be operating successfully with slave labor, the negroes being mostly owned by the company. The enterprise was of $100,000 capital, and employed 128 operatives, including children; there were 5000 spindles and 120 looms, the product being heavy brown shirting and Southern stripe. "The superintendent is decidedly of the opinion that slave labor is cheaper for cotton manufacture than free white labor. The average cost per annum of those employed in this mill, he says, does not exceed $75. Slaves not sufficiently strong to work in the cotton fields can attend to the looms and spindles in the cotton mills. . . ." The average cost of a white operative per year was said to be $116, so that those using slaves, it was claimed, enjoyed "over thirty per cent saved in the cost of labor alone."[100]

---

will be much less there [in the South] than anywhere else, so that it will not be surprising if in the course of a few years, those Southern factories should manufacture coarse cotton goods, and sell them in the public markets, at one-half the price, at which they are manufactured in England. There are several cotton factories in Tennessee operated entirely by *slave* labor, there not being a white man in the mill but the superintendent . . ." (ibid.). Montgomery instanced other cases of actual or intended use of negro labor at Richmond and Petersburg, and went so far as to say "there is every reason to believe that it is better adapted to the manufactory than to the field, and that the negro character is susceptible of a high degree of manufacturing cultivation. . . . This kind of labor will be much cheaper, and far more certain and controllable. The manufacturer will have nothing to do with strikes, or other interruptions that frequently produce serious delay and loss to the employer " (A Practical Detail of the Cotton Manufacture of the United States of America (1840), p. 192). He estimated the total expense for the services of the best negro workmen for a whole year at $170, females and young men being cheaper. Gregg's quotation from Montgomery is not quite accurate, though perfectly exact in spirit. Further extenuation is brought to Gregg in the statement of Mr. Kohn that " The history of the early efforts of the industry in this State indicate that slave labor was very largely used " (Cotton Mills of S. C., p. 24). Buckingham, writing three years before Gregg, implied that it would be the natural thing to use negroes at least equally with whites (Slave States of America, vol. i, p. 171). The Rocky Mount Mill, in North Carolina, employed negroes from 1820 to 1851 on the coarser yarns, most of the product going to country merchants near the factory, but some to the Philadelphia market. In 1849 negroes were the only operatives (Thompson, pp. 250–251).

[100] The health of the blacks in the mill was said to be better than that of whites in the same occupations (quoted from New York

DeBow approved the recommendation of a Tennesseean that slave labor be applied to the manufacture of cotton and wool throughout the South, "such labor having been found most advantageous wherever adopted."[101]   It may

Herald, in DeBow, vol. ii, p. 127, note). Another observer said that the experienced white overseers from the North, at first prejudiced against the slave labor, testified to its equal efficiency and even superiority in many respects as compared with white. The negroes were tested out at spinning, but later learned to weave, and turned out full quantity of cloth. "The resources of the South are great, and it should be gratifying to all who view these facts, with the eye of a statesman and philanthropist, that the sources of profitable employment and support to our rapidly-increasing African labor are illimitable, and must remove all motives for emigration to other countries" (ibid., vol. i, p. 232). In 1847 the plant was declared to have done a "fine business" for three years previous (Columbia Telegraph, quoted in Kohn, Cotton Mills of S. C., p. 18). Other reports of this mill do not paint so bright a picture. The son of a man who relinquished the superintendency in 1838 said the mill was owned by slaveholders who chose to use some of their negroes in this way—they were planters first and manufacturers second. The negro labor was not successful (Charles McDonald, int., Charlotte). One manager of the mill was reported as saying that slave labor failed there because of the malarial condition of the neighborhood and because the negroes' fingers were clumsy (William Banks, int., Columbia). Mr. Kohn states that the factory was operated largely by slave labor until the close of the Civil War, when whites were installed, and quotes Hammond's Handbook to the effect that 90 slaves in charge of a white overseer were "capable of learning within reasonable limits" (Cotton Mills of S. C., p. 16). This factory, perhaps the best known of those employing negro operatives, is said to have been burned by Federal troops entering Columbia. The ruins, across the river, about three miles above the city, are still to be seen, flanked by a grove on a small plateau overlooking the stream. The foundations and maybe one or two stories were of stone. The race, now empty of water, is stone-lined and deep, and huge wooden beams and parts of the rude shafting remain in the wheel-pit. The dam flung across the river seems still in tolerable condition, though the sluice is widened by years of neglect. Mr. Kohn says the establishment was hampered by lack of capital, and quotes Gregg to the effect that the capitalization of the plant was not more than sufficient to pay for the expensive dam (Cotton Mills of S. C., p. 17). Except in the weaving department, blacks were employed in the DeKalb factory in South Carolina for several years, thirty belonging to the company, which thought they compared favorably with white operatives. Wages of negroes were 18¾ cents a day and board; whites who succeeded them, exclusive of the weavers, were given from 13 to 36 cents a day. References to wages in old mills in Georgia and Alabama seem to indicate that there must have been some negro employes (Ingle, pp. 75-76). Cf. Kohn, ibid., p. 16.

[101] Industrial Resources, vol. ii, p. 124.

be concluded that slave operatives in ante-bellum mills were common. The attempt of Alexander and Haskell, both perfectly familiar with the negro and the economic conditions prevailing in South Carolina at that time, to employ blacks in the Congaree Mill, the first erected in Columbia after the war, must indicate that they were repeating a familiar practice.[102] It will be seen presently that the rare later efforts to use negroes were considered experimental and watched with doubt by outsiders.

It must be observed that, partly as a suggestion from pre-war usages, partly as an evidence of disposition sometimes shown to overlook the labor supply so naturally found in the poor whites, and partly springing from the speculative frame of mind that prevailed just before the industry took its real rise, the possibility of employing negroes in cotton mills was much in the air in 1880, certainly in South Carolina. The chief source of information, the Blackman Report, contains clear indication of the activity with which the public imagination was working at the time. Few new mills were building; the remoter history of the industry had lapsed for the moment into the background; the new development had not commenced. In contemplating the mills then in operation, there was the feeling that they were not important as types of the past nor as presages of what was to come. That there was to be a new story there was no doubt. Thus in this interval between sterile past and dynamic future, inquiries might be poorly informed and answers afterwards shown to be mistaken—very often the creeping of the chrysalis from the old cocoon was not noticed. But knowledge was being gathered, stock was being taken, resolve was forming to meet the challenge that was rightly guessed to be impending.

The Blackman survey of cotton mills operating in South

---

[102] William Banks, int., Columbia. The experiment lasted a year or more, but the negroes were found to be poorly adapted to the work; a fire disabled the plant after this trial, and it was converted into a warehouse. Cf. Kohn, Cotton Mills of S. C., p. 24, and Tompkins, Cotton Mill, Commercial Features, pp. 109–110.

Carolina in 1880, made for the News and Courier, while rarely mentioning the finding of negroes in the factories then, often comments upon the exclusive employment of whites.[103]   Probably ante-bellum experience was responsible for survival of negro operatives in the Saluda Cotton Factory.   Blackman found in this mill a hundred operatives, twenty-five of whom were colored, ranging in age from eight years up.   Operatives lived in homes owned by the factory.   Asked as to the feasibility of employing negro operatives, the superintendent replied that " at his factory he had worked mixed operatives with great advantage.   The negro was as capable of instruction in the business as the white male or female, and could afford to work much cheaper, as they lived so much cheaper.   The negro labor he found was easily controlled. . . ."[104]

Blackman in his visits to the mills had a stock question designed to bring out the pros and cons of negro labor.   He received answers from which it must have appeared pretty evident that negroes were not destined to play a progressive part in the history of the industry.   These discouraging replies were based on disbelief in the suitability of working negroes and whites together, on the inadaptability of negroes to the employment, and on the plentifulness of whites offering for service in the mills.   One of the owners of a large factory said negroes were not apt enough to learn the business properly, whites would not work in the same room with negroes, and as most of the work was paid for by the piece, the labor if mixed must necessarily give unsatisfactory results.[105]

---

[103] Thus of Glendale: " The factory employs 120 operatives, all of whom are white " (p. 10).   Cf. as to Langley, p. 7, and Red Bank, p. 8.

[104] Ibid., p. 9.

[105] Ibid., p. 10.   An officer of a little establishment said: " The whites and blacks will not work together, and we have an abundance of white labor, which is certainly superior to any class of colored labor that we could employ " (ibid., p. 8).   Cf. ibid., p. 11.   The summary of the report correctly said: " There is . . . considerable diversity of opinion on the subject of labor, but it appears that the preponderance is in favor of white labor, as more dexterous and trustworthy, and we assume that this difference will become more

The failure of a mill at Concord, promoted and managed by a negro and worked by negro operatives, cannot be taken as a strong argument against the feasibility of using the negro in the textile development of the South. This venture was tried under such adverse circumstances as to make it practically without value as an indication one way or the other. The mill was projected in 1896 by Warren Coleman, born in slavery and said to have been the illegitimate son of a prominent North Carolinian. Coleman had made money as a merchant in Concord and had built perhaps as many as a hundred "shacks" which he rented out to negroes; it was supposed that he was worth as much as $50,000. His natural father is reported to have assisted him to get his start in life, and to have advised about the mill project. The idea was that the factory should be a negro undertaking. The colored press commented enthusiastically upon the appeals for subscriptions to stock, $50,000 was raised and the company organized in 1897 with Coleman as secretary and treasurer. The enterprise looking promising, the capital stock was increased to $100,000, some white people in the community subscribing to encourage the effort. Negroes all over the State took the small shares, which could be paid in trifling instalments. But many of the poor negroes who had subscribed could not meet the payments—some of the washerwomen made hardly more in all than their investment obligations amounted to, and many of the artizans who had agreed to work out their subscriptions in assisting with the erection of the plant disappointed the management. It took four years to complete the building, and when the mill was ready for operation, Coleman had had to assume much of the forfeited stock. A white superintendent from Easthampton, Massachusetts, was employed. The factory was handicapped by second-hand English machinery; the yarn market was depressed;

marked as finer classes of goods are more generally made. The difficulty in obtaining operatives is not great. . . ." One superintendent had declared, however, that in his opinion, a mill could be run with negro operatives entirely, directed by skilled whites, at a 40 per cent saving (ibid., pp. 5–6).

other Concord mills were making little profit. The yarn market pulled up, but Coleman's plant failed to pay, and ran only off and on after the first year. Coleman died in 1904 and a few months later the factory was sold under the mortgage. It was said the negroes made clever enough operatives, learning quickly, and the manager at the last attributed the failure to other factors than labor—poor machinery, insufficient capital, unaccustomed administration. Operation of the plant was loose; sometimes the mill would stand idle for hours waiting for cotton or fuel. Some of the operatives would be considered good average workers in any Southern mill, though while white spinners at Concord were receiving ten to twelve and one half cents per side, the negroes could command only five or six cents, making only about $2.50 per week. Being old, the machinery had to be run slowly to give good results; the negro overseers showed favoritism and were harsh in docking operatives. The manager believed that under favorable circumstances, near a city where more intelligent negroes might be gotten, a mill could be run successfully with white overseers and colored operatives.[106]

In an attempt to use negro hands in the old plant of the Charleston Manufacturing Company, the direct management was of the best, capital was sufficient and the machinery was new. But because of peculiar local circumstances attendant upon this experiment, it does not reflect much light upon the apparently satisfactory character of the labor in the Concord mill. Before telling of the Charleston experience, however, it is curious to notice that one of the great pioneers in the cotton mill movement in South Carolina, H. P. Hammett, in 1880, answering questions designed to bring out points in which Charleston as a prospective manufacturing place was interested, predicted success for such a scheme as afterwards proved a failure: "I should think

---

[106] For the story of this mill I am indebted almost entirely to Mr. Thompson's "From the Cotton Field to the Cotton Mill," amended in minor particulars by an interview with Mr. Charles McDonald at Charlotte.

that a yarn mill in Charleston properly constructed to make
coarse yarns alone out of the rejected and cheap cottons
that could be bought there might be run to great advantage
and profit to the owners. I rather think negroes could be
used to do coarse yarn work. I think that they could be
trained to make very fair goods. I don't think the labor
would be much cheaper than with white operatives. We
give our operatives good wages and take care of their
morals."[107]

The plant, which for some time had been idle, was bought
through the initiative of a successful up-country manufacturer in cooperation with Charleston men who had been interested in the former company. It operated first with
white labor and was a failure. After about a year it was
determined to try negro operatives. Enthusiasm of much
the same sort as had marked the original enterprise, directed
now, however, toward the opportunity for negroes instead
of poor whites as factory workers, was evinced. But again
the projectors relied upon their own *a priori* opinions much
more, it may be thought, than upon assurances proceeding
from a study of the abilities and willingness of the negroes
whom they wanted to employ. They felt so keenly that the
plan *ought* to succeed that they did not inquire greatly
whether it *would* succeed. " The superintendent of the
mill and myself," said one of the stockholders, got the colored preachers and a negro ex-policeman down here at the
bank and showed them the opportunity for the colored people if they would go into the mill and make good operatives.
They saw it too, and as far as we know did all they could,
but they couldn't make efficiency where it wasn't. The
negroes lost a great opening."[108]

---

[107] Blackman, ibid., p. 17.

[108] George W. Williams, int., Charleston. Another of the investors gave a similar account: " We were assured the colored people
would work for low wages, less than whites, and would be faithful,
but they turned out to be just the reverse. We had everybody exhorting them, telling them now was their opportunity, and that if
the experiment succeeded here, mills all over the South would be
open to them. But when a circus would come, they would all troop

The superintendent declared that he had educated 3000 negro operatives to the work and made them competent, but that on any one day he could not get 300 of them in the mill. White operatives were used in the picking and carding rooms, separated, of course, from the negroes up stairs, employment of some whites being necessary to provide enough workers to run the plant.[109] The mill operated for about a year with negro labor, and the unsuccessful venture was discontinued. "We had the best management and fine machinery, and all the money necessary. It was the labor. I am absolutely convinced it was the labor."[110]

The failure at Charleston had the effect on some mill men of confirming their disbelief in negro labor, but with others did not daunt their faith in the theoretical soundness, at least, of the proposal.[111]

---

away to it. It was a sight to see them" (W. P. Carrington, int., Charleston). The negroes, shunning "the opportunity of their lives, would go for oysters in the oyster season, and then for strawberries in the strawberry season" (Williams, ibid.).

[109] F. Q. O'Neill, int., Charleston.

[110] Ibid. One of those who had worked hardest to prove negro operatives suitable, said: "If a white man will get 92 per cent out of a machine, a negro will get 76 per cent only and be satisfied" (George W. Williams, int., Charleston). Mr. Thompson thinks one reason for the unsatisfactory issue of the experiment was that the mill as worked by negroes was expected to pay dividends on a capitalization enlarged by installation of new machinery. Mr. Montgomery, chiefly responsible for the enterprise, is reported to have assigned the distractions of the city as cause for the failure (pp. 251–252). A stockholder attributed non-success to malign influence of selling agents of the mill: "The commission house took every means to show the colored labor unprofitable. Those negro women could tie a knot at a spindle as well as white women could." One of those interested in the company still believed the plan of having negro operatives was abandoned too soon, that the mill was on the eve of making money when the machinery was moved to Gainesville, Georgia (William M. Bird, int., Charleston). Cf. Tompkins, Cotton Mill, Commercial Features, pp. 109–110.

[111] The superintendent of a large up-country mill said that the superintendency of the Charleston mill was offered him at the time negro labor was to be installed, and that he promptly declined the position. "The negroes' average of intelligence is so low that you cannot organize them. If you could pick them from all over the State, you might accomplish something, but taking them as they come, you cannot accomplish anything" (W. J. Britton, int., Spartanburg). A mill president of Augusta, speaking of the prevalent belief that cotton cannot be profitably manufactured in a seaport

Evidence gathered at first hand, even after fifteen years, still bears out Mr. Thompson's observation that the mill men of the South have thought of negro labor in a speculative way only, as a remote possibility or necessity. Since Mr. Thompson wrote, however, the South has approached measurably closer, in common conception of manufacturers, to a genuine and widespread shortage of operatives, and has felt this condition in an increase in wages not entirely consequent upon the European war. Steadily the question of employing negroes in the mills has gained a place in the minds of manufacturers. The hope of continuing the favorable labor differential, in spite of child labor legisla-

in the South, gave his reaction in brisk sentences: "I have no sympathy with this view. If you can command the managerial skill, and you can surely get the machinery, you can run a cotton mill in a seaport as well as anywhere else. At once Manchester and New Bedford and Lowell come into your mind—they have all got spinning climates. In the South there is, of course, the labor problem, most of the operatives coming from the up-country. But there are labor troubles in anything. You will have labor troubles in running a shoe factory in New England or in picking prickly apples in the Zulu Islands. So far as I am concerned, if I wanted to operate a mill at the coast, say Charleston, I would employ negroes. I wouldn't work them as those people worked them. I would not pay them half as much as white labor, but just as much. There is no reason why colored labor will not prove profitable." An expert in cotton mill practice said: "A negro can run a ginning outfit as well as a white man, and is tickled to death with it. The great trouble with negro labor for cotton mills is poor adaptability to organization. If I was going to run a mill with negroes, I would want to be right on the ground and study them, and not follow the experiment of trying to run the mill in Charleston with the president living in Spartanburg. I don't see why colored operatives cannot be used in cheap mills" (J. H. M. Beatty, int., Columbia, Jan. 3, 1917). A superintendent eminently practical declared: "The only trouble with negro labor is the mixing of the races. If a mill could be run exclusively with negro operatives, there would be no difficulty. Why, we have negro bricklayers, tailors, decorators, and these do handsome work; negro women are good seamstresses; there are negro dentists and doctors. I don't see why piccaninnies won't make good factory hands, spinning and weaving. There is nothing lacking in their capacity to learn" (George T. Lynch, int., Augusta). And a mill official whose family name is synonymous with the founding of the industry in the South said that while his fellow-manufacturers would want to hang him if they thought he expressed such a belief, he saw no real reason why negroes cannot be profitably and suitably used as operatives.

tion and the entrance of trade unionism, may lead to further tests of negro operatives.[112]

---

[112] Cf. the writer's "The End of Child Labor," in Survey, Aug. 23, 1919, pp. 749–750. Tompkins in 1895 said: "It is impossible for me to come to a conclusion as to whether the colored people would make successful mill hands or not. . . . I would be willing to be one of 100 persons to subscribe $1,500 each for a mill to be operated by colored people until by losses it should be determined that the experiment was a failure. . . . This experiment is important to the whole South. . . . With white labor alone it will be only a few years before we reach the limit of supply. Then we will without doubt have the same laws, the same experience and the same accessories [sic] of new labor from various sources that New England has had." Foreseeing child labor laws and legislation governing hours of work in the South, he felt that "the general conditions will constantly approach closer and closer to those that have been already brought about in old and New England." While he had no doubt of the negro's intelligence, he thought he lacked tenacity of purpose where the work was monotonous, and that in the warm rooms of a mill, doing light work, he was apt to fall asleep (Cultivation, Picking, Baling and Manufacturing of Cotton, p. 11 ff. Cf. ibid., p. 15 ff.). Mr. Thompson wrote that "speaking broadly the difficulty with negro operatives is not an intellectual one," believing that the chief failings of all negro labor are moral and temperamental. Drawbacks are dislike of the negro of working alone, insufficient ambition and pride in his work; daily association in the same employment might make the negro less respectful to the white man (Cotton Field to Cotton Mill, pp. 249–250). However, this student admitted that bettered standards of life might enable the negro to enter occupations which growing scarcity of white workers must open to him (ibid., p. 266). Cf. Tompkins, Cotton Mill, Commercial Features, pp. 109–110. Relying upon disqualifications usually noted, Mr. Copeland concluded that "There is little likelihood that the negro will become the mill operative of the future," and that "he would require more supervising than his labor would be worth." This writer is mistaken in saying that "Before the Civil War the use of slaves in the factories was occasionally suggested." As has been seen, they were in several instances actually used; in declaring that "no competent business man has yet ventured to make a real test" of negro labor, he overlooks the management of the mill in Charleston (p. 47 ff.). Cf. Uttley, p. 45. Mr. Goldsmith says dogmatically that "The negroes cannot be utilized in the manufacture of cotton" (p. 10). In a discerning summary of reasons for non-employment of negroes in the mills, Murphy placed chief stress on the natural preference of managers for the stronger race, it being often difficult to employ the two together (pp. 103–104). In conversation, Mr. Kohn confirmed the position taken in his writings, and emphasized the hurtful absenteeism of negro labor (interview, Columbia, Jan. 5, 1917). A deterrent to the employment of negroes at the emergence of the mill period not sufficiently dwelt upon, is found in the bitter hatred, born of political and racial fear, that followed the war and Reconstruction. For an excellent statement illustrating this point, see testimony of Lewis W. Parker in report of Hearing before

Not only do opinions differ in regard to negro labor, but facts point in contrary directions. A hosiery manufacturing company which began using negroes in one plant in 1904 has recently installed colored help in two more factories, in all three cases due to shortage of white operatives. Wages of these operatives run from 20 to 40 per cent lower than for white knitting mill hands; they get no better than 80 per cent production from the machines; special care must be used to hold absenteeism in check; difference in production of negro and white workers is not so great as difference in wages, but the number of " seconds " turned out by negroes is greater than in the case of whites. The cost of supervision is higher with negroes, but under practiced management their skill in these mills, as judged by fineness of work, has more than doubled. Negroes offer themselves in sufficient numbers to allow of some selection. All are piece workers. Only superintendents and foremen are white. The judgment of the manager is that where white operatives can be secured, negro labor in textile mills should not be attempted. He could readily understand why a silk mill operated in the South with colored hands had failed, and uses negroes only on coarse work.

It is pleasant, in a study such as this, in which many conclusions as to broad social conditions must be reached by inference, to come upon a part of the subject in which there is an absolute expression of facts under consideration. In speaking of wages paid in cotton mills of the South there are, happily, some figures to form the center of the discussion. Although occasionally distorting the image a little, the wages, in the instance of this industry in the South, constitute a mirror to reflect complicated economic phenomena in a way to make them realizable and concrete. Much evidence which, after passage of time, is undiscoverable in itself, many factors which no one would even think to look for as bearing upon the problem, are unfalteringly assimi-

House Committee of Judiciary upon proposed constitutional amendment giving congress power to regulate hours of employes in factories, April 29, 1902, part 2, pp. 11–12.

lated in the wage scale. Wages paid the operatives are a composite photograph not only of the state of the industry at the time of its commencement, but of the agricultural, social, commercial and educational situation of the South at and just previous to the period here treated.

It will be found that wages varied very markedly from one locality to another for practically identical work; this, so far from weakening the force of what has just been observed, strengthens it, for it has been impressed all along that there was in the South only that standardization which proceeded from the weight of poverty; that it is impossible, as to most aspects, properly to speak of industry in the section as a whole, but only of the particular facts for separate communities.

In these pages regarding wages the reader should keep in mind not only preceding discussions in this chapter—as to condition of the poor whites before they entered the mills, the generally superabundant supply of native white people, the large proportion of women and children in the first mill populations—but larger aspects of the whole study as well. The part played by labor in forming an argument, selfish or philanthropic, for the building of factories; the earnestness with which communities cooperated to raise capital in the face of meagre resources; the faith with which projectors of enterprises reached out for support from the North; the character of plants erected and of machinery put in them; the relations with creditors and commission merchants—all these have their bearing. If it be true that the cotton mills of the South rested to a large extent upon plentiful supply of native white labor, then wages paid to operatives afford a convenient indication of the level from which the industry took its rise.

First to glance at some ante-bellum wages. It is said that in the early fifties $116 per year was the average cost of white labor; then average wages on the basis of 300 working days amounted to thirty-nine cents.[113]

---

[113] A table given by Montgomery for 1831 includes only two South-

In 1856 Olmsted wrote that there were from 15,000 to 20,000 spindles running in Columbus, the largest manufacturing place south of Richmond. "The operatives of the cotton-mills are said to be mainly 'Cracker-girls' (poor whites from the country), who earn, in good times, by piece-work, from $8 to $12 per month." Workers in all Columbus factories of various sorts were declared to be "in such a condition that, if temporarily thrown out of employment, great numbers of them are at once reduced to a state of destitution, and are dependent upon credit or charity for their daily food."[114]

At a time when negro labor was dearer than that of free whites, when slaves were better looked after than white people doing similar work, it is not surprising that there should have been no social watchfulness of the conditions of employment of the latter.[115]

Slavery precluded moral and economic alertness on the part of the public. As comes out more clearly in post-bellum days, it was a miracle if there was work for men and women to do; everyone was far from quarrelling with the terms of engagement.[116]

---

ern States, Maryland and Virginia. Average weekly wages of males in Maryland amounted to $3.87 and of females $1.91; male operatives in Virginia received $2.73 per week and females $1.58 (Practical Detail of Cotton Manufactures, p. 161). Cf. ibid., p. 133. In 1849 in the DeKalb factory in South Carolina operatives exclusive of weavers received from 13 to 36 cents per day; in the same year the average wage at Vaucluse was 37 cents, most of the hands being women and children; 300 hands in an Augusta mill averaged $3.05 per week; in an Alabama town the average was $8 per month; at Columbus the pay was from 12 to 75 cents per day for operatives, and for overseers from $1 to $1.25 (Ingle, pp. 75–76).

[114] Seaboard Slave States, pp. 547–548. "Public entertainments were being held at the time of my visit, the profits to be applied to the relief of operatives in mills which had been stopped by the effects of a late flood of the river." (Cf. ibid., p. 543.)

[115] Cf. Olmsted, p. 543.

[116] The position of the South in 1860 can be fancied when it is said of the entire country at the same date that "One or two states had passed laws regulating hours of labor; but none had thought of the cost to the race of hard toil and long hours for women and children, and most men regarded the builder of a mill as a public benefactor because he furnished employment to just this element in the population" (Dodd, Expansion and Conflict, pp. 209–210).

An Alabama cotton manufacturer declared in 1878 it was cheaper by 42 cents per hand per day to operate a mill in his State than in Massachusetts.[117]

In 1883 a New Hampshire hosiery manufacturer purposed establishing a mill at Columbia, South Carolina, and said he could run the plant there "without counting the cost of raw material (which he could procure . . . at less cost than further North) at least twenty-five per cent cheaper, in the cost of labor alone, than he could in New England."[118] Major Hammett, showing the advantage of the South over the North, especially in the manufacture of coarse goods, estimated that the difference in labor amounted to not less than one and one half cents per pound.[119]

A writer in the New York Times observed that "a Fall River, Lowell, or Manchester operative would hardly be able to live on the $4 a week which will make a Georgia operative's family comfortable. There is an abundance of native white labor to be had at from 50 to 60 cents a day."[120]

Coming to a typical mill of the early eighties, it was reported of Clifton, in South Carolina, proposing to employ four hundred native whites, that wages would amount to 50 cents to $1 per day.[121] In one of the little note books giving informal estimates for the Charleston Manufacturing Company, there is a memorandum indicating that a good superintendent would cost $4000 a year, and "Labor 25 cts to 1.50 pr day" with the additional remark: "these wages paid in cotton mills in the State—good authority for this statement."

---

[117] It is difficult to tell how much of this saving was imputed to lower wages, and the problem is not much helped by the calculation that a 4000-spindle, 125-loom plant in Alabama had a cost for labor and mill expenses amounting to $63.44 per day (Haralson, in Burney, Handbook of Alabama, p. 271 ff.).

[118] Manufacturers' Record, Baltimore, Feb. 1, 1883.

[119] Quoted from Atlanta Constitution, in ibid.

[120] Quoted in News and Courier, Charleston, Nov. 5, 1881. Low wages were ascribed to low cost of living.

[121] News and Courier, Charleston, May 21, 1881. This plant had 17,000 spindles, 500 looms, and a capital stock of $500,000.

It must be apparent that low wages paid to operatives in Southern mills were bound up with the low cost of living. Remuneration which would otherwise seem impossibly small becomes understandable when expenses of the operatives are seen to have been very little. In order to know the condition of the workers, it is obviously necessary to keep in mind real wages and not money wages. It must be noticed that lower wages prevailing in the South, however accompanied by greater purchasing power and by other payment by the mills in kind, showed the less advanced economic position of the South as compared with other parts of the country. Also, the standard of life of the Southern operative was lower than that of the New England operative, and however completely Southern wages allowed the former to reach his standard of life, he was probably not so well off as his New England brother who saved no more money.

In estimating the real income of workers in the Southern mills it must be remembered that the companies made up a considerable part of the pay in goods and services rather than in coin, and this practice of the early establishments has in large measure endured through the years, affording one of the most striking particulars in which the old economic system, born of slavery and fostering a paternalistic attitude of master toward servant, of employer toward employe, has persisted into a new day. A little mill in the deep country, which got its start shortly before the industrial era, manufactured the coarsest yarns on 880 spindles, and had 600 acres of cultivated land and a gin. Twelve operatives, all white, received an average wage of 33½ cents per day, and 120 persons in all were dependent upon the factory for support. The very low pay and the number of those looking to the mill for a living occasions less surprise when it is learned that the company furnished its operatives with houses free of rent.[122]

---

[122] Blackman, p. 11. A factory a little larger, but otherwise about similar, on a waterpower located eighteen miles from the railroad, employed 65 white operatives at an average wage of 40 cents for

15

Low wages were partly due to the limited money economy. Companies frequently could easily bear the prime
living costs of their operatives and their families, when the
equivalent amount could not well have been paid in cash.
The smaller the quantity of money required, the more convenient it was for manufacturers cramped for capital. The
company store, which became a widespread institution, as
well as being a necessity in isolated factory locations, was
designed to limit the amount of circulating capital required
by the mill management. The company-owned village has
been an extension of the company store. At Piedmont, with
300 operatives and 600 dependents in all, $50,000 was suf-
ficient to cover the annual pay roll, including salaries, the
average wage for spinners being 50 cents a day. Operatives lived in seventy-seven tenement houses furnished free
of rent by the company.[123] In such "free villages" many
lesser gifts are implied in remission of rents. Often wood
might be cut from the company's land and cows pastured in
the company's fields, and garden patches about the houses
were well-nigh universal. In these first villages of the
Campaign years poor whites from the neighborhood, desperate for a means of livelihood, thanked the mill for all
their needs.

Whatever other factors contributed to the low scale of
wages, the primary cause, of course, was the lean condition
of the South and the relatively small number of jobs as
contrasted with the large number of those wanting work.
Wages were really a question of what the factories could
pay, rather than of what the people might ask. With
economic progress, as agriculture has become more prosperous and industrial plants thicker, wages have steadily
risen.

It has been noticed that wages varied greatly from place
to place. At Crawfordsville, for example, wages were 33½
cents a day; Fork Shoals, not far away and a mill almost

spinners; there were 200 people dependent upon the factory, which
provided houses free (ibid., p. 13).

[123] Ibid., p. 16.

precisely circumstanced, paid about 40 cents a day. This is attributable not only to want of knowledge of workpeople in one neighborhood of conditions of pay and of living prevailing in another, but to the extreme provincialism of employers as well. An important factor besides was wide variableness of circumstances of employment from one locality to another. One mill might have operatives for some years already in its service, and as unwilling to leave for the farms again as they were not likely to go to another factory paying more wages; relative proximity of a mill to a city or town, controlling to some extent the agricultural rents and value of farm produce, and the ease or difficulty with which families could move their few effects, as well as the outlook of the people upon whom the plant drew for operatives, would make a difference in wages. The proportion of women and children employed would have a vital bearing. These things influenced also the operating costs of the factories, and thus indirectly as well as directly helped to determine the amount of money that might be paid in wages. These considerations apply more conspicuously to the mills of the seventies than to those of the eighties, but the distinction is one of degree and not of kind. The larger and more numerous factories became, the less, of course, such forces prevailed.

The summary of the Blackman Report said there were 2,612 operatives in South Carolina in 1880, upon whom 8,143 persons were dependent for support. The amount paid out in wages monthly was $38,159, and the rate of wages for spinners ranged from 25 cents to 78 cents a day, " according to the situation and the character of the labor." The Valley Falls factory, near to Crawfordsville and Fork Shoals, mentioned above, was making profit on coarse yarns although the machinery was old and " despite . . . the great disadvantage of being situated in an almost inaccessible region." Fifteen operatives were employed at an average wage of 40 cents a day.[124]

---

[124] Ibid., p. 11. At Reedy River, a larger mill in the same locality,

The only indication found of dissatisfaction in the early years with prevailing wages paid is that contained in the following item which appeared in 1882: "Last Monday morning four of the 'warpers' employed in the Rock Hill Cotton Factory waited upon the superintendent and demanded an advance in wages. Their demands were not considered. They were told that their services were no longer wanted at any price. They left and their places were supplied immediately."[125]

Hard times in the industry, especially in the Augusta district, where mills had never seemed to ride on the crest of the wave, were responsible for sharp wage reductions in 1884 in some of the largest factories. In May one cut officers' salaries 20 per cent and employes' wages 15 per cent, and another reduced both salaries and wages 15 per cent. The policy was inaugurated to allow continued sales at market prices,[126] but was only partly efficacious, for the

the average pay of the 65 operatives was 50 cents a day (ibid., p. 13). At Glendale, where 60 per cent of the 120 operatives were women and children, wages averaged 67 cents a day (ibid., p. 10). Langley in 1879 made coarse shirtings and drills as well as yarns, and paid its operatives, two-thirds of them female, an average of 78 cents per day (ibid., p. 7). Not only might wages vary from mill to mill, but the range might be wide in a single factory. Thus at Glendale the highest was $1.50 per day and the lowest 12½ cents (ibid.). Persistence of variations in wages between mills may be strikingly seen in facts gathered by Mr. Kohn (Cotton Mills of S. C., p. 43). A table of wages paid annually by the mills of South Carolina, and of the capital and spindleage of these factories, published in 1883, yields little that is helpful because "capital" sometimes meant paid up capital and sometimes allowed capital; a comparison of spindleage with wages is not more helpful, because a part of the wages was undoubtedly paid for a greater or less amount of weaving. Two mills with combined capital of $600,000 and 32,368 spindles paid in wages $180,000 a year; Clifton and Piedmont each had $500,000 capital and paid annually $100,000 in wages, but the former had 19,000 spindles and the latter 23,000. These factories were probably making a larger proportion of yarns than Langley, which, with $400,000 capital and only 10,000 spindles, paid in wages $87,500 a year. Another mill, with less than half as many spindles, paid $18,000 a year for wages, or about one fifth as much as Langley. The factory with the smallest capital was expending in wages only $2400 annually (Columbia correspondent of Augusta Chronicle and Constitutionalist, quoted in Manufacturers' Record, Baltimore, Jan. 18, 1883).

[125] News and Courier, Charleston, Jan. 23.
[126] Evening News, Augusta, May 28, 1884.

Enterprise mill soon shut down, and by the time it resumed in October the King and Augusta mills had reduced wages 25 per cent.[127]

In the history of the industry in the South, increasing cost of living and, more importantly, growth of mills and diminishing supply of labor have given to wages an upward trend that, despite lapses and spurts, has been strong and inevitable; wages have advanced not gradually, but in jumps mainly as a consequence of accelerated mill building, though wage reductions in periods of slump have to considerable extent been avoided through absorption of the field from the factory, the opportunity open to operatives to return to cotton raising.

The low wage scale paid in the South as contrasted with other textile sections, notably New England, has often been remarked. The advantage flowing to the Southern manufacturer from cheap labor, partially offset by the lower price received for Southern goods in many cases, and by inability of unskilled workers to get full production from expensive machinery, has proved more persistent than that resulting from other factors.[128]

In assuming that, in real wages, Southern operatives have been as well off as those of New England, it must be remembered that the lower level on which Southern mills have been conducted has involved certain very definite social disutilities which do not appear in any calculation of expenses of living. Such are the results of child labor, long hours of work, poor schooling, mischievous abetting of harmful politics, a contracted economic outlook linked with difficulty in working through the mills to better employments.

That the mills have brought a better living, generally speaking, than most other employments open to the people,

---

[127] Chronicle, Augusta, Oct. 21, 1884.
[128] Cf. Kohn, Cotton Mills of S. C., p. 33 ff.; Uttley, p. 56; Thompson, pp. 152–153; Tompkins, Storing and Marketing of Cotton, in transactions of New England Cotton Manufacturers' Assn., vol. 77, pp. 10–11.

must be patent from the comparative ease with which factories have obtained labor.[129]   Apologists for Southern mills regularly, and others less disingenuous frequently, have laid stress on the favorable " family wage " received by operatives.[130]   The error here would seem to be too evident to require correction.   To the extent that the head of the family, certainly if assisted by one or two other adult members, cannot by his wages provide for those dependent upon him, the employing industry is socially parasitic.   With the entire, or nearly the entire family in the mill, children competing fatally with their elders, money income, augmented by many payments in kind, has been only about sufficient to support tolerable existence.

It has been observed that Southern mill wages have advanced in jerks.   Such a sharp rise came in the years leading to the panic of 1907, when the increase was 25 per cent, more or less.[131]   Besides paying higher wages, many mills introduced bonus plans.[132]   In some cases these were not bonuses at all, but simply wages, operatives working through the noon hour or otherwise speeding up to earn them, but the bonus and less obvious devices took on stronger significance in the hands of employers in the period of sharper competition for operatives during the European War.   In February of 1917 it was said: " Few industries can boast of an enterprise which would actually lose money in certain lines in order to benefit its workers, and yet that is just what the Loray Mills are doing.   For example, they sell wood and coal to their workers at actual cost always,

---

[129] Cf. Thompson, p. 159. Comparison of mill wages with those in arrgriculture, here given, lose force from the consideration that food might be given to farm workers and, besides, account must be taken of the depressing effect of negroes working in the country. Cf. Kohn, Cotton Mills of S. C., p. 50.

[130] Cf. Kohn, Cotton Mills of S. C., for many references.

[131] Cf. Thompson, pp. 159 ff.; Goldsmith, p. 10; Kohn, Cotton Mills of S. C., pp. 33, 36 and 39. Statements of increased incomes to specific families in the years 1902 to 1907 are without point, because of addition of new members to the working group and increase in ages and skill of operatives during the period. Cf. Thompson, ibid., pp. 148–149.

[132] Cf. Kohn, Cotton Mills of S. C., p. 49.

but during the past two months they have been furnishing their help coal at a price fifty cents per ton cheaper than the mills actually pay for the coal delivered to them."[133]

Just as mills have had to compete in welfare work to hold their operatives, it is clear that these extra concessions were simply a convenient avoidance of cash payments. It might have been foretold that increases in money wages would not be allowed to stand frankly as such. The event proved that these were usually painted as "voluntary" on the part of the companies.[134] These things are not worth mentioning either as naïve subterfuges of employers or more naïve efforts of writers to create an impression favorable to hard-set manufacturers, but are interesting as showing now a canny continuance of practices which were sincere and acceptable in the earlier history of the Southern industry. Wage advances were general and rapid in succession, and without doubt many employers would have given these out of pure goodwill to their operatives and to let them share in enormously mounting profits. But it did not need the negro migration that left farm vacancies, unprecedentedly high prices for cotton, army drafts that took their thousands and war construction that held out unbelievable wage opportunities, joining with the first concerted union attention to the South as an unorganized field with resulting strikes at Anderson, Graniteville, and Columbus, to make it plain that the great stimulus back of increases in pay was the necessity of the mill managements.[135]

---

[133] Charlotte News, Textile Ed. Throughout this survey and a like one of the Columbia Record in 1916 are any number of similar references. In estimating the gratuity of the mills, it is well to note an observation of a North Carolina manufacturer: "Wages, though mill men may not recognize the fact, tend to be determined by the cost of living in the particular mill village. At High Shoals, where wood is $1.50 a cord, wages are less than at Charlotte, where wood is $4 a cord" (Sterling Graydon, int., Charlotte, Sept. 4, 1916).

[134] Cf. Textile Editions of Columbia Record, 1916, and Charlotte News, 1917, the writer's "End of Child Labor," in Survey, Aug. 23, 1919, and Mill News, Charlotte, quoted in Literary Digest, Dec. 9, 1916.

[135] Before these phenomena appeared, Tompkins said: "The pay of operatives rarely varies in the South with the price of goods . . ." (Cotton Mill, Commercial Features, p. 55).

CHAPTER IV

THE RÔLE OF CAPITAL

The achievement represented in the rise of cotton mills in the South is not more clearly apparent than in the story of how capital was gathered and how financial operations of the factories were conducted. Here was an agricultural community made poor by war, economically disorganized by Emancipation and estranged from the capable North through Reconstruction, face to face with an unaccustomed task needing wealth, concert at home and cooperation from without. No new industrial movement has been a shorter time in the talking stage; the South met the acid test of purpose by plunging instantly into actual performance.

Investments in Southern cotton mills increased about $2,-000,000 each decade after 1840 until that of 1870–1880, when the advance was roughly $6,000,000—from $11,-088,315 to $17,375,897. The figures for the decade 1880–1890 reflect the suddenness and rapidity of the growth once the undertaking was entered upon; capital trebled to $53,-821,303 and by 1900 had reached $124,596,879.[1] The forward leap was marked right from 1880. In the fall of 1882 it was estimated that the new paid up capital, not including increases from earnings, had amounted in the two years previous to between $15,000,000 and $18,000,000.[2]

It was of the genius of the movement that Southern capital should be drawn upon to the limit. It will presently be seen how valuably this was augmented from the North,

---

[1] U. S. Census of Manufactures, 1900. In such an aggregate, these figures may be taken as sufficiently accurate; a local estimate for South Carolina in 1880 was a little under the census return. Cf. Blackman, p. 3.

[2] Baltimore Journal of Commerce and Manufacturers' Record, Sept. 2, 1882. Cf. Manufacturers' Record, Baltimore, March 8, 1883. In Augusta, between 1880 and 1883, two mills were built and five enlarged, making 63,000 new spindles, 2200 new looms, and representing an added investment of some $3,000,000 (ibid., Feb. 15, 1883).

but as to both amount and importance it is right to say that
"the chief sources of capital employed in starting the mills
were local."[3]   While recognizing the extent of outside assistance, an acquainted observer accurately said: "The
great majority of cotton mills in the South represent the
sacrifices and great efforts of the communities in which they
are situated.   In the East the cotton mill is built from the
capital of the rich; in the South it is built from the combined capital of many of little means."[4]   It has already
been remarked that a symptom of the Cotton Mill Campaign was the location of factories in towns rather than on
isolated water powers, and this was because community
enterprise was coming forward.[5]   "A most gratifying feature connected with the establishment of cotton mills in the
South," it was declared in 1881, "is that the great bulk of
the capital employed in their operation has been furnished
by Southern people. . . . More than three-fourths of the
capital invested . . . has been subscribed by our own people."[6]   Southern savings were almost under compulsion to

---

[3] S. S. Broadus, Decatur, letter, Jan. 27, 1915. Cf. Edmonds, Facts
about South, p. 32. Many interviews supported this point.

[4] Testimony of Lewis W. Parker, Hearing before House Committee of Judiciary, 1902, part 2, p. 12.

[5] J. A. Chapman, int., Spartanburg, Sept. 5, 1916. In explaining
how a place without wealth could establish the industry, Tompkins
overstated the fact in saying that "every one of the towns and cities
of the southeast that are now manufacturing places built their first
factory out of native resources and without outside help" (A Plan
to Raise Capital, p. 25).

[6] News and Courier, Charleston, Sept. 1. Cf. quotation from C.
C. Baldwin in ibid., July 11, 1881. "The industry is distinctly a
home enterprise, founded and fostered by natives of the State," says
Mr. Thompson, who agrees that 90 per cent of the mill capital of
North Carolina was native (Cotton Field to Cotton Mill, p. 81).
Cf. ibid., p. 59 ff.; Augusta Trade Review, Oct., 1884. There is
abundant support for the assertion that "the industry taken as a
whole is almost strictly a North Carolina achievement" (Charlotte
News, Textile Ed., 1917). Cf. ibid. as to Rhyne's mills and other
instances. Twenty years after the commencement of the development, it was estimated that 80 per cent of South Carolina mill stock
was owned in the State; as will be seen later, some of this had gravi-
tated South from Northern hands, but against it might be set off
shares held elsewhere in the South (Kohn, Cotton Mills of S. C.,
ed. of 1903, p. 32 ff.). One of the founders said that early in the
period over 65 per cent of the capital invested in South Carolina was
native (E. A. Smyth, int., Greenville).

become cotton mill shares: "We may look in vain for the dawn of an era of enterprise . . . so long as thousands and millions of money are deposited in our banks on four per cent interest, when its judicious investment in manufactures would more than quadruple that rate. . . ."[7]

Many specific instances show the embodiment of this spirit. The considerable cotton industry of Columbus was wiped out by the capturing Federal army in 1865, and within fifteen years had been rebuilt by local capital to the point where the mills took nearly 17,000 bales.[8] Right after the War, a Northern observer believed that Charleston did not possess recuperative power for its rebuilding, that unless New England sent energy and capital the city would remain a wreck.[9] Yet by 1881 Charleston was leading the industrial advance in the State and furnishing a model of home enterprise in the Charleston Manufacturing Company.[10] It was declared in 1865 that all the mercantile stocks in Columbia, in the heart of the devastated area, could be bought for $20,000.[11] In a decade and a half the citizens were buying out New England interests which had failed to develop the water power and plant cotton manufactures, subscriptions of $55,000 being received in one hour and reaching $117,000 in two weeks.[12]

---

[7] News and Observer, Raleigh, Nov. 9, 1880. Cf. ibid., Dec. 24, 1880, as to Edward Richardson. "I am tired of hearing the cry of 'We want Yankee brains and enterprise.' We don't want any such thing; we want Southern brains and enterprise. What the South wants is common sense and action" (C. M. Clay, quoted in Gannon, p. 18). Mills before the war, being usually neighborhood affairs, regularly had local capital, ordinarily from a few investors (cf. Thompson, p. 51). Perhaps the most ambitious suggestion for home subscriptions contemplated the building of mills by groups of fifteen planters who should take $4000 in stock each; nothing came of the plan (cf. Barbee, Cotton Question, p. 138 ff.).

[8] Observer, Raleigh, Sept. 10, 1880.

[9] Andrews, p. 3.

[10] It was said that more than three-fifths of the capital was contributed in Charleston (News and Courier, Charleston, July 6, 1881. George W. Williams, int., Charleston).

[11] Andrews, p. 34.

[12] News and Courier, Charleston, March 17, 31, 1881. Cf. Charlotte News, Textile Ed., 1917, regarding Hope Mills. An enterpriser in a small South Carolina town announced in the local paper:

Not only was a large proportion of the stock held locally, but it was chiefly native investors that actually paid in cash; it will be seen soon that machinery manufacturers received stock in return for equipment.[13]

It frequently happened that after local capital, largely from community spirit, had been adventured generally in a first enterprise, succeeding mills would be erected by a small number of investors as private establishments.[14] Also, even with initial mills, stock after a few years tended to come into the hands of the larger investors who had been central in the subscription.[15]

It has been observed that Gregg, before the War, plead that the dormant wealth of Charleston might be directed into the industrial development of South Carolina.[16] In

"I am now engaged in getting up a mill of 2,500 spindles to manufacture yarn at this place. I do not expect to seek a dollar of foreign subscription, but I want our own citizens throughout the county to be interested in it and to help me build and operate it" (D. J. Winn, in Sumpter Southron, quoted in News and Courier, Charleston, March 31, 1881). Cf. ibid., Jan. 21, 25, 27, 1881. "The project of establishing a manufactory for cotton near Walhalla is being mooted. An informal meeting of some of the citizens of that place was held . . . and stock to the amount of nearly $10,000 was subscribed by the few present. It is believed strongly that as much as $25,000 will be subscribed in that neighborhood, and if the people of the county will join in the enterprise as much as $50,000 might be made available" (ibid., Feb. 26, 1881). The instances of the first mills at Salisbury and Laurens, applicable here, have been recited. Mills at Rockingham were built principally with money from "home people" of that and adjoining counties (William Entwistle, int., Rockingham). Cf. Columbia Record, Textile Ed., 1916, as to mills at Greenwood, Ninety-Six and Lancaster; Grady, pp. 197-198; Tompkins, History of Mecklenburg, vol. ii, p. 198; News and Courier, Charleston, March 17, 1881; Baltimore Journal of Commerce and Manufacturers' Record, June 24, 1882, as to Southern subscriptions to Atlanta Exposition.

[13] Benjamin Gossett, int., Anderson.

[14] Cf. Tompkins, Cotton Mill, Commercial Features, pp. 29-30. When the Charleston mill, which had been peculiarly public in its inception, was to be sold in 1899, the little group of intending purchasers prepared for the transaction with secrecy (Bird Memoranda). Some who had withheld subscriptions from the first Salisbury mill went in on the second, and the third was distinctly private in character (Theodore F. Klutz and O. D. Davis, interviews, Salisbury).

[15] Hudson Millar, int., Charlotte, N. C., Sept. 4, 1916.

[16] Speech on Blue Ridge Railroad, pp. 6-7, 29.

the eighties his wish was amply, if tardily, satisfied. It was
principally Charleston capital which developed such up-
country mills as Piedmont, Pacolet, Clifton and Pelzer,[17]
and many smaller factories drew partially on that city.[18]
Many Charleston men, besides, went out as mill builders.

Gregg succeeded in persuading South Carolina to grant
limited liability to incorporators of industrial enterprises,[19]
and here again after events showed his wisdom. When,
during the Cotton Mill Campaign, poor communities felt a
stirring which wealthy individuals had not experienced, the
companies were regularly incorporated; also, established
factories wishing to enlarge sought this facility.[20]

Noticing that many towns which despaired of being able
to project a cotton mill yet had building and loan associations with accumulated cash in excess of the amount necessary for a factory, Tompkins took the lead in applying the
building and loan principle to manufacturing enterprise.
Under his guidance a score of plants, mostly in the Carolinas, were successfully set going; the instalment payment
was usually 50 cents a week, though sometimes $1.00 or as
little as 25 cents. The mill might be erected as capital came
in, or might be completed sooner with money borrowed on
endorsement of directors or notes of subscribers used as
collateral.[21] The instalment plan did not come into use

---

[17] E. A. Smyth, int., Greenville.

[18] Mills at Sumter and Anderson, after exhausting local resources,
appealed successfully to Charleston investors (News and Courier,
Charleston, Dec. 17, 1881; Marshall Orr, int., Anderson).

[19] Cf. Propriety of Granting Charters of Incorporation, p. 4 ff.;
Domestic Industry, p. 16.

[20] The South Carolina legislature in the 1882 session granted charters to nine mills with an aggregate capital of $1,725,500 (Manufac-
turers' Record, Baltimore, Jan. 11, 1883). By 1910 the South showed
20 mills owned by individuals, 13 by firms and 620 by corporations
(U. S. Census of Manufactures, 1910, Cotton Manufactures, p. 44).
The old subscription list of the Bivingsville mill, 1856, in the possession of Mr. J. B. Cleveland, of Spartanburg, contrasts with the
model charters explained in Tompkins' writings (cf. Tompkins,
Water Power on the Catawba River, p. 20 ff.).

[21] Cf. Tompkins, Plan to Raise Capital. With a mill operated before all capital was paid in, earnings would balance interest; sometimes profits were so large that a plant under these circumstances
even paid dividends (cf. Thompson, p. 82 ff.). In one instance half

right at first, and was generally employed in modest enterprises.[22]

Turning now to financial participation from without the
section, it is to be remembered that by 1880 the Southern
attitude toward Northern assistance was warmly, even ardently cordial. Willingness to welcome help of Northern
money in Southern mills was a test of earnestness in the
new program, the characteristic mark of conquest over
hurtful pride and estranging rancor. The wish for nationalism and for industrialism on the part of the South was
necessarily one. Immediately after the War only the wisest
men championed the entrance of Northern enterprise, and
found the up-country far more favorable to this view than
the low-country.[23] But fifteen years afterwards, Southern
sentiment responded outspokenly to even the imperfect sympathies of Edward Atkinson.[24] In connection with the Atlanta Exposition it was said: "We have in the midst of us
the raw material . . . of a magnificent prosperity. We
lack knowledge, population and capital. These may be
slowly accumulated in the course of years, or they may be
rapidly by well directed efforts to obtain them from beyond
our own borders. We advocate the latter plan."[25] A competent interpreter of South to North asserted: "I say on
the strength of recent and extended observation that whatever of antagonism to Northern capital may have existed in
the South has disappeared. I never met it, at any time.
. . ."[26] Grady was representative in regretting "that our

the subscription was paid down and the balance piecemeal (J. L.
Hartsell, int., Concord).
   [22] The mill built by negroes at Concord was virtually shut up to
this method.
   [23] Cf. Andrews, pp. 79–80, 176, 320, 378.
   [24] Cf. Atkinson, Address at Atlanta, preface, p. 4; p. 8.
   [25] News and Courier, Charleston, March 14, 1881. A country correspondent declared that the South could not afford to remain solid;
that the party that could guarantee the safety of incoming capital
was the party for South Carolina (ibid., May 25, 1881).
   [26] C. C. Baldwin, quoted in News and Courier, Charleston, July
11, 1881. The slave States, themselves emancipated, stood "with a
warm and generous recognition of the right of all men of every
section of their own country, and of every foreign land, to come into
their territory, whether with muscle or money, and share with their

brothers from the North have not taken larger part with us in this work" of building up the South.[27]

Before speaking of solicitation of capital from particular sources, some general bids for outside assistance may be mentioned. Exemption of new cotton factories from taxation, if losing to a State a few thousands, might be expected to induce Northern capitalists to invest in the industry. "Once here, they will be so pleased with our advantages that they will never think of leaving us."[28]   The widespread rebuttal which met the statement of Edward Atkinson that he "could not conscientiously recommend investments in Southern cotton mills" showed how keenly the South desired Northern capital.[29]   "Unfriendly comments" drove him to conciliation.   Superiorities of South over North were set forth in a business-like way, much in the manner of a prospectus, often concluding with a suggestion

own people in developing its riches" (Richmond Industrial South, quoted in Baltimore Journal of Commerce and Manufacturers' Record, June 17, 1882). ". . . Southern investment encourages Northern capital to come into the same field, and the rate of progress is far more rapid than if it depended on either Southern savings or Northern capital alone" (News and Courier, Charleston, Sept. 1, 1881). Cf. Daily Dispatch, Richmond, March 5, 1880, as to Northern money in a railroad project.

[27] Expressions of suspicion were rare; a small paper, out of the current, said: "Well enough is it to talk about repelling Northern capital by discriminating legislation, but far better have no Northern capital than have it holding native noses down to the grindstone. The half-starved mountain wolf refused to change places with the sleek mastiff that wore a master's collar" (Winnsboro News, quoted in News and Courier, Charleston, July 7, 1881).

[28] "One mill owner, himself a Northern man, stated that if their advantages were fully understood at the North, a great many Northern capitalists would make investments in factories at the South" (Observer, Raleigh, Feb. 13, 1880). An Augusta correspondent of a Cincinnati paper, reciting the success of mills in the Southern city, gave this data "for the information of the loose capital which is floating around Cincinnati, seeking five or six per cent investments . . ." (quoted in Manufacturers' Record, Baltimore, Jan. 4, 1883). Cf. Baltimore Journal of Commerce and Manufacturers' Record, June 3, 1882.

[29] Atkinson, Address at Atlanta, p. 27; cf. p. 14. It turned out that above other benefits of the Atlanta Exposition was "the confidence begotten in Northern capitalists by the astonishing display of material wealth and the opportunities offered them of making permanent investments . . ." (Baltimore Journal of Commerce and Manufacturers' Record, Sept. 28, 1882).

that "to the anxious capitalists tired of a petty 4 per cent . . . such facts are not without interest. They go to support the claim that the Southern mill has an advantage of from 10 to 20 per cent over its New England competitor."[30]

Not all appeals for outside help gave promise of realization. Such was the "Cotton Syndicate" proposed to link Southern plantations with Manchester weaving mills. The abortive project is interesting, though, as indicating how even farmers could look to cotton manufacturing for salvation.[31] Some Southern men made active hunters after Northern investors: "Mr. D. L. Love, the pioneer of cotton factories in Huntsville, left for New England . . . for

---

[30] Atlanta correspondence of New York Times, quoted in News and Courier, Charleston, Nov. 5, 1881. Southern papers eagerly presented news of successful enterprises in order to attract Northern attention (cf. Manufacturers' Record, Baltimore, Nov. 23, 1882). "We are persuaded that once the folks in New England, who have surplus money awaiting employment, thoroughly investigate the points Richmond presents for a safe lodgment of that capital in manufacturing, the flow will start this way" (Dispatch, quoted in News and Courier, Charleston, March 25, 1881).

[31] Cotton lands lacking value, planters requiring capital and profits being diminished in charges of middle men, the National Cotton Planters' Association of America in 1882 sponsored a scheme by which Southern farmers should erect spinning mills on the railroads, to be equipped with machinery supplied by Manchester manufacturers and operated for three years by English workers; farmers would supply food for these operatives and pay four cents a pound for the spinning of their staple. The Manchester men would be guaranteed 10 per cent profit on their stock by mortgage on plantations. Thus Manchester would be certainly supplied with yarn, the Southern cotton growers could borrow on their lands from the Bank of England, all charges between field and mill would be saved, as well as interest on capital for buying cotton and all expenses for sale of goods! (cf. Baltimore Journal of Commerce and Manufacturers' Record, July 15, 22, Sept. 2, 1882). The hardly more likely plan of the Region of the Savannah Colonization Association has been noticed already. The frequent reports in these years of English manufacturers or capitalists about to acquire extensive Southern cotton interests were without foundation. Lumber and minerals, too, were said to be constantly on the point of English exploitation. Cf. News and Courier, Charleston, Nov. 10, 1881; Baltimore Journal of Commerce and Manufacturers' Record, Aug. 26, 1882; Manufacturer's Record, Baltimore, Nov. 23, Dec. 21, 1882; Feb. 8, March 8, 1883. A Southern cotton manufacturer, English by birth and early experience, who has seen the whole development, said that no English capital came to mills of the South in any quantity (William Entwistle, int., Rockingham). This was confirmed by Tracy I. Hickman, int., Augusta.

continuous exertion for the establishment of factories in the South." Projects for mills in Mississippi, Alabama and Tennessee were declared promising; old enterprises were to be set running again and a Connecticut manufacturer wishing to relocate was to be brought to Huntsville.[32] With passing years welcome to Northern capital became, of course, more wide-spread, but it could not gain in sincerity.[33]

Southern overtures to Northern capital were matched by Northern liberality toward Southern opportunities. It will be seen later that most Northern support came not from investors as such, but from commission men, machinery makers and from manufacturers establishing plants in the cotton fields. The impression of the president of the National Cotton Planters' Association was well-nigh universal: "I have been for some weeks in New York and Boston, and I find capitalists entirely willing to back any scheme which is founded on any right basis. Cotton mills are especially attractive. . . ."[34] Ready subscriptions from the North to the Atlanta Exposition had significance for the future.[35]

Occasionally, even in the first years, the mountain moved to Mahomet, as the Southerners must have viewed it; Northern mills or cotton firms sought to manufacture in the South. There was even an instance, that of Athens, where a town by embarrassing delays lost the placement of a fac-

---

[32] Huntsville Democrat, quoted in News and Courier, Charleston, July 30, 1881. An Atlanta man conducted New York capitalists in an inspection of a Georgia water power; it was bought to propel a cotton mill (Manufacturers' Record, Baltimore, March 1, 1883). "Outside capital . . . is beginning to seek this Southern field to aid in a more rapid and thorough work of restoration. . . . This movement needs a wise encouragment by public and private approval" (News and Courier, Charleston, June 28, 1881).

[33] Cf. Charlotte Daily Observer, Nov. 4, 1897; Tompkins, Storing and Marketing of Cotton, pp. 11–12.

[34] Baltimore Journal of Commerce and Manufacturers' Record, July 1, 1882.

[35] News and Courier, Charleston, April 1, 1881. Cf. ibid., May 21, 1881; Baltimore Journal of Commerce and Manufacturers' Record, Sept. 2, 1882; Daily Dispatch, Richmond, March 25, 1880; Manufacturers' Record, Baltimore, Dec. 14, 1882, March 1, 1883.

tory by a New York firm that was otherwise certain.[36] An interesting, though incorrect view, applicable at most to the South Carolina up-country, has it that " the first movement was from the North to the South. Northern capital was looking for investment; due to the proximity to raw cotton and labor it came to the South. Camperdown and Batesville had only Northern money in them. The idea began to smoulder; other mills came into being, Southern enterprise appealing to Northern capital."[37]

Unsolicited transfer of capital from North to South, especially where plants were founded outright by Northern interests, was not prominent in the opening decade of the period.[38]

Given a Southern community of restricted means intent upon establishing a cotton mill and yet unable to appeal effectively to general capital sources because venturing upon an untried experiment, and the natural thing happened: the local projector would exhaust home resources, likely securing enough money to erect the building, and then would ask makers of cotton manufacturing machinery to take part payment in stock, and apply to commission firms handling goods to subscribe, usually in return for the agency for the product. Thus special inducements were offered and there was redoubled interest in putting the plant in operation promptly. " A promoter had to have his home money first. He would get, say, $50,000; he would go to the machinery men and explain that he had so much subscribed, and would

[36] Baltimore Journal of Commerce and Manufacturers' Record, Oct. 14, 1882. " Mr. Boyd, a capitalist of Providence . . . is in Georgia in behalf of several New England capitalists, and is prospecting for the best place in the State to erect a large cotton factory " (News and Courier, Charleston, April 9, 1881). Cf. Clark, in South in Building of Nation, vol. vi, pp. 266–267; Dry Goods Economist, Jubilee Number, 1896, p. 79; Murphy, Present South, appendix, p. 317.

[37] Mrs. M. P. Gridley, int., Greenville.

[38] A South Carolina town refused to cooperate with a Philadelphia firm which wished to build a mill to use machinery from a Pennsylvania mill that had failed, but the community erected a factory on its own account, stimulated by neighboring Southern enterprise (J. A. Brock, int., Anderson). Cf. Tompkins, Cotton Mill, Commercial Features, p. 39.

16

they sell him the equipment and how much would they take in stock. Commission and machinery firms would give him 40 to 50 per cent of his total capital. If a man had no previous mill connections, his local subscriptions would be his sole backing."[39] It seems the best opinion that machinery manufacturers took more stock than commission houses—anywhere from a fourth to a half the price of the equipment, depending partly upon demand for their product at the time.[40] However, as will be seen, commission firms often supplied ready money for working capital. Even as to these predisposed helpers there was weight in the reflection that "nothing so attracts investors in other States as the knowledge that people on the ground have proved their faith in an undertaking by putting money in it."[41]

---

[39] W. J. Thackston, int., Greenville. "In most places where a new mill is proposed, an idea is prevalent that if half the money is raised at home, then somebody from somewhere will furnish the other half" (Tompkins, Cotton Mill, Commercial Features, p. 39). This statement needs the reminder that local ponds were regularly dragged and redragged.

[40] W. J. Thackston, int., Greenville; W. W. Ball, int., Columbia, Jan. 3, 1917.

[41] News and Courier, Charleston, March 8, 1881. "Books have been opened in Newton, Alabama, for subscriptions to a cotton factory at that place, and Northern capitalists have pledged $100,000 as soon as Newton raises $50,000" (Athens Banner, quoted in Baltimore Journal of Commerce and Manufacturers' Record, June 24, 1882; cf. Manufacturers' Record, Baltimore, March 8, 1883). When a movement was started for a factory at Vicksburg, nearly $200,000 was subscribed in the city, and it was expected that as much more would come from the "East," and that these latter stockholders would manage and equip the plant (News and Courier, Charleston, Aug. 12, 1881). Commission houses participated in the Charleston Manufacturing Company: ". . . the books of subscription to the stock of this company were closed yesterday. . . . Our citizens responded well to the call made upon them, and the full amount of stock desired in Charleston for the immediate organization of the company was subscribed . . ." (ibid., March 16, 1881; cf. ibid., March 15). Of $500,000 wanted for a factory at Gaffney, it was felt that $200,000 could be raised in the county. "The other $300,000 will be obtained at the North" (ibid., Oct. 24, 1881). A typical distribution of stock was that of the Clifton mill, with half of its $500,000 capitalization paid up; $50,000 was held in Boston, $150,000 in Charleston, and $200,000 in Spartanburg, the latter being the local community (ibid., May 21, 1881). Cf. Blackman, p 17, as to Piedmont. Half the stock of Langley was held in New York, the other half equally divided between Augusta and Charleston (ibid., p. 7).

Sometimes it was proposed to inaugurate a small mill completely and then seek outside aid in extension of plant: "It is said that fifteen thousand dollars will set in motion over five hundred spindles, and continual additions can be made. . . . We believe there is money enough in the county, here and there, to make at least a modest beginning so as to attract outside capital."[42]

"If a Southern promoter had no business connections at the North, he went immediately to the machinery and commission men as those most interested."[43] It will be interesting to notice some details of this soliciting method. Many Southern mill projectors entering uncertainly an unfamiliar field would stop in Baltimore to call on the commission house of Woodward, Baldwin & Co., and there were given a kindly reception that bolstered up self-confidence. "Many times we would not know promoters that came, but going about the South we would hear of their enterprises. They would bring letters of introduction, and be in town several days. A party of gentlemen might put up money to erect the building and buy machinery, coming out of the arrangement with more or less indebtedness to the machinery people and lacking working capital. The proposition would be broached to us to take the account of the mill and put up sufficient money to operate the plant. In other cases they would set out to raise $100,000, get half this amount, and come to us. We would subscribe to some

---

[42] Winnsboro News, quoted in News and Courier, Charleston, Feb. 8, 1881. Cf. item from Chester Bulletin in ibid. The first mill at Gaffney (the initial enterprise projected, referred to in the previous note, did not eventuate) had $50,000 capital and 5000 spindles and drew nearly entirely upon local resources. When a second plant was built, costing $800,000, machinery firms took much of the stock (H. D. Wheat, int., Gaffney, S. C., Sept. 13, 1916). A small Texas mill had room for more machinery. "Up to this time home capital alone has been put in it. An invitation is extended to foreign capitalists for more capital. At least $50,000 more can be used to great advantage" (Baltimore Journal of Commerce and Manufacturers' Record, Aug. 12, 1882). Cf. as to Rock Hill Factory, News and Courier, Charleston, Jan. 12, 14, 1882.

[43] Tracy I. Hickman, int., Augusta. Cf. Copeland, pp. 49–50.

of the stock and then see friends who might be interested in the project and secure additional subscriptions."[44]

Sometimes it was felt a commission house was tying too many strings to its offered subscription, and its assistance was refused; on the other hand, a firm subscribing unconditionally might create an impression resulting in its receiving the agency.[45]

If the Cotton Mill Campaign in the South did not evoke great outward misgiving on the part of the New England industry, it was reflected in the sharply increased business

---

[44] The commission firm might thus lend influence that was as valuable as direct participation. "We generally required that they should have local subscriptions, local officers and local board. They usually had this arranged for. Then they would perhaps put in a member of the firm of subscribing agents who would attend the meetings. This kept the commission house in touch with the mill, but the business of the firm was to sell and not to manufacture the goods. I do not know that we exacted this last as a requirement. It was recognized as a proper thing to do; the mills wanted it" (Summerfield Baldwin, Sr., int., Baltimore). This firm, especially through William H. Baldwin, had much to do with the establishment of the industry in the South, and everywhere in the mill districts one hears it cordially spoken of. Participation of this and a Boston house in the Charleston Manufacturing Company was representative (cf. News and Courier, Charleston, March 29, May 17, 1881). Much stock was secured in Boston through friendly offices of the commission merchants there (William M. Bird, int., Charleston). Lockwood, of Providence, engineer for the mill, took stock and influenced his friends to do so (A. B. Murray, int., Charleston). Southerners who had before hardly more than seen a cotton mill, were given rapid acquaintance with the industry by visits to plants with their Northern allies.

[45] A. N. Wood, int., Gaffney, S. C., Sept. 13, 1916. "A Boston man told me he would take stock if the King Mill would make colored goods and give him the selling agency. I told him that if he took only a little stock he would have little to say about how the goods were manipulated, and if he didn't take any, he wouldn't have anything to say" (Charles Estes, int., Augusta). As the market for machinery in the South developed, equipment manufacturers became readier participants. An active solicitor who placed little stock of his first mill, in the eighties, with them, had their willing help for a second plant, erected ten years afterwards. In the first instance the enterpriser utilized any connection he had with men of wealth, however slight. He approached many persons he did not know at all. Often the commission house for another Southern mill would be appealed to. A Southern company proposing to buy machinery outright, likely going in debt for part of it, might find the manufacturers willing to take stock, and so would increase the capitalization of the mill. Cf. Manufacturers' Record, Baltimore, March 22, 1883; News and Courier, Charleston, April 6, 1881.

of Northern machinery manufacturers. For obvious reasons, most of the machinery was of American rather than
English make. Unacquainted Southern spinners could not
buy from a distance even had they not required the close
credit relations which domestic machinery men were ready
to give them. Just at first some second-hand equipment
was installed, less from desire of New England mills to put
this off on their new rivals, than from innocence and necessity of Southern beginners. The number of Southern spindles, which had increased during the seventies from 327,871
only to 548,048, from 1880 to 1890 increased to 1,554,000
and by 1900 stood at 4,299,988; Southern looms in 1870
numbered 6,256, advanced by 1880 to 11,898, shot up in the
next decade to 36,266, and in 1900 were 110,015.[46] Yarns
that had been selling at 14 and 15 cents went in 1880 to 28
cents; established mills joined with new plants in rushing
for machinery, for more money was to be made now in six
months than before in two years. Prosperity resulted to
makers of all equipment.[47] In June of 1882 a single Southern railroad transported twenty-two car loads of machinery
from Boston shops, and the same manufacturers notified
carriers that they were working on three hundred car loads
to be delivered by early fall.[48] Shops which made for the
Southern trade enlarged their capacity.[49] It was reported

---

[46] U. S. Census of Manufactures, 1900, Cotton Manufactures, pp.
56–57.

[47] William Entwistle, int., Rockingham. Southern mill men did
not balk at the high price caused by a 37½ per cent tariff on machinery, though it was occasionally complained of. The whole increase of business of machinery makers was not due, of course, to
the South; the entire industry was reviving from the depression
since 1873; probably, however, a larger proportion of Northern mills
installed English equipment.

[48] Baltimore Journal of Commerce and Manufacturers' Record,
July 22, 1882. Twenty-four car loads came to Augusta in one week
for the King Mill (Manufacturers' Record, Baltimore, Jan. 18, 1883).
Cf. quotation from Detroit Free Press in Observer, Raleigh, Aug.
31, 1880.

[49] Cf. Baltimore Journal of Commerce and Manufacturers' Record,
July 29, Sept. 2, 1882; Manufacturers' Record, Baltimore, March 8,
1883.

that in two and a half years after 1880 the South had invested $12,000,000 in cotton machinery.[50]

Southern mills with new machinery throughout (it was quickly learned that old equipment was a bad bargain at any price) had an advantage over Northern mills that contributed to profits.[51]

This spurt of the machine shops was caused both by anxiety of Southern mills to buy and solicitude of Northern makers to sell. They were kept closely in touch with one another by trade papers.[52] Agents were sent to at least one Southern State to encourage the building of mills.[53] Mill engineers buying machinery for new plants sometimes collected commissions from the makers, and superintendents were accused of the same practice.[54]

---

[50] Baltimore Journal of Commerce and Manufacturers' Record, July 29, 1882; cf. quotation from American Machinist in ibid., Aug. 19, 1882. New orders were being chronicled continuously; cf. Manufacturers' Record, Baltimore, Nov. 30, 1880, March 8, 1883; Baltimore Journal of Commerce and Manufacturers' Record, June 17, Sept. 9, Oct. 7, Nov. 18, 1882; News and Courier, Charleston, Feb. 26, March 4, 25, 1881. The demand for machinery is indicated in the fact that intending users met the makers much more than half way to investigate the Clement Attachment (cf. Blackman, pp. 18–19). Also, worn machinery was in some cases transferred from one Southern mill to another, though rapidly depreciating in effectiveness (John W. Fries, int., Winston-Salem; Manufacturers' Record, Baltimore, Dec. 28, 1882). In this connection it is interesting that some New England mills in the active period following the Armistice, despite full knowledge of its drawbacks, have been driven to install used equipment. By 1884 the shops were over the first rush; times were disturbed, and this idleness, as will be seen, made them anxious to stimulate Southern business again. Cf. Chronicle, Augusta, Aug. 24, 1884.

[51] Cf. Southern Cotton Spinners' Assn., proceed. 7th Annual Convention, p. 67. Probably no Southern plant installed altogether old machinery (H. D. Wheat, int., Gaffney).

[52] Cf. Baltimore Journal of Commerce and Manufacturers' Record, June 10, July 15, Aug. 5, Sept. 30, 1882; Manufacturers' Record, Baltimore, March 1, 29, 1883.

[53] Thompson, pp. 65–66.

[54] Charles Estes, int., Augusta. Equipment manufacturers might supply building plans to companies which did not engage an engineer (William Entwistle, int., Rockingham). Besides, it was said in 1882 that a dozen young Southerners were gaining experience in Lowell machine shops, to be able to operate mills at home afterwards (Baltimore Journal of Commerce and Manufacturers' Record, Aug. 26, 1882).

The principal difference between the participation of commission houses and machinery makers lies in the fact that the former regularly retained their stock in Southern mills, whereas the latter realized upon their holdings as soon as possible. The one group, therefore, so far as concerns investment, had a continuing and the other a passing connection with the industry. Machinery men accepted stock simply in order to sell their product; having no relation to the output of the factories, they had no wish for a voice in their conduct.[55]

It is generally declared that Southern mills have no complaint against their treatment by machinery firms, these having been liberal and cooperative, except that the industry as a whole and individual plants were encouraged to expand beyond wise limits to create a market for equipment.[56]

---

[55] Confirmation of this point is universal. Sometimes they would sell immediately at a discount, having loaded the price of the machinery to compensate for this loss; sometimes they waited longer, but rarely held on for dividends (interviews with Summerfield Baldwin, Jr., Baltimore; W. W. Ball, Columbia, Jan. 3, 1917; Sterling Graydon, Charlotte; J. W. Norwood, Greenville, S. C., Sept. 9, 1916; Joseph H. Separk, Gastonia; F. Q. O'Neill, Charleston, Dec. 27, 1916). " The machinery men sold out at 94 or 95. I told them to retain their stock, that it would be profitable. But they replied that to sell was their practice " (William Entwistle. int., Rockingham). Most of the shares thus thrown on the market came into local ownership. " At a South Carolina print-cloth mill I was told that 62 per cent of the stock was originally held by Northern machinists, but that by now it had all come South again and was held to a large extent locally " (see T. W. Uttley, Cotton Spinning and Manufacturing in U. S., pp. 46-47). Sometimes, certainly in South Carolina, when a mill was to be built, dealers in tin, lumber, brick and paint would be asked how much stock they would take if awarded contracts (J. B. Cleveland, int., Spartanburg, Sept. 8, 1916). It is likely that such shares were quickly resold.

[56] David Clark, int., Charlotte; J. W. Norwood, int., Greenville. South Carolina mills, with capital in larger units, may have suffered more in this regard than North Carolina plants. It is said that rebates and other benefits were given to purchasers of machinery for cash, while buyers on time were assured the latter was as advantageous a plan. Tompkins was the Southern representative of many machinery firms; besides plants that he built outright, he equipped perhaps 150 mills. Both as commercial agent and as publicist he encouraged erection of factories, but never with any hint of chicanery attaching to his activities, though he was obliged to have some factories sold for debt (Sterling Graydon, int., Charlotte). Not all agents have had this record; a North Carolina mill had to

A common failing of the mills, in the train of which came many embarrassments and drawbacks, was lack of working capital. This was due partly to insufficiency of ready money in the South, partly to need of large sums for purchase of quantities of cotton for coarse spinning, and was not unconnected, perhaps, with willingness of a community unacquainted with industry to rest satisfied when visible investment had been cared for. Also, original provision for enlargement of plant, while ultimately economical, was immediately expensive, rendering some capital unproductive.[57] Tompkins was giving advice for the typical enterprise when he counselled that $75,000 was the least that should be subscribed for a mill in a new section, and that while this did not allow of 10 to 20 per cent of capital stock being set aside for working capital, as was wisest, still most companies started without this facility, either borrowing from a home bank or consigning product to a commission house and drawing against it for 75 to 90 per cent of its value. So far from possessing running capital, mills often began operation with indebtedness on the plant.[58]

be reorganized before it commenced operation, and while local investors were scared off by the project to double its spindleage, machinery manufacturers encouraged the enlargement and took preferred stock, of which there came to be an actual majority. A machinery representative is president. The mill is less successful than those about it.

[57] Southern cotton factories from the beginning have developed water power, installed boilers and erected buildings with a view to extension; this showed as much faith in the future of the industry on the part of projectors as it did solicitude for future work on the part of engineers and machinery manufacturers supplying plans (cf. Uttley, p. 47). Sixty-four per cent of new spindles in 1903 were credited to established mills (ibid., p. 44). A 25,000-spindle, 600-loom mill that cost, with provision for 15,000 more spindles and their complement of looms, $28.65 per spindle, was to cost, when fully equipped, $16 per spindle (ibid., p. 48). Here was a wider difference than Tompkins calculated when he said that building with a view to doubling capacity would cost about 7 per cent more at the outset (Cotton Mill, Commercial Features, p. 51 ff.). For typical instances at the opening of the period, cf. Baltimore Journal of Commerce and Manufacturers' Record, July 22, 1882, as to Rome Cotton Factory, and ibid., Oct. 28, 1882, as to Huguenot Mill.

[58] "The capital proposed for the Darlington mill is $280,000. Of this $140,000 has been subscribed and the work of construction begun" (News and Courier, Charleston, "South Carolina in 1884").

Hurtful refusal of Southern banks to cash drafts for goods sold directly to Southern merchants, remarked by a Virginia governor in the fifties,[59] became a no less compromising inability to finance the industry in the eighties. Nor could Southern mills look to Northern banks—the industry was too untried, the banks too far away. The factories needed friends at court, agencies involved in the future of the new enterprises. Commission firms were the natural resort. Said a manufacturer not liking this recourse: " The Yankees asserted first we could not run because of climate. We did it. Then they said we could make coarse goods, but not fine goods. Well, we are doing it. The North made two guesses out of three, and was mistaken in them. It did not make the guess that we could not run without money. But you find Southern mills failing and going to the Eastern men to whom they were in debt."[60]

Believing need for working capital had led mills into damaging connections with agents for goods, it was declared that companies would have done better to depart from practice and issue bonds at the outset to provide themselves

" One of the special disadvantages under which Southern mills have to work is that often they have very little working capital and at the beginning think that all they have to do is to pay for the mill, if, indeed, they do that " (S. S. Broadus, Decatur, letter). " Most Southern mills when built had to borrow their total working capital, and this is still done. Many borrowed to build the plant. It is not wrong for a mill to borrow a little fixed capital, say $3 or $4 on the spindle " (Summerfield Baldwin, Jr., int., Baltimore).

[59] Cf. Clark, in South in Building of Nation, vol. v, p. 324.

[60] J. H. M. Beatty, int , Columbia. Mr. Copeland has recognized that " It is available cash rather than geographical location, which determines who will be able to buy cotton when the price falls " (see pp. 36–37). " The unsuccessful mills are often so because of slavery to the commission houses through which they sell their product. Too many Southern mills have been built with insufficient working capital or with none at all. . . . The commission houses, many of which have banking connections, gladly advance 75 to 90 per cent of the market value of unsold goods, charging the mill double the rate of interest which they themselves must pay for the money. Thus interest charges often eat up profits " (Thompson, pp. 89–90). Mr. Law referred to commercial paper placed with banks, and not to more entangling alliances, when he declared latterly that a cotton mill is properly a seasonal borrower for the purchase of raw material (John A. Law, Cotton Mill Credits, in proceed. Robt. Morris Club, National Association of Credit Men, 1916, pp. 24–25).

with ready money. "A mill could issue $500,000 in bonds at 6 per cent, carrying this $30,000 interest and pay a man in New York $15,000 to sell its product. For borrowing the same sum from the commission house, the mill must pay $50,000, and for this privilege must give, besides, a terrific bonus of 4 per cent on sales. The difficulty could have been avoided had the mills been capitalized at enough in the beginning."[61]

With the exception of the labor factor, scarcely any relations of the mills have been so continuous and uniform through the history of the industry as those with commission houses selling the product. It has been explained how, through taking stock and lending working capital, these firms became a characteristic part of the enterprise. It is very difficult to generalize as to whether their influence has

---

[61] Tracy I. Hickman, int., Augusta. "Mills with no working capital began life with their credit strained; so they were in the grip of commission firms which lent them money" (W. W. Ball, int., Columbia, Jan. 3, 1917). Lack of capital sometimes entailed equipment with second-hand machinery. This was probably the cause with Montgomery's first mill at Spartanburg, built by instalment payments (L. G. Potter, int., Gaffney, S. C., Sept. 13, 1916). Later, a mill at Bessemer City, N. C., installed old machinery and put a mortgage upon it (G. W. Ragan, int., Gastonia). For a typical advertisement of old machinery for sale by a New England mill, cf. News and Courier, Charleston, April 19, 1881. The establishment of Piedmont fell in hard times; for three months while the machinery was being installed, the only pay of the workmen was credit for groceries at a store in Greenville, the mill giving a note in guarantee (W. J. Thackston, int., Greenville). A commission firm was of great assistance. Hammett had to mortgage some of his private property (James D. Hammett, int., Anderson, Sept. 11, 1916). The Charleston Manufacturing Company had contemplated setting aside $75,000 of the $500,000 capital for preliminary and running expenses, but quicksand was struck in making the foundations and this money had to be spent in piling (William M. Bird, int., Charleston). Lack of running capital precluded success. Bonds to the extent of $250,000 were issued soon after operation commenced (A. B. Murray, int., Charleston). It is asserted that the King Mill, at Augusta, is the only one built and run within its original capital stock; a fourth of its million-dollar capitalization was reserved for running expenses (Charles Estes, int., Augusta; a contemporary newspaper article gives a maximum of $181,979.57 for this purpose; cf. Evening News, Augusta, Jan. 23, 1884). In the depression in 1884 mills without surplus capital were seriously embarrassed (Chronicle, Augusta, Sept. 11, 1884). It is said that bad management was responsible for fewer failures than insufficient working capital (Tracy I. Hickman, int., Augusta).

been good or bad. It is best to understand that, for a good many years at the outset, mills could not have come into being without assistance from commission men, and then, in the spirit of Tompkins' position that well-disposed houses have been advantageous allies but that many abuses need to be eliminated, to state the usual complaints and defenses.

It was early felt that if a mill was to secure full prices and prompt sales, the executive officer must be a good merchant, correcting his reliance on the commission firm by personal knowledge of markets.[62] After some years of experience, reasons for this circumspection could be enumerated. Pointing out that selling agents found subtler means of exploitation than the commission rate, a standard 5 per cent, a manufacturer said that an indictment of firms guilty of malpractice would include the following counts: (1) Beating other commission men to the market was preferred to shuffling in the competition and trying to make a sale that would in the end, if successful, bring a higher commission —so they would offer the mill's product at a figure below the current price. (2) Agents would sell a mill out further ahead than was wise from the manufacturer's standpoint. (3) Suppose a mill has been holding its product in hope of a rise, but the commission house, advising that no advance will come soon, dumps the goods on the market. The market falls further. Then, to prevent product from piling up in stock, the agents apply to sell it. It has been suspected that commission firms sometimes in such cases sold goods to themselves for purposes of speculation, they being in a position to know that the market would recover later. Here they reaped their percentage on bogus sales and a profit on the speculation. Where a house acts as exclusive agent for the output of a factory, guaranteeing accounts,

---

[62] Cf. comment on a statement of Hammett's, in Manufacturers' Record, Baltimore, Feb. 1, 1883. There were many later expressions; cf. Tompkins, Cotton Mill, Commercial Features, p. 128 ff. Precautions were to be taken at the very start; in deciding on the goods a new mill should make, it should be remembered that the commission firm was likely to advise that particular product in which it specialized, and this would not necessarily be profitable in the long run (ibid., p. 56 ff.).

it is best considered that the goods are sold to the house outright, to do with as it will. It is the duty of the mill management under such an arangement, of course, to keep up
with the market and insure fair play. (4) A commission
firm might tell a mill its product was bringing less than was
the case, the firm keeping the difference. This was theft.
(5) Where the yarn of a mill was made of cotton superior
to that used by its competitors, the agents would not always take pains to explain this and so get a better price
than the average; demand for yarn of that count might be
supplied from lower grade goods, the difference in commissions not making it worth while to push the finer product.
And yet the commission men were supposed to represent
the interests of their clients. (6) A firm might even seek
to accomplish the buyer's interest exclusively. Suppose it
did not handle all the product of a mill, but sometimes
placed it in specific orders. Seeing a chance to sell goods,
the commission house, knowing the factories of the district,
would shop around and get the bottom price from the most
necessitous maker, and offer this to its client.[63]

---

[63] Sterling Graydon, int., Charlotte. Several of these and additional points are brought out by Tompkins (Cotton Mill, Commercial Features, p. 128 ff.) ; agents have thrown cancelled orders back
upon the mills without much scrutiny into claims of the purchaser;
on the other hand, they have been too accommodating about holding
goods and advancing money on these, so that interest account absorbed the mill's assets. It has been a custom for commission firms
not to reveal to mill managements names of customers. Out of this
has grown much suspicion and perhaps some misdealing. Said an
official : " Some years ago a mill in which I was a stockholder had a
lot of goods piled up while prices were at rock bottom. The commission house wanted to sell the goods. The mill begged the house
not to sell; we were confident the market would recover. But the
firm wrote back that the mill owed it $200,000, and that unless this
was paid the stock would be sold. The commission house knew the
mill could not pay the amount then, and the goods were disposed
of at a great loss. I have always thought the selling agent bought
on his own account."   In another instance a mill received through a
commission firm an order for 10,000 pounds of yarn to be delivered
each month for ten months. The mill shipped the first batch, but
when time came to deliver the second, was advised by the house that
the market had gone off some points, and not to deliver. Months
passed with no more deliveries until the tenth month arrived. By
now the price was above that named in the contract, and the mill
was instructed to ship goods covering the entire order. Expostula-

Observing that a mill partly owned by a commission house frequently must see its goods sold under the market and that factories that would not have come into being except for assistance of selling agents were built as feeders for commission firms and not to make money for local stockholders, a progressive manufacturer advised that interference by agents be eliminated at any cost; on the whole, their influence in the Southern textile industry has been bad.[64] Stock in mills about Greenville, once largely held at the North, is coming to the locality of the factories; commission men were not sorry to ruin a mill if they could be indemnified in charges first.[65]

The story is not one entirely of condemnation. Some commission firms have had close and thoroughly helpful relations with Southern mills, lending not only financial support but valuable business judgment. Rates of commission have declined one-third since the eighties.[66] Many bad

tion was unavailing, the commission house replying that the customer would be lost if pressed upon the fault, and that unless the yarn was delivered the house would sever relations with the mill. The director who wished to sever connections was bought out. It was his conviction that the selling agent was his own touchy customer. This sort of experience has led many to the conclusion that the only way is to sell to the house direct, demanding payment from it and not knowing or caring where the product goes (Charles E. Johnson, int., Raleigh). There was a famous case in South Carolina where a mill owing a commission house an amount equal to a fourth of its capitalization and feeling itself mistreated, changed agents, borrowing from the new firm money to pay the old debt. But the offended agents secured enough stock to control the mill, and finally sapped it. The same commission house, it is asserted, tried in every way to show that colored labor was unprofitable in a mill in which it had been installed in an extremity. Commission men, especially where they had banking interests, found it profitable to borrow money in the North at 3 or 3½ per cent and lend it to Southern mills at 6 and 7 per cent. This caused much dissatisfaction, particularly when the sums going to the agents in commission were considered (Tompkins, ibid.; William M. Bird, int., Charleston). Commissions have in special cases, where a firm was eager to secure agency of a mill, been as low as 2 or 3 per cent (F. Q. O'Neill, int., Charleston. W. W. Ball, int., Columbia, Jan. 3, 1917).

[64] Joseph H. Separk, int., Gastonia.

[65] Clement F. Haynsworth, int., Greenville. Lancashire half a century after the South, developed the same devices for financing new mills as have here been described, with the same drawbacks attending. Cf. Copeland, pp. 317–318.

[66] Summerfield Baldwin, Jr., int., Baltimore.

practices have disappeared. It is probably true that along with regret for early faults must go the recognition that, whether participation of commission men was damaging or beneficial, it was necessary and that the industry owes its establishment as much to them as to any other factor.[67] It is to be borne in mind, too, that the mills were started by men new to that industry and, in many cases, to all industry; these might be too quick to charge exploitation by powerful agents a thousand miles away in the North. Also, selling houses had the money motive, not the patriotic one present with local projectors.[68]

There is an evident movement in the South away from any reliance upon outside commission houses. This manifests itself in action by sales through brokers or directly to jobbers and mills, by patronage of Southern selling agents, and by establishment by groups of mills of sales offices in the North. Moreover, that the South is thinking of a still better solution is apparent in frequent mention of the possibility of building up a distributing point within the sec-

---

[67] J. A. Chapman, int., Spartanburg; C. S. Morris, int., Salisbury.

[68] As early as 1903 a spirit of conciliation toward commission men, of letting bygones be bygones, was shown in the Southern Cotton Spinners' Association (proceed. 7th Annual Convention, p. 162). It should be clear to the reader why selling houses, in contrast to machinery manufacturers, retained their mill shares. Critics at the South have charged this degree of control permitted peremptory methods in disposal of product that proved harmful; on the other hand, this may be interpreted as a proper watchfulness over enterprises being credited with large sums at a time when money could not be gotten by them otherwise (cf. Copeland, p. 197). "This Southern development would have been delayed twenty years if the commission men had not taken hold. Southern promoters absolutely did not have enough money at home to accomplish it. Besides, it was credit extended to projectors of mills by selling houses that gave them a measure of credit with machinery people." Commission firms have had to keep large capitals ready against calls of their Southern clients; over advances have usually been made just on the credit of the mill (Summerfield Baldwin, Sr., int., Baltimore). Frequently money was lent to mills at less than local rates, even had banks been willing to furnish funds (Washington Clark, int., Columbia. Cf., as to slightness of available banking facilities, Hammond, pp. 160–161). Commission percentages were not so high where mills were not heavy borrowers (J. A. Chapman, int., Spartanburg). The fact that selling houses placed little real money at disposal of the mills, except in advance on goods, does not modify the importance of their assistance.

tion that will make dependence upon Philadelphia and New York no longer necessary. It is generally recognized that this last cannot be accomplished until finishing plants have become numerous in the South, until financial support of outside selling firms is not required, and until diversity of prices for identical product, largely resulting from participation of commission firms, disappears. The Panama Canal, development of banking resources, competition itself through extension of the industry, and, all in all, total maturing of Southern economic life, will hasten realization of this ideal.[69] There are enough who believe that the strong tradition, mainly in favor of New York, cannot be broken down, and that other obstacles preclude complete conduct of the industry, in manufacture and commerce, within the South. But others accept and challenge these difficulties in much the same spirit that characterized the founders of mills forty years ago. These cannot see the logic of sending goods to the North to be bleached and finished when the South has every facility for these processes if only they are taken advantage of; if it was once raw cotton that was to be manufactured near the source, it is now goods in the grey that are not to be wastefully shipped away and shipped back.

Before the Southern industry as such took its rise, before Northern selling firms came into the field, the majority of mills relied mainly upon local, or certainly Southern, demand for their product. Exchange of yarn for butter and beeswax by the smallest factories was matched in somewhat more extended barter of larger mills. Such practices survived the war, and were occasionally present even after a commission house took charge of part of the output of a plant.[70] Even in the eighties some mills had traveling salesmen covering the South, and others were terminating brief connections with commission houses and selling direct or

[69] George W. Williams, Charleston; Thomas Purse, Savannah, Ga., Dec. 26, 1916, interviews.

[70] Cf. Thompson, p. 51; Daily Dispatch, Richmond, Jan. 2, 1880; William Banks, Columbia, and W. J. Thackston, Greenville, gave instances in interviews.

through brokers (the latter giving the mill right of accept-
ance or rejection of orders, costing far less and involving
risk that was small beside commission charges) ; but for
the most part this was the day of leaning upon selling
agents.[71]   From this dependence the South is emerging
and returning to the old self-reliance, but a self-sufficiency
accompanied by improved facilities and wider outlook.
Distributing companies formed by chains of Southern mills,
especially where under united ownership, are becoming factors in Northern markets; with more commercial knowledge direct selling by individual mills loses its dangers.[72]
True, international representation has not yet come, but
this may lie just over the horizon.[73]

It has been said that merchants were often mill builders.
These sometimes got outside capital from other sources
than machinery and commission men, namely, from those
with whom they had commercial dealings, but even in this
instance there were special reasons prompting investment.
Concord presents typical cases. The largest manufacturer
of the place went to the town as clerk in a general store
and later went in business for himself. He determined to
build a factory, securing some $60,000 in local subscrip-
tions. Then he went to the firms from which he bought

---

[71] Copeland, p. 216; Charles Estes, Augusta; W. R. Odell, Concord, interviews.

[72] Copeland, pp. 172, 209; C. B. Armstrong, int., Gastonia; for references to new selling methods, see Charlotte News, Textile Ed.,
1917.

[73] Cf. Law, in proceed. Morris Club, National Assn. Credit Men,
1916, p. 23; Tompkins, The South's Position in American Affairs, p.
5 ff. An interesting approach to later developments was the formation of the Cone Export and Commission Co., sometimes known as
the "Plaid Trust," in 1891. The firm sought to represent all the
Southern plaid mills, these buying stock and securing a measure of
control in the enterprise. It came too early to succeed, unity proving
impossible; it can hardly be called an effort by a commission house
to anticipate autonomous action on the part of the factories. (Information as to this project is contained in an announcement by the
Company issued in May, 1891, giving quotations from the Daily
Commercial Bulletin, N. Y., May 14, and Dry Goods Chronicle, May
23, 1891; cf. Copeland, p. 206, and as to a somewhat similar organization, p. 161 ff.; Mrs. Moses Cone, Baltimore, Md., Nov. 14, 1916;
Bernard Cone, Greensboro; R. G. Vaughn, Greensboro, Aug. 30,
1916, interviews.)

"brogans," and cloth and to which he shipped raw cotton, explaining to them his plans and showing that a mill would enable the town to grow and permit him to do a larger merchandise business with these wholesalers. It was almost worth the subscription to keep his business, so each firm bought $5000 of stock.[74] The only shares of another Concord company owned outside of North Carolina are held by Baltimore men who had business relations with the merchant who built the mill.[75] Sometimes mercantile connections of many years before were recalled to serve a purpose in the eighties.[76]

Much of the early mill building consisted of extension of plant by means of earnings. Tompkins indicated that profits to the amount of 5 per cent of capital were ordinarily devoted to this extension, but in frequent individual cases much more than this was found available.[77] Often by the time a mill was put in operation a company had exhausted credit facilities and local capital resources; the large earnings brought a new increment of cash and additional command over credit, which were employed in augmentation of plant.[78] Vaucluse was built from the profits of Graniteville and a third plant, the Hickman, was created with money borrowed.[79]

While many mills with extended plant have little more

---

[74] J. L. Hartsell, int., Concord. Years later, when merchandising is no longer thought of, this manufacturer can readily get subscriptions, it is said, from retired wholesale dealers of New York, Philadelphia and Boston (Charles McDonald, int., Charlotte).

[75] Ibid.

[76] Charles Estes, int., Augusta.

[77] Cotton Mill, Commercial Features, p. 172. Besides, he confused new construction with upkeep.

[78] Benjamin Gossett, int., Anderson. There might be combination of methods. The 5000-spindle Williamston Mill issued extra stock to $300,000, increasing spindleage to 15,000; afterwards the plant grew to have 32,000 spindles, all on earnings and credit.

[79] Tracy I. Hickman, int., Augusta. Cf. Blackman, p. 5. The Gaffney mill erected a two-story addition from the first three years' earnings (L. Baker, int., Gaffney). The Arlington Mill, Gastonia, organized with $130,000 capital and 3000 spindles, after three years issued a stock dividend of $45,000 and increased its spindles to 9500, and by later earnings enlarged to 12,000. Cf. Charlotte News, Textile Ed., 1917, as to Cliffside and McAden mills.

17

than their original capitalization, that of others has been increased by additional issues of stock, frequently to subscribers at a reduction. Though thus put out at 75 or 80, the industry was profitable enough to keep shares at the par of 100.[80] "The stockholders of the Matthews Cotton Factory, at Selman," it was reported, "have resolved to increase the capital stock from $100,000 to $300,000. Extensive plans for enlargement have been determined on, and they will be commensurate with the amount of increased stock taken."[81] The Anderson mill, capitalization of which was raised from $100,000 to $250,000 and by three more increases to $800,000, had a debt on the plant in the beginning; earnings going to take care of this, and further credit probably being difficult, stock issues were resorted to for enlargements. Machinery and commission men participated heavily.[82] Local brokers negotiated for the entire additional stock of the Enterprise Factory, Augusta; it was understood that one man and his friends would take $140,000 of the $350,000 issue.[83]

It was characteristic of the establishing of an industry among people not very familiar with financial devices, with few investors beside those interested in cotton manufactur-

---

[80] Increasing capital to $1,000,000, stock of the Sibley mill was offered to original subscribers in pro rata amounts, any not so taken to be sold in the general market at not less than par. The directors were empowered, too, to issue $100,000 in bonds (circular letter of William C. Sibley, Augusta, April 26, 1882, in Raworth scrapbook). It is said now that $500,000 in stock should have been issued to build the Hickman mill, rather than borrowing for this purpose (Tracy I. Hickman, int., Augusta).

[81] Manufacturers' Record, Baltimore, Dec. 21, 1882. At reorganization of the Charleston Manufacturing Co., $300,000 fresh capital was subscribed and equipment of the plant was completed (A. B. Murray, int., Charleston).

[82] J. A. Brock, int., Anderson. Most of the original shareholders increased their subscriptions to the Cannon Mill before the plant was completed (J. L. Hartsell, int., Concord). Enlargement of capital and plant often was undertaken in this early stage. In a period of similar activity thirty-five years later, companies at Gastonia had hardly received their charters before deciding to increase capitalization. Clifton and Trough Shoals mills intended to double capacity and capital when a successful beginning had been made (Blackman, pp. 10–11; News and Courier, Charleston, Feb. 10, 1882).

[83] News and Courier, Charleston, Feb. 24, 1881.

ing as such, and with commission houses and machinery makers to assist, that bonds and preferred stock should have been employed rarely. "The people just put in their money and made it go as far as it would, without thought of preferred stock and bonds. Mills were generally small because the money did not go far."[84] Also, if fixed assets in land, buildings and machinery were mortgaged by issuance of bonds, there was only material in course of manufacture and finished product on which to base commercial credit. It is said that in most instances where bonds were sold, the practice was found to be bad.[85] No case has been discovered where preferred stock or bonds were issued at the outset; it was when a mill got into trouble, needed additional capital or had to be reorganized that such helps were turned to.[86] A mill at Bessemer City was under-capitalized, the projector could not persuade stockholders to increase their subscriptions, and so machinery could not be installed. The promoter built a second mill and a third which were

---

[84] T. C. Leak, int., Rockingham.

[85] W. J. Thackston, letter, Greenville, S. C., Nov. 25, 1916.

[86] Tracy I. Hickman, Augusta; F. Q. O'Neill, Charleston, interviews. Cf. U. S. Census of Manufactures, 1900, "Cotton Manufactures," p. 31. The following from the report of the president of the Enterprise factory to the stockholders in 1885 is sufficiently revealing to bear quotation: "Four months ago, when the Board of Directors took charge of your property, they found it burdened with a floating debt of $200,550.25, largely the result of embezzlement on the part of its former President. . . . The company had also issued second mortgage bonds on property, to the amount of $150,000.00, with which to pay off such debts as were most urgent, but, not finding a ready sale for these bonds in their then crippled condition, the President had hypothecated them to the extent of their issue, as collateral to secure creditors. . . . It was determined to issue preferred stock to the amount of $250,000.00, and with the proceeds pay off the debts of the company, take up the second mortgage bonds, and operate the mill. Since then there has been $148,200.00 subscribed to the preferred stock, of which $85,750.00 has been collected. We have already taken up and destroyed $100,000.00 of the second mortgage bonds, and paid $95,121.34 of the outstanding indebtedness. There remains $101,800.00 of the preferred stock not yet taken, but your Board believe, that in the improved condition of the company, it will not be necessary to dispose of more than one-half of it" to care for all indebtedness except $42,000 to machinery makers, to be paid by company's notes running for ten years. It was hoped soon to redeem the preferred stock (Raworth Scrapbook). Cf. Augusta Trade Review, Oct., 1884, as to Augusta Factory.

bon'ded. Neither venture succeeded.[87] Earnings having
been slight because of a bad market for goods, it was decided in 1884 to cut down the proportion of overhead expense of the Sibley mill by completing the equipment of the
plant; this was thought advantageous, too, because makers
were not busy and machinery could be purchased cheaply.
Not all of the previously authorized bonds had been sold;
the directors recommended an additional issue and urged
that shareholders follow the example of the directors in
subscribing as heavily as possible. This course would pre-
serve the ownership of the property, make 6 per cent earnings possible and arrest the decline in value of stock.[88]

In some instances, as in Columbia and Charleston, local
banks were of substantial assistance in furnishing working

[87] S. N. Boyce and J. Lee Robinson, int., Gastonia.

[88] See annual report of President Sibley in Chronicle and Constitutionalist, Augusta, May 1, 1884. In two weeks nearly two-thirds
of the bonds had been placed and the president, "notwithstanding
the disappointments of the past," had "more faith now than he ever
had in the final success of the company" (ibid., May 14, 1884).
Striking difficulties with commencement of operation, the Charleston
mill issued bonds to half the value of its property (A. B. Murray,
int., Charleston). Later, an instructive operation took place between an involved South Carolina mill and its commission house.
The plant cost $21 per spindle—$1,748,000—but there was a debt of
$9.64 to the spindle, the company being capitalized at $976,700, all
common stock. The net indebtedness had run as high as $830,000,
but at the time of this episode it stood at $510,000. Trouble of a
serious nature being discovered in the books, the mill would have
gone into the hands of receivers unless relief had come. The commission house was so heavily interested that it had to act, and took
$500,000 of preferred stock at par, though a banking house would
not have given above 80. Other creditors insisted upon payment of
their accounts, and the selling firm had to put up $560,000 to care
for these items, making its total interest in the company well over
a million dollars. Though the original debt of mill to commission
house had been liquidated through conversion into preferred stock,
by the whole operation this obligation was greater than before, and
there was an increase in stock from $980,000 to $1,500,000. Conditions speedily improved from this date. In a case such as this the
preferred stock would ordinarily be offered to the shareholders who,
however, were not usually able to take it. Though there are statements to the contrary, one of wide observation did not know of an
instance where a commission house bought into a healthy mill to gain
control of it. Probably a similar happening was the taking of all the
bonds of a mill by a firm of selling agents thirty years ago (A. A.
Thompson, int., Raleigh). Cf. Columbia Record, Textile Ed., 1916,
as to Lydia mills.

funds, but such assistance was far from general. Reasons for this have been noticed. Banks were few and had slender resources.[89] Industry and banking, developing together, were mutually helpful, but neither could greatly take the initiative. Interest rates were high. Even latterly, mills borrowed at 7 and 8 per cent, and besides were compelled to keep a balance of 20 per cent of the loans, on deposit without interest. On the other hand, commission firms might lend at less than these rates and require no balance. Northern mills could get money from banks at half the interest paid in the South.[90] Southern banks assisted the mills indirectly to some extent by loans to stockholders on their shares.[91]

As early as 1884 it was suggested in the South that those contemplating the founding of mills should consider the plan of securing subscriptions from operatives, popular in England.[92] In the nature of things, the scheme could not have been employed in that stage of the development. Probably it was not relied upon to any extent until, recently, half the stock in a Gastonia mill was taken by operatives.[93]

Leaving now the means of acquiring capital, the subject of profits and dividends is to be examined. In 1890 it was estimated that for the country at large profits in cotton

[89] Immediately after the war, the largest bank in Charlotte had a capital of only $20,000 (Hudson Millar, int., Charlotte). The rate of growth of Southern banking is eloquent of former leanness (cf. John Skelton Williams, The Billion Arrives, p. 7).

[90] Summerfield Baldwin, Jr., Baltimore; Benjamin Gossett, Anderson; interviews; S. S. Broadus, Decatur, letter. Generally, conditions have improved. A good mill can sell paper through brokers at 4 per cent and commission. (Summerfield Baldwin, ibid.; C. B. Armstrong, int., Gastonia). Richmond banks have come to bear important part in the Southern industry. One group of mills at some seasons has owed Richmond as much as $4,000,000.

[91] August Kohn, int., Columbia. Barely worthy of mention is the fact that mills sometimes, with more or less surrender of strictly local control, got assistance from established manufacturers in the South. Or a factory might merge entirely with a group of mills skilfully managed.

[92] An Augusta paper of Nov. 6, referring to earlier publication in New Orleans Times-Democrat, in Raworth Scrapbook.

[93] Charlotte News, Textile Ed., 1917. In limited adoption, the plan has frequently been used as an employer's device. Cf. ibid., as to Saxony Spinning Mill, Lincolnton.

manufactures, allowing only for ordinary repairs, were 7.59 per cent, or, deducting 3 per cent of the value of plant to care for depreciation, 5.83 per cent.[94] The estimated average rate of dividends paid by New England mills from 1889 to 1908 was 7.7 per cent.[95] Such calculations are not fairly comparable, and yet some statements as to earnings of Southern factories will help to give a notion of the relative position of the industry in that section. Experience in the Carolinas showed that mills on all classes of goods made there could have a profit of from 10 to 30 per cent.[96] The same competent observer thought that the average annual net profit of the best mills for the first twenty years of the period was 15 per cent.[97] But assertions vary widely, even considering differences in periods embraced. One with knowledge of the industry believed average profits from 1880 to 1914 were not as high as 10 per cent,[98] while a writer on the subject said that South Carolina investors would have been better off financially had they put their money in real estate mortgages at 7 per cent.[99]

Besides the confusion between profits and dividends, statements as to earnings are difficult of comparison because uniformity of calculation was lacking. A common error was to quote dividends paid on capitalization rather than earnings on total investment. Plant cost of some mills was as much as four times their capital. Dividends might be paid on shares, neglecting large liabilities of stockholders; sometimes, also, gains seemed great because stated in terms of paid up capital only.[100] Even late in the period

---

[94] U. S. Census of Manufactures, Cotton Manufacture, p. 167.

[95] Copeland, p. 263.

[96] Tompkins, Cotton Mill, Commercial Features, p. 51. That this was true for the smallest as well as the largest plants is verified by the case of the 1000-spindle Fingerville Factory (cf. Blackman, p. 11).

[97] Tompkins, Cotton Mill, Commercial Features, p. 172; cf. Thompson, p. 88.

[98] John W. Fries, int., Winston-Salem.

[99] August Kohn, int., Columbia.

[100] Thirty-five years after the mills around Greenville were founded, plants costing $21.08 per spindle were capitalized at $12.72 per spindle. Dividends on actual plant cost have not been over 12 per cent (W. J. Thackston, int., Greenville; cf. Goldsmith, p. 6).

there was occasion for the advice of a trained manufacturer that all profits not required for dividends be not
passed to surplus without providing for depreciation, working capital, and reserve for paying plant debt.[101] A friend
of the Southern industry right at the outset sought to discredit the overstatement of promoters of the Clement Attachment that 28⅝ per cent could be made on a capital of
$6000, showing that they had included no charges for super-
intendence, commission and freight, insurance, taxes and
wear and tear, and allowed too little for incidental expenses.[102]

Mills in the beginning, from reasons that have been
noted—general prosperity of the time, newness of equipment, nearness to raw cotton, cheapness of power and labor,
length of working hours, unexploited home market—were
extraordinarily profitable. "A cotton factory which is not
making money now had better close up at once," it was said
in 1880.[103] Two years later it was recited that the Augusta
Factory in the previous seventeen years had paid an average of 14½ per cent dividends besides laying aside a surplus of $350,000; Langley for several years had been pay-

"In the old days it took four or five years to pay for the plant if
they did not make the mistake of trying to pay normal dividends
instead of liquidating this debt" (Benjamin Gossett, int., Anderson).
It has even been said that all mills were undercapitalized and started
out in debt (Marshall Orr, Anderson; A. N. Wood, Gaffney, interviews). Machinery makers and commission firms, anxious to increase their business, were severely blamed for inducing too great
extension without sufficient capitalization, but this writer found the
conditions bettering latterly (Law, pp. 19-20).

[101] Tompkins, Cotton Mill, Commercial Features, pp. 83-84. He
was appreciative, however, of the wisdom of a surplus to guarantee
equality of dividends. It will be noticed later that failure to allow
for depreciation was all too common; cf. ibid., pp. 82, 172; Thompson, pp. 88, 67-68.

[102] Daily Constitution, Atlanta, Feb. 20, 1880. For a few of many
instances illustrating neglect to offset depreciation, see Blackman,
pp. 7, 10, 13. "In no case have we heard of any mill declaring less
than 10 per cent annual dividends, and in every case in which only
this per cent was declared a large amount was taken from the earnings and used for repairs, additions to machinery and increasing the
. . . capacity of the mills" (Baltimore Journal of Commerce and
Manufacturers' Record, June 3, 1882). Here, evidently, upkeep and
extension were looked to rather than depreciation.

[103] Blackman, p. 12. This was probably Hammett.

ing from 15 to 20 per cent and had an accumulated surplus of $200,000. The Wesson mills in Mississippi had just paid a dividend of 26 per cent, the Troup factory in the same State had paid 24 per cent, and a mill in Tennessee had touched 50 per cent. Such facts were often cited to show that the Southern industry, though young and hampered by untrained management and operatives and lack of capital, was more prosperous than that of the North. A New England estimate was quoted to the effect that fifty leading establishments of that section in the previous five years had paid average annual dividends of less than 7 per cent.[104]

The profitableness of Graniteville was often pointed to; there came to be almost a Graniteville legend in this regard. Dividends under Gregg amounted, in various statements, anywhere from 7 to 12½ per cent. The mill was in bad condition when Hickman became president in 1867, being in debt and paying 12 per cent interest. There is no

[104] Baltimore Journal of Commerce and Manufacturers' Record, June 3, 1882. For minor variations of these statements, cf. ibid., Sept. 2, 1882. There was believed to be room for indefinite expansion of cotton manufacture in South Carolina, "inasmuch as the Carolina mills pay expenses when the New England mills run at a loss, make money when the New England mills only pay expenses and make still larger profits than the New England mills when these pay well (Blackman, p. 19; cf. ibid., statement of Twitchell, p. 11). Cf. Baltimore Journal of Commerce and Manufacturers' Record, Nov. 4, 1882, quotation from Bradstreet's and Manufacturers' Record, Baltimore, Feb. 1, 1883, statement of Hammett. The Boston Commercial Bulletin said: "The advantages of cotton manufacture are with the South decidedly, the profits of the business there having shown an average dividend of 15½ per cent against 7⅔ per cent in the North during the year 1882" (ibid., April 5, 1883). Reviewing the generally unsatisfactory condition of Northern mills from 1890 to 1900, attributed in large part to successful competition of Southern enterprises, it was declared: "Prior to the close of the census year there had been scarcely any interruption of the exceeding prosperity of Southern spinners. They did not curtail production when many Northern manufacturers were in a state bordering upon despair; on the contrary, a large number of their mills were running day and night. They did not seek to dispose of their product by auction, but sold all they could make at prices which gave their stockholders handsome dividends" (U. S. Census of Manufactures, 1900, Cotton Manufactures, p. 20; cf. ibid., pp. 28–29). Cf. News and Courier, Charleston, Sept. 13, 1881, interview with Francis Cogin.

doubt about the improvement that took place—the plant was enlarged and bettered and stock was increased in value.[105]

While competition was slight, mills run in any sort of way made money.[106] Stock in South Carolina mills in 1880 was worth, on the average, more than 125. Exclusive of a Clement Attachment mill, where 50 per cent was made, profits ranged from 18 to 25½ per cent. It was said that in the next year any ordinary factory ought to pay as well.[107] Demonstrated fact encouraged one estimate that spinning mills in the South at large should make 50 per cent.[108] In 1882 "authenticated statistics" were declared to show that investments in Southern mills with good, bad and indifferent management were receiving average dividends of 22 per cent.[109] It was not unusual for mills in these years to make 30 per cent to 75 per cent profit.[110]

---

[105] Clark, in South in Building of Nation, vol. v, pp. 324–325; Blackman, pp. 4–5; News and Courier, Charleston, Feb. 23, April 25, 1881; Boston Journal of Commerce, July 29, 1882; Augusta Trade Review, Oct., 1884; Tracy I. Hickman, int., Augusta, Dec. 29, 1916. As to profitableness of Georgia and Alabama mills in the seventies, see Clark, ibid., vol. vi, p. 256; Berney, Handbook of Alabama, p. 271; News and Courier, Charleston, Sept. 13, Aug. 18, 1881.

[106] Benjamin Gossett, int., Anderson. When a new superintendent took hold at a North Carolina mill he found half the looms idle, and yet the plant was highly successful (William Entwistle, int., Rockingham).

[107] Blackman, leading article and pp. 3, 8, 16, 18.

[108] Daily Constitution, Atlanta, March 18, 1880.

[109] Baltimore Journal of Commerce and Manufacturers' Record, June 24. Clark says that investments this year amounted to $10,-000,000; this is not surprising when it is remembered that large, well-conducted corporations were paying dividends of 17 to 24 per cent.

[110] Sterling Graydon, Charlotte; William Entwistle, Rockingham, interviews. The Augusta Factory made 17 per cent in six months (News and Courier, Charleston, Aug. 18, 1881; cf. Daily Constitution, Atlanta, Jan. 6, 1880). Other mills made from 26 to 29 per cent (Baltimore Journal of Commerce and Manufacturers' Record, June 24, 1882). Even mills in bad situations and with poor equipment made large sums. A little factory eight miles from the nearest place and hauling over wretched roads paid 25 per cent on the investment; machinery was old, capacity limited and the mill ran only 278 days in the year. Yarns sold at 23 cents per pound cost 2.44 cents to manufacture, and the demand could not be nearly supplied—the total output might have been sold to one man (Blackman, pp. 11–12).

If Vaucluse was the only mill established before 1880 that paid anything in the first year of operation,[111] its record was matched regularly after that date. Twenty-four per cent was made the first year by a Georgia mill, and a Spartanburg company after six months paid a 4 per cent dividend and proposed to increase its capital to $1,000,000.[112]

Without following this subject through remaining years, it may be mentioned that 1882 was in some respects not so easy for Southern cotton manufacturers as the two years previous,[113] and that, though experiencing general alarm and a few disasters in 1884, 1893 and 1896, the industry quickly recovered from these backsets.[114] Following the great activity of mill building which began about 1900, Southern earnings were approximating the low averages of New England plants twenty-five years earlier.[115] With some exceptions,[116] mills did only fairly well through the next decade, and many were in bad condition financially when the advent of the Great War lifted them all into prosperity. The liveliest successes of the eighties were repeated and surpassed. A right new mill at Gastonia with $150,000 capital after a short period of operation paid a stock dividend of 20 per cent and made $155,000 net profit for the year. Generally, mills at this place that did not make 75 per cent were thought poorly managed, numbers made their entire capitalization in twelve months and some even higher.[117] Other localities throughout the South found themselves hardly less blessed; with profits as the

---

[111] Ibid., p. 6.

[112] Baltimore Journal of Commerce and Manufacturers' Record, June 3, Aug. 26, 1882. For notice of typical factories paying unevenly but averaging about 20 per cent, cf. Blackman, pp. 10, 13, 15; Deutsche Zeitung, Charleston, Feb. 28, 1881; News and Courier, Charleston, Sept. 7, 1881. For some less conclusive references to profits see ibid., Jan. 25, Feb. 26, April 4, 1881.

[113] Manufacturers' Record, Baltimore, Feb. 1, 1883; A. B. Murray, int., Charleston.

[114] Clark, in South in Building of Nation, vol. vi, pp. 281, 284–286.

[115] Cf. Goldsmith, p. 6.

[116] Murphy, p. 16; Law, pp. 23–24.

[117] S. N. Boyce and J. Lee Robinson, G. W. Ragan, C. B. Armstrong, Gastonia, interviews; J. Lee Robinson, letter, Gastonia, Nov. 28, 1916.

incentive, factories sprang up as suddenly and widely as in the Cotton Mill Campaign.[118]

There is a relation between percentage of profit and size of plant. The magnitude of mills, of a part, of course, with degree of concentration of investment, is an interesting subject, indicating differences in development of the industry in various States. It is convenient to compare South Carolina and North Carolina in this regard. Factories of the former State tended to be fewer in number but greater in capacity than those of the latter, and wove as well as spun. Furthermore, the impulse toward cotton manufacturing was felt later in North than in South Carolina. Several reasons may be assigned for these facts. The considerable capital of Charleston, as it had earlier been largely responsible for Graniteville and Langley, later played the leading part in the founding of such mills as Piedmont and Pelzer. These big weaving mills set a standard; also, as has been noticed, Charleston money was a resource to South Carolina local communities pretty generally. North Carolina had no city the size of Charleston; Wilmington was not so good a port and did not possess so much capital available for investment. Little neighborhoods were shut up to their own initiative and means. Moreover, there had always been less social unity in North Carolina; with much Scotch blood, the people were individualists. Most of the time small merchants had to be mill projectors, and this was agreeable, too, because personal control over modest units was preferred to a pooling of resources in the hands of an important capitalist. These things explain, also, why the development commenced later in North Carolina. More people had to be converted than in a State where a few could set a powerful example. Even where North Carolina had weaving mills, these were generally smaller than those of South Carolina. It is to be observed that whereas the principal mill mergers of South

---

[118] W. J. Thackston, int., Greenville; Literary Digest, N. Y., Dec. 9, 1916; cf. files of all trade papers, especially Manufacturers' Record, Baltimore.

Carolina showed concentration of management, in the out-standing case in North Carolina constituent mills remained semi-autonomous. When a tradition was established, it tended to maintain itself.[119]

With local capital in greater supply in South Carolina, commission and machinery firms were more interested and engineers were more regularly engaged, so large plants were encouraged. In undertaking the development of power and manufacturing at Columbia, it was pointed out by engineers that a 16,000-spindle mill would cost $27 per spindle and yield 17 per cent profit; plant cost would be proportionately less if equipment was 20,000 spindles and the complement of looms, and earnings should be 21 per cent; 26,000 spindles ought to bring earnings of 25 per cent.[120]

Later, a conscious, concerted movement toward mills, lifting spindleage above the 30,000 point, in which North Carolina patterned after South Carolina, was typified in the erection of the great Olympia plant at Columbia. The animating spirit was evidenced by a speaker before cotton manufacturers in 1903: "I believe thoroughly in organizations of such magnitude that will justify the employment of the very best skill to be obtained in systematic management." There was much to be saved in purchase of supplies and materials. "A weakly fitted up mill under poor management is worthless; the same mill under good management is even then sadly handicapped." But merger with

[119] David Clark, Hudson Millar, Charlotte; E. A. Smyth, Greenville; Charles E. Johnson, Raleigh; W. K. Boyd, Durham, N. C., Sept. 18, 1916; J. A. Chapman, Spartanburg; J. H. M. Beatty, Columbia, interviews. Georgia was much like South Carolina. Speaking of the limitations of North Carolina, it was said: "Our people hadn't the money; they all had to scratch to get anything to put into cotton mills, and then it wasn't much" (W. R. Odell, int., Concord).

[120] News and Courier, Charleston, April 13, 1881; cf. Law, p. 19. As early as 1883 South Carolina had several mills which would be ranked as large even today—four companies with capitalization of half a million or more, with others of size (cf. Manufacturers' Record, Baltimore, Jan. 18, 1883). There were, of course, mills as small as any in North Carolina, but these dated from previous years (cf. as to Valley Falls and Reedy River, the former of only $5000 capital, Blackman, pp. 11, 13).

other plants would bring increased financial facilities. " The
tendency to concentrate and build mills with a larger number of spindles than formerly is a move in the right direction."[121] But it was soon learned that very large separate
mills and close mergers of several plants were of uncertain
success, disadvantages more than offsetting advantages.[122]
Small, isolated plants bought local cotton at a saving and
paid no higher commissions on product; some could burn
wood; operatives were few and individually known; a superintendent could be developed from the working force
and did well enough on a limited number of standard
yarns; living in a small place was cheaper.[123] Time has

---

[121] " The record of the past three years shows a large number of
plants erected in the South of from 25,000 spindles up to that grand
specimen of push and enterprise—the Olympia Mills—which has
104,000 spindles in one mill and all in one room " (see Southern Cotton Spinners' Assn., proceed. 7th Annual Convention, address of E.
W. Thomas, p. 149 ff.). Cf. Clark, in South in Building of Nation,
vol. vi, pp. 287-288. Greenville had the example of the success of
such large mills as Pelzer as contrasted with the smaller Huguenot
and Camperdown factories; there was the strong impression that
individual mills of limited size were not easily financed (Clement F.
Haynsworth, int., Greenville). " The Loray Mill in Gastonia was
built about the same time as Olympia; small mills had succeeded, and
they thought big ones would succeed even better " (S. N. Boyce
and J. Lee Robinson, int., Gastonia).

[122] " Attention is being paid to the danger of having too large
units, the prevailing opinion in the South being that no special economies from increased size are obtainable after say 50,000 to 60,000 are
reached. A notable disaster to stockholders and near-disaster to
creditors in recent years has taught the lesson that an unwieldy
combination of plants scattered geographically has no advantage,
through concentration of purchasing or selling, that can possibly
offset the diminution of the personal equation in relations with employees or scrutiny of details, usually given by the executive in
charge of smaller units " (Law, p. 19; cf. Tompkins, Cotton Mill,
Commercial Features, p. 55). The promoter of the chief amalgama-
tion in South Carolina believed he would save in overhead expense;
the main benefit was in financing, for much money was offered at
3 per cent when the merger went together, whereas the individual
mills had never borrowed at less than 5 per cent. Any other savings
were more than counterbalanced by expensively lax supervision.
Failure resulted (J. H. M. Beatty, int., Columbia). In the principal
North Carolina chain, while ownership is virtually identical, each
mill has its own directors and must stand on its own bottom financially. Some economies of combination are deliberately sacrificed to
maintain efficiency of superintendence (James W. Cannon, int.,
Concord).

[123] Cf. Thompson, p. 90 ff.

taken away some of these benefits, but the best present opinion is that well situated units of about 10,000 spindles are most economical.[124]

There was little buying and selling of mill stocks in the first part of the period, and for several reasons. Factories were so often looked upon as family affairs, part and parcel of the communities which established them. Local subscribers, small and large, put in their money as an investment, and most of those who could purchase shares did so at first. Mills were successful, moreover, and brought dividends. To outsiders the industry was an experiment; private investors were not attracted. There were few agencies in the South for handling the securities. Consequently, notices of value of stocks usually meant really book value.[125]

It has been seen that in 1880 the shares of South Carolina mills were reported as being worth on the average $125. Three years later all were above par except five, which were at par; Langley was highest, selling at $173.[126] The stock of the Wesson mill in Mississippi, paying 26 per cent dividends, stood at more than 300.[127] Shares in the Merrimack mills, in Alabama, par value $1000, sold for $1620.[128]

[124] Building since 1914 has shown this. "I had rather run four mills of 10,000 spindles each than one of 40,000 spindles" (C. B. Armstrong, int., Gastonia). This would have to be modified some in the case of cloth mills.

[125] "The stock of the company sold for $63 a share in 1867, and now is quoted at $123. Even this figure is not a fair estimate of what it is worth because nobody wants to sell. I could go in the market tomorrow and run it up to $130, or even $150, just by offering that for it. This is not what we want, however" (Hickman, of Graniteville, quoted in Blackman (1880), p. 4. A Rockingham mill has been owned by the same stockholders for the forty years since its establishment (Charlotte News, Textile Ed., 1917, as to Roberdell Mill No. 1). Stock in the first mill at Salisbury could not be bought; 60 per cent of it was owned by women who received it by inheritance (O. D. Davis, int., Salisbury). Where there was a market at the opening of the period it was local, mills taking charge of their own sales (Tracy I. Hickman, Augusta; William Entwistle, Rockingham, interviews).

[126] Manufacturers' Record, Baltimore, Jan. 18, 1883. The stock of Graniteville and Vaucluse had climbed to 170. For similar facts as to Augusta factories, cf. Baltimore Journal of Commerce and Manufacturers' Record, Sept. 2, 1882; News and Observer, Raleigh, Nov. 16, 1880.

[127] News and Courier, Charleston, Jan. 14, 1882.

[128] Observer, Raleigh, Aug. 26, 1880.

Besides the usual causes, Southern mill stocks have varied in value because the business was subject to sharp fluctuations, companies were irregular in providing surplus to insure constant dividends and in offsetting depreciation,[129] skill in management was so largely hit-or-miss, commission firms sometimes interfered hurtfully and, as will be remarked, machinery makers dumped their shares in large blocks. Pacolet once had to alter its product and so its machinery; preferred stock was issued and common fell from 300 to below par.[130] Within two years after a commission firm had gained control of a South Carolina mill following a fight with local stockholders, shares that had been at 175 dropped to par.[131]

An active market for the stocks developed in Charleston about 1890 and in the up-country somewhat later. A good many brokers made a specialty of these securities. The business was assisted by machinery builders disposing of their holdings at concessions. One firm handled in one year about $2,000,000 worth of securities thus thrown on the market.[132] Charlestonians had been heavy subscribers to new ventures in the State, but about 1900 stopped because they could buy at less than par.[133]

The financial history of Southern mills has exhibited physical differentials becoming less and less important, and skill in management becoming more and more important. Atkinson's admonition that success in cotton manufacture meant a small margin of profit on a large capital was, after

---

[129] Cf. Tompkins, Cotton Mill, Commercial Features, p. 85.

[130] A. N. Wood, int., Gaffney. Stock in Graniteville and mills at Augusta, which earlier led the field, went far below par (Tracy I. Hickman, int., Augusta).

[131] W. W. Ball, int., Columbia, Jan. 3, 1917.

[132] W. J. Thackston, letter, Greenville. When machinery manufacturers were taking part payment in stock, equipment was in great demand and high in price. Makers could therefore sell their shares quickly at 50 cents on the dollar and still make money (Washington Clark, int., Columbia). Commission men, retaining their shares, sometimes made money; a firm that took stock when it received the agency of a mill and offered to sell at 50 later succeeded in selling at 300 (Walter Montgomery, int., Spartanburg, S. C., Sept. 5, 1916).

[133] W. W. Ball, int., Columbia, Jan. 3, 1917.

all, of only delayed applicability in the new industry.[134]   At the opening of the period, as has been seen, "they didn't run mills, but just put them up and they made money. Long hours of labor and low wages made the difference between that time and this.   But old superiorities have passed.   Mills that stayed in the old rut went to the wall. It is necessary to *operate* mills in the South today."[135] Management of investments in land and negroes was not the best equipment for industrial control.   As the South had grown a staple commodity, raw cotton, and grew too much of it, so it manufactured staple cotton goods, following the impulse mechanically.[136]   Inexperienced men founding the industry in 1880 made money; the same type entering the business twenty years later, as at Bessemer City, found they could not exist.[137]   By this time, in the same mill in which average management would yield 10 per cent profit, superior management might bring 25 per cent and inferior operation a loss of 5 per cent.[138]   The margin between the price of middling cotton and of print cloth made from it between 1881 and 1910 worked down, though not without great irregularity, from 108.52 to 59.24.[139]   And

---

[134] Cf. News and Courier, Charleston, Dec. 5, 1881, and the writer's "Factors in Future of Cotton Manufacture," in Manufacturers' Record, Baltimore, May 10, 1917.

[135] W. J. Britton, int., Spartanburg.   Social position and good intent too often had to serve in place of industrial ability, though after 1880 there were few instances approaching an episode during the Civil War, when, at reorganization of an Augusta mill, a governor was given $100,000 in stock for his influence as a director (Charles Estes, int., Augusta).   Often general capability, disregarding accustomed financial methods of corporate undertakings, succeeded through sheer force, but in other cases a slump in the business would take enterprises out of the hands of the original management (Chronicle, Augusta, Jan. 28, 1886; Henry E. Litchford, int., Richmond, Aug. 29, 1916).

[136] Landon A. Thomas, int., Augusta.   Initiative in the trend toward closely supervised plants making specialty products, already appearing, is fundamentally a problem of the common school, awakening public intelligence.   Cf. Georgia Industrial Assn., proceed. 4th Annual Convention, pp. 46-47.

[137] S. N. Boyce and J. Lee Robinson, G. W. Ragan, Gastonia, interviews.

[138] Tompkins, Cotton Mill, Commercial Features, p. 173.

[139] Copeland, appendix, p. 394.

training gained in manufacturing has made apparent a lack of development of commercial attributes which are as necessary a part of the mill man's equipment.[140] There has been a gradual evolution from first projectors, who were really transplanted slaveholders, through a somewhat later group composed of business and professional men, to the newer type of manufacturers who conceive it their work to make money on fabricated product and not in speculation on raw cotton or any other gamble, who are not afraid of competition with New England and the world, who relish technical information and know they had better manage a few plants well than many poorly.[141]

A qualified observer has said that in the Southern industry the total losses on an investment of $100,000,000 have not amounted to 20 per cent, and that this is remarkable when it is remembered how few managers began with knowledge of the business.[142]

Gregg assigned five main causes of failure of mills in South Carolina in his day. These were injudicious selection of machinery and character of goods to be made, lack of steady and cheap motive power, poor location, lack of moral training of operatives, and want of sufficient capital.[143] The first and last of these reasons are the only ones

---

[140] See Georgia Industrial Assn., proceed. 4th Annual Convention, address of J. J. Spalding, pp. 46–47.

[141] Cf. the writer's "Factors in Future of Cotton Manufacture," in Manufacturers' Record, Baltimore, May 10, 1917; Tompkins, Cotton Mill, Commercial Features, pp. 30 ff., 63; Plan to Raise Capital, p. 18; J. H. M. Beatty, Columbia, Jan. 3, 1917; Landon A. Thomas, Augusta; Joseph H. Separk, Gastonia, interviews. It is true that in this process young men technically trained have not yet made themselves available for large leadership, so that others without their advantages are still called upon (W. W. Ball, int., Columbia, Jan. 3, 1917).

[142] W. J. Thackston, int., Greenville; cf. Law, p. 18. There is some truth in a statement that as a rule the local investor has not made much on dividends, but has received, with everybody, a large indirect, social benefit from the establishment of the industry (M. L. Bonham, int., Anderson). Small local shareholders, if dividends did not begin promptly, sometimes sold, very often to the mill promoter (J. W. Norwood, int., Greenville).

[143] Quoted in Kohn, Cotton Mills of S. C., p. 18.

18

that may be said to have held in the later period.[144] Misfortunes following untrained management were not mentioned by Gregg, probably because he could not foresee competitive conditions that were to come.

It has been remarked that a good many mills were sold just prior to the opening of the Cotton Mill Campaign. Some of these were old factories that had been run down, or their owners had died; either they failed, or were bought up when the industry was receiving renovation and there was a demand for plants that could be improved.[145] The mills sold in the eighties were decidedly exceptions.[146] However, 1884 saw losses and partial shut-downs while debts accumulated. Graniteville went backward for the first time in seventeen years. Recovery in special cases was the slower because mills were just launching out.[147]

Surrounded by cotton, the price of the raw material playing so large a part in coarse goods manufacture, and having some capital at their disposal, the temptation for mill executives to speculate in the staple has been an evil. Two men worked together in promoting manufactures at Gastonia; one was content to make or lose as a spinner, and succeeded, while the other after a time counted too heavily on his skill in manipulation of cotton deals and met with disaster. About 1900 the stock of an excellent South Carolina mill went to 150, and the promoter erected a second large plant. With good credit, mill president and town were ruined in two years; he gambled in cotton and the

---

[144] Old machinery was always a bad bargain, but when it was bought the mills were making money and soon could scrap this equipment and profit by the experience; standard goods were manufactured and, as will be noticed presently, losses on these were because of sudden change in the market rather than through mistaken choice of product.
[145] Cf. Blackman, p. 12.
[146] Cf. Savannah Morning News, July 7, 1882. The Charleston factory changed hands at a loss totalling $499,000 (Bird Memoranda).
[147] Cf. Chronicle, Augusta, May 28, July 29, 1884; Jan. 29, April 23, 1885; Jan. 28, March 10, 1886, and other clippings arranged in the Raworth Scrapbook; there are printed reports of the president of the Sibley mill dated April 28, 1886, and Oct. 23, 1888.

market went against him.[148] A sympathetic critic of the Southern industry has said that " The principal occasion of financial disaster . . . has been that of speculation. It is true that in some instances this has been merely the final plunge of desperate unsuccessful management. In other cases, however, both directors and stockholders have known that earnings greater than possible from legitimate manufacturing were being shown. They winked at the excessive profits and deserved little sympathy when they sustained losses."[149]

There has been little fraud on the part of mill men. In the beginning there could scarcely have been any, so intimately were communities acquainted with the enterprises.[150] The scandal in the great Parker merger recently has been the conspicuous exception; the experience did much to turn favor away from closely centralized financial control. This failure was a moral blow not only to the industry, but to the section.[151]

Another cause of failure has been payment of too high salaries, with extension of plant to make these seem plausible. Also, superintendents have been accused of receiving commissions on machinery and supplies bought by them.[152]

---

[148] Cf. Columbia Record, Textile Ed., 1916, respecting Union and Buffalo mills.

[149] Law, p. 21 ff. " Profits thus obtained are absolutely demoralizing to efficiency in management or the working out of small economies—the legitimate source of success—and are hurtful to the general industry, in that they create fictitious costs, apparently justifying sales of product at really destructive prices. . . . My belief is that the cotton manufacturer who now indulges in such speculation is the exception." There have been examples of what might be called speculation in finished product, too. A gingham mill at Rock Hill had been operating successfully; the market dropped, but prospects were thought to be good and cloth was stored in warehouses until it represented a value greater than the capitalization of the company. The style in ginghams changed, and the plant had to be sold (cf. Columbia Record, Textile Ed., 1916).

[150] There seems to have been allegation of fraud in the case of the small Fork Shoals factory in 1881. This was an old and isolated mill (cf. News and Courier, Charleston, April 23).

[151] W. J. Thackston, int., Greenville.

[152] Charles Estes, int., Augusta. In the case of one Augusta mill, it is alleged, the president did not inspect matters narrowly; the

Extensions involving debt, especially from the nineties forward, were a source of misfortune. The Gaffney mill after three profitable first years built a warranted addition, but then followed a big new plant and a finishing mill that saddled the company with obligations under which it could not succeed, business being depressed.[153]

Coleman's mill at Concord, not unnaturally for a first enterprise by negroes, was badly managed and became in debt to local capitalists, who foreclosed.[154] Everyone had been willing to lend to the reliable Graniteville mill without anxiety as to payment of principal, until suddenly creditors became solicitous for their money, precipitating reorganization of the company in 1915.

Though there is complaint that too many mills were built in a short period, so that profits fell away,[155] it may be concluded that where enterprises have not succeeded their difficulties have been due to untrained management and lack of capital rather than to untoward conditions or limited opportunities in the industry.[156]

---

superintendent would send certified bills to him and he would make out New York checks for the amounts, the superintendent getting his benefit from such payments.

[153] L. Baker, int., Gaffney. The Laurens mill borrowed $150,000 to give the plant 30,000 spindles and other enlargements ensued and contributed to embarrassments of the company later. Whaley in Columbia built the little Richland mill and then Granby, and both did well. Then he proposed to build the greatest mill on earth under one roof, and exhausted the credit of his previous factories (W. W. Ball, int., Columbia, Jan. 3, 1917). "Many mills were built with a debt of $10 per spindle [the average cost being about $20], believing they could pay up in a few years at the high earnings of $4 or $5 per spindle. Many of these were caught with big debts and declining earnings" (Summerfield Baldwin, Jr., int., Baltimore).

[154] Charles McDonald, int., Charlotte.

[155] James D. Hammett, Anderson; Mrs. M. P. Gridley, Greenville, interviews.

[156] Julius Koester, H. R. Buist, Charleston; Thomas Purse, Savannah; August Kohn, Columbia, interviews.

INDEX

Agriculture, exclusive devotion to, vii; character of, in antebellum South, 30 (note); use of primitive methods in, 27; indications of revival of, in N. C., 73, 81; improvement in, 86–87; at low ebb in seventies, 144–146; closely joined with industry, 173 ff., depressed condition of, 173–176.

Atkinson, Edward, his views on proximity to raw material, 64–65; on preparation of cotton, 65; significance of Atlanta speech, 75 and note; his character, purposes and influence, 117 ff.; attitude of South toward, 237, 238.

Baker, L., quoted, 101 (note); his leadership at Gaffney, S. C., 128–129.

Banks, unimportant participation of, 249, 260–261.

Bonds, 258–260.

Borrowing. See Capital and Commission Houses.

Brown, W. G., quoted, vii.

Capital, availability of, to antebellum South, 23, 24; in Southern industry 1850–60, 44; home, to be drawn upon, 83; investments as result of Atlanta Exposition, 124 and note; English, negligible, 149–150; would come with immigration, 205; investment of local, 232–237; attitude toward outside, 237–241; investment by machinery makers and commission firms, 241 ff.; lack of working, 248 ff.; of Charleston, 267; borrowing, 261 and note, 267 (note).

Charleston, S. C., ordinance of, against use of steam engine,

33 and note; neglect of State industry by, 37–38; changed spirit of, 81–82 and note, 111; concern of, for public welfare, 127; scarcity of operatives in, 193–196; negro operatives in, 216–218; capital of, 267.

Charleston Manufacturing Company, organization of, 71; reasons for inception of, 97, 127, 132, 133–134, 157; labor troubles of, 193–196; negro operatives in old plant of, 216–218.

Child labor, necessary and natural at first, 95.

Civil War, not a fortuitous event, 43; as block to declared industrial beginnings, 46 (note); lack of manufactures to assist in, 53; opened door to Southern upbuilding, 53–55, 85.

Clark, V. S., his views on period 1840–60, 22–26; on whole antebellum period, 41–43.

Clay, C. M., on slavery as cause of Southern inaction, 51 (note).

Clement Attachment, 74, 154, 263.

Climate, modified by humidifiers, 67 (note).

Coleman, Warren, 215–216.

Columbia, S. C., peculiar sufferer in Civil War, 83 (note), 128 (note); canal project at, 128; advantage of location at, 224; self-help in, 234.

Commission Houses, participation of, 241 ff.; as lenders of working capital, 248 ff; "Plaid Trust," 256 (note).

Copeland, M. T., on location of mills, 184–185; on negro operatives, 220 (note).